EUROSLA
Yearbook

VOLUME 14 (2014)

Edited by

Leah Roberts
University of York

Ineke Vedder
University of Amsterdam

Jan H. Hulstijn
University of Amsterdam

John Benjamins Publishing Company
Amsterdam/Philadelphia

Editorial Board
Camilla Bardel, Stockholm University
Inge Bartning, Stockholm University
Theo Bongaerts, Radboud University Nijmegen
Vivian Cook, University of Newcastle
Jean-Marc Dewaele, Birkbeck College, University of London
Christine Dimroth, University of Münster
Tess Fitzpatrick, Cardiff University
Fanny Forsberg Lundell, Stockholm University
Aline Godfroid, Michigan State University
Marianne Gullberg, Lund University
Ayşe Gürel, Bogaziçi University
Alex Housen, Vrije Universiteit Brussel
Martin Howard, University College Cork
Jan H. Hulstijn, University of Amsterdam
Barış Kabak, Konstanz University
Peter Jordens, Free University Amsterdam
Batia Laufer, University of Haifa
Patsy M. Lightbown, Concordia University
Sarah Ann Liszka, University of Greenwich
Theodoros Marinis, University of Reading
Emma Marsden, University of York
Leyla Martı, Bogaziçi University
Paul Meara, Swansea University
Carmen Muñoz, University of Barcelona
Florence Myles, University of Newcastle
Mitsuhiko Ota, University of Edinburgh
Gabriele Pallotti, University of Modena and Reggio Emilia
Despina Papadopoulou, Aristotle University of Thessaloniki
Simona Pekarek Doehler, University of Basel
Carmen Pérez Vidal, University Pompeu Fabra
María del Pilar García Mayo, University of the Basque Country
Rebekah Rast, The American University of Paris
Vera Regan, University College Dublin
Jason Rothman, University of Reading
Sarah Schimke, University of Münster
David Singleton, Trinity College, Dublin
Roumyana Slabakova, University of Southampton
Antonella Sorace, Edinburgh University
Danijela Trenkic, University of York
Ianthi Maria Tsimpli, University of Reading
Josje Verhagen, Utrecht University
Georges Daniel Véronique, Université de Provence
Shigenori Wakabayashi, Chuo University
Martha Young-Scholten, University of Newcastle

Table of contents

Acknowledgements   V
Introduction   VII

Linguistic correlates to communicative proficiency levels
of the CEFR: The case of syntactic complexity in written L2 English,
L3 French and L4 Italian   1
    Henrik Gyllstad, Jonas Granfeldt, Petra Bernardini and Marie Källkvist

The effects of time in the development of complexity and accuracy
during study abroad: A study of French and Chinese learners of English   31
    Julia Jensen and Martin Howard

An analysis of complexity in primary school L2 English learning   65
    Heather Hilton and Carine Royer

Aspect in L2 English: A longitudinal study of four Japanese child returnees   79
    *Neal Snape, John Matthews, Makiko Hirakawa, Yahiro Hirakawa
    and Hironobu Hosoi*

Effectiveness of implicit negative feedback in a foreign language
classroom: The role of input, frequency and saliency   111
    Nadia Mifka Profozic

Adjectival modification in L2 Spanish Noun Phrases   143
    Pedro Guijarro-Fuentes

Interfaces in the interpretation of mood alternation in L2 Spanish:
Morpho-phonology, semantics and pragmatics   173
    Aoife Ahern, José Amenós Pons and Pedro Guijarro-Fuentes

Word order and case in the comprehension of L2 German
by L1 English speakers   201
Tom Rankin

When Germans begin to learn Swedish: Which is the transfer source
for function words, content words and syntax?   225
Christina Lindqvist and Ylva Falk

Cross-linguistic influence and formulaic language: Recurrent word
sequences in French learner writing   240
Magali Paquot

Acknowledgements

Eurosla Yearbook 14 comprises 10 papers from the EUROSLA conferences in Amsterdam, the Netherlands, in August 2013 and Poznán, Poland, in September 2012.

The 2013 conference was organized by a committee of members of the research group CASLA (Cognitive Approaches to Second Language Acquisition) of the Amsterdam Center for Language and Communication (ACLC) of the University of Amsterdam. Members of the organizing committee, chaired by Folkert Kuiken, were Sible Andringa, Klaartje Duijm, Jan Hulstijn, Rob Schoonen, Tessa Spätgens, Margarita Steinel and Ineke Vedder.

The organising committee would like to express their gratitude to the University of Amsterdam for hosting the conference, the Conference Office of the University of Amsterdam, and the Amsterdam City Council. We particularly thank Louise Gunning-Schepers (President of the Executive Board of the University of Amsterdam) and Pieter Hilhorst (Alderperson Amsterdam City Council) who opened the conference. The organising committee is grateful to the student volunteers for their invaluable help throughout the conference and to Thijs Geerts (Faculty of Humanities) for his work on the conference website. The organisers would also like to thank John Benjamins Publishing Company, the Language Learning journal, Bijzonder Fonds Neerlandistiek (Dutch Studies), Multilingual Matters, Oxford University Press, Springer, Cambridge English Language Assessment, Cambridge University Press, Anéla (Dutch Association for Applied linguistics), Routledge, Taylor & Francis Group, and Cambridge Scholars Publishing, for their financial support.

The organisers also wish to thank the members of the Scientific Committee, who devoted their precious time to reviewing the many submissions, and all the presenters, section chairs and workshop discussants who contributed to the success of the conference. We also thank the plenary speakers Alison Mackey (Georgetown University, and Lancaster University), Marianne Nikolov (University of Pécs), Pavel Trofimovich (Concordia University Montreal) and Rens Bod (University of Amsterdam), as well as the invited speakers and discussants of the Language Learning Round Table, William O'Grady (University of Hawai'i at Manoa), Wander Lowie & Marjolein Verspoor (University of Groningen),

Christine Dimroth (University of Osnabrück) and Manfred Pienemann (University of Paderborn, and Newcastle University).

The Yearbook editors would like to that all those who submitted their papers for consideration. We are also extremely grateful to the Yearbook reviewers, who gave their valuable time to review the papers, and without whom this volume would not have been possible: Maria Dimitrakopoulou, Violetta Demonte, Tiina Eilola, Fanny Fosberg Lundell, Alison Gabriele, Ayşe Gürel, Bjørn Hammerstrøm, Jan Hulstijn, Carrie Jackson, Jill Jaegerski, Scott Jarvis, Seon Jeon, Tihana Kraš, Àngels Llanes Baró, Wander Lowie, Cristobal Lozano, Theo Marinis, Kevin McManus, Carmen Munoz, Muiris O'laire, Jason Rothman, Rapael Salaberry, Sarah Schimke, Ludovica Serratrice, Ianthi Tsimpli, Josje Verhagen, and Keiko Yoshioda.

Leah Roberts, University of York
Ineke Vedder, University of Amsterdam
Jan Hulstijn, University of Amsterdam

Introduction

This year's volume opens with a set of papers on the general topic of complexity. Firstly, Gyllstad, Granfeldt, Bernardini and Källkvist report on a study – a contribution to the empirical underpinning of the Common European Framework of Reference for Languages (CEFR) – which aims to identify linguistic correlates to the proficiency levels defined by the CEFR. The study was conducted in a Swedish school setting, focusing on English, French and Italian, and examined the relationship between CEFR levels (A1–C2) assigned by experienced raters to learners' written texts and three measures of syntactic complexity (based on length of t-unit, subclause ratio, and mean length of clause). Data were elicited through two written tasks (a short letter and a narrative) completed by pupils of L2 English (N = 54) in years four, nine and the final year of upper-secondary school, L3 French (N = 38) in year nine and the final year of upper-secondary school, and L4 Italian (N = 28) in the final year of upper-secondary school and first year of university. The results showed that, globally, there were weak to medium-strong correlations between assigned CEFR levels and the three measures of syntactic complexity in English, French and Italian. Furthermore, it was found that syntactic complexity was homogeneous across the three languages at CEFR level A, whereas syntactic complexity was different across languages at CEFR level B, especially in the data for English and French. The results demonstrate that two of the three general measures of syntactic complexity show a greater sensitivity at the levels of proficiency covered in this study: both Mean length of T-unit and Mean number of subordinate clauses/T-unit are capable of discriminating between CEFR levels A and B within French and English.

In the next paper, Jensen and Howard report on a longitudinal study of French and Chinese learners of English over a nine month Study Abroad period. The results for complexity and accuracy suggest that the extent to which time, or LoS abroad, influences development in complexity and accuracy is inconsistent, or at least, subject to a great deal of variation at the individual level. This underlying individual variation is evident by the non-linear fashion in which learners progress or regress over time. The actual extent to which LoS abroad influences such progression or regression is also subject to individual variation.

In the context of a Complex Systems (CS) approach to language acquisition and teaching research, Hilton and Royer describe in the next paper the potential of using Geometric Data Analysis (GDA) to explore langauge acquisition data, particularly on how one can investigate the complex relationships between individual features and early L2 skill. Using classroom data from beginning learners of English in a primary school context in France; their participants performed four different tasks at two times during their first year of English and also completed a variety of psychometric tests and questionnaires measuring various cognitive, verbal, affective et conative characteristics. As the authors note, since variability is the norm in classroom behavior and in language acquisition, individual characteristics must be an important part of the information that should be considered in our studies, and our observational tools should be able to reflect a large number of characteristics and the interactions between them. The authors state that the field will need to accept that CDS research must start with small-scale or even individual studies, in which numerous qualitative and quantitative measurements are taken on very few learners at a time (Lowie & Verspoor 2013; Mackey 2013). We will have to build up slowly to "group" perspectives – where groups are defined in a data-driven way, and not necessarily by institutional level or age. The authors show that Geometric Data Analysis is an interesting means of uncovering structure in data, and how it can help to formulate qualitative interpretations of objectively-measured variables, and they outline ideas for future research within the complex systems paradigm.

We stay in the language classroom for the next paper, by Snape, Matthews, Hirakawa, Hirakawa and Hosoi who investigate the question of language attrition, focusing on four Japanese child returnees who had lived in the U.S. between 8 and 12 years before returning to Japan. Data was collected on three separate occasions over a period of 12 months in which their English proficiency was assessed by TOEIC and C-test scores, and they undertook an Acceptability Judgment Task (AJT). Despite the returnees' exposure and daily use of English having decreased since returning to Japan, only slight L2 attrition of English was found in the domain of aspect for one returnee. Overall, the results indicate that rather than L2 language loss, the returnees managed to maintain their competence in the L2 aspectual domain.

Nadia Mifka Profozic reports on a study investigating the effectiveness of recasts and clarification requests in a French as a foreign language classroom, with three classes of high school students in New Zealand. The study targeted the acquisition of the *passé composé* and the *imparfait* using picture-based and written narrative tasks designed to encourage communication and to elicit the use of past tense. Overall, the results indicate that recasts were more effective for acquisition of the *passé composé* whereas both recasts and clarification requests proved beneficial for acquisition of the *imparfait* at this early stage of learning. Also, a comparison between more advanced and less advanced learners suggest that only the 'low proficiency' learners benefited from clarification requests.

The next set of papers focuses acquisition of syntax, and in particular, on cross-linguistic influences. Guijarro-Fuentes presents the results of a study on Chinese learners of Spanish, investigating the extent to which adult learners are (un)able to acquire new functional features that result in a L2 grammar that is mentally structured like the native target language. The author examine their data in the light of competing hypotheses: the *Interpretability Hypothesis* (*IH*, Hawkins & Hattori 2006; Tsimpli & Dimitrakopoulou 2007) and the *Feature Reassembly Hypothesis* (Lardiere 2009). The results of the two reported experimental tasks show that parametrically different uninterpretable and interpretable features are not totally accessible to adult L2 learners, but that proficiency level and individual differences figure largely in the implementation of them, causing target deviant patterns. The author argue that contrary to the *IH*, their results show initial underspecification of the [+/−] interpretable features in interlanguage grammars and a gradual process which would first mimic L1-consistency before becoming native-like.

In the next paper, Ahern, Amenós Pons and Guijarro-Fuentes present the results of a study comparing French and English L2 learners of Spanish testing their interpretation of mood choice in *if*-conditional constructions (conditional utterances containing both regular and irregular indicative and subjunctive forms). Irrespective of the learners' different L1s, the learner groups performed similarly in the written task. The authors argue that their findings demonstrate that feature re-assembly in L2 Spanish is not trouble-free, as simple current feature accounts would advocate, even if those features exist in the learners' L1.

Continuing with the theme of L1 influences, Rankin explores some of the learnability implications of Full Transfer at the initial state of L2A. His study investigates L1 English-speaking learners' comprehension of L2 German questions and relative clauses is tested on the basis of a picture interpretation task. The patterns of (mis)interpretation of the German clauses in his study suggest that lower-intermediate proficiency learners still access the L1 syntax in order to parse L2 input. Ranking takes these findings to indicate that learners are influenced by L1 word order patterns in assigning thematic roles in L2 clauses and discusses them in light of approaches to L2 parsing and processing which attribute different roles to L1 influence.

In the next paper, Linqvist and Falk explore the role of the L1 and the L2 in L3 oral production, both as regards syntax and the lexicon, in the film retellings of 11 German L3 learners of Swedish. Previous research has shown that both L1 and L2 are used in L3 oral production, and different explanatory factors have been put forward, e.g. (psycho)typology and L2 status. However, these factors do not explain why function words tend to come from L2 while content words seem to be transferred from both L1 and L2 to a larger extent. The transfer patterns in L3 that the authors observe in their analysis of lexical and syntactic transfer largely support the predictions from the declarative/procedural model (Paradis 2009) which state that syntactic transfer will come from L2; transfer of function words from L2; and transfer of content words from both L1 and L2.

Taking a usage-based perspective, in the final paper Paquot investigates transfer effects on French EFL learners' use of recurrent word sequences focusing on a large dataset of two- to four-word lexical bundles overrepresented in the French component of the *International Corpus of Learner English* (ICLE) as compared to nine other ICLE learner sub-corpora. In her results, the different manifestations of L1 influence displayed in the learners' idiosyncratic use of lexical bundles are traced back to various properties of French words and word combinations, among which their discourse function and frequency of use seem to play a crucial role.

We hope you agree that this year's Yearbook exemplifies some of the excellent work being undertaken in the field of SLA today.

Leah Roberts, University of York
Ineke Vedder, University of Amsterdam
Jan Hulstijn, University of Amsterdam

Linguistic correlates to communicative proficiency levels of the CEFR

The case of syntactic complexity in written L2 English, L3 French and L4 Italian

Henrik Gyllstad, Jonas Granfeldt, Petra Bernardini and Marie Källkvist
Lund University

This study is a contribution to the empirical underpinning of the Common European Framework of Reference for Languages (CEFR), and it aims to identify linguistic correlates to the proficiency levels defined by the CEFR. The study was conducted in a Swedish school setting, focusing on English, French and Italian, and examined the relationship between CEFR levels (A1–C2) assigned by experienced raters to learners' written texts and three measures of syntactic complexity (based on length of t-unit, subclause ratio, and mean length of clause (cf. Norris & Ortega, 2009)). Data were elicited through two written tasks (a short letter and a narrative) completed by pupils of L2 English (N = 54) in years four, nine and the final year of upper-secondary school, L3 French (N = 38) in year nine and the final year of upper-secondary school, and L4 Italian (N = 28) in the final year of upper-secondary school and first year of university. The results showed that, globally, there were weak to medium-strong correlations between assigned CEFR levels and the three measures of syntactic complexity in English, French and Italian. Furthermore, it was found that syntactic complexity was homogeneous across the three languages at CEFR level A, whereas syntactic complexity was different across languages at CEFR level B, especially in the data for English and French. Consequences for the empirical validity of the CEFR framework and the nature of the three measures of complexity are discussed.

Introduction

The *Common European Framework of Reference: teaching, learning and assessment* (Council of Europe, 2001, henceforth CEFR) is now widely referred to and used in modern language syllabuses and in proficiency tests, in Europe and beyond (Figueras, 2012; Leung & Lewkowicz, 2012). Its empirical validity has been questioned, however (Hulstijn, 2007), and in a recent volume focusing on the relationship between the communicatively defined CEFR levels and the linguistic constructions produced by users on these levels, members of the SLATE research group (Second Language Acquisition and Testing in Europe, see http://www.slate.eu.org/) emphasize the need for research that connects the CEFR to both language testing and language acquisition (Hulstijn, Alderson & Schoonen, 2010). A general concern in this regard is the validity of the framework's descriptive scales of language proficiency. Specifically, Hulstijn, Alderson & Schoonen (2010) advance a set of research questions, two of which are immediately relevant here:

> What are the linguistic profiles at every CEFR level for the two productive language skills (speaking and writing) and what are the linguistic features typical of the two receptive skills (listening and reading) at every CEFR level?
>
> To what extent do common or different profile features exist across the seven target languages investigated by researchers in the SLATE group (Dutch, English, Finnish, French, German, Italian and Swedish)?
>
> (Hulstijn, Alderson & Schoonen, 2010: 17–18)

In an attempt to respond to the SLATE call for more CEFR-related acquisition research, and with a clear bearing on the above research questions, this paper aims to investigate the relation between assessed CEFR levels and a set of general measures of syntactic complexity in written data in L2 English, L3 French and L4 Italian. To set the scene for our empirical study, we first provide some relevant background to the CEFR. We then outline some current issues and challenges, before accounting for the notion of complexity and explaining why we believe (syntactic) complexity to be a relevant concept when addressing the research questions above. Finally, we review some previous studies that have investigated CEFR levels and linguistic correlates.

Background

The CEFR

The CEFR is a rich document and provides, among other things, a language-independent description of language use and a definition of communicative proficiency at six levels. The levels (A1, A2, B1, B2, C1 and C2) align with three broad proficiency bands: Basic User (A), Independent User (B) and Advanced User (C). The CEFR is action-oriented; language users are viewed as social agents who take part in communicative activities in relation to other agents and social institutions.

CEFR level	Descriptor
A2	Can write short, simple formulaic notes relating to matters in areas of immediate need.
B1	Can convey information and ideas on abstract as well as concrete topics, check information and ask about or explain problems with reasonable precision.

Figure 1. Example of CEFR level descriptors.

These activities necessarily involve language in a broad sense and the CEFR describes *what* a learner can do with respect to a specific task at a certain level of communicative proficiency and *how well* he or she can do it. Consider as an illustration the example in Figure 1 of descriptors at the adjacent levels A2 and B1 from the scale entitled *Overall written interaction* (Council of Europe, 2001:83).

The CEFR encompasses four categories of language activities of this type (reception, production, interaction and mediation). These activities are further specified with respect to domains of language use (i.e. personal, public etc.) and three types of parameters regarding situational context, text type and external constraints on language use (Little, 2007). In addition to the functional scales of Chapter 4 on language use and the language user (*cf.* example above), Chapter 5 of the CEFR specifies the learner's/user's competences. The scales in this chapter define linguistic, pragmatic and socio-linguistic competences needed to carry out the activities. In particular, Chapter 5 presents communicative language competences. As in the rest of the CEFR, the scales in Chapter 5 are language independent. There is thus no mention of particular languages like French, English or Italian but examples (words and sentences) are provided in descriptors and in surrounding texts. Even though not explicitly stated, the underlying assumption of the CEFR must be that a particular communicative activity requires the same level of language proficiency in all languages involved. There should be no difference, then, with respect to communicative difficulty when writing a formal letter in French or in Swedish. Furthermore, the language-independent approach in the CEFR implies that communicative tasks and the proficiency needed to carry them out are learned in the same order and at approximately the same pace in all languages.

The CEFR represents a major step forward in establishing a common European basis for teaching, learning and assessment of languages in Europe. Since its publication in English in 2001, the CEFR has been translated into more than 35 languages. It is fair to say that the framework has had enormous success in the sense that it has been adopted by a large number of stakeholders in the European language sector. An increasingly large number of language programmes make use of the CEFR for curricula development; major language tests under the ALTE hospice (see www.alte.org) are aligned to the CEFR, and policy makers rely on the CEFR when creating entrance exams. Needless to say, such a wide-spread and influential framework should remain open to debate and improvements. Currently, a number of issues and questions remain unexplored. In the next subsection we briefly outline a few that are of particular relevance to the present study.

Three current issues and open questions with respect to the CEFR

On a first critical note, the relative absence of empirical underpinnings of CEFR descriptors and scales has been pointed out (Alderson, 2007; Hulstijn, 2007). In fact, descriptors and scales in the CEFR originate from previous proficiency scales and were initially screened for relevance by experienced language teachers. Scales and descriptors were subsequently subjected to different kinds of quality assessments, including the use of Item Response Theory (IRT) in the form of Rasch analyses in several steps (North, 2007). Nevertheless, there is an urgent need for empirical validation of descriptors and levels on the basis of performance data from language learners' production and comprehension.

A second observation concerns the inter-relationship between activity-oriented scales in Chapter 4 (*cf.* example above) and competence-based scales in Chapter 5. The way scales are presented in the CEFR gives the impression that they should be read together in such a way that learners that are at, say, level A2 with respect to e.g., *Overall written interaction* (Council of Europe, 2001: 83) are simultaneously at the same A2 level with respect to competence-based scales, like e.g., *Vocabulary control* (Council of Europe, 2001: 112). In his paper, Hulstijn (2007: 664) discusses such a "parallel" reading of CEFR scales from a Second Language Acquisition (SLA) perspective. Hulstijn notes that SLA research has shown that there are at least three types of L2 users: (a) learners who can do few things but with high linguistic quality, (b) learners who can do many language tasks but with low linguistic quality and (c) learners whose range of language tasks is parallel to their linguistic ability. Hulstijn notes that, as a result of the way the CEFR presents its scales, only the third type is included. We can add to Hulstijn's argument that possible inter-relationships between different scales remain an empirical question, and the answer can only be found if the first critical point (*cf.* above) is properly addressed. To the best of our knowledge, only once does the CEFR recognise the existence of "uneven profiles" (Council of Europe, 2001: 17), i.e. users who are at different levels of proficiency in different activities, but nothing is said about the frequency or specificities of such potential users.

Continuing on this last point, several researchers have pointed out that the definition of language proficiency in the CEFR could more generally benefit from taking into account findings in SLA research (see contributions in Bartning, Martin & Vedder (2010) and references below). In particular, the rather brief and general descriptors of linguistic competences in Chapter 5.2 could be improved and specified by integrating results on the acquisition of particular languages. There is now a considerable body of corpus-based studies on L2 development and L2 performance in many European languages, including classic large-scale projects like European Science Foundation (Perdue 1995) and recent quasi-experimental projects like the WISP-project (*cf.* Hulstijn, Schoonen, de Jong, Steinel & Florijn, 2012).

Taken together, the three points briefly outlined above represent the motivation for our current project. In the present paper we limit ourselves to two types of language activities, written interaction and creative writing. We investigate learner production and discuss the notion of (syntactic) complexity in relation to this production. As we show in the following sections, the notion of complexity forms an important part of the definition of communicative linguistic competence in the CEFR. At the same time, SLA researchers are currently discussing the construct and operationalization of linguistic complexity. This makes complexity an ideal candidate for bringing the two perspectives together (*cf.* the third point above). By so doing we hope to contribute to the further development of the CEFR.

Complexity in the CEFR

The notion of complexity is frequently referred to in the CEFR. In the Swedish translation, we find no less than 59 occurrences of adjectival uses of *complex* with various nouns and 90 occurrences of its antonym *simple/basic*. The CEFR talks about *complex language, complex speech, complex material, simple syntax, simple information* etc. Therefore, it is fair to say that the notions of complexity and simplicity are well-represented in the CEFR. At no point, however, does the CEFR define what complexity (or its opposite) is.

If we look more closely at Chapter 5, these terms are used in several scales and at several proficiency levels. A detailed analysis of the terminology used in all scales in Chapter 5 reveals the results presented in Table 1. From this 'key word in context' (KWIC)-type of analysis it is possible to make four observations. Firstly, there is frequent use of the terms *complex, simple* and *basic* in these scales. Secondly, these terms are used at some but not all levels; they are particularly frequent at levels A1 and A2. Thirdly, there is an overall development starting in simple, basic and short sentences, structures and patterns, and developing into increasingly more complex and longer sentences, structures and patterns. Lastly, but importantly, our analysis revealed a gradient turning point at level B1. The

Table 1. References to complex vs simple/basic in two scales for linguistic competence.

CEFR level	Simple – complex
C2	"complex language"
C1	
B2	"some complex sentence forms", "longer complex stretches of speech"
B1	"expressing more complex thoughts", "simple face-to-face conversation"
A2	"basic language", "basic language functions", "basic sentence patterns", "simple sentences", "simple structures", "simple needs", "simple connectors"
A1	"basic range of simple expressions", "few simple grammatical structures", "very basic linear connectors"

descriptors below B1 include the adjectives *simple* and *basic* while descriptors at B1 use both *simple* and *complex*, and descriptors above B1 only use the adjective *complex*. It is thus possible to interpret level B1 as the threshold level where the CEFR assumes that the users reorganise their linguistic system in such a way that it becomes increasingly complex.

Complexity in L2 research

In SLA, complexity is often regarded as one of the legs in the triad Complexity-Accuracy-Fluency (Skehan, 1998). It is acknowledged, however, that complexity is the most elusive of the three to define (Housen & Kuiken, 2009). In their discussion of complexity, Housen & Kuiken (2009) distinguish between *cognitive* and *linguistic complexity*. In this paper, our focus is on the latter of the two.

Linguistic complexity in a L2 has been defined as the size, elaborateness, richness, and diversity of some level of the interlanguage system (Housen & Kuiken, 2009). It is thus possible to talk about, e.g. phonological complexity, lexical complexity, and syntactic complexity. The operationalization of linguistic complexity also presents major challenges. How can linguistic complexity be measured reliably, across languages and in different types of tasks, and with different types of learners? With respect to syntactic complexity, the literature distinguishes in this case between *general* and *specific* measures (see Norris & Ortega, 2009). The former are typically language-independent measures of length and degree of subordination, whereas the latter are typically language-specific constructions or morphemes for which developmental trajectories are known. In this latter case, syntactic complexity emerges as a dynamic and developmentally sensitive measure based on acquisitional timing.

It has been suggested that general measures of syntactic complexity display a linear correlation with overall language proficiency (Wolfe-Quintero, Inagaki & Kim, 1998). Recently, Norris & Ortega (2009), while acknowledging the findings of Wolf-Quintero and colleagues (1998), argued that also general measures need to be adjusted to the development of the learner. Therefore they proposed an organic and dynamic approach to operationalizing syntactic complexity in L2 performance. In short, they suggested three measures that jointly can account for the growth of complexity in L2 performance, defined in the following way (Norris & Ortega, 2009: 561):

1. Overall or general complexity measured by a length-based measure (i.e. length of T-units)
2. Complexity via subordination measured by a subclause-ratio measure (i.e. subordinate clauses / T-unit)
3. Subclausal complexity via phrasal elaboration measured by mean length of clause.

Norris & Ortega argue that the last measure, mean length of clause, is particularly important for capturing development among more advanced learners and that it differs from other length-based measures in crucial ways:

> When the average length of all finite clauses (counted regardless of their status as independent, dependent, or subordinate) is calculated, any increases can only result from the addition of pre- or postmodification within a phrase (via adjectives, adverbs, prepositional phrases, or nonfinite clauses) or as a result of the use of nominalizations, or the process of reduction of clauses into phrases which help to condense information […]. Thus, mean length of clause is radically different from the other length-based measures […]. Despite its sharing a superficial similarity with the other length-based calculations, clause length taps a more narrowly defined source of complexification; it must be considered a specific measure that taps complexification subclausally, that is, at the phrasal level.
> (Norris & Ortega, 2009: 561)

They furthermore conclude that the relationship between the three measures is not necessarily a linear, and there may not be a linear relationship with overall language proficiency either. They suggest that syntactic complexity may initially develop linearly along the length and subordinate clause axes but only up to a certain point. After this point, which remains to be identified, complexity might increase in other ways.

Previous research

Two types of previous research related to the CEFR are relevant to the present paper. On the one hand, the CEFR has been supplemented with language-specific material, like *Niveau B2 pour le français* (Beacco, Bouquet & Pourquier, 2004). These additions provide detailed inventories of language functions, words and structures for specific CEFR levels. While certainly useful for many purposes, the approach taken in these publications is, however, still top-down and these large inventories appear not to be the result of empirical research of what learners actually do. An example of work that does rely on learner performances can be found in the English Profile Programme, based on the Cambridge Learner Corpus (Hawkins & Filipović, 2012). On a general level, this research has shown that the mean length of utterance (MLU) increases steadily as learners progress across the CEFR levels with A2 = 7.9; B1 = 10.8; B2 = 14.2; C1 = 17.3; and C2 = 19.0 (Hawkins & Filipović, 2012: 23). This increase in MLU, a measure seen as an indicator of learning, is argued to stem from the fact that learners' output becomes more expressive, as well as longer and syntactically more complex: "…with added length comes added complexity of sentence structure and the generation and use of more complex sentence types" (Hawkins & Filipović, 2012: 23).

It seems this latter type of research is more in line with the kind of work advocated by the SLATE network researchers, who have approached the CEFR from a learner perspective. While acknowledging the importance of the CEFR and its potential, the research focus in SLATE is on matching the description of linguistic competences in Chapter 5 with the functional levels for different language activities in Chapter 4. The overarching research question was formulated in Hulstijn, Alderson & Schoonen (2010: 17): "Which linguistic features of learner performance (for a given target language) are typical at each of the six CEFR levels?", and a first set of results on Dutch, Finnish, French, English, Italian and Spanish were published in a dedicated volume edited by Bartning, Martin & Vedder (2010). For the purposes of the present study, a closer look at some of these studies is warranted.

Forsberg & Bartning (2010) investigated to what extent morphosyntax, discourse organisation and use of formulaic language could be matched with the six CEFR levels (A1–C2), analysing written data from Swedish university-level students (N = 42) learning French. Each student was assigned to one of the CEFR levels through taking the DIALANG vocabulary placement test and the diagnostic test measuring written skills, together with a self-assessment test. They then completed two written tasks (a summary of a film or a book, and a written text specific to each CEFR level). In terms of relevance to the present study, significant differences were found between adjacent CEFR levels for morphosyntactic deviances (errors, such as lack of subject-verb agreement or incorrect gender on articles) up to the B2 level. It should be noted, however, that the data for the A1 and C1 levels were not submitted to any statistical analyses due to there being too few values.

Martin, Mustonen, Reiman & Seilonen (2010) conducted a study on learners of L2 Finnish, including young learners in grades 7–9 in Finnish schools and adults taking a national proficiency certificate exam (> 20 different L1 backgrounds). The data set consisted of 669 texts, covering three text types: an informal message, a formal message, and an argumentative text. Three domains were studied: the use of cases, transitive constructions and passive constructions. Each text had been independently rated to be at a given CEFR level (A1–C2). The researchers found that targeted structures occurred more frequently and accurately as a function of higher CEFR levels, but no quantitative measure of complexity was used since no such measure was deemed "sufficiently refined" (2010:75).

Furthermore, in a study targeting L2 Dutch, Spanish and Italian, Kuiken, Vedder & Gilabert (2010) looked at the relation between communicative adequacy and syntactic complexity, lexical diversity and accuracy in adult university-level learners' written production. The participants (N = 103) came from a wide range of L1 backgrounds and they varied in proficiency level from A2 to C1, although the majority were in the A2 to B1 range. Their judged proficiency was based on a C-test. The two tasks were argumentative written texts. Each written text was assessed by 3–4 raters in terms of its judged CEFR level. Syntactic complexity was operationalized as the number of clauses per T-unit and a subclause ratio. The results showed significant correlations between rated communicative adequacy and measured lexical diversity and accuracy, but not for syntactic complexity. The authors argue that the results suggest that rated levels for linguistic complexity were guided more by the range of vocabulary used and the accuracy of learners' production than by the observed two measures of complexity (clauses per T-unit and subclause ratio). The authors also concluded that if participants were split up on the basis of proficiency levels, the correlations between holistically assessed linguistic complexity and communicative adequacy were stronger for the higher proficiency groups than for the lower proficiency groups for the three targeted languages.

In a more recent study by Prodeau, Lopez & Véronique (2012) written production from 40 learners of French (with a variety of L1s), taken from the *Test de Connaissance de français*, was analysed. All texts were rated according to the CEFR by several experienced raters. Half of the texts were rated as belonging to B1 and the other half as belonging to B2. All texts were examined for different linguistic features, whether correct or not, in an attempt to find out whether learners at these two different CEFR levels use different linguistic means. Prodeau and colleagues found no morphosyntactic (nominal or verbal) features capable of discriminating between these two CEFR levels. However, the authors suggest that text length could be used to distinguish the two levels (2012:63).

Summing up previous findings, we find that studies differ on several points, including target L2s, L1s of the learners, CEFR-levels involved, types of measures (specific or general) used and linguistic task type. Considering these notable differences in design, it is perhaps not surprising that it is difficult to draw conclusions and generalize from these studies. This in itself motivates further research on this topic. In our view cross-linguistic comparison is important in studies in this domain since the CEFR is a language-independent framework. At this point of research, a comparison across languages seems, however, more feasible if the dependent variables are general (complexity) measures, like in the study by Kuiken, Vedder & Gilabert (2010). In the present study, we keep the L1 close to constant (Swedish for all learners). Furthermore, following suggestions by Norris & Ortega (2009), we add a third syntactic complexity measure (mean length of clause) which is argued to be specifically suited to capture developments at higher proficiency levels. Against this background, we developed three research questions, to which we now turn.

1. What is the correlation between the three general measures of syntactic complexity – Mean length of T-unit, Mean number of subordinate clauses per T-unit, and Mean length of clause – and the rated CEFR levels?
2. For the three general measures of syntactic complexity, are there differences:
   a. between languages within the same CEFR level?
   b. between CEFR levels within the same language?

Method

Participants

Our data set consists of texts from a total of 120 unique participants writing in the three targeted languages: L2 English: N = 54; L3 French: N = 38; L4 Italian: N = 28. The L2 learners of English were at three different levels in the Swedish school system: 19 were in year 4 (10–11 years old, 45% female); 14 were in year 9 (15–16 years old, 64% female), and 21 were in their final year of upper secondary school (17–19 years of age, 62% female). The L3 learners of French were at two different levels (L3 classes are available as an option from year 6): 22 were in year 9 (15–16 years of age, 59% female) and 16 were in their final year of upper-secondary school (18–19 years old, 69% female). The L4 learners of Italian were either

Table 2. Participants from the three target languages and their school level.

	Year 4	Year 9	Year 12	University
	Compulsory school		Upper-secondary school	Tertiary level
L2 English	X N = 19	X N = 14	X N = 21	
L3 French		X N = 22	X N = 16	
L4 Italian			X N = 21	X N = 7

in the final year of upper secondary school or from university. Italian as a L4 is offered only at upper-secondary school. Of these, 21 (18–19 years, 43% female) were in their final year of upper-secondary school and 7 (25–67 years old, 57% female) were at university at a level which requires completed courses in Italian from the final year of upper-secondary school.

Data collection procedures

All participants were enrolled in different schools in a city in southern Sweden and were recruited through personal contacts with teachers or head teachers at the schools. Intact classes were approached and asked to participate by completing two written tasks on computer online. Participants were told that their participation was voluntary and that they could withdraw their participation at any time.

A website was specifically designed for data collection, containing three separate sections to be completed by each participant. The use of an online platform not only facilitated data collection across groups and locations, it was also felt to have face validity with the participants in the sense that writing on a computer online would have more appeal than a traditional paper-and-pencil format. The first section of the website was used to gather background information, asking students to state their full names, date of birth, school year and name of school, language(s) used in the home, amount and type of exposure to the target language at hand, and to indicate on a scale the ease with which they were able to type on a computer, ranging from 'very easy' to 'very difficult'. Once these background details had been entered, students clicked to save the information and continued to Section 2, which provided instructions for task 1 and a box in which to type their text. Once task 1 had been completed, students clicked on a button to save the text, and continued to Section 3, which provided instructions for task 2 and a box in which to type their text. Once students had completed text 2, they clicked on a button to save their text and leave the website. Where possible, data were collected in computer rooms at the schools, but in cases where such facilities were unavailable, students were asked to come to a computer room at the local university to complete the tasks.

Participants were allowed 40 minutes to complete both tasks on computer. No language support (dictionaries, grammars etc.) was allowed. All participants were able to complete both tasks within the allotted time frame, apart from two year-4 pupils, who needed slightly more time.

The tasks

For the purpose of targeting somewhat different domains, registers, functions and linguistic structures, we used two tasks with all participants. The tasks were somewhat adapted versions of two tasks (#2 and #5) used by Alanen, Huhta & Tarnanen (2010) in a CEFR-linked study of young and adult learners' L2 English and L2 Finnish in Finland (the Cefling project). Details about the tasks are provided in Table 3.

Task 1 instructed students to write an email message to their teacher. It was made somewhat easier for the year-4 pupils (10–11 years of age) than for the year-9 students (15–16 years old) and the students in their final year of upper-secondary school (19–20 years of age). In task 2, students were asked to write a story about something nice or exciting that had happened to them, with the purpose of eliciting a narrative text. The instructions were identical for L2 English learners in year 4 and year 9, and for L3 learners of French in year 9, whereas the instructions for learners of English, French and Italian in their final year of upper-secondary

Table 3. The two tasks used in the study (adapted from Alanen, Huhta & Tarnanen, 2010: 32).

Task	Domain, register and functions
Task 1 E-mail message to a teacher	*Domain and register*: personal life, school, informal or formal *Functions*: argumentation or expressing obligation/necessity, asking for information *Linguistic structures*: questions, negation, tense, locative expressions
Task 2 Story	*Domain and register*: personal life, informal *Functions*: describing and narrating, argumentation or expressing an opinion, liking or dislike *Linguistic structures*: tense, agreement

school or first year of university (Italian) were identical. All the task instructions can be found in Appendix 1.

The CEFR raters

A total of eight CEFR raters were asked to read the texts and provide a CEFR score ranging from A1 to C2. Of these, seven were trained and experienced raters. The least experienced rater (R4 for Italian) did not have any formal CEFR rating training but was an experienced teacher, well familiar with the CEFR framework. Two of the raters assessed the English texts, two rated the texts written in French, and four rated the Italian texts (R1 and R2 for the upper-secondary school texts, and R3 and R4 for the university-level texts). Details on the raters are provided in Table 4 below.

The raters assessed the texts independently of each other. The procedure was as follows. The raters received the texts in pdf format and were also provided with a CEFR scale (Appendix 2) that had been compiled from several of the CEFR scales. The scale consisted of 'can-do statements', and linguistic form and/or accuracy was never mentioned. The raters were asked to: (a) rate each text using the CEFR scale provided (A1, A2, B1, B2, C1 and C2), (b) indicate the degree of certainty of each rating on a 4-point scale ranging from 'completely certain' to 'completely uncertain', and (c) to provide an alternative CEFR rating if, and only if, the indicated degree of certainty was low (i.e. 'uncertain' or 'completely uncertain'). Raters entered the information in a spreadsheet provided by the researchers. The spreadsheet also contained a column where raters could enter any additional information they considered relevant to the assessment task.

Table 4. Details on the raters and their backgrounds.

	English		French		Italian			
	R1	R2	R1	R2	R1	R2	R3	R4
Age	61	57	61	57	52	51	36	34
Training in CEFR rating	Yes	Yes	Yes	Yes	Yes	Yes	Yes	No
Frequency of CEFR rating	Several times a year	Every day	Every day	Sometimes	Several times a year	Several times a year	Once or twice a year	No
Approx. number of rated texts	< 200	> 1500	"More than I can say"	> 100	> 200	> 300	> 200	0

Coding and analysis of the data

Text files were automatically converted to basic CHAT-format using the textin tool in the CLAN toolbox (MacWhinney, 2000). All files were manually segmented and coded for T-units and tokens and types of dependent clauses. Analyses to generate descriptive statistics were run using a combination of utility programs in the CLAN toolbox. Examples from each of the three target languages in this study along with their respective coding are provided below:

(1) English
[$_{\text{T-UNIT}}$ [$_{\text{MATRIX}}$ I hope] [$_{\text{SUBCLAUSE}}$ that I will be back in school on monday]].

(2) French
[$_{\text{T-UNIT}}$ [$_{\text{MATRIX}}$ Je suis desolé] [$_{\text{SUBCLAUSE}}$ que je n' étais pas en
    I am sorry   that I was NEG in
l'école   la semaine dernière]].
the school the week last

(3) Italian
[[$_{\text{SUBCLAUSE}}$ Quando ero   un bambino] [$_{\text{MATRIX}}$ ho   giocato
       when   (I)was a kid   (I)have played
calcio spesso]].
soccer often

On the basis of the coded data, three measures of syntactic complexity were computed. For an individual learner text, Mean length of T-unit was computed as the total number of words divided by the total number of T-units in the text. Likewise, Mean number of subordinate clauses was computed as the total number of subordinate clauses divided by the total number of T-units in the text. Following the definition in Norris & Ortega (2009: 561), Mean length of clause was computed on all finite clauses, counted regardless of their status as matrix or subordinate clauses. A matrix clause was defined here as a main clause minus a possible subordinate clause. Overt subordinators (e.g. *that, que, quando*) were analysed as heading the subordinate clause.

Results

The distribution of texts and rated CEFR levels

Table 5 presents the distribution of texts from all three languages across the CEFR levels. The distribution in the table is based on averaged scores, where the CEFR

Table 5. Distribution of rated texts across the six main CEFR levels and intermediate levels for each language.

	A1		A2		B1		B2		C1	C2
English	15	11	17	6	24	14	16	1		
French	7	25	11	14	9	6	2	2		
Italian	5	4	20	14	7	5				

ratings (A1–C2) were first transformed into a numerical value (1–6). Then the two scores were added and an average was calculated for each text. For example, a rating of A1 (= a score of 1) and A2 (= a score of 2) for a text yields a combined score of 1.5 (3 divided by 2). Thus, the A1 row in the table contains texts that were given a rating of A1 from both raters, and the A2 row texts that were rated A2 by both raters etc. The columns in-between the major six CEFR levels contain texts where the raters provided different CEFR scores. For example, the column in-between A1 and A2 contains 11 English texts. These texts were rated as A1 by one of the raters and A2 by the other.

As is evident from the distribution in Table 5, the texts in our data set ranged predominately between A1 and B2, with very few texts rated above the B2 level. A question that arises, of course, is how to classify the texts that straddle two CEFR levels. One analysis would entail treating these as belonging to the lower of the two levels, as both raters assessed it as being at least on that lower level. However, we chose to present them as residing in-between the six CEFR levels. Support for this solution can be found in the CEFR where, sometimes, the six levels are further subdivided into A1.1 and A1.2 etc., yielding a total of 12 theoretical levels.

Inter-rater reliability

As a first step, we established the level of inter-rater reliability (Bachman 2004) based on the raters' CEFR scores. Since we had two raters assigning a CEFR score to each of the participating students' two texts, we converted the assigned CEFR scores for each rated text into an ordinal scale ranging from 1 to 6, where an original CEFR score of A1 was replaced by the score of 1, and a score of C2 by the score of 6, and the scores in between accordingly, in a logical fashion. We then computed the consistency by using Cronbach's alpha. The obtained coefficients are shown in Table 6 below.

As can be seen in Table 6, high coefficients were obtained for the three languages involved. According to DeVellis (1991: 85), a coefficient of > .9 corresponds to "excellent" reliability, whereas a value of > .8 represents "very good" reliability. The obtained high inter-rater reliability values, close to .8 or higher for all three

Table 6. Inter-rater reliability of the assigned CEFR scores (based on the original data sets).

Data set	Number of cases	Cronbach's alpha
Ratings of English texts	104 pairs	.93
Ratings of French texts	76 pairs	.80
Ratings of Italian texts	56 pairs	.78

languages, meant that further analyses involving correlations between assigned CEFR ratings and other variables would be meaningful.

Research Question 1: What is the deree of correlation between the three general measures of syntactic complexity and the rated CEFR levels?

In order to address RQ1 correlations were computed. This was based on a total of 235 texts generated by the participants. In this analysis, we took an average of the two ratings for each text. For example, a text that was rated as A1 and A2, respectively, was assigned a numeric score of 1.5 (with A1 = 1, and A2 = 2, which gives us 1 + 2 = 3, and 3 ÷ 2 = 1.5). The chosen statistic was Kendall's tau (τ), a non-parametric correlation, since the data set contained a large number of tied ranks (Field, 2005: 131). The obtained correlation values together with the squared correlation values are shown in Table 7. The squared values tell us how much of the variability in the respective syntactic complexity variable can be explained by the assigned CEFR score.

As can be seen, significant correlations were observed for all complexity measures across all three languages. This means that the higher the average CEFR

Table 7. Kendall's tau correlation coefficients (τ) and correlation coefficients squared (τ^2) based on English N = 104 (texts); French N = 76 (texts); Italian N = 55 (texts).

	Complexity Measure 1 N of words per T-Unit		Complexity Measure 2 N of words per clause		Complexity Measure 3 N of clauses per T-Unit	
	τ	τ^2	τ	τ^2	τ	τ^2
English CEFR scores	.48**	.23	.31**	.10	.46**	.21
French CEFR scores	.46**	.21	.21*	.04	.54**	.30
Italian CEFR scores	.38**	.14	.27**	.07	.35**	.12

** Correlation is significant at the .01 level (2-tailed).
* Correlation is significant at the .05 level (2-tailed).

score, the more syntactically complex the text is. For all three languages, there is a trend visible in slightly lower correlations overall for the second measure targeting complexity via subordination, i.e. the number of words per clause. Also, the correlations for Italian are generally lower than for English and French.

Overall the correlations are of medium strength and the squared values show that, taken on their own, each measure can at best only explain between 20 to 30 per cent of the variation in the CEFR ranking data. In itself this is not a surprising finding since it would require a combination of features to explain a larger proportion of variation, but it is interesting to note that the measure Clauses per T-unit consistently has the weakest explanatory power among the three. Given the distribution of CEFR ratings in the data (mainly A2–B1), this result confirms the argument of Norris and Ortega (2009) that Clauses per T-unit is a measure suited to capture development at higher levels of proficiency.

Research Question 2: For the three general measures of syntactic complexity, are there differences: (a) between languages within the same CEFR level?; (b) between CEFR levels within the same language?

In order to address RQ2, we used as our point of departure a simpler analysis model with only three theoretical CEFR levels: A (basic), B (independent) and C (proficient). This simplification was made as some texts, especially in the French data, were given disparate ratings (cf. Table 5 above). Thus, texts rated either A1 or A2 were merged into a new category called A. In a similar fashion, texts rated either B1 or B2 were grouped into a category called B. No text could, however, be classified into category C, so only two CEFR levels were retained (A and B). Texts where the ratings straddled one of the main categories of the CEFR, e.g., a text rated A2 and B1, were excluded from this analysis (3 English texts, 12 French texts and 9 Italian texts). This resulted in a data set consisting of 211 texts. The descriptive statistics for this analysis can be seen in Table 8. Starting with English, from a purely descriptive point of view, we see that the mean values for level B texts are higher than level A texts for all three measures. In fact, this is the case also for French and Italian. However, until we have subjected our data to inferential statistical tests, we cannot know for sure whether these differences are also statistically significant. In order to properly address RQ2, then, we ran an ANOVA.

This analysis was carried out on transformed mean scores (square root) in order to adjust for group means that were not normally distributed. We furthermore used tests that are robust against violations of a regular ANOVA, for example unequal sample sizes (Games-Howell post hoc test (Field, 2005: 341)). The ANOVA showed that there were significant differences between CEFR levels A and B in the

Table 8. Descriptive statistics for measures of syntactic complexity for the assessed texts.

CEFR category	Number of texts	Mean number of words per T-unit (SD)	Mean number of words per clause (SD)	Mean number of clauses per T-unit (SD)
English A	43	7.10 (2.29)	5.54 (1.59)	1.30 (0.38)
English B	58	11.62 (2.65)	6.37 (0.74)	1.83 (0.39)
French A	42	6.76 (1.66)	6.03 (1.28)	1.12 (0.16)
French B	22	9.57 (2.15)	7.00 (1.24)	1.36 (0.20)
Italian A	33	6.23 (2.45)	5.51 (1.88)	1.12 (0.16)
Italian B	13	8.14 (3.07)	6.29 (1.18)	1.27 (0.28)

means for all three syntactic complexity measures, for Mean words per T-Unit, $F(5, 205) = 36.09$, $p < .001$, $r = .47$; for Mean words per clause, $F(5, 205) = 6.24$, $p < .001$, $r = .13$; and for Mean clause per T-Unit, $F(5, 205) = 42.33$, $p < .001$, $r = .51$. The effect sizes thus range from a small effect for the second measure (.13), to a large (.51) and close to large (.47) effect for the third and first measures, respectively. This set of results answers partly the second part of our research question.

In order to answer the remaining parts of RQ2, we turn to the data in Figures 2–4 and Tables 9–11. The figures show error bar graphs for the mean of each measure and each language with 95% confidence intervals for the span of estimated population means, whereas the tables indicate significant differences between CEFR levels for the three complexity measures, as revealed through the post hoc tests. In the following we present the results for each measure in turn and discuss the results in the following order: first we compare the measure across languages for the same CEFR-level; then we compare the measure across CEFR levels within each language.

First, as Figure 2 and Table 9 show, the measure of syntactic complexity, Mean words per T-Unit, shows no significant differences across languages at the rated

Table 9. Table of significant differences for Mean words per T-unit for CEFR-rated English, French and Italian texts.

	English A	English B	French A	French B	Italian A
English A					
English B	***				
French A	no	***			
French B	**	*	***		
Italian A	no	***	no	***	
Italian B	no	*	no	no	no

*** = significant at p < .001; ** = significant at p < .01; * = significant at p < .05.

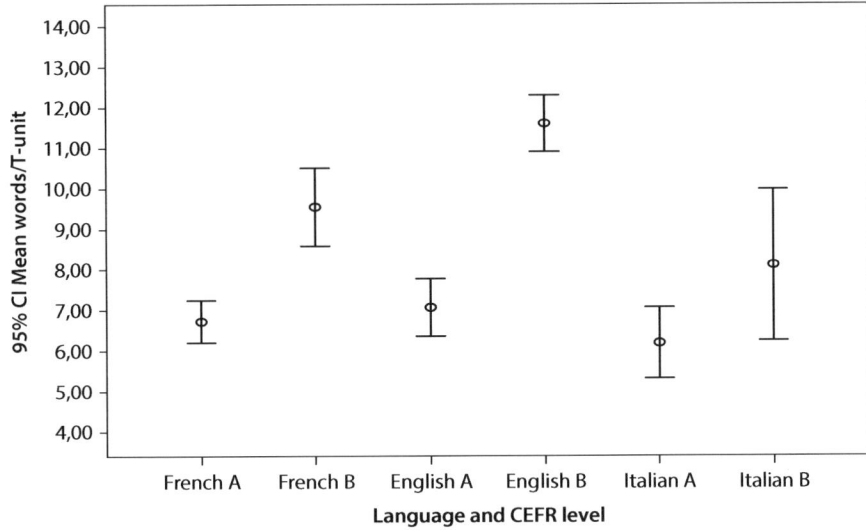

Figure 2. Error bar graphs for Mean words per T-Unit for CEFR-rated English, French and Italian texts. The circle in the middle of each bar represents the mean, and the vertical bar shows the confidence interval (span of estimated population mean) around that mean.

CEFR A level, but there were significant differences between the B levels in English and French and in English and Italian. Second, we found significant differences between rated CEFR levels within two languages, English and French, but not in Italian.

As shown in Figure 3 and Table 10, for Mean words per Clause, no differences between languages within either of the two CEFR levels were found. Looking at the results between rated CEFR levels within languages, however, there were again significant differences for English and French, but not for Italian.

Table 10. Significant differences for Mean words per Clause for CEFR-rated English, French and Italian texts.

	English A	English B	French A	French B	Italian A
English A					
English B	**				
French A	no	no			
French B	**	no	*		
Italian A	no	no	no	**	
Italian B	no	no	no	no	no

*** = significant at p < .001; ** = significant at p < .01; * = significant at p < .05.

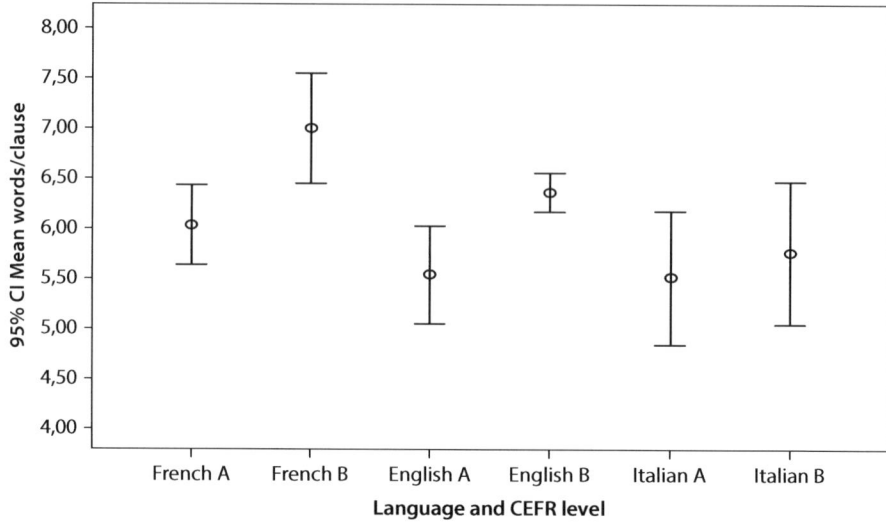

Figure 3. Error bar graphs for Mean words per Clause for CEFR-rated English, French and Italian texts. The circle in the middle of each bar represents the mean, and the vertical bar shows the confidence interval (span of estimated population mean) around that mean.

As to the last of the three complexity measures – Mean clause per T-Unit – the values in Figure 4 and Table 11 indicate that no differences existed between languages within the rated CEFR A level, whereas the English mean was highly significantly different from the French and Italian means for the rated CEFR level B, but no significant differences emerged between the latter two. For within languages, again there were differences for English (A versus B) and French (A versus B), but not for Italian.

Table 11. Table of significant differences for Mean clause per T-unit for CEFR-rated English, French and Italian texts.

	English A	English B	French A	French B	Italian A
English A					
English B	***				
French A	no	***			
French B	no	***	***		
Italian A	no	***	no	***	
Italian B	no	***	no	no	no

*** = significant at p < .001; ** = significant at p < .01; * = significant at p < .05.

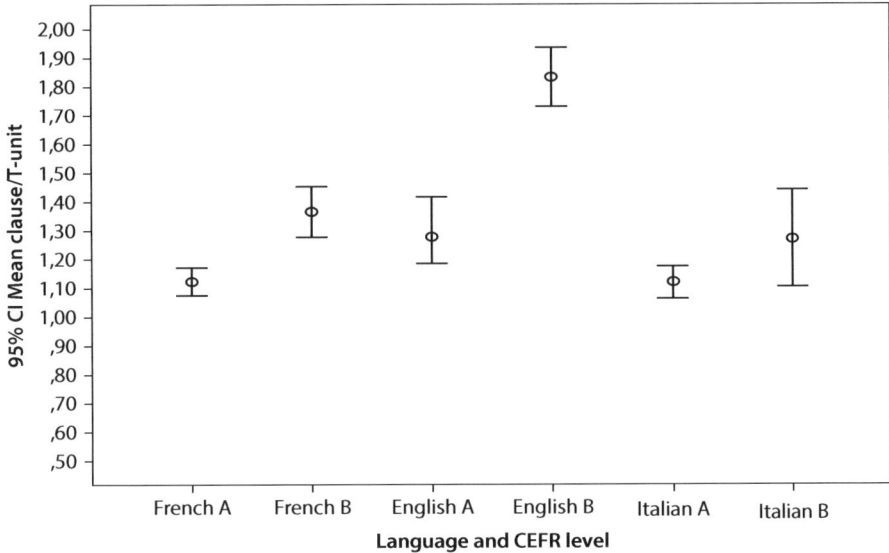

Figure 4. Error bar graphs for Mean clause per T-Unit for CEFR-rated English, French and Italian texts. The circle in the middle of each bar represents the mean, and the vertical bar shows the confidence interval (span of estimated population mean) around that mean.

Discussion

This paper set out to empirically investigate whether communicative proficiency levels of the CEFR can meaningfully (a) be characterized in terms of linguistic profiles, and (b) to what extent these profiles are different in written data from three foreign languages, namely English, French and Italian.

On the one hand, the study is motivated by the fact that although the CEFR is the most wide-spread framework for languages in Europe and its present importance for language policy makers cannot be overstated, little empirical research in relation to the CEFR has been carried out to date. The present study is thus an attempt to contribute to the empirical underpinnings of the CEFR. On the other hand, the study is also motivated by the fact that the few previous studies that have been carried out so far have yielded inconclusive results. For one and the same language (e.g. French), some studies have found that CEFR levels can be separated by (measures of) linguistic features (Forsberg & Bartning, 2010), while others have not (Prodeau, Lopez & Véronique, 2012). It might be suggested that the absence of consistent results in previous research is due to variability in design, populations and materials. In the present study we explicitly aimed at keeping constant a number of background variables.

We opted for three general measures of syntactic complexity as measures of linguistic proficiency. This choice was motivated by the fact that previous SLA studies have found these measures to be suitable for tapping into development of linguistic proficiency (Wolfe-Quintero, Inagaki & Kim, 1998; Housen & Kuiken, 2009; Norris & Ortega, 2009) and by the fact that the notion of Complexity is widely referred to in the CEFR when defining proficiency levels (cf. above). Finally we also found that these general measures lent themselves to operationalization in a sufficiently clear and similar way for the three languages we aimed to compare.

Against this background, we formulated two research questions. These addressed the degree of correlation between three general measures of syntactic complexity and rated CEFR levels (A1–B2), and, also in terms of syntactic complexity, the question of whether there were differences both between languages within the same CEFR level and between CEFR levels within the same language. In the following we discuss our findings in relation to our research questions. Two main results emerge: CEFR levels matter and so do measures of syntactic complexity.

Our results show that, overall and within in each language, there is a linear positive significant correlation between all three measures of syntactic complexity and rated CEFR levels. This result answers the first RQ but also provides a first affirmative answer to the broader question of whether communicatively defined CEFR levels can be characterized in terms of linguistic profiles, in our case in terms of measures of syntactic complexity. More interestingly, the results with respect to the second RQ revealed that CEFR levels are not equal. When the rated CEFR level A was compared across languages, we found no significant differences for any of the three measures of syntactic complexity. This can be interpreted as suggesting that the linguistic profile at CEFR level A is rather homogeneous. Put differently, we can say that, independently of language, learners at CEFR level A do not vary significantly in syntactic complexity. The fact that CEFR level A does not differ across the three languages can also be interpreted in support of the language-independent approach adopted by the CEFR. Some aspects of linguistic proficiency, at least at this initial stage, are possible to define without reference to a particular language. At CEFR level B, however, for two of the measures (Mean length of T-unit and Mean number of subordinate clauses / T-unit) differences between languages were observed, especially between English and French (cf. Tables 9–11). The reason why measures for CEFR level B in Italian did not show significant differences (except for Mean length of T-unit) compared to French and English might be explained by the fewer number of texts (e.g. 13 texts, cf. Table 8) rated at this level for this language. One way of interpreting the difference between CEFR level A (syntactic complexity homogenous across languages) and CEFR level B (syntactic complexity different across languages) would be to suggest that it is from CEFR level B and onwards that learners have developed a sufficiently rich linguistic repertoire for differences to emerge. The limited linguistic proficiency at CEFR level A might not, as it were, provide enough room for variation in terms of sentence elaboration and clause combining. Continuing along this line of reasoning, we might also suggest that it is from CEFR level B and onwards that language-specific properties begin to affect the data. We know yet very little about possible typological effects on general measures of syntactic complexity in different languages, but we can suspect that they matter. In this particular study we compared one Germanic language with two Romance languages. However, French and English share many structural properties while Italian is clearly different (e.g. pro-drop). The effect of the typological factor is a topic for further research (Granfeldt, Bernardini, Gyllstad & Källkvist, forthcoming), but the results in this study can be interpreted as showing that this effect might emerge only at CEFR level B.

Moreover, our analysis of the CEFR scales revealed that it was precisely at CEFR level B1 that the authors of the CEFR start referring to the notion of complexity. Below B1, scales systematically used the terms *simple* and/or *basic*. The finding that B1 is a threshold with respect to complexity fits with the observation that syntactic complexity from this point onwards seems to differ depending on the specific language involved.

Our results do not only show that CEFR levels matter, however, but also that measures matter. In fact, two of the three general measures of syntactic complexity show a greater sensitivity at the levels of proficiency we covered in this study. Both Mean length of T-unit and Mean number of subordinate clauses /T-unit are capable of discriminating between CEFR levels A and B within French and English. Again, the results for Italian are different but this may be due to the distribution of the data or sample size. The third measure, Mean length of clause, is only capable of discriminating between English A and B CEFR levels. These results suggest that the first two measures are better suited to tap into development of syntactic complexity at the initial and intermediate stages of linguistic proficiency. The result also indirectly confirms Norris & Ortega's suggestion (2009) that Mean length of clause is a better measure for more advanced proficiency levels. In addition, our results corroborate the findings in Prodeau, Lopez & Véronique (2012), who suggested that text length is a reliable way of discriminating between adjacent CEFR levels. It should be noted, though, that our design is very different.

The present study is limited in a number of ways. In relation to the major research questions outlined by the SLATE group, it is true that by considering only general measures of syntactic complexity and not specific measures (i.e. specific target constructions, morphology etc.) we can only gain a limited understanding of linguistic profiles at different CEFR levels. We have argued that the general measures are a good starting point, since they could easily be operationalized for all three languages in an identical way. Other studies within our project have examined individual languages and specific features (Rosenberg, 2011; Granfeldt & Ågren, 2013; Bernardini, 2013). A second limitation concerns a lack of control of how our raters interpreted the criteria in the CEFR scales, which may have led to a certain amount of circularity in our design. We ensured that raters had had appropriate training in assessing communicative proficiency with CEFR and that they had sufficient experience in using the framework for this purpose, but we did not carry out any post-rating interviews with them. As one reviewer notes, there is thus a potential risk that at least some rater(s) interpreted various references to "basic", "simple" and "complex" in the CEFR scales (cf. Appendix 2) as meaning length of T-units or number of subordinate clauses. We can exclude the possibility that raters consciously counted words or clauses while assessing but not that they might have unconsciously been affected by such linguistic properties of the learner texts. A third limitation concerns the more advanced levels of proficiency. As pointed out above (cf. Table 5), no learner text, not even in English, was rated at the C-level by two independent raters. We speculate that this is the major reason as to why the measure Mean length of clause only marginally correlates with rated CEFR levels, but without data from levels C1 and C2, this remains a speculation.

Finally, we would like to address some possible avenues for future research. When investigating several languages, it would be beneficial to use raters capable of rating in more than one language. Even though high agreement can be reached within rater pairs for one language, it is desirable to obtain also high agreement between the same pairs in different languages. Another question for future research is the potential value of native speaker comparison data. Even though the performance of native speakers is not at the heart of the CEFR and its purposes, such comparisons could provide a useful baseline, for example as a means of validation.

Acknowledgements

We would like to thank the Joint Faculties of Humanities and Theology at Lund University for funding the study. We are also indebted to all participating students and their teachers; without their generosity this study would not have been possible. We would also like to thank: our raters for assessing the texts; Maisa Martin, Pirjo Lehtonen and colleagues at Jyväskylä University for sharing their tasks with us; Alexander Kapranov, Jessica Rosenberg and Federica Sala for coding some of the data. Finally, we would like to express our gratitude to two anonymous reviewers for insightful comments on the first draft of this paper.

References

Alanen, R., Huhta, A. and Tarnanen, M. 2010. "Designing and assessing L2 writing tasks across CEFR proficiency levels." In *Communicative Proficiency and Linguistic Development: Intersections between SLA and Language Testing Research* [Eurosla Monographs Series 1], I. Bartning, M. Martin and I. Vedder (eds), 21–56. European Second Language Association. http://eurosla.org/monographs/EM01/EM01home.html

Alderson, C.J. 2007. "The CEFR and the need for more research." *The Modern Language Journal* 91: 658–662. DOI: 10.1111/j.1540-4781.2007.00627_4.x

Bachman, L. 2004. *Statistical Analyses for Language Assessment*. Cambridge: Cambridge University Press. DOI: 10.1017/CBO9780511667350

Bartning, I., Martin, M. and Vedder, I. (eds). 2010. *Communicative Proficiency and Linguistic Development: Intersections between SLA and Language Testing Research* [Eurosla Monographs Series 1]. European Second Language Association. http://eurosla.org/monographs/EM01/EM01home.html

Beacco, J., Bouquet, S. and Pourquier, R. 2004. *Niveau B2 pour le français: un référentiel*. Paris: Didier.

Bernardini, P. 2013. "Abilità comunicativa (QCER) ed effettive produzioni linguistiche in italiano L4." Paper presented at *XCIS, X Congresso Italianisti Scandinavi Reykjavík*, 13–15 July, 2013.

Council of Europe. 2001. *Common European Framework of Reference for Languages: Learning, Teaching, Assessment*. Cambridge: Cambridge University Press.

DeVellis, R.F. 1991. *Scale Development*. Newbury Park, NJ: Sage Publications.

Field, A. 2005. *Discovering Statistics using SPSS*. London: Sage.

Figueras, N. 2012. "The impact of the CEFR." *The English Language Teaching Journal* 66: 477–485. DOI: 10.1093/elt/ccs037

Forsberg, F. and Bartning, I. 2010. "Can linguistic features discriminate between the communicative CEFR-levels? A pilot study of written L2 French." In *Communicative Proficiency and Linguistic Development: Intersections between SLA and Language Testing Research* [Eurosla Monographs Series 1], I. Bartning, M. Martin and I. Vedder (eds), 133–158. European Second Language Association. http://eurosla.org/monographs/EM01/EM01home.html

Granfeldt, J., Bernardini, P., Gyllstad, H. and Källkvist, M. Forthcoming. "Linguistic complexity in the CEFR and in L2 English, L3 French and L4 Italian: On the role of target language typology for measuring language proficiency". Paper accepted for *ReN workshop at the AILA 2014 Conference*, Brisbane.

Granfeldt, J. and Ågren, M. 2013. "Stages of processability and levels of proficiency in the common European framework of reference for languages. The case of L3 French." In *Language Acquisition and Use in Multilingual Contexts. Theory and Practice* [Travaux de l'Institut de linguistique de Lund 52], A. Flyman-Mattsson and C. Norrby (eds), 28–38. Lund: Lund University.

Hawkins, J.A. and Filipović, L. 2012. *Critical Features in L2 English. Specifying the Reference Levels of the Common European Framework* [English Profile Studies 1]. Cambridge: Cambridge University Press.

Housen, A. and Kuiken, F. 2009. "Complexity, accuracy, and fluency in second language acquisition". *Applied Linguistics* 30: 461–473. DOI: 10.1093/applin/amp048

Hulstijn, J.H. 2007. "The Shaky Ground beneath the CEFR: Quantitative and qualitative dimensions of language proficiency." *The Modern Language Journal* 91: 663–667.
DOI: 10.1111/j.1540-4781.2007.00627_5.x

Hulstijn, J.H., Alderson, J.C. and Schoonen, R. 2010. "Developmental stages in second-language acquisition and levels of second-language proficiency: Are there links between them?" In *Communicative Proficiency and Linguistic Development: Intersections between SLA and Language Testing Research* [Eurosla Monographs Series 1], I. Bartning, M. Martin and I. Vedder (eds), 11–20. European Second Language Association. http://eurosla.org/monographs/EM01/EM01home.html

Hulstijn, J.H., Schoonen, R., de Jong, N.H., Steinel, M.P. and Florijn, A. 2012. "Linguistic competences of learners of Dutch as a second language at the b1 and b2 levels of speaking proficiency of the common European framework of reference for languages (CEFR)". *Language Testing* 29: 203–221. DOI: 10.1177/0265532211419826

Kuiken, F., Vedder, I. and Gilabert, R. 2010. "Communicative adequacy and linguistic complexity in L2 writing." In *Communicative Proficiency and Linguistic Development: Intersections between SLA and Language Testing Research* [Eurosla Monographs Series 1], I. Bartning, M. Martin and I. Vedder (eds), 81–100. European Second Language Association. http://eurosla.org/monographs/EM01/EM01home.html

Leung, C. and Lewkowicz, J. 2012. "Language communication and communicative competence: A view from contemporary classrooms". *Language and Education* 1: 1–17.
DOI: 10.5923/j.edu.20110101.01

Little, D. 2007. "The common European framework of reference for languages: Perspectives on the making of supranational language education policy." *The Modern Language Journal* 91: 645–655. DOI: 10.1111/j.1540-4781.2007.00627_2.x

MacWhinney, B. 2000. *The CHILDES Project: Tools for Analyzing Talk*, 3rd edition. Mahwah, NJ: Lawrence Erlbaum Associates.

Martin, M., Mustonen, S., Reiman, N. and Seilonen, M. 2010. "On becoming an independent user." In *Communicative Proficiency and Linguistic Development: Intersections between SLA and Language Testing Research* [Eurosla Monographs Series 1], I. Bartning, M. Martin and I. Vedder (eds), 57–80. European Second Language Association. http://eurosla.org/monographs/EM01/EM01home.html

Norris, J.M. and Ortega, L. 2009. "Towards an organic approach to investigating CAF in instructed SLA: The case of complexity". *Applied Linguistics* 30: 555–578.
DOI: 10.1093/applin/amp044

North, B. 2007. "The CEFR illustrative descriptor scales." *The Modern Language Journal* 91: 656–659. DOI: 10.1111/j.1540-4781.2007.00627_3.x

Prodeau, M., Lopez, S. and Véronique, D. 2012. "Acquisition of French as a second language: Do developmental stages correlate with CEFR levels?" *Apples – Journal of Applied Language Studies* 6 (1): 47–68.

Rosenberg, J. 2011. *Existe-t-il des corrélations entre les stades de développement morphosyntaxique et les niveaux proposés du Cadre européen commun de référence ? Une étude de productions écrites par des apprenants suédophones de français L2*. Unpublished Bachelor thesis in French Linguistics. Centre for Languages and Literature: Lund university.

Skehan, P. 1998. *A Cognitive Approach to Language Learning*. Oxford: Oxford University Press.

Wolfe-Quintero, K., Inagaki, S. and Kim, H. 1998. *Second Language Development in Writing: Measures of Fluency, Accuracy, & Complexity*. Honolulu: University of Hawaii Press.

Appendix 1

Task 1

Instructions for year-4 pupils: "Email message to your teacher: You have been absent from school for one week. Please send an email message to your teacher. Tell your teacher why you have been absent. Ask one question about the homework, and two questions about the lessons you have missed. Write in English." (our translation from Swedish)

Instructions for students in year 9 (translated from Swedish, instructions were identical for learners of English and French): "Email message to your teacher: You have been absent from school for one week. Soon you will sit an English (French) test. Please ask your teacher two questions regarding the test. Ask two questions about what happened over the week when you were away. Remember to begin and to end your email message in an appropriate way. Write in English (French)."

Instructions for students in their final year of upper-secondary school or first year at university (translated from Swedish, instructions were identical for learners of English, French and Italian): "Email message to your teacher: You have been absent from school for one week. You have been given an assignment that is due next week. Send an email to your teacher. Tell your teacher why you have been absent. Ask two questions about the assignment. Ask two questions about the course content. Write in English (French or Italian).

Task 2

Instructions for students of English in year 4 and students of English and French in year 9: "Please write a story about something fun, nice or exciting that has happened to you. What happened? Why was the event fun, nice or exciting? Write in English (French)."

Instructions for students of English, French and Italian in the final year of upper-secondary school or university: "Please write about a special event that occurred or a special experience that you have had that you can still remember. What happened? Why is the event or experience memorable? Write in English (French or Italian)."

Appendix 2

The rating scale used in the study, compiled from several CEFR scales

	Overall written production	Written interaction	Correspondence & notes, messages, forms	Creative writing & thematic development & coherence and cohesion
A1	Can write simple isolated phrases and sentences.	Can ask for or pass on personal details in written form.	Can write a short simple postcard. Can write numbers and dates, own name, nationality, address, age, date of birth or arrival in the country, etc. such as on a hotel registration form.	Can write simple phrases and sentences about themselves and imaginary people, where they live and what they do. Can link words or groups of words with very basic linear connectors like 'and' or 'then'.
A2	Can write a series of simple phrases and sentences linked with simple connectors like 'and', 'but' and 'because'.	Can write short, simple formulaic notes relating to matters in areas of immediate need.	Can write very simple personal letters expressing thanks and apology. Can take a short, simple message provided he/she can ask for repetition and reformulation. Can write short, simple notes and messages relating to matters in areas of immediate need.	Can write about everyday aspects of his/her environment, e.g. people, places, a job or study experience in linked sentences. Can write very short, basic descriptions of events, past activities and personal experiences. Can write a series of simple phrases and sentences about their family, living conditions, educational background, present or most recent job. Can write short, simple imaginary biographies and simple poems about people. Can tell a narrative or describe something in a simple list of points. Can use the most frequently occurring connectors to link simple sentences in order to tell a narrative or describe something as a simple list of points. Can link groups of words with simple connectors like 'and', 'but' and 'because'.

… Linguistic correlates to the CEFR

	Overall written production	Written interaction	Correspondence & notes, messages, forms	Creative writing & thematic development & coherence and cohesion
B1	Can write straightforward connected texts on a range of familiar subjects within his/her field of interest, by linking a series of shorter discrete elements into a linear sequence.	Can convey information and ideas on abstract as well as concrete topics, check information and ask about or explain problems with reasonable precision. Can write personal letters and notes asking for or conveying simple information of immediate relevance, getting across the point he/she feels to be important.	Can write personal letters giving news and expressing thoughts about abstract or cultural topics such as music, films. Can write personal letters describing experiences, feelings and events in some detail. Can write notes conveying simple information of immediate relevance to friends, service people, teachers and others who feature in his/her everyday life, getting across comprehensibly the points he/she feels are important. Can take messages communicating enquiries, explaining problems.	Can write straightforward, detailed descriptions on a range of familiar subjects within his/her field of interest. Can write accounts of experiences, describing feelings and reactions in simple connected text. Can write a description of an event, a recent trip – real or imagined. Can narrate a narrative. Can reasonably fluently relate a straightforward narrative or description as a linear sequence of points. Can link a series of shorter, discrete simple elements into a connected, linear sequence of points.
B2	Can write clear, detailed texts on a variety of subjects related to his/her field of interest, synthesising and evaluating information and arguments from a number of sources.	Can express news and views effectively in writing, and relate to those of others.	Can write letters conveying degrees of emotion and highlighting the personal significance of events and experiences and commenting on the correspondent's news and views.	Can write clear, detailed descriptions of real or imaginary events and experiences, marking the relationship between ideas in clear connected text, and following established conventions of the genre concerned. Can write clear, detailed descriptions on a variety of subjects related to his/her field of interest. Can write a review of a film, book or play. Can develop a clear description or narrative, expanding and supporting his/her main points with relevant supporting detail and examples. Can use a limited number of cohesive devices to link his/her utterances into clear, coherent discourse, though there may be some 'jumpiness' in a long contribution. Can use a variety of linking words efficiently to mark clearly the relationships between ideas.

	Overall written production	Written interaction	Correspondence & notes, messages, forms	Creative writing & thematic development & coherence and cohesion
C1	Can write clear, well-structured texts of complex subjects, underlining the relevant salient issues, expanding and supporting points of view at some length with subsidiary points, reasons and relevant examples, and rounding off with an appropriate conclusion.	Can express him/herself with clarity and precision, relating to the addressee flexibly and effectively.	Can express him/herself with clarity and precision in personal correspondence, using language flexibly and effectively, including emotional, allusive and joking usage.	Can write clear, detailed, well-structured and developed descriptions and imaginative texts in an assured, personal, natural style appropriate to the reader in mind. Can give elaborate descriptions and narratives, integrating sub-themes, developing particular points and rounding off with an appropriate conclusion. Can produce clear, smoothly flowing, well-structured speech, showing controlled use of organisational patterns, connectors and cohesive devices.
C2	Can write clear, smoothly flowing, complex texts in an appropriate and effective style and a logical structure which helps the reader to find significant points.	As C1	As C1	Can write clear, smoothly flowing, and fully engrossing stories and descriptions of experience in a style appropriate to the genre adopted. Can create coherent and cohesive text making full and appropriate use of a variety of organisational patterns and a wide range of cohesive devices.

The effects of time in the development of complexity and accuracy during study abroad
A study of French and Chinese learners of English

Julia Jensen and Martin Howard
University College Cork

Reflecting the current age of mammoth globalisation and the desirability of having a second language in today's world, study abroad (SA) is becoming increasingly popular amongst university students across many disciplines. Moreover, with the EU identifying a target of 20% participation in SA in 2010, the value of this activity is also being recognised on an intergovernmental level. Participants in SA programmes stand to gain not only invaluable experiences, in terms of expanding their social and cultural knowledge, but also in developing their second language (L2). While there now exists a multitude of SLA studies situated within this unique learning context, such studies vary enormously in the duration of their learner-participants' stay in the target language community. Indeed, a review of the current literature indicates that the duration of SA in the existing research ranges from a couple of weeks to a full year. Given such diversity, it is difficult to draw substantive conclusions on the effect of duration of SA on L2 development, although a limited number of important studies have explored the issue (e.g. Davidson, 2010; Dwyer, 2004; Llanes & Muñoz, 2009; Serrano et al., 2012). Against this background, the current paper reports on a longitudinal study of French and Chinese learners of English over a nine month SA period. Initial, medial and final interview data were analysed in terms of Complexity and Accuracy which are considered two important, and often rivalrous, features of language performance (Ellis & Barkhuizen, 2005). The results of the study point to considerable individual variation, both within individuals (variation across observations) and between individuals (variation across participants) in scope of development, making it difficult to capture language gains in terms of a neat, linear pattern over time.

1. Introduction

As a growing subfield of SLA, Study Abroad (SA) has received substantial attention from SLA researchers as it provides a highly interesting context of L2 acquisition. Different learning contexts, be they classroom, immersion, naturalistic or SA, may have a fundamental effect on language learning outcomes as different contexts entail, both qualitatively and quantitatively, varying patterns of language exposure (Freed, 1995; Pérez-Vidal & Juan-Garau, 2011). Curiously, while SA has proven to be highly beneficial in certain areas, such as fluency, sociolinguistic competence and lexical development, it appears to have a less positive effect on grammatical development compared to the classroom setting. Studies such as Dechert et al. (1984), Freed (1991) and Collentine (2004) have pointed to the relatively limited grammatical gains made during SA. Inquiries into the SA context have tended to vary enormously in the duration of their learner-participants' stay in the target language community, with the length of stay (LoS) generally ranging from a couple of weeks to a full calendar year (Davidson, 2010; Dwyer, 2004; Llanes & Muñoz, 2009; Serrano, 2010; Serrano et al., 2012). Given such differences in LoS, it is unclear whether the limited linguistic development that some studies report simply reflects an effect for time, whereby the duration of SA was not sufficient for the learners to evidence significant gains, or whether SA genuinely did not impact development irrespective of the time period investigated. It thus remains unclear whether the learners investigated would have evidenced development had they spent longer in the target language community.

With a view to quantifying the extent of learners' development over time, the present study explores development in relation to complexity and accuracy which have long been regarded as important features of L2 development and as a means by which L2 proficiency can be measured (Skehan, 1998; Ellis 2003; Ellis & Barkhuizen, 2005; Housen & Kuiken, 2009). Typically, complexity and accuracy are measured alongside a third construct, fluency. These three components together are referred to as CAF. There are several reasons to investigate language development in terms of this neat triad, including the assumption that it provides a "sophisticated framework for investigating the multicomponent nature of language use and development" (Polat & Kim, 2014: 186). Although fluency features in the larger project underlying this paper, the current paper focuses specifically on complexity and accuracy, reflecting our focus here on grammatical development during SA. The study also recognises the evolutionary nature of language and the subsequent need for a developmental yardstick by which L2 development can be measured longitudinally. As such, a Developmental Index is proposed as a means of illustrating the relationship between time and linguistic development in complexity and accuracy.

In the following, we will first review the existing literature pertaining to the role of time in SA and we will then present an overview of the current study. Subsequently, we will introduce the proposed Developmental Index of CAF before presenting the results for complexity and accuracy. We conclude with a discussion of the results, limitations of the study and directions for future research.

2. Literature review

Arguably, one of the fundamental issues which a theory of SLA must account for is the role of learning context on L2 learning processes and outcomes (Pérez-Vidal & Juan-Garau, 2009). SA has received much attention from SLA researchers as it allows an interesting comparison of the effects of naturalistic exposure on classroom learners spending a period of residence abroad. As Freed (1995) has illustrated, SA differs considerably from the foreign language classroom, insofar as it constitutes a context in which learners are exposed to copious amounts of the target language as well as providing the opportunity for extensive interaction with, and feedback from, native speakers. Contemporary research studies within this growing subfield of SLA acknowledge the role of a period spent abroad in L2 development but also highlight the need for broader, context-sensitive enquiries which examine specific qualitative changes in learner language proficiencies (Long, 1997 cited in Collentine & Freed, 2004).

Much of the SLA research which has employed a SA contextual approach has focused on the development of oral proficiencies, such as fluency as well as lexical, pragmatic and sociolinguistic competence (Churchill & DuFon, 2006). In the case of lexical development, studies generally point to the significant lexical gains made during SA in terms of an increased lexical repertoire, along with more native-like organisation of lexical collocations (see, for example, Ife et al., 2000). Concerning pragmatic gains, Rasouli Khorshidi (2013) offers an insightful comparative study of learners in an At Home (AH) context and an SA context. Results from the study indicate that there was significant development in the SA learners' pragmatic knowledge compared to the AH group. In a review of the literature surrounding the development of sociolinguistic competence during SA, Regan (1998: 82) concludes that "study and living abroad has significant benefits for the acquisition of sociolinguistic competence."

In contrast to such positive gains, findings are more contradictory in the case of grammatical development. For example, studies such as Dechert et al. (1984), Freed (1991) and Collentine (2004) have reported relatively limited grammatical gains arising from a period of residence abroad compared to a classroom setting. Conversely, other studies, which have generally been of longer duration (Howard,

2005; Sasaki, 2007, 2009; Serrano et al., 2012), have reported gains in both spoken and written production emerging as a result of SA, pointing to a possible effect for time in grammatical development during SA.

On this count, Serrano (2010) conducted an extensive review of studies in which researchers employed a comparative approach in their investigation of the learning effects of AH regular classrooms and SA contexts in an ambitious attempt to "critically assess the dimensions investigated, the methodology used and the main findings reported" (Serrano, 2010: 149). She notes that the studies reviewed vary in terms of the number of participants involved, their respective proficiency level in the L2 and the time period investigated. In her concluding remarks, Serrano (2010: 159) suggests that "future studies should try to collect their data at several points in time."

As a factor which may constrain the scope of linguistic development, time has received minimal attention within the SA literature, although a limited number of important studies have explored the issue (Davidson, 2010; Dwyer, 2004; Llanes & Muñoz, 2009; Serrano, 2010; Serrano et al., 2012; Llanes, 2012; Pérez-Vidal et al., 2012). This trend is particularly surprising since in order to compare the oftentimes contradictory findings across studies, it is imperative to control for the factor of time.

Perhaps one of the most extensive studies on the effects of time is that conducted by Davidson (2010), whereby he tracked the language development of 1,881 U.S. learners of Russian, participating in formal language study programmes at Russian universities for periods of 2, 4, and 9 months. The study examines development in terms of speaking, listening and reading by means of pre- and post-programme test score differences. The results indicate that a positive correlation does indeed exist between length of stay and L2 development of such skills.

In another large-scale study, Dwyer (2004) examines end of academic term evaluation results by drawing on the IES (formerly known as the Institute of European Studies) data pool, which encompasses over 50 years of data. More than 17,000 SA alumni were available to survey and comparisons of a large range of types of programmes rendered analysis across educational models and cultures possible. The study concludes that "the greatest gains across all outcome categories are made by full year students" (Dwyer, 2004: 161).

Llanes and Muñoz (2009) present comparative findings for a short-term SA programme, comparing learners who stayed for 3 weeks with those who stayed for 4 weeks. Their results indicate that even a small difference in duration of stay (1 week) plays a role in the development of linguistic features (such as oral fluency), with greater gains evident in those learners staying for 4 weeks than those staying for just 3 weeks. These important findings serve to illustrate the potential of time to impact L2 development, even in the short-term.

In her review of a set of 16 articles that compared linguistic development within the AH and SA context, Serrano (2010) notes that only one of the studies reviewed was conducted over a full academic year (Isabelli & Nishida, 2005). Similarly, in her state-of-the-art overview of the evidence available on L2 gains during SA, Llanes (2011) notes that the type of SA programme least investigated in the literature is short-term SA programmes (less than eight weeks), followed by full academic year SA programmes. As such, the most frequently investigated SA programmes are those which run for one semester, a fact which the author attributes to the general trend underlying SA programme choice. Llanes also underlines the overwhelming focus on North American undergraduate L2 learners, suggesting that future researchers concentrate on other populations "in parts of the world other than the USA" (Llanes, 2011:211).

Subsequently, Serrano et al. (2012) employed a longitudinal design to analyze the spoken and written progress made by 14 Spanish-speaking learners of English during a full academic year at a British university. In line with previous inquiries, they find that improvement in written production is more likely to occur over longer time periods, whereas gains in oral production may be evident after as little as a few months. Their results offer an appealing explanation as to why some studies, which have focused on the development of accuracy in short-term stays, have observed relatively little improvement. In their concluding comments, the authors refer to length of stay as "an influential variable in terms of the progress that is to be expected for oral and written skills" (Serrano et al., 2012:155).

While these studies serve to illuminate the issue of time, research into SLA and duration of SA is nonetheless seen to be limited (Dwyer, 2004; Davidson, 2010). With this in mind, further investigation is needed to deepen our understanding of the specific effects of length of stay in the target language community on L2 development.

3. The study

3.1 Theoretical perspective

The theoretical framework employed in this study is taken from Dynamic Systems Theory (Verspoor et al., 2011), underpinned by the Trade-off hypothesis as proposed by Skehan (Skehan, 1998, 2001, 2003; Skehan & Foster, 1999, 2001). Originally, Dynamic Systems Theory (DST) developed as a branch of physics and was applied to problems relating to, for example, the dynamics of nonlinear systems within the physical sciences (de Bot et al., 2007). In the early 1990's, DST gained interest among researchers working in a wider array of areas as the potential for the application of DST to the more human and natural sciences became apparent (Waldrop, 1992; Mohanan, 1992). Larsen-Freeman (1997) called attention to the similarities among complex nonlinear systems occurring in nature, and language acquisition (Larsen-Freeman, 1997: 142). Following Larsen-Freeman's pioneering work, DST has appeared in studies from other SLA researchers (Herdina & Jessner, 2002; Larsen-Freeman, 2002; Verspoor et al., 2004, 2011; de Bot & Makoni, 2005), although the literature on the application of DST in SLA remains somewhat limited (de Bot et al., 2007). Although DST does not have its origins in language research, it does provide a "general formalism which is useful for describing any system consisting of many interacting parts" (Keijzer, 2001: 178). At the core of DST is the concept of *Complete Interconnectedness* pertaining to the assumption that "all variables are interrelated, and therefore changes in one variable will have an impact on all other variables that are part of the system" (de Bot et al., 2007: 8). DST also posits that systems are in a constant state of flux irrespective of their initial states, and that they develop not only through interaction with their environment but also over time (de Bot et al., 2007). Taking into account the intrinsic nature of time and variability within DST, Ortega and Byrnes (2008) promote the adaptation of this theoretical approach in longitudinal studies of advanced L2 capacities.

Within this framework, Complexity, Accuracy and Fluency (CAF) are conceived as a multidimensional and dynamic system of interrelating subsystems which is conditioned by external factors such as context and time (Larsen-Freeman, 2009; Norris & Ortega, 2009). Larsen-Freeman (2009: 582) comments on the interdependency and multidimensionality of the CAF components, stating that "if we examine the dimensions one by one we miss their interaction and the fact that the way they interact changes with time as well." However, approaches in earlier work on SA have mainly focused on individual components such as general oral skills or fluency (Churchill & DuFon, 2006). Additionally, many studies have been cross-sectional in nature rendering it difficult to track development longitudinally within the same learner cohort.

The 'Trade-Off' Hypothesis, as proposed by Skehan (1998), was originally developed as a means to explain the effects of task complexity on L2 oral production (Skehan, 1998, 2001, 2003; Skehan & Foster, 1999, 2001). In Skehan's view, increased task difficulty leads to decreased attentional resources to devote to form over meaning. Central to the 'Trade-off' Hypothesis is the concept of limited attentional capacity, whereby it is accepted that CAF requires working memory involvement and the commitment of attentional resources and that focusing on one aspect of the CAF triad may have a negative impact on the other aspects (Skehan, 2009). As such, under certain conditions, raised performance in accuracy may be at the expense of performance in complexity and vice versa. Situating the study within this framework of dynamic and interrelated systems allows for the tracking of not only how complexity and accuracy develop individually over the duration of the study, but also how the relationship between each develops. Furthermore, the approach examines whether development in certain components of CAF is more tangible than others, at what stage development emerges, and whether it plateaus after a certain amount of time.

3.2 Research questions

The study is guided by the following research questions:

a. To what extent does length of stay (LoS) abroad influence development in Complexity and Accuracy?
b. How does development in Complexity and Accuracy differ during SA?

3.3 Methodology

3.3.1 *Participants*

The participants in the study were eighteen university learners of English, ten from France and eight from China, thirteen of them female, five of them male. Although female participation was distinctly higher than that of male participation, such a trend is reflective of the general trend in SA participation. According to a study conducted by the European Parliament in 2010, entitled "Improving the Participation in the ERASMUS Programme," the majority of ERASMUS students are under 25 and female (Vossensteyn et al., 2010). The participants of the study were aged between 20 and 23 years, and spent a full academic year, approximately nine months, enrolled full-time at a university in an English-speaking country. The details of the participants, in relation to their gender, age, nationality, years of L2 instruction, previous SA experiences and the academic disciplines to which they belonged is summarised in Table 1.

As Table 1 illustrates, there was some diversity in relation to the university degrees that the participants were pursuing at the time of the study, insofar as all of the French learners, apart from one (FR10), were majoring in English. In contrast, while the Chinese learners were majoring in another subject area, English was also a core subject of their degree programme. All of the participants had studied English for at least six years and received all of their tuition at the host institution through the target language. At both a linguistic and extralinguistic level, the learners reflect the advanced instructed learner profile proposed by Bartning (1997, 2009). That is to say, in terms of their socio-biographical characteristics, the learners had been studying English for a number of years in an instructed

Table 1. The participants

ID	Gender	Age	Nationality	Years of L2 instruction	Previous SA experience	Major
FR1	F	20	French	10		English
FR2	F	21	French	9	1 week	English
FR3	F	21	French	15	10 days	English
FR4	F	20	French	11	2 weeks	English
FR5	F	21	French	10	1 week	English
FR6	F	20	French	10		English
FR7	F	21	French	11		English
FR8	M	20	French	14	4 weeks	English
FR9	M	21	French	13	1 week	English
FR10	M	22	French	10		Chemistry
CH1	F	21	Chinese	8		Economics
CH2	F	21	Chinese	13	6 weeks	Economics
CH3	F	20	Chinese	12		Economics
CH4	F	21	Chinese	9		Economics
CH5	F	22	Chinese	12		Economics
CH6	F	22	Chinese	6		Linguistics (Chinese)
CH7	M	22	Chinese	11		Finance
CH8	M	23	Chinese	13		Microelectronics

setting, where their metalinguistic knowledge had been significantly developed through their explicit study of the language system. Moreover, in terms of their motivation, the learners are at the upper end of the scale, having chosen to study English for their degree programme, while also opting to spend time in the target language community as part of their studies. At a linguistic level, as advanced learners, while the target language features are considered to be less emerging than emerged, the learners' use of those features is characterised by considerable linguistic variation. As Bartning notes, such variation is a distinguishing characteristic of the advanced learner variety, whereby it remains for the learner to gain increasing control over use of the target language forms in real time.

While various sub-stages constitute the more global advanced learner variety, we did not administer any specific language proficiency test at the commencement of the study. While learner progress may be dependent on the learners' overall proficiency level (e.g., Hart et al., 1994), the study foregoes an analysis of any potential impact of initial proficiency level. Rather, our focus is on the scope and nature of development across different measures of CAF development during SA. As such, the proficiency level of the participants at the onset of SA was deemed to be quantifiable by means of their initial score in CAF upon arrival in the TL country. In the case of our Chinese participants, however, we note that they had all passed the IELTS (International English Language Testing System) examination prior to the commencement of SA.

With regards to the learners' living arrangements during SA, fifteen of the participants lived in student accommodation, of which twelve lived with at least one native English speaker. The remaining three participants lived in shared private accommodation, also with at least one native English speaker. Concerning their patterns of input exposure during SA, the participants reported using the L2 in a variety of different situations with a variety of individuals, such as instructors, native and non-native speaker friends, classmates, housemates and service personnel. Notwithstanding, the amount of time spent engaged in these activities varied greatly across participants, and highlights the need in future research to explore any correlation between L2 development and such input and interaction factors as type, frequency, duration and intensity of L2 interaction, as well as the specificity of the social networks that learners create during study abroad (for discussion, see Howard, 2011a, 2011b).

3.3.2 Data collection

The methodological approach to this inquiry is quantitative in nature underpinned by a qualitative perspective. The learners in this study were interviewed three times (T_1, T_2 and T_3) over the course of a full academic year, at intervals of approximately three months. In each of these data collection situations, the methodological approach took the form of the Labovian sociolinguistic interview (Labov, 1984). The interviews are semi-structured in nature and aim to elicit natural, spontaneous discourse. This interview technique is designed to minimise the observer's paradox whereby learners may adjust how they speak when observed, leading to possible changes in register and speaking style. This effect was minimised by the researcher through the adaptation of a position of lesser authority and by allowing for tangential shifting, or contributions by the interviewee that shifted the conversational topic away from the original question (Labov, 1984). During these interviews, the participants were engaged in one-to-one conversations with the researcher for 45 to 60 minutes. Each set of interviews began with an array of biographical questions, leading to more detailed questions relating to, for example, family life, personal interests, their SA sojourn and future aspirations. Every effort was made to ensure that participants discussed past, present, future and hypothetical events. These data were transcribed into standard orthography for the purposes of an analysis of the learners' development in two widely used constructs of language performance, complexity and accuracy (Ellis & Barkhuizen, 2005).

Additionally, participants were asked to complete slightly adapted versions of the pre- and post-test versions of the Language Contact Profile (LCP), as developed by Freed et al. (2004). The pre-test LCP was administered upon completion of the second sociolinguistic interview (T_2) which allowed for the gathering of data pertaining to the participants' language learning history, contact and interaction with native speakers and levels of interaction with the target language, prior to, and during the initial period of study abroad. At the end of the third sociolinguistic interview (T_3), participants completed the post-test version of the LCP which detailed L2 use with native speakers of the target language (e.g. friends, housemates, lecturers, service personnel etc.). The post-test version of the LCP also included a section entitled "reflection" wherein participants were asked to rate their study abroad experiences, in terms of the perceived level of benefit and/or difficulty. In both the pre- and post-test LCPs, the L2 learners were asked to quantify their L2 usage during study abroad, with a view to illuminating the potential of input and interactional issues to impact development in CAF. These questionnaires were administered through English, in the presence of the researcher who was on hand to answer any questions.

3.3.3 Coding of complexity

Complexity has been defined as "the extent to which the language produced in performing a task is elaborate and varied" (Ellis, 2003: 340). Each sociolinguistic interview was coded for syntactic complexity by enumerating the total number of words, the total number of clauses and the total number of AS-units (see *3.3.4. Coding of accuracy* for a description of AS-units). The total word count was not seen to include one-word minor utterances such as *yeah, Okay, mhm* and echoic responses. Furthermore, false starts, self-corrections and functionless repetitions were also excluded from the total word count. In terms of determining clause boundaries and status, definitions and examples provided by Foster et al. (2000) were followed closely. An independent clause was defined as "minimally a clause including a finite verb" (Foster et al., 2000: 365). Following conclusions made by Norris and Ortega (2009) relating to best measurement practice, three aspects of syntactic complexity were analysed, namely, overall complexity, complexity by subordination and complexity by phrasal/subclausal elaboration. These three aspects of syntactic complexity were investigated through the employment of three measures, which will be described in the following section.

3.3.3.1 Measures of complexity

3.3.3.1.1 Words per AS-unit (WPerAS).
Overall complexity was ascertained to relate to the average length of AS-units. This figure was obtained by dividing the total number of words by the total number of AS-units. For example, if a learner

produced 4,000 words and 300 AS-units, their average number of words per AS-unit would be 13.33.

3.3.3.1.2 *Clauses per AS-unit (ClPerAS).* Complexity by subordination was calculated as the average number of clauses per AS-unit. In relation to the term *clauses*, both finite and non-finite clauses were considered. This figure was obtained by dividing the total number of clauses by the total number of AS-units. In this instance, if a learner produced 500 clauses and 300 AS-units, their average number of clauses per AS-unit would be 1.66.

3.3.3.1.3 *Words per clause (WPerCl).* Complexity by phrasal/subclausal elaboration was deemed to relate to the mean length of a clause (MLC) and was calculated by dividing the total number of words by the total number of clauses. For instance, if a learner produces 4000 words and 500 clauses, the mean length of clauses produced would be 8 words.

3.3.4 Coding of accuracy

Accuracy has been defined as "the conformity of second language knowledge to target language norms" (Wolfe-Quintero et al., 1998:4). As Foster et al. (2000:354) aptly put it, "the analysis of spoken language requires a principled way of dividing transcribed data into units in order to assess features such as accuracy." The first step in the analysis of accuracy was thus the selection of a base unit. In this regard, the analysis of speech unit, or AS-unit, was chosen for a number of reasons. The AS-unit is one of the only units of speech available with a comprehensive, accessible definition and identified conditions for determining where the unit boundary lies. An AS-unit is defined as "a single speaker's utterance consisting of an independent clause, or sub-clausal unit, together with any subordinate clause(s) associated with either" (Foster et al., 2000:365). Additionally, the AS-unit also offers three different levels of application, allowing for the systematic exclusion of certain data which if included, have the potential to skew results. As the Labovian sociolinguistic interview is semi-structured and thus highly interactional, level two was applied, allowing for the systematic exclusion of one-word minor utterances such as *yeah, Okay, mhm* and echoic responses, which could potentially distort the perception of performance if included.

3.3.4.1 *Measures of accuracy*
Following the methodological approach outlined in Llanes and Muñoz (2009), three quantitative measures of accuracy were computed: the ratio of error-free AS-units per total number of AS-units (ErrFreeAS), the average number of errors per clause (ErrPerCl) and the AS-unit error rate (ASErr).

3.3.4.1.1 *Error-free AS-unit Ratio (ErrFreeAS).* This ratio was obtained by dividing the total number of error-free AS-units by the total number of AS-units. In this regard, if a learner produces 180 AS-units, 100 of which are error-free, their ErrFreeAS ratio would be 0.5555. This would indicate that 55.5% of the learner's entire speech production was error-free.

3.3.4.1.2 *Average number of errors per clause (ErrPerCl).* The average number of errors per clause was obtained by dividing the total number of errors by the total number of clauses. In this regard, if a learner produces 400 clauses and a total of 200 errors, their average number of errors per clause would be .5, revealing an average of one error per every two clauses produced.

3.3.4.1.3 *AS-unit error rate (ASErr).* The AS-unit error rate was obtained by dividing the total number of errors by the total number of AS-units. For example, if a learner produced a total of 200 errors and 180 AS-units, their AS-unit error rate would be 1.11.

3.4 The Developmental Index (DI)

A final and pressing consideration of this study is the way in which development in CAF could be represented with a numerical value. The term developmental index (DI) was first coined by child language acquisition researcher Kenji Hakuta in 1975. Subsequent researchers such as Larsen-Freeman (1978, 2006) have reiterated the need for such an index of development, concluding that it would provide SLA with a "developmental yardstick by which researchers could expediently and reliably gauge a learner's proficiency in a second language" (Larsen-Freeman, 1978: 439). Larsen-Freeman and Ellis (2009) explore CAF within a complex, dynamic systems view and conclude that language progress could not be totally accounted for by performance in one of these subsystems alone, due to the interrelated nature of the CAF components. Wang (2009) discusses both the theoretical and the empirical difficulties in establishing a developmental index of SLA and concludes that "some objective measures that can reflect learners' development in fluency, complexity and accuracy as well as discriminate a specific population will be regarded as valid to depict the status quo of this group" (Wang, 2009: 34).

In an effort to gauge linguistic development in CAF over time, the following equation was devised:

$$\text{Developmental Index of CAF } (DI_{CAF}) = DI_C + DI_A + DI_F$$

Each of the three components within this equation (DI_C, DI_A and DI_F) is made up of three parts, corresponding to the measures used to gauge each respective component of CAF. For example, DI_C can be expanded to include the following, where $(T_2 - T_1)$ calculates progress over the first semester and $(T_3 - T_2)$ calculates progress over the second semester:

$$DI_C = [WPerAS\{(T_2 - T_1) + (T_3 - T_2)\}] + [ClPerAS\{(T_2 - T_1) + (T_3 - T_2)\}] + [WPerCl\{(T_2 - T_1) + (T_3 - T_2)\}]$$

Similarly, the accuracy component (DI_A) of the DI_{CAF} equation may be elaborated to include the three measures used to gauge accuracy:

$$DI_A = [ErrFreeAS\{(T_2-T_1)+(T_3-T_2)\}] + [ErrPerCl(-1)\{(T_2-T_1)+(T_3-T_2)\}] + [ASErr(-1)\{(T_2 - T_1) + (T_3 - T_2)\}]$$

Note that the DI_A equation additionally contains (-1) for the case of ErrPerCl and ASErr as a negative value in either of these measures actually denotes progress over time. In the example of FR3 (a female learner from France) in our study (Figure 1 below), her ASErr at T_1 was 1.2108 relative to a score of 1 at T_2 and 0.6510 at T_3. In the relevant section of the equation then $[(-1)\{(T_2 - T_1) + (T_3 - T_2)\}]$, the (-1) serves to transform the otherwise negative score of -0.5597, which is actually reflective of a decrease in the AS-Unit error rate, to 0.5597 which denotes an overall increase in accuracy within that measure.

The DI_F component of the equation may also be expanded to include the three measures which are currently being applied to the data in this project, for example:

$$DI_F = [SPM^*\{(T_2 - T_1) + (T_3 - T_2)\}] + [SPPM\{(T_2 - T_1) + (T_3 - T_2)\}] + [AR\{(T_2 - T_1) + (T_3 - T_2)\}]$$
* SPM = Syllables per minute; SPPM = Silent pauses per minute

In theory, the full DI_{CAF} equation should account for individual development in the CAF components over time by calculating the differences in scores for each measure between T_1 and T_2 $(T_2 - T_1)$ and T_2 and T_3 $(T_3 - T_2)$. Furthermore, it is possible to note changes in these scores as the SA period progresses by simply

FR3	AS-unit error rate (ASErr)
Time 1 (T_1)	1.2108
Time 2 (T_2)	1
Time 3 (T_3)	0.6510
$(T_2 - T_1) + (T_3 - T_2)$	−0.5597
$[(-1)\{(T_2 - T_1) + (T_3 - T_2)\}]$	0.5597

Figure 1. ASErr scores for FR3

restricting the time period in question within the formula. For example, if the DI_C needs to be obtained for the first semester only (e.g. $T_2 - T_1$) the equation would be condensed to include only values representative of the time period investigated:

$$DI_C (T_2 - T_1) = [WPerAS\{(T_2 - T_1)\}] + [ClPerAS\{(T_2 - T_1)\}] + [WPerCl\{(T_2 - T_1)\}]$$

Moreover, the DI_{CAF} formula may be further limited to the initial scores only (e.g. $DI_C(T_1) + DI_A(T_1) + DI_F(T_1)$) in order to gauge or enumerate the learners' initial proficiency level in CAF.

4. Results

As mentioned, the study explores development within the framework of CAF. So far, the data have been analysed in relation to the accuracy and syntactic complexity components, with the analysis of fluency constituting the next stage of the project. The findings presented here therefore focus exclusively on accuracy and syntactic complexity. In both cases, we present the results for the individual learners, as opposed to at group level, reflecting the considerable individual variation between the learners whereby a group analysis would skew the results. Indeed, such group analysis fails to capture the individual progression and regression observed across the learners at each stage of the study.

4.1 Syntactic complexity development

By applying the DI_C equation to each participant's scores for each syntactic complexity measure over the course of the study, a sliding scale from least to most complex is produced (Figure 2). If we examine the DI_C equation in relation to, for example, CH4's scores, in each measure of complexity, we see that CH4's language became more complex as time progressed, as her final DI_C score is marked by a positive value.

$$DI_C CH4 = [WPerAS\{4.3341\}] + [ClPerAS\{0.5526\}] + [WPerCl\{-0.1349\}] = 4.7518$$

From the table (Figure 2) it is possible to note the learner with the highest overall DI_C score, and the learner with the lowest. In this instance, CH4 (a female learner from China) has the highest DI_C score (4.7518), while FR3 (a female learner from France) has the lowest (−4.2890). It is also noteworthy that there are a lot of cases of regression within the WPerCl column, suggesting that this measure is more

ID	Overall Complexity WPerAS $(T_2 - T_1) + (T_3 - T_2)$	Complexity by Subordination ClPerAS $(T_2 - T_1) + (T_3 - T_2)$	Complexity by phrasal/ subclausal elaboration WPerCl $(T_2 - T_1) + (T_3 - T_2)$	DI_C
FR3	−3.6397	−0.4603	−0.1890	−4.2890
CH1	−0.4022	0.1159	−0.6949	−0.9811
FR1	−0.0610	−0.0255	0.0556	−0.0310
CH6	0.6240	0.1416	−0.3589	0.4068
CH8	0.4298	0.0736	−0.0725	0.4308
FR5	0.3146	−0.1149	0.6378	0.8375
CH3	1.0485	0.2121	−0.3776	0.8831
FR7	1.1628	0.1960	−0.1171	1.2418
FR6	1.3708	0.2024	−0.1014	1.4717
FR2	1.4163	0.2317	−0.1673	1.4806
CH2	2.0434	0.4511	−0.9594	1.5351
CH7	1.7160	0.2441	−0.0295	1.9306
FR8	1.5799	0.0671	0.4243	2.0714
FR4	2.7737	0.2111	0.6178	3.6026
CH5	3.3722	0.3882	0.1845	3.9449
FR9	3.1687	0.1990	0.7848	4.1524
FR10	3.2064	0.1862	0.9107	4.3033
CH4	4.3341	0.5526	−0.1349	4.7518

Figure 2. Overall differences in scores over time $(T_2 - T_1) + (T_3 - T_2)$ for each syntactic complexity measure as well as the subsequent DI_C score for the entire sample

difficult to progress on compared to the other measures of complexity, given the finite amount of words possible within any given clause. Moreover, it has been suggested that the WPerCl measure is most suitable for higher-level participants, revealing a possible effect for proficiency level (Norris & Ortega, 2009). Additionally, the results presented for the number of clauses per unit (ClPerAS) measure are also likely to have been influenced by proficiency, since this measure has "proven to increase together with the proficiency level of L2 learners" (Housen et al., 2012: 145). As such, a threshold has been also posited for ClPerAS in relation to learner proficiency level (Norris & Ortega, 2009).

The graphs in Figure 3 provide a more detailed view of the effect of time on development within each complexity measure investigated. In terms of overall complexity, for example, it can be noted that some learners (FR10, FR8, CH5, CH4 and CH3; 5 of the total group) continuously increased the average length of their AS-units as time progressed. However, the average length of the AS-units produced by the remaining learners fluctuated over time. Similarly, upon examining the complexity by subordination measure, it becomes apparent that only

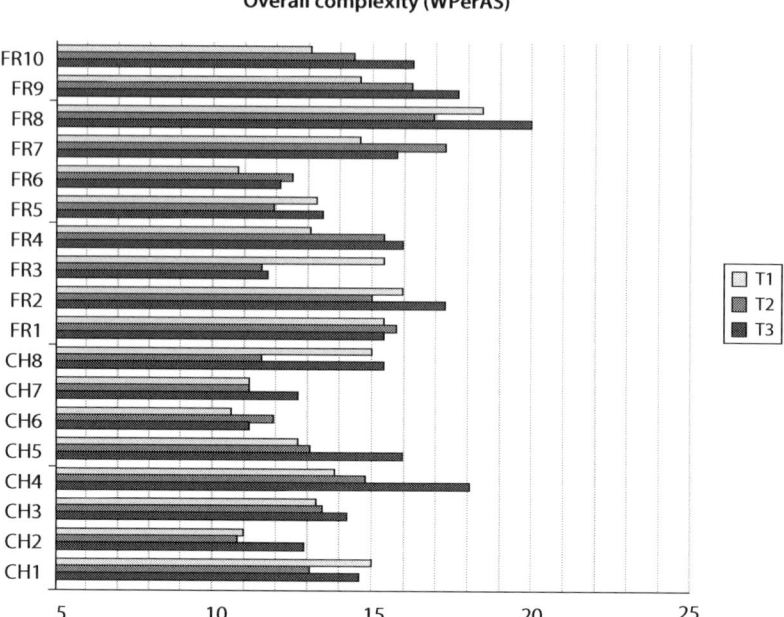

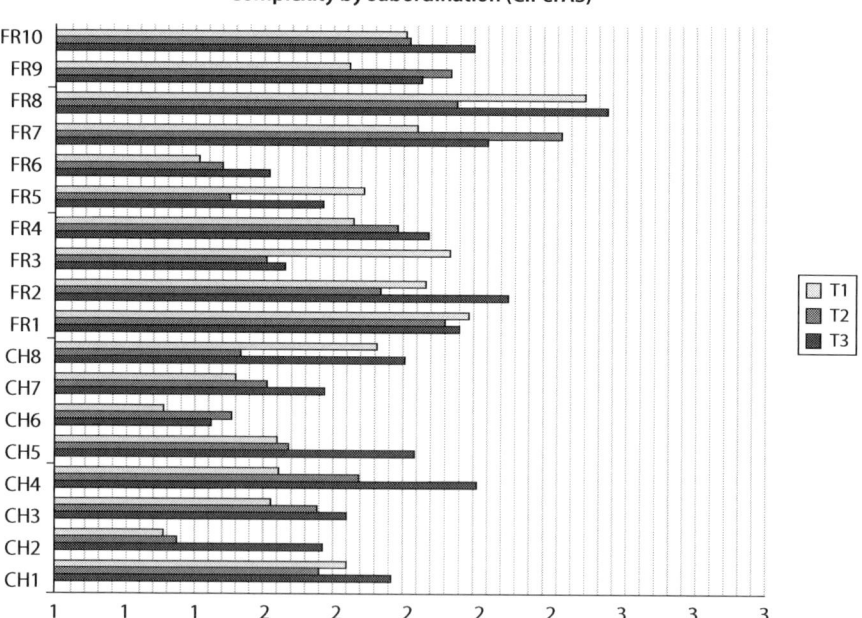

Figure 3. The effect of time on three complexity measures

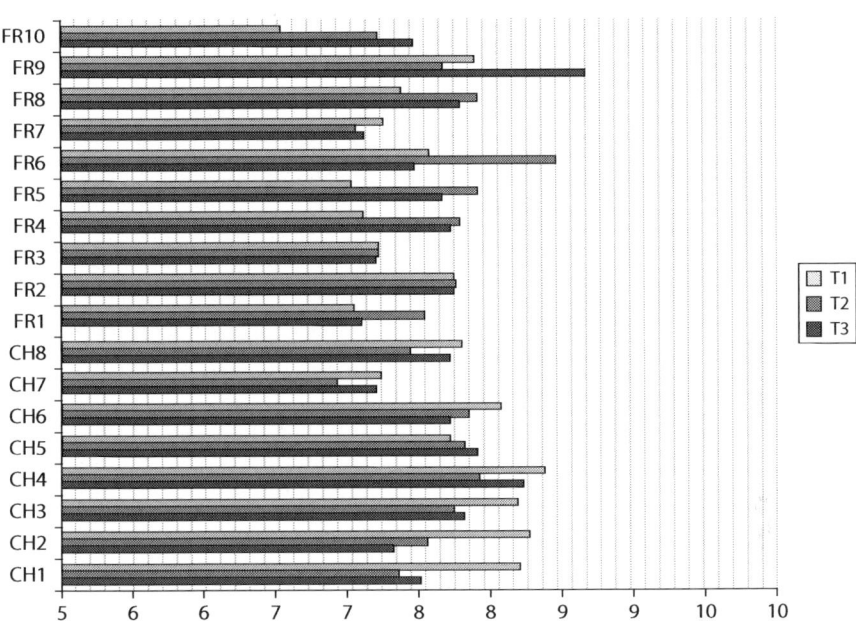

Figure 3. (*continued*)

8 learners (FR10, FR6, FR4, CH7, CH5, CH4, CH3 and CH2) out of the total sample saw a continued linear increase in the average number of clauses they produced per AS-unit over time, whereas the remaining 10 learners either produced more or less clauses per AS-unit as time progressed. In terms of complexity by phrasal/subclausal elaboration, only 2 learners (FR10 and CH5) within the entire sample continually increased their average number of words per clause over the time period investigated, with the remaining 16 learners producing either more or less words.

Figure 4 illustrates that the extent of development within complexity is also subject to individual variation as a function of the measure used to gauge complexity. For example, FR2's complexity by subordination score after two semesters of SA was 0.232, suggesting that as the SA period progressed, FR2 produced more clauses per AS-unit. Additionally, FR2's score in overall complexity after two semesters of SA was 1.416, suggesting that her average number of words also increased over the course of SA. However, with a score of −0.1673 for complexity by phrasal/subclausal elaboration after two semesters of SA, FR2's average number of words per clause fell slightly as time progressed. Overall, only five learners within the entire sample saw an increase in their scores for all three complexity measures over the course of SA.

48   Julia Jensen and Martin Howard

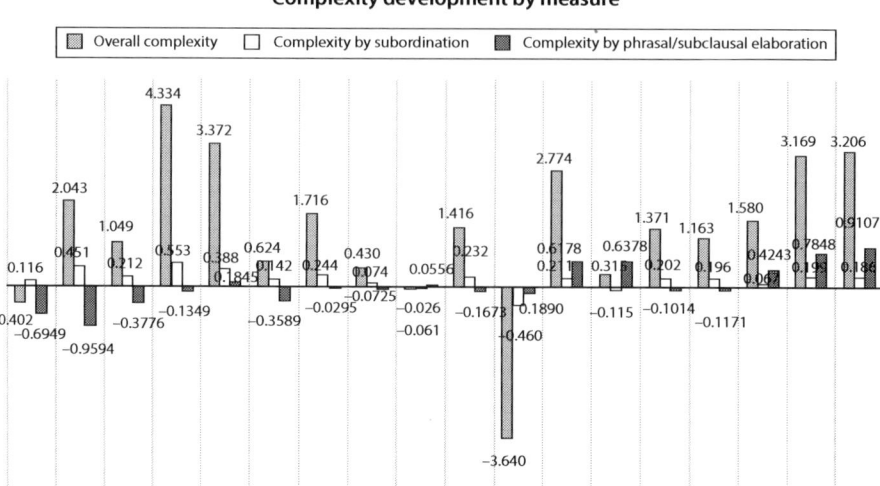

* Development in complexity after 1 semester was calculated as:
$DI_C(T_2 - T_1) = [WPerAS\{(T_2 - T_1)\}] + [ClPerAS\{(T_2 - T_1)\}] + [WPerCl\{(T_2 - T_1)\}]$.

** Development after 2 semesters was calculated as:
$DI_C(T_3 - T_2) = [WPerAS\{(T_3 - T_2)\}] + [ClPerAS\{(T_3 - T_2)\}] + [WPerCl\{(T_3 - T_2)\}]$.

Figure 4. Development in the three complexity measures after two semesters of SA

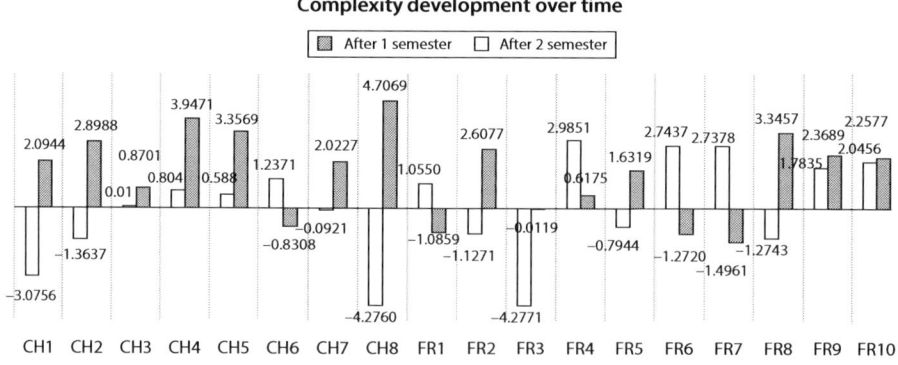

Figure 5. Complexity development after 1 semester and after 2 semesters

Results presented in Figure 5 compare global DI_C scores after one semester $(T_2 - T_1)$ and after two semesters $(T_3 - T_2)$ of SA. The chart illustrates how development in complexity fluctuates over time. Some learners, such as CH1, for example, became less complex over the course of the first semester and then became more complex during the second semester. Other learners, such as FR1, progressed in complexity after one semester and regressed after two. From a Dynamic Systems Theory perspective, this trend of non-linear and aberrative development may constitute an effect for time and be in part due to the evolutionary nature of L2 development.

4.2 Accuracy development

By applying the DI_A equation to each participant's scores for each accuracy measure, a sliding scale from the learner with the least to most accurate language is produced (Figure 6). If we examine the DI_A equation in relation to, for example, CH4's scores, in each measure of accuracy, we see that CH4's language became less accurate as time progressed, as her final DI_A score is marked by a negative value.

$$DI_A \text{ CH4} = [\{-0.0771\}] + \{0.0282\} + \{-0.3242\}] = -0.3732$$

	ErrFreeAS $(T_2 - T_1) + (T_3 - T_2)$	ErrPerCl $[(-1(T_2 - T_1) + (T_3 - T_2)\}]$	ASErr $[(-1(T_2 - T_1) + (T_3 - T_2)\}]$	DI_A
CH4	−0.0771	0.0282	−0.3242	−0.3732
FR9	−0.1361	−0.0474	−0.1582	−0.3416
CH5	−0.0917	0.0059	−0.1851	−0.2709
CH8	−0.0469	−0.0137	−0.0774	−0.1380
FR4	−0.0728	0.0046	−0.0482	−0.1164
CH2	−0.0740	0.0651	−0.0766	−0.0855
FR5	0.0091	−0.0152	0.0022	−0.0038
FR1	0.0419	0.0165	0.0423	0.1007
FR2	0.0737	0.0305	0.0268	0.1309
FR6	−0.0104	0.1238	0.1214	0.2348
FR10	0.0604	0.0735	0.1013	0.2352
FR7	0.0335	0.0950	0.1552	0.2836
FR8	0.0732	0.0794	0.1872	0.3398
CH7	0.1095	0.1690	0.1538	0.4322
CH3	0.1074	0.1614	0.1667	0.4355
CH6	0.0493	0.2321	0.2289	0.5103
CH1	0.1020	0.2016	0.3303	0.6338
FR3	0.1576	0.1790	0.5597	0.8963

Figure 6. Overall differences in scores over time $(T_2 - T_1) + (T_3 - T_2)$ for each accuracy measure as well as the subsequent DI_A score for the entire sample

From the table (Figure 6), it is possible to note the learner with the highest overall DI_A score, and the learner with the lowest. In this instance, FR3 (a female learner from France) has the highest DI_A score (0.8963), while CH4 (a female learner from the People's Republic of China) has the lowest (−0.3732). This result is particularly interesting as these two learners also appeared as the highest and lowest in complexity, yet at opposite sides of the scale. This finding is supportive of the Trade-Off hypothesis (Skehan, 1998), as these two learners may have experienced a "tension between form" resulting from "attention directed to using challenging language (complexity) relative to conservative, less advanced language, but greater accuracy" (Skehan 1998, cited in Skehan, 2009: 511). Indeed, such differences across measures point to the limitations of controlling for proficiency level in terms of a single test score, insofar as learners differ in the progress they demonstrate between measures compared to their initial scores at time I.

The graphs in Figure 7 serve to illustrate the effect of time on the extent of development within each accuracy measure investigated. In terms of error-free AS-unit ratio (ErrFreeAS) for example, it can be noted that 5 learners (FR10, FR3, FR1, CH3 and CH1) of the total sample continuously increased their average number of error-free AS-units per total number of AS-units as time progressed. Upon examining the average number of errors per clause scores, it becomes apparent that 9 learners (FR10, FR8, FR7, FR6, FR2, CH7, CH6, CH3 and CH1)

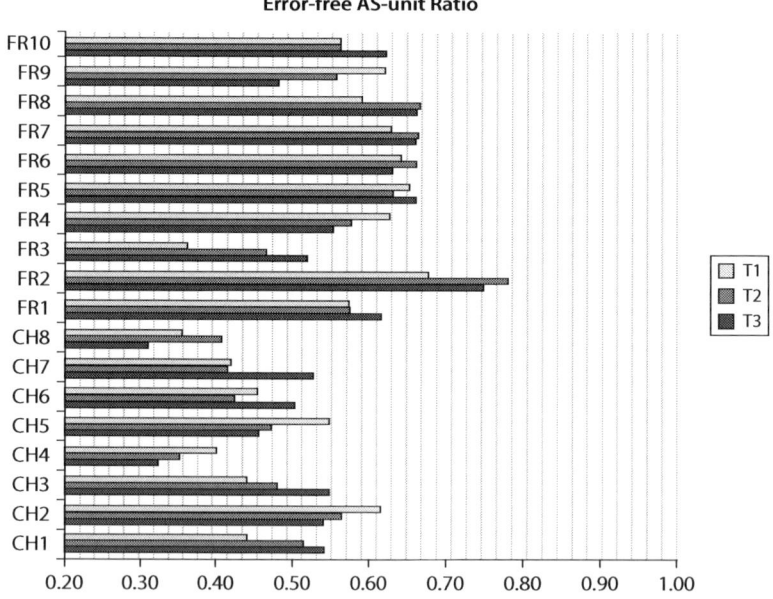

Figure 7. The effect of time on three accuracy measures

The effects of time in the development of complexity and accuracy during SA 51

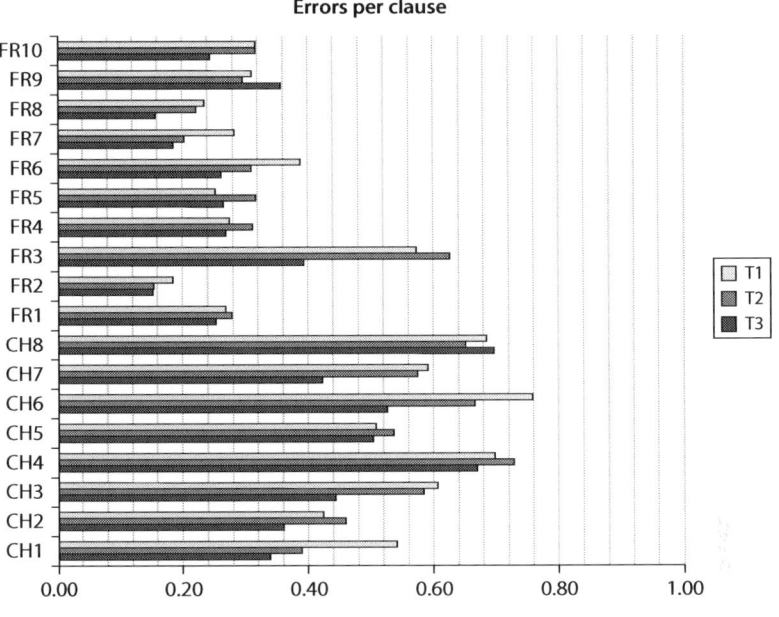

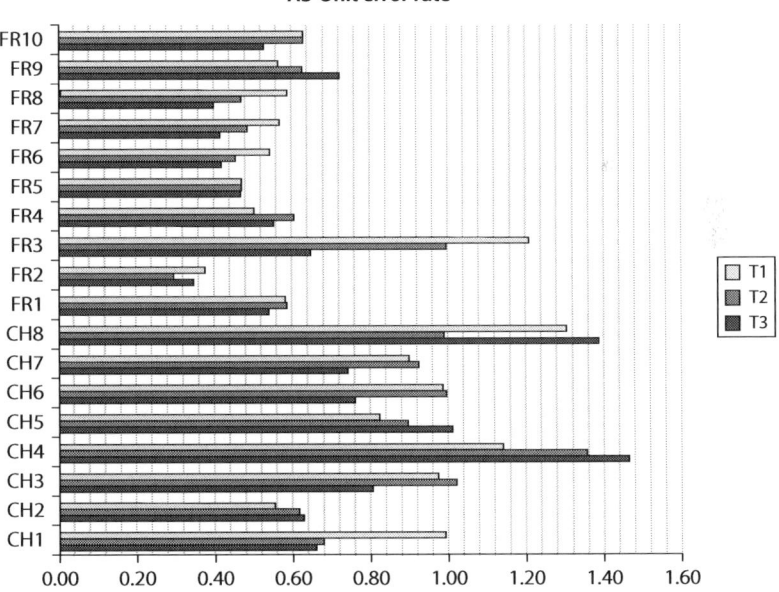

Figure 7. (*continued*)

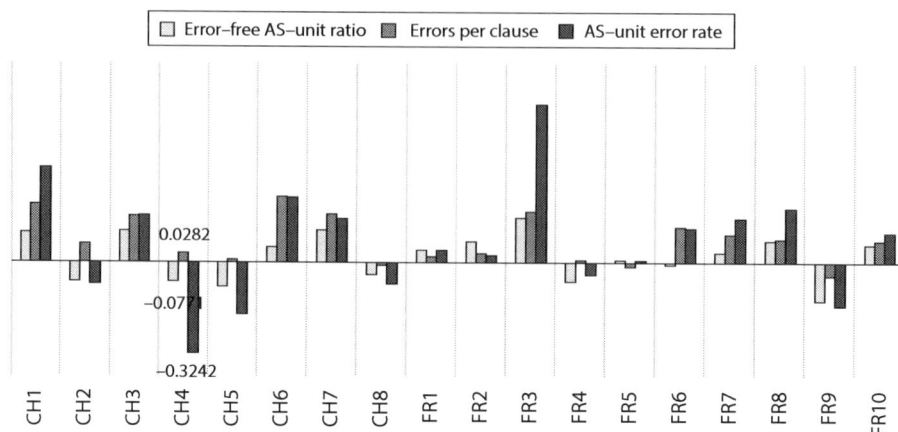

Figure 8. Development in the three accuracy measures after two semesters of SA

out of the total sample saw a linear decrease in the average number of errors they produced per clause over time, whereas the other half of the sample either produced more or less errors per clause as time progressed. In terms of AS-unit error rate, 6 learners (FR10, FR8, FR7, FR6, FR3 and CH1) of the entire sample gradually decreased their rate of error in a linear manner over the course of SA. Of the remaining sample, 3 learners (FR9, CH5 and CH4) continuously produced more errors per AS-Unit as time progressed.

Figure 8 serves to illustrate the extent of individual variation in development within the different measures of accuracy over the course of the SA period.

As was evident with complexity development, individual learners both progress and regress based on the part of accuracy investigated. For example, CH4's AS-unit error rate score after two semesters of SA was –0.3242, suggesting that as the SA period progressed, CH4 produced less errors per AS-unit. On the other hand, CH4's average number of errors per clause score after two semesters of SA was 0.0282, suggesting that CH4 produced more errors per clause as time progressed. However, with a score of –0.0771 for error-free AS-unit ratio (obtained by dividing the total number of error-free AS-units by the total number of AS-units) after two semesters of SA, CH4 produced slightly more error-free AS-units relative to the total number of AS-units as time progressed. In the case of CH4, who scored the highest DI_C, it is interesting to note the types of errors produced at T_1, T_2 and T_3 (see Figure 9 below), as her increased number of errors may be directly correlated with her attempt to use more complex structures. Following Bardovi-Harlig and Bofman (1989), oral errors were classified as either morphological, syntactic or lexical. Morphological errors were those related to nominal

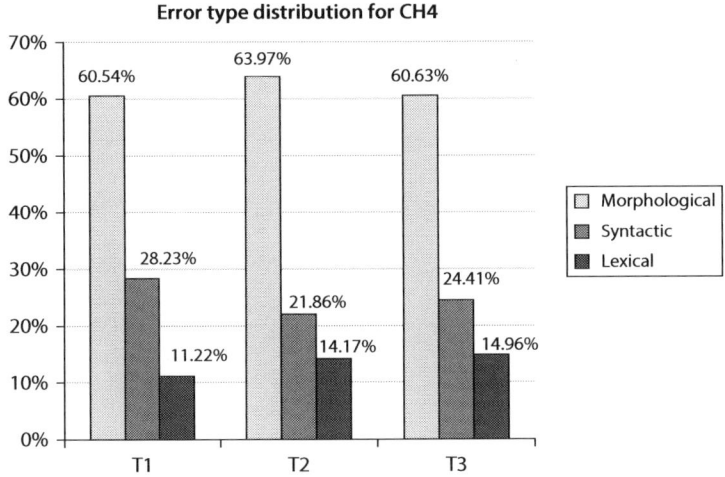

Figure 9. Error type distribution

morphology, verbal morphology, derivational morphology, articles, determiners and prepositions. Syntactic errors were those relating to word order, combining sentences and absence of constituents. Finally, lexical errors concerned idiomatic expressions and words.

From Figure 9, we can note that CH4 consistently produced a large number of morphological errors over the course of SA. Interestingly, her number of syntactic errors decreased from T_1 to T_2 yet increased from T_2 to T_3. Moreover, CH4's lexical errors rise in a linear manner as SA progresses, although the extent of this increase seems to taper off during the second semester. In the case of CH4, these findings indicate a direct correlation between the production of more words per AS-unit as well as more clauses per AS-unit (using more complex language), and the production of more syntactic and lexical errors.

Finally, results presented in Figure 10 compare global DI_A scores after one semester ($T_2 - T_1$) and after two semesters ($T_3 - T_2$) of SA, illustrating the extent to which time impacts development in accuracy. Some learners, such as CH8, for example, became more accurate over the course of the first semester and then became less accurate during the second semester. Other learners, such as FR1 regressed in accuracy after one semester and progressed after two. Again, this trend of non-linear development in accuracy over time further supports a theory of Dynamic Systems.

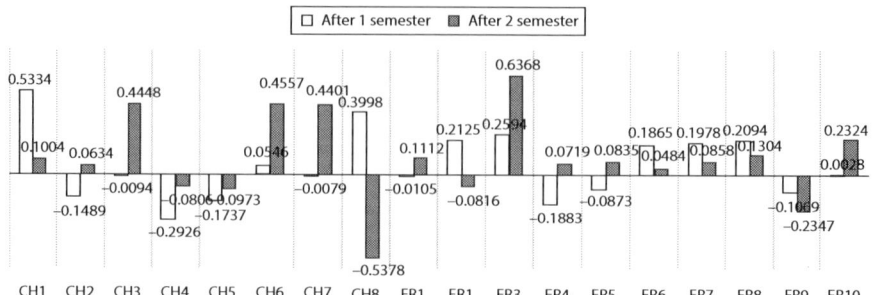

* Development in accuracy after 1 semester was calculated as:
$DI_A(T_2 - T_1) = [ErrFreeAS\{(T_2 - T_1)\}] + [ErrPerCl\{(T_2 - T_1)\}] + [ASErr\{(T_2 - T_1)\}]$.

** Development after 2 semesters was calculated as:
$DI_A(T_3 - T_2) = [ErrFreeAS\{(T_3 - T_2)\}] + [ErrPerCl\{(T_3 - T_2)\}] + [ASErr\{(T_3 - T_2)\}]$.

Figure 10. Accuracy development after 1 semester* and after 2 semesters**

4.3 Accuracy development vs. complexity development

Comparing global development in complexity and accuracy, Figure 11 further confirms the belief that "various components emerge at various levels, to various degrees, and at various times" (Wang, 2009: 33).

As the chart illustrates, underlying development in complexity and accuracy is a great deal of individual variation. While some learners progress in both of these language components over time (e.g. FR2, FR6, FR10, FR7, FR8, CH7, CH3 and CH6), the other learners either become more or less accurate or complex, but not both. However, none of the learners' language became both less accurate and less complex over the time period investigated. Of the total sample, 15 learners

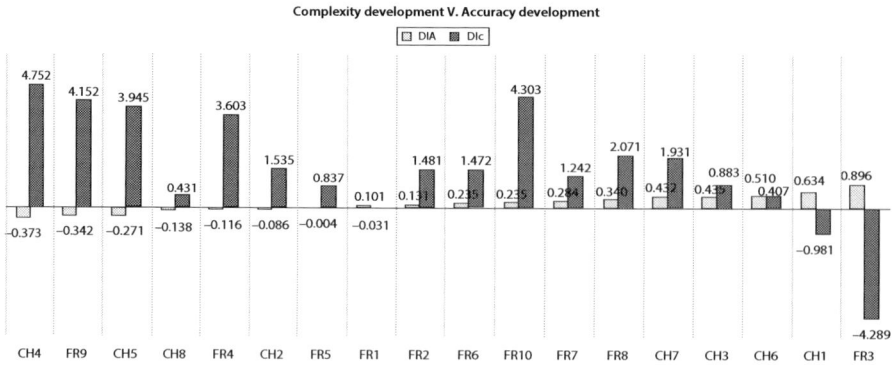

Figure 11. Global DI_C scores plotted against global DI_A scores after two semesters of SA

increased their DI_C score over the course of SA compared to 11 learners who increased their DI_A score, leading to the finding that development in complexity may be more tangible than development in accuracy after two semesters of SA. Only 8 learners of the entire sample (44.4%) saw increases in both their DI_A and DI_C scores. Given the small number of learners, we forego statistical analysis of such differences, and present them simply for information. The learner who saw the greatest gains in accuracy (0.8963), FR3, also exhibited the lowest scores for complexity (−4.2890). Likewise, the learner who saw the greatest gains in complexity (4.7518), CH4, exhibited the lowest score for accuracy (−0.3732). This finding is supportive of the Trade-Off Hypothesis (Skehan, 1998) in that these learners may have focused on either the complexity or accuracy aspect of the CAF triad, leading to a negative impact on the other aspects (Skehan, 2009).

5. Discussion

In this section, we review the findings presented in relation to the two research questions we asked at the start of the study. The first research question asked:

a. To what extent does length of stay (LoS) abroad influence development in complexity and accuracy?

The results for complexity and accuracy suggest that the extent to which time, or LoS abroad, influences development in complexity and accuracy is inconsistent, or at least, subject to a great deal of variation at the individual level. This underlying individual variation, which characterises advancement in both of these aspects of CAF, is evident by the non-linear fashion in which learners progress or regress over time. The actual extent to which LoS abroad influences such progression or regression is also subject to individual variation. Over the course of the first semester (between T_1 and T_2) for example, 10 learners (or 55.5%) progressed in complexity compared to 13 learners (or 72.2%) who progressed over the course of the second semester (between T_2 and T_3), suggesting that advancement in this language component became tangible to more learners as the LoS abroad increased. However, of the 10 learners who originally progressed in complexity after 1 semester of SA, only 6 continued to progress during the second semester, suggesting a plateau effect in the development of complexity for some learners as time progressed. In relation to complexity development, it is important to consider the differences between the two groups of learners. These differences can be considered in terms of cross-linguistic influence (CLI), which is the term commonly used to describe the effects that a first language can have on the learning of an L2 and is viewed as "one of the central processes in second language acquisition" (Llama et al., 2010: 39). The decision to investigate Chinese and French learners of English as an L2 thus served a dual purpose. Firstly, the French and Chinese learners came from very different cultural backgrounds and, as such, might experience different patterns or levels of acculturation, or simply, the process by which learners acquire and adapt to the practices of a new culture (Antonakopoulou, 2013), allowing the study to track any changes and/or differences in amount and type of exposure to the L2, as it related to levels of social integration and acculturation. Secondly, there is evidence to suggest that native speakers of a language which is linguistically *close* to the target language will attain a higher level of proficiency in the L2 than speakers of a native language which is linguistically *distant* (Chiswick & Miller, 2004). French and Chinese are two widely-spoken and widely different languages, and are viewed as either typologically close (with an alphabetic writing system) to the L1 (French), or typologically distant (with a logographic writing system) to the L1 (Chinese) (for a full account of linguistic distance in SLA, see Chiswick & Miller, 2004). Moreover, Chinese differs from English in its lack of polysyllabic words, higher homophone density, smaller inventory of syllables, use of distinctive tones and a dual vocabulary (Duanmu, 2006). As such, the Chinese learners' L1 may have had a greater impact on their complexity development (in terms of, for example, length of units) than the French. On this count, however, the findings are somewhat counterintuitive as seven of the eight Chinese participants produced more words per AS-unit (WPerAS) over the course of SA, with only one learner (CH1) steadily producing shorter units as time progressed (see Figure 2). If we examine the words per clause (WPerCl) measure, however, we note that six of the eight Chinese learners (compared to two of the ten French learners) produced fewer words per clause at the end of SA than at the outset (Figure 2), pointing to a possible effect for cross-linguistic influence. Given such differences between measures, it is difficult to draw any substantive conclusions about the role of the learners' L1, in this case, Chinese, in their development of complexity.

In terms of accuracy development, 8 learners (or 44.4%) became more accurate between T_1 and T_2, compared to 13 learners (or 72.2%) between T_2 and T_3, suggesting that development in accuracy was also more tangible as the LoS abroad increased (based on DI_A scores in Figure 6), similar to complexity. Differences were also evident between the French and the Chinese learners in relation to accuracy development. Over the course of the first semester ($T_2 - T_1$) only three of the Chinese learners (CH1, CH6 and CH8) increased their overall DI_A score, compared to six of the ten French learners. Over the course of the second semester ($T_3 - T_2$) more learners (both Chinese and French, six and eight of each respectively) scored more positively in the DI_A. In terms of the different accuracy measures employed, the most interesting finding relates to the learners' rate of error (ASErr), whereby four of the eight Chinese learners' rate of error (within AS-units) actually increased as the SA period progressed, compared to only two of the ten French learners. Overall then, with the clear majority (72.2%) of all learners evidencing gains within both complexity and accuracy during the second semester of SA, it appears that development in both of these language aspects became more tangible over time. This finding is in line with the findings presented by Serrano et al. (2012: 149) whose study reported that "the progress experienced by students abroad during the first and second semester in oral and written production differs."

The second research question asked:

b. How does development in Complexity and Accuracy differ during SA?

As mentioned above, development in complexity and accuracy differs in terms of LoS abroad as learners experience different levels of development as time progresses. More learners progressed in complexity over the course of the first semester of SA (55.5%) compared to those who progressed in accuracy during this time period (44.4%). Conversely, an equal number of learners progressed in complexity and accuracy over the course of the second semester (72.2%).

Although the findings presented point to some differences between the learners in their development on accuracy and complexity during SA, it is difficult to draw substantive conclusions as to the reason for these differences while considering just two of the three CAF aspects. Indeed, the study recognises the multidimensionality of CAF and regards it as a dynamic system of interrelating subsystems (Larsen-Freeman, 2009; Norris & Ortega, 2009). In other words, although the results for complexity and accuracy are supportive of the 'Trade-Off' hypothesis (Skehan, 1998), it is accepted within this study that the attributes of a learner's language, such as CAF, should be regarded and investigated as an interrelated triad. As such, our analysis and subsequent findings for the fluency component of CAF will be invaluable in drawing definitive conclusions on this matter.

6. Conclusion

In summary, the findings point to considerable individual variation in the development of both complexity and accuracy during SA, with some learners evidencing progress while others do not. Equally, variation is also evident at the individual level after one semester of SA and after two semesters of SA, such that there is no linear pattern of development across all learners. Rather, at best, it seems that some learners progress from T_1 to T_2, while others regress. Similarly, between T_2 and T_3, some of the learners who had previously progressed may now have regressed, while those who had regressed may now have progressed. It is noteworthy, however, that the scope of progression or regression is relatively small, such that there is no sudden spurt of development evident at any stage of the study.

Taken together, the findings point to the underlying complexity of the issue of time and L2 development in a study abroad context. As we have outlined, this complexity relates to the different perspectives on the role of time that emerge depending on the actual measure of L2 development investigated, as well as the individual variation between the learners at the different stages of the study. Moreover, differences are also evident among the French and Chinese learners such that drawing substantive conclusions on the effects of LoS becomes problematic, with some learners evidencing gains in both/either complexity and/or accuracy from T_1 to T_2 and then regression from T_2 to T_3, and vice versa. While the findings presented for accuracy and complexity remain to be complemented by those concerning fluency, the individual variation between the learners highlights the importance of exploring factors underlying such variation in the SA context. Given that a neat pattern of development does not emerge across the learners or within the individual learner, the findings presented will be further complemented with data from the pre- and post-test versions of the LCP (Freed et al., 2004). These data will provide further insight into the potential of social, input and extralinguistic factors at play during SA to constrain individual learner development at particular moments in time, while promoting development at others. Space precludes presentation of these findings here. While the findings on complexity and accuracy highlight the complexity of development, it is important to note that they are subject to some limitations. In the following, we note those limitations, and highlight some areas for future research in the area.

7. Limitations and directions for future research

With regard to the study we have presented, an initial potential limitation of the findings concerns the relatively small sample size involved (n = 18). The sample size is partly attributed to the longitudinal design of the study, and the consequent level of commitment required from each participant in terms of participant retention. However, given the relatively small number of longitudinal studies within SA research, especially over a full academic year, it is precisely this type of study that can truly illuminate the intricacies of longitudinal development over time within the same learner cohort. Moreover, in this study, the limitation concerning sample size is minimised in part due to the volume of data collected from each learner, amounting to over 36 hours of interview recordings and 200,000 words in transcriptions. In relation to the findings, the small sample size is, however, problematic in generalising the findings to a wider population representative of a larger group of SA learners. Notwithstanding, as the results point to considerable individual variation, the issue of the generalisation of the findings may be less the issue than the need to illuminate such individual variation. Indeed, such individual variation in SA findings is noteworthy across studies, such that there is considerable need to explore the socio-biographical, social and extralinguistic factors giving rise to such individual variation. In the case of our study here, our qualitative data will provide complementary insights in the future, but they are beyond the scope of the paper presented here.

A second limitation in the study concerns the fact, as already mentioned, that no independent proficiency test was administered at the outset of the study. Instead, the learners' initial proficiency in the well-defined constructs of complexity and accuracy (Skehan, 1998) was enumerated by employing the proposed developmental index of CAF. While the role of proficiency level was not the focus of this study, it is noteworthy that some studies within an SA framework already report an effect for proficiency level, whereby less advanced learners make greater gains than more advanced learners. Such differences are seen to reflect the simple fact that less advanced learners have more to gain, but also that they are not necessarily constrained by their less extensive communicative resources compared to their more advanced counterparts (see Freed, 1995).

In sum, notwithstanding such issues of proficiency level and other socio-biographical, social and extralinguistic factors which may potentially be at play, our findings point to considerable intra-learner variation across the different measures of development. Given such variation within the individual learner, the relationship between those factors and the various ways in which progression and regression have emerged in this study suggest that such a relationship may be especially complex. While future research should undoubtedly explore the specificity of the relationship holding, there is also considerable need to explain such intra-learner variation in terms of the factors which allow a learner to evidence progression on some measures, but not all, while also simultaneously demonstrating regression on others. While recent SA research has taken a considerable social turn, our findings would suggest that there remains a need for in-depth linguistic-oriented analysis of the learner's linguistic development during SA. In sum, such development would seem not to be a case of all or nothing, but very much dependent on the specific measure of development employed. A further related area of fruitful investigation in the future concerns the benefits of including a native speaker group as a point of comparison. In particular, while it would be interesting to see if similar inter-individual differences are characteristic, such a comparison with L2 learners would allow for an interesting yardstick of the scope of learner development during SA in the potential direction of target language norms. Taken together, such issues point to the rich insights that future SA research can bring to the CAF paradigm within SLA.

Acknowledgements

We would like to thank the anonymous reviewers for their valuable input and suggestions on an earlier version of this chapter. The project on which the study is based was generously funded by a Strategic Research Fund award at University College Cork to whom we also extend our gratitude.

References

Antonakopoulou, E. 2013. "Sociocultural adaptation of U.S. education abroad students in Greece: The effects of program duration and intervention." *Frontiers: The Interdisciplinary Journal of Study Abroad* XXIII: Fall 2013.

Bartning, I. 1997. "L'apprenant dit avancé et son acquisition d'une langue étrangère. Tour d'horizon et esquisse d'une caractérisation de la variété avancée." *Acquisition et Interaction en Langue Etrangère* 9: 9–50.

Bartning, I. 2009. "The advanced learner variety: 10 years later." In *The Advanced Learner Variety. The Case of French*, F. Myles and E. Labeau (eds.), 11–40. Bern: Lang.

Bardovi-Harlig, K. and Bofman, T. 1989. "Attainment of syntactic and morphological accuracy by advanced language learners." *Studies in Second Language Acquisition* 11 (1): 17–34. DOI: 10.1017/S0272263100007816

Chiswick, B.R. and Miller, P.W. 2004. "Linguistic distance: A quantitative measure of the distance between English and other languages." *Journal of Multilingual and Multicultural Development* 26 (1): 1–16. DOI: 10.1080/14790710508668395

Churchill, E. and DuFon, M. 2006. *Language Learners in Study Abroad Contexts*. Clevedon / Toronto: Multilingual Matters.

Collentine, J. 2004. "The effects of learning contexts on morphosyntactic and lexical development." *Studies in Second Language Acquisition* 26 (2): 227–248.

Collentine, J. and Freed, B. 2004. "Learning context and its effects on second language acquisition." *Studies in Second Language Acquisition* 26 (2): 153–171.

Davidson, D. 2010. "Study abroad: When, how long, and with what results? New data from the Russian front." *Foreign Language Annals* 43 (1): 6–26. DOI: 10.1111/j.1944-9720.2010.01057.x

De Bot, K., Lowie, W. and Verspoor, M. 2007. "A dynamic systems theory approach to second language acquisition." *Bilingualism: Language and Cognition* 10 (1): 7–21. DOI: 10.1017/S1366728906002732

De Bot, K. and Makoni, S. 2005. *Language and Aging in Multilingual Societies: Dynamic Perspectives*. Clevedon / Toronto: Multilingual Matters.

Dechert, H.W., Mohle, D. and Raupach, M. 1984. *Second Language Productions.* Tubingen: Gunter Narr.

Duanmu, S. 2006. "Chinese (Mandarin): Phonology." In *Encyclopedia of Language and Linguistics*, 2nd Edition, K. Brown (ed.), 351–355. Oxford: Elsevier. DOI: 10.1016/B0-08-044854-2/00096-1

Dwyer, M. 2004. "More is better: The impact of study abroad program duration." *Frontiers: The Interdisciplinary Journal of Study Abroad* X: 151–164.

Ellis, R. 2003. *Task-based Language Learning and Teaching.* Oxford: Oxford University Press.

Ellis, R. and Barkhuizen, P. 2005. *Analysing Learner Language.* Oxford: Oxford University Press.

Freed, B.F. 1991 "Language learning in a study abroad context: The effects of interactive and non-interactive out-of-class contact on grammatical achievement and oral proficiency." In *Linguistics, Language Teaching and Language Acquisition: The Interdependence of Theory, Practice and Research*, J. Alatis (ed.), 459–477. Washington DC: Georgetown University Press.

Freed, B.F. 1995. "What makes us think that students who study abroad become fluent?" In *Second Language Acquisition in a Study Abroad Context*, B.F. Freed (ed.), 123–148. Amsterdam: John Benjamins. DOI: 10.1075/sibil.9.09fre

Freed, B.F., Dewey, D.P., Segalowitz, N. and Halter, R. 2004. "The language contact profile." *Studies in Second Language Acquisition* 26 (2): 349–356.

Foster, P., Tonkyn, A. and Wigglesworth, G. 2000. "Measuring spoken language: A unit for all reasons." *Applied Linguistics* 21 (3): 354–375. DOI: 10.1093/applin/21.3.354

Hakuta, K. 1975. "Learning to speak a second language: What exactly does the child learn?" In *Developmental Psycholinguistics: Theory and Applications*, D.P. Dato (ed.), 193–207. Washington DC: Georgetown University Press.

Hart, D.S., Lapkin, S. and Swain, M. 1994. "Impact of a six-month bilingual exchange program: attitudes and achievement." Report to the Department of the Secretary of State. Toronto: OISE Modern Language Centre.

Herdina, P. and Jessner, U. 2002. *A Dynamic Model of Multilingualism: Perspectives of Change in Psycholinguistics.* Clevedon / Toronto: Multilingual Matters.

Housen, A. and Kuiken, F. 2009. "Complexity, accuracy and fluency in second language acquisition." *Applied Linguistics* 30 (4): 461–473. DOI: 10.1093/applin/amp048

Housen, A., Kuiken, F. and Vedder, I. 2012. *Dimensions of L2 Performance and Proficiency: Complexity, Accuracy and Fluency in SLA.* Amsterdam: John Benjamins. DOI: 10.1075/lllt.32

Howard, M. 2005. "Second language acquisition in a study abroad context: A comparative investigation of the effects of study abroad and foreign language instruction on the L2 learner's grammatical development." In *Investigations in Instructed Second Language Acquisition*, A. Housen and M. Pierrard (eds.), 495–530. Berlin / New York: Mouton de Gruyter. DOI: 10.1515/9783110197372.4.495

Howard, M. 2011a. "Input perspectives on the role of learning context in second language acquisition. An introduction to the special issue." *Input and Learning Context in Second Language Acquisition*, Special issue of *International Review of Applied Linguistics* 49 (3): 71–82.

Howard, M. 2011b. "Lessons from the world of SLA on the impact of learning context in L2 acquisition. Insights from study abroad research." In *Discours, acquisition et didactique des langues. Les termes d'un dialogue*, P. Trévisiol-Okamura and G. Komur-Thilloy (eds.), 87–104. Paris: Orizons.

Ife, A., Vives Boix, G. and Meara, P. 2000. "The impact of study abroad on vocabulary development among different proficient groups." *Spanish Applied Linguistics* 4 (1): 55–84.

Isabelli, C.A. and Nishida, C. 2005. "Development of the Spanish subjunctive in a nine month study-abroad setting." In *Selected Proceedings of the 6th Conference on the Acquisition of Spanish and Portuguese as First and Second Languages*, D. Eddington (ed.), 78–91. Somerville, MA: Cascadilla Press.

Keijzer, M. 2001. *Representation and Behavior*. Massachusetts: MIT Press.

Labov, W. 1984. "Field methods of the project on linguistic change and variation." In *Language in Use*, J. Baugh and J. Scherzer (eds.), 43–70. Englewood Cliffs: Prentice Hall.

Larsen-Freeman, D. 1978. "An ESL index of development?." *TESOL Quarterly* 12 (4): 439–448. DOI: 10.2307/3586142

Larsen-Freeman, D. 1997. "Chaos/complexity science and second language acquisition." *Applied Linguistics* 18 (2): 141–165. DOI: 10.1093/applin/18.2.141

Larsen-Freeman, D. 2002. "Language acquisition and language use from a chaos/complexity theory perspective." In *Language Acquisition and Language Socialization: Ecological Perspectives*, C. Kramsch (ed.), 33–46. London: Continuum.

Larsen-Freeman, D. 2006. "The emergence of complexity, fluency, and accuracy in the oral and written production of five Chinese learners of English." *Applied Linguistics* 27 (4): 590–619. DOI: 10.1093/applin/aml029

Larsen-Freeman, D. 2009. "Adjusting expectations: The study of complexity, accuracy, and fluency in second language acquisition." *Applied Linguistics* 30 (4): 579–589. DOI: 10.1093/applin/amp043

Larsen-Freeman, D. and Ellis, R. 2009. *Language as a Complex Adaptive System*. Oxford: Wiley-Blackwell.

Llama, R., Cardoso, W. and Collins, L. 2010. "The influence of language distance and language status on the acquisition of L3 phonology." *International Journal of Multilingualism* 7 (1): 39–57. DOI: 10.1080/14790710902972255

Llanes, À. and Muñoz, C. 2009. "A short stay abroad: Does it make a difference?" *System* 37 (3): 353–365. DOI: 10.1016/j.system.2009.03.001

Llanes, À. 2011. "The Many Faces of Study Abroad: An Update on the Research on L2 Gains Emerged During a Study Abroad Experience." *International Journal of Multilingualism* 8 (3): 189–215. DOI: 10.1080/14790718.2010.550297

Llanes, À. 2012. "The impact of study abroad and age on second language accuracy development." In *Intensive Exposure Experiences in Second Language Learning*, C. Muñoz (ed.), 193–212. Bristol: Multilingual Matters.

Long, M. 1997. "Construct validity in SLA research: A response to Firth and Wagner." *Modern Language Journal* 81: 318–323. DOI: 10.1111/j.1540-4781.1997.tb05487.x

Mohanan, K.P. 1992. "Emergence of complexity in phonological development." In *Child Phonological Development*, C. Ferguson, L. Menn and C. Stoel-Gammon (eds.), 635–662. Timonium, MD: York Press.

Norris, J.M. and Ortega, L. 2009. "Towards an organic approach to investigating CAF in instructed SLA: The case of complexity." *Applied Linguistics* 30 (4): 555–578. DOI: 10.1093/applin/amp044

Ortega, L. and Byrnes, H. 2008. *The Longitudinal Study of Advanced L2 Capacities*. London: Routledge.

Pérez-Vidal, C. and Juan-Garau, M. 2009. "The effects of study abroad (SA) on written performance." *EUROSLA Yearbook* 9: 269–295. DOI: 10.1075/eurosla.9.13per

Pérez-Vidal, C. and Juan-Garau, M. 2011. "The effect of context and input conditions on oral and written development: A study abroad perspective." *International Review of Applied Linguistics* 49 (2): 157–185. DOI: 10.1515/iral.2011.008

Pérez-Vidal, C., Juan-Garau, M. Mora, J.C. and Valls-Ferrer, M. 2012. "Oral and written development in formal instruction and study abroad: Differential effects of learning context." In *Intensive Exposure Experiences in Second Language Learning*, C. Muñoz (ed.), 193–212. Bristol: Multilingual Matters.

Polat, B. and Kim, Y. 2014. "Dynamics of complexity and accuracy: A longitudinal case study of advanced untutored development." *Applied Linguistics* 35 (2): 184–207.

Rasouli Khorshidi, H. 2013. "Study abroad and interlanguage pragmatic development in request and apology speech acts among Iranian learners." *English Language Teaching* 6 (5): 62–70.

Regan, V. 1998. "Sociolinguistics and language learning in a study abroad context." *Frontiers: The Interdisciplinary Journal of Study Abroad* 4 (3): 61–91.

Sasaki, M. 2007. "Effects of study-abroad experiences on EFL writers: a multiple data analysis." *Modern Language Journal* 91 (4): 602–620. DOI: 10.1111/j.1540-4781.2007.00625.x

Sasaki, M. 2009. "Changes in English as a foreign language students' writing over 3.5 years: a sociocognitive account." In *Writing in Foreign Language Contexts: Learning, Teaching, and Research*, R. Manchon (ed.), 49–76. Bristol / Toronto: Multilingual Matters.

Serrano. S. 2010. "Learning languages in study abroad and at home contexts: A critical review of comparative studies." *Porta Linguarum* 13: 149–163.

Serrano, S., Tragant, E. and Llanes, À. 2012. "A longitudinal analysis of the effects of one year abroad." *Canadian Modern Language Review* 68 (2): 138–163. DOI: 10.3138/cmlr.68.2.138

Skehan, P. 1998. *A Cognitive Approach to Language Learning*. Oxford: Oxford University Press.

Skehan, P. 2001. "Tasks and language performance." In *Researching Pedagogic Tasks: Second Language Learning, Teaching, and Testing*, M. Bygate, P. Skehan and M. Swain (eds.), 167–186. London: Longman.

Skehan, P. 2003. "Task based instruction." *Language Teaching* 36: 1–14. DOI: 10.1017/S026144480200188X

Skehan, P. 2009. "Modelling second language performance: Integrating complexity, accuracy, fluency, and lexis." *Applied Linguistics* 30 (4): 510–532. DOI: 10.1093/applin/amp047

Skehan, P. and Foster, P. 1999. "The influence of task structure and processing conditions on narrative retellings." *Language Learning* 49 (1): 93–120. DOI: 10.1111/1467-9922.00071

Skehan, P. and Foster, P. 2001. "Cognition and tasks." In *Cognition and Second Language Learning*, P. Robinson (ed.), 183–205. New York: Cambridge University Press. DOI: 10.1017/CBO9781139524780.009

Verspoor, M., de Bot, K. and Lowie, W. 2004. "Dynamic systems theory and variation: A case study in L2 writing." In *Words in Their Places: A Festschrift for J. Lachlan Mackenzie*, H. Aertsen, M. Hannay and R. Lyall (eds), 407–421. Amsterdam: Free University Press.

Verspoor, M., de Bot, K. and Lowie, W. 2011. *A Dynamic Approach to Second Language Development: Methods and Techniques*. Amsterdam: John Benjamins. DOI: 10.1075/lllt.29

Vossensteyn, H., Beerkens, M., Cremonini, L., Besançon, B., Focken, N., Leurs, B., McCoshan, A., Mozuraityte, N., Huisman, J., Souto Otero, M. and de Wit, H. 2010. "Improving the participation in the ERASMUS programme." In *Directorate General for Internal Policies, Policy Department B: Structural and Cohesion Policies Culture and Education*, European Commission, Brussels.

Waldrop, M.M. 1992. *Complexity: The Emerging Science at the Edge of Order and Chaos*. New York: Simon and Schuster.

Wang, W. 2009. "Interlanguage theory and emergentism: Reconciliation in second language developmental index studies." *English Language Teaching* 2 (1): 31–36.

Wolfe-Quintero, K., Inagaki, S. and Kim, H.-Y. 1998. *Second Language Development in Writing. Measures of Fluency, Accuracy and Complexity*. University of Hawai'i: Second Language Teaching and Curriculum Center.

An analysis of complexity in primary school L2 English learning

Heather Hilton and Carine Royer
Université Lyon 2 (France) / Université de Cergy-Pontoise (France)

In the context of a Complex Systems (CS) approach to language acquisition and teaching research, this paper will use Geometric Data Analysis (GDA, l'*Analyse géométrique des données*: Benzécri 1973; Le Roux & Rouanet 2010) to explore data collected from beginning learners of English (n = 54) in a primary school context in France. The study was initially designed along classical "group comparison" lines (six-year-olds vs. eight-year-olds), and not from the start for CS analysis; participants performed four different tasks in English at two times during their first year of English; they also completed a variety of psychometric tests and questionnaires measuring various cognitive, verbal, affective et conative characteristics. We will begin by looking at classic nonparametric comparisons of the two groups of learners and correlations between the psychometric tests and performance on the English tasks. These univariate statistics do not actually turn up very much structure in the data set, and we will use multivariate GDA for a closer look at the complex relationships between individual features and early L2 skill.

Introduction

In the language sciences, the emergentist framework for language acquisition research was first adopted by researchers working in the field of child language development, and notably by Elizabeth Bates and Brian MacWhinney, as they developed and refined their "Competition Model" (Bates & MacWhinney 1987; MacWhinney 1987; MacWhinney & Bates 1989; Bates & Goodman 1999; MacWhinney 1997b, 1999, 2001). The emergentist paradigm that now dominates L1 acquisition theory has, from the start, incorporated research on second language acquisition by bilingual children, and MacWhinney himself introduced the model into the field of second language acquisition (SLA) research (MacWhinney 1992; MacWhinney 1997a), where it was quickly taken up (Ellis 1996; Ellis 1998).

The adoption of an emergentist model has led SLA researchers to discover the complex dynamic systems paradigm that has been adopted by L1 researchers (van Geert 1991; Thelen & Smith 1994; van Geert 2006; van Geert 2010) to consider the interactions of multiple factors that influence the emergence of language knowledge and skill (de Bot et al. 2007; Ellis 2007; van Geert 2007; Larsen-Freeman & Cameron 2008). In a promising trend for our young field of scientific investigation,[1] the emergentist construct appears to interest researchers operating in the various "branches" of SLA research (McLaughlin 1989) – cognitive, linguistic and interactionist – which up to now have tended to operate separately or even exclusively (a certain hostile scepticism characterizing some of the theoretical stances taken in the 1980s and early 1990s). The complex dynamic systems (CDS) paradigm offers an excellent opportunity for researchers from the three historic branches of SLA to pool data and share methods, as we tackle increasingly richer data sets from a more mature theoretical perspective (Ellis 2007: 23).

Ideally, an L2 study designed for CDS analysis would involve (as it does in the L1 literature) closely following an individual over time, taking frequent measures that reflect multiple factors developing over time, and attempting to identify the characteristics of the interactions that bring about the emergence of new knowledge and skills (van Geert 2013; de Bot 2013), no doubt using the sophisticated mathematical algorithms that are needed to find structure in "big data" (Beslon 2012). Irregularities or variability in these measures will no longer be discarded as statistical "noise," but rather scrutinized as important indicators of "how learning happens" (Larsen-Freeman & Cameron 2008: 40). The data described here was not taken from a study intended for CDS analysis from the start, and some of it is still being transcribed and coded; the discussion that follows is not, therefore, an illustration of a complete CDS approach to language acquisition research, nor will we propose detailed interpretations of the phenomena observed. We will, however, be looking at individual variability, and considering ways of looking for structure in complex (but relatively traditional) data sets. One particular set of mathematical techniques – used for what French social scientists call "Geometrical Data Analysis" (*Analyse géométrique des données*; Le Roux 2013) – appears to be well-suited for this type of analysis.

---

1. The *European Second Language Association* (EUROSLA) having been founded just twenty-four years ago.

The Paris8 Primary English project

An exploratory project on early language learning in two French primary schools was originally designed along classical "group comparison" lines, by researchers connected with the linguistic branch of SLA research. Fifty-four beginning learners of English as a foreign language were followed during their first year of classroom study over the 2012–2013 school year: one group of 25 six-year-olds (all first-graders born in 2006), and one group of 29 eight-year-olds (all third-graders born in 2004). The two schools participating in the study belong to the same *regroupement scolaire* in the Seine-et-Marne region east of Paris, in which the full range of primary classes is distributed among small schools in neighboring rural villages; the children participating in the study therefore have the same socio-economic background (there are even eight pairs of siblings in the two groups). September 2012 marked the first time that English was offered to first-graders in this system, which explains how we managed to observe two different age groups beginning English in the same school system the same year. Parental consent was obtained for each child's participation in all phases of the project.

Each individual learner possesses a unique combination of skills and characteristics that influences or shapes his interactions with new materials, information, instructors and classmates in any educational setting or learning experience. "Variables" that come into play in any learning experience may be cognitive (attention, working memory, perceptual preferences), social (personality, interactional knowledge and skill, relationships to others), or conative (relating to motivation or desire to learn); phonological memory and prior verbal knowledge have also been shown to play a role in classroom *language* learning (Papagno, Valentine & Baddeley 1991; Carroll 1993; texts in Robinson 2002). In order to know more about the 54 children participating in the Paris8 project – and to reflect more fully the complexity of the learning phenomena observed – eleven tests and questionnaires were administered to each child in French. Each instrument was chosen as a measure of one characteristic (cognitive, verbal, social or conative) that has been shown to contribute to the emergence of new language knowledge and skill; the list of variables, and of the tests used to reflect each one, is presented in Table 1. Four measures relate to cognitive capacity and function: tests of attentional capacity, working memory capacity and span, and phonological memory. There are also four measures reflecting L1 verbal memory and skill (that is, verbal learning prior to this first classroom experience): French listening and vocabulary tests, and metalinguistic syllable and phoneme suppression tasks. To reflect some aspects of personality the children performed a risk-aversion task, and their teachers completed the social competence scale from the *Socio-affective Profile* questionnaire. With the exception of the syllable and phoneme suppression tasks (administered

Table 1. Variables measured in the Paris8 Primary English project
(* indicates tasks included in the analyses that follow)

Individual variables		Instrument
executive function in WM	sustained attention* digit span* WM span (reverse digit)*	Weschler, D. (2007) *WISC-IV*. Paris: ECPA.
phonological memory	nonword repetition*	Casalis, S. (2000) *Répétition de logotomes*. Lille: Université de Lille.
L1 verbal skill	L1 listening*	Khomsi, A. (2001) *Evaluation du langage oral*. Paris: ECPA.
L1 verbal knowledge	L1 vocabulary*	
metalinguistic skill	syllable suppression* phoneme suppression*	Ecalle, J. (2007) *THaPho: test d'habiletés phonologiques*. Dardilly: Mot à mot.
personality: risk-taking	risk aversion task	Baratgin, J. & Jamet, F. (under development at the Université Paris 8).
social competence	questionnaire	Dumas et al. (1997) *Profil socio-affectif*. Paris: ECPA.
motivation for English	smiley questionnaire*	adapted from *ELLiE* project questionnaire (Enever 2011)
linguistic profile	parent questionnaire*	adapted from *ELLiE* project, with in-house questionnaire

collectively), all cognitive and verbal tests and the risk aversion task were administered individually by trained psychometrists. The children also completed a "smiley" questionnaire designed to reflect their motivation for learning English (adapted from the *Early Language Learning in Europe* project), in December and May of the project year. Their parents completed a linguistic profile questionnaire (also based on *ELLiE* project instruments), designed to identify plurilingual participants, family attitudes towards language learning, and exposure to English by the children in their homes.

Various researchers have insisted on the dynamic nature of constructs such as personality, motivation, or memory (for example, Dörnyei 2009: 243), and they tend to reject the sorts of standardized measures that are listed in Table 1 as being too static to represent individual traits that are themselves complex systems. We are fully cognizant of (and in agreement with) these positions, but did not dispose of a more dynamic means of reflecting such traits in the limited amount of time during which we had access to the children participating in the project. We will therefore rely on these well-known measures, considering each one as a sort of snapshot view of one capacity that a child may enlist as s/he comes to grips with a new language, and hoping to uncover through our analyses of the data those "higher order combinations of different attributes" (*ibid*) that determine various attractor states in the emergence of L2 knowledge and skill.

We took similar "snapshots" of emerging L2 knowledge and skill at three different times during the school year (early December, mid-February, late May). The children were asked to complete four tasks in English, each at two of these times: a phoneme discrimination task (in December and May), a listening task, an elicited imitation task, and a free production task (all in February and May). All four of these tasks were administered individually, in a one-on-one session with adult SLA researchers whom the children grew familiar with over the school year. In the phoneme discrimination task the child indicated whether two English CVC syllables were the same or different (the differences being minimal pairs targeting vowel or consonant contrasts); the listening task involved selecting an appropriate picture after hearing an English statement. In elicited imitation the child simply repeated an English phrase or sentence, and in free production s/he commented in English on pictures of objects or scenes. All of the audio stimuli for the first three tasks were recorded, and played to the child on a laptop computer through padded headphones (reducing outside noise); the responses for the two production tasks were recorded in *Audacity* on the same laptop.

To obtain a sample of environmental, methodological and behavioral factors that are also part of the complex system from which L2 skill emerges, we filmed one week of English lessons at each of our three visits to the schools (December, February, May), for a total of four hours of filmed lessons for each class. These video files are being transcribed and annotated, for detailed analyses of the types of activities and classroom interaction the children engaged in in each class. Both of the teachers participating in the project were also interviewed, so that we could obtain additional information on their methodological choices, their English program for the year, their attitudes towards the English lessons, and their perception of the French national syllabus for primary language teaching.

Analyzing the data set with traditional statistics

We will not be analyzing our complete data set here, but focusing on the measures of cognitive, verbal, and conative variables, and possible relationships between these features and the children's performance on the two receptive English tasks (phoneme discrimination and listening) and the free production task. We will start with traditional univariate group comparisons and correlations, and move on to Geometric Analysis of the same data, in order to illustrate the ways in which this type of multivariate analysis can uncover "hidden structure in complex data"

Table 2. Group results, French tests (cognitive and verbal characteristics) and English tasks

	1st graders	3rd graders	Group comparisons (Mann-Whitney)
Group characteristics and numbers			
n =	25	29	
girls/boys	15/10	17/12	
L1 French monolinguals/ bi- or plurilinguals	21/4	26/3	
Individual differences (tests in French)			
French vocabulary test	15.9	17.5	3rd > 1st* ($U = 195.0$, $p < .01$)
French listening test	13.2	17.2	3rd > 1st*** ($U = 43.0$, $p < .0001$)
Test of sustained attention	11.8	10.8	1st = 3rd ($U = 283.0$, $p = .17$)
Digit Span (WM capacity)	5.8	7.3	3rd > 1st* ($U = 184.5$, $p < .01$)
Reverse Digit Span (WM span)	4.6	5.3	1st = 3rd ($U = 264.5$, $p = .08$)
Nonword repetition (phonological memory)	94.1	86.9	1st > 3rd** ($U = 170.0$, $p < .001$)
Metalinguistic skill (phoneme suppression)	5.0	5.4	1st ≈ 3rd ($U = 247.5$, $p = .053$)
Metalinguistic skill (syllable suppression)	5.4	5.7	1st = 3rd ($U = 308.0$, $p = .40$)
Tasks in English and motivation for English			
Motivation for English in December	21.5	20.0	1st = 3rd ($U = 254.5$, $p = .18$)
minimum	12	9	
maximum	24	24	
Motivation for English in May	22.3	20.0	1st > 3rd (m) ($U = 206.0$, $p = .03$)
minimum	18	7	
maximum	24	24	
English phoneme discrimination (Dec.)	21.3	20.4	1st = 3rd ($U = 273$, $p = .25$)
minimum	12	14	
maximum	28	24	
English listening (Dec + May combined score)	15.1	15.8	1st = 3rd ($U = 281.0$, $p = .40$)
minimum	10	9	
maximum	22	21	
English production (nb of utterances)	9.1	13.5	3rd > 1st** ($U = 115.0$, $p = .001$)
minimum	3	0	
maximum	14	25	
English production (MLU)	1.3	2.7	3rd > 1st*** ($U = 69.5$, $p < .0001$)
minimum	1	0	
maximum	3.86	4.5	
English production (error rate)	2.1	11.5	3rd > 1st*** ($U = 84.0$, $p < .0001$)
minimum	0	0	
maximum	14.3	44	

(Le Roux 2013). Scores for the English phoneme discrimination and listening tasks consist of one point for each correct response (with a possible total of 30 points for each test); free production is measured by the number of words and utterances produced, mean length of utterance (MLU, in words), and error rate (per 100 words). Table 2 presents the results by group (first-graders, third-graders) for the various tasks and questionnaires that have been scored to date, with group comparisons (Mann-Whitney's U) reported in column 4.

These classic nonparametric group comparisons do show a few interesting characteristics of our six- and eight-year-old groups. It is probably non-trivial to note that the first-graders – who are, of course, less advanced in L1 listening skill than third-graders (French Listening Test) – perform as well on the English listening tasks as the eight-year-olds. This particular group of six-year-olds is better at nonword repetition, which may partially explain why they are also as good as the eight-year-olds on the English auditory discrimination task, although the "teacher" variable no doubt also contributes to the performance observed (the first-grade teacher majored in English and lived in the US for two years; the third-grade teacher reported herself as "ill-at-ease" with English pronunciation, in particular). The motivational level of the six-year-olds remains marginally higher than the eight-year-olds at the end of the school year; this may be an institutional effect, or a factor related to age (older learners becoming less enthusiastic about school as time goes by). The third-graders were more "chatty" than the first-graders in the English speaking task, producing longer utterances and more of them, which, in turn, provides greater margin for error (so a higher error rate).

Spearman correlations (run on all of these scores) indicate only two significant pairings of verbal or cognitive variables and emerging English skill. Performance on the L1 phoneme suppression task was correlated with scores on the English listening task ($rs = .493$, $p < .001$), suggesting a possible role for metalinguistic skill in the realization of the type of task proposed. Nonword repetition correlated negatively with error rate in the production task ($rs = .414$, $p < .01$), indicating a possible relationship between phonological memory and ability to extract grammatical patterns from communicative-style classroom input.

"Geometric Analysis" of available data

These results hint at possible complex relationships between individual differences and emergent English skills, so we decided to plunge deeper into the data, using the techniques of Geometrical (or Geometric) Data Analysis (*Analyse géométrique des données* or simply *Analyse des données*) developed by French mathematicians in the 1950s and '60s, and adapted for the social sciences by Jean-Paul Benzécri

(Benzécri 1973, 1982). Working closely with Benzécri, French sociologist Pierre Bourdieu found in geometrical Correspondence Analysis (*l'Analyse des correspondances*) "a relational procedure whose philosophy fully expresses what in my view constitutes social reality" (Preface to the German edition of *Le Métier de sociologue*; cited in English by Le Roux & Rouanet 2010:5). The set of procedures developed by Benzécri are designed for the analysis of qualitative data, which must be formatted from the start for Correspondence Analysis (Le Roux 2013). The analysis of our quantitative test scores will involve procedures based on Principle Component Analysis (Pearson 1901; Hotelling 1933). Generally, in Geometric Data Analysis, multivariate factor analysis and orthogonal scaling are used to provide a geometrical representation of correspondences existing in complex data sets (Martin 2004; Le Roux & Rouanet 2010); these techniques seem particularly well-suited to the analysis of complex phenomena:

> PCA analyzes a data table representing observations described by several dependent variables [...]. Its goal is to extract the important information from the data table and to express this information as a set of new orthogonal variables called principal components. PCA [...] represents the pattern of similarity of the observations and the variables by displaying them as points in maps.
>
> (Abdi & Williams 2010:434)

The following Geometric Analysis of our primary school data was carried out using the SPAD7 software suite (Coheris), under the guidance of some of the mathematicians who have helped develop its programs.

In the first step, Principle Component Analysis (PCA) is carried out on the cognitive, verbal, and motivation scores, to prepare the data for cluster analysis. Hierarchical clustering algorithms identify patterns of similarity in the relation of each subject to these principle components; SPAD7 recommends "cutting" the cluster tree at eight or five branches. For the analyses presented here we opted for eight clusters, to avoid losing information on particular profiles that may be less well-represented in a pool of only 54 subjects. Table 3 summarizes the significant characteristics of the children in each cluster (measures where the children in the cluster scored significantly higher or lower than their peers, column 2), giving numbers of children in each cluster (column 3), as well as their age and sex (columns 4 through 7). Although half of the clusters (2, 4, 6, 7) contain children of only one age group, and "cluster" 3 contains only one child, the three remaining clusters (1, 5, and 8) are larger and mixed, revealing cross-group similarities that univariate statistics miss.

The second step in our Data Analysis is to perform PCA on the scores obtained on our English tasks; this identifies two receptive components (the auditory discrimination task and the cumulative listening score), and two production

Table 3. Clusters of learners (cognitive, verbal & motivational factors) identified through PCA; grey boxes indicate that the group (age or gender) is significantly represented in the cluster (WM = working memory, NWR = nonword repetition)

Cluster	Characteristics	n =	Age 6	Age 8	F	M
cl1	high WM capacity, NWR, metalinguistic skill, motivation	13	6	7	12	1
cl2	low attention	2	2	0	1	1
"cl"3	(one child) low L1 listening and vocabulary; high motivation	1	1	0	0	1
cl4	low L1 listening, low WM capacity	6	6	0	5	1
cl5	high attention; low L1 listening and metalinguistic skill	11	9	2	4	7
cl6	high L1 listening; low motivation	5	0	5	2	3
cl7	low NWR (problems with phonological memory)	2	0	2	0	2
cl8	high L1 listening and vocabulary; low executive function in WM (attention, capacity), and low NWR	14	1	13	8	6

components (number of words produced and mean length of utterance) as significant performance factors. The SPAD software uses the results of this PCA to define a two-dimensional data matrix: "The variables are plotted as points in the component space using their loadings as coordinates" (Abdi & Williams 2010: 444). In Figure 1, performance in English describes two axes, one productive (MLU and number of words produced, "axe 1") and one receptive (auditory discrimination and listening scores, "axe 2").

In the third step of the analysis (Figure 2), the individual learners – each color-coded according to the cluster s/he belongs to (following step one) – are situated in the geometrical space defined by PCA of the English scores in step two. To help visualize possible differences in performance between the clusters, the software can calculate ellipses representing the geometrical dispersion of the bigger clusters (1, 4, 5, 6 and 8). The number of subjects in each of these clusters is still quite small, and we provide the ellipses here essentially to illustrate the sorts of data presentation that are possible with Geometric Analysis; they do suggest that children with different patterns of cognitive and verbal abilities do perform differently in beginning English production and comprehension. For example, the ellipse encompassing the thirteen children in cluster 1 (high working memory capacity and phonological memory, good metalinguistic skill and high motivation; dashed line) illustrates performance that is skewed away from the right-hand side of the first axis (productive performance), towards high L2 receptive performance (top of the second axis) – although this large ellipse illustrates a certain dispersion in the performances observed. The smallest ellipse, encompassing the eleven children in cluster 5 (high attentional capacity, but low L1 listening and

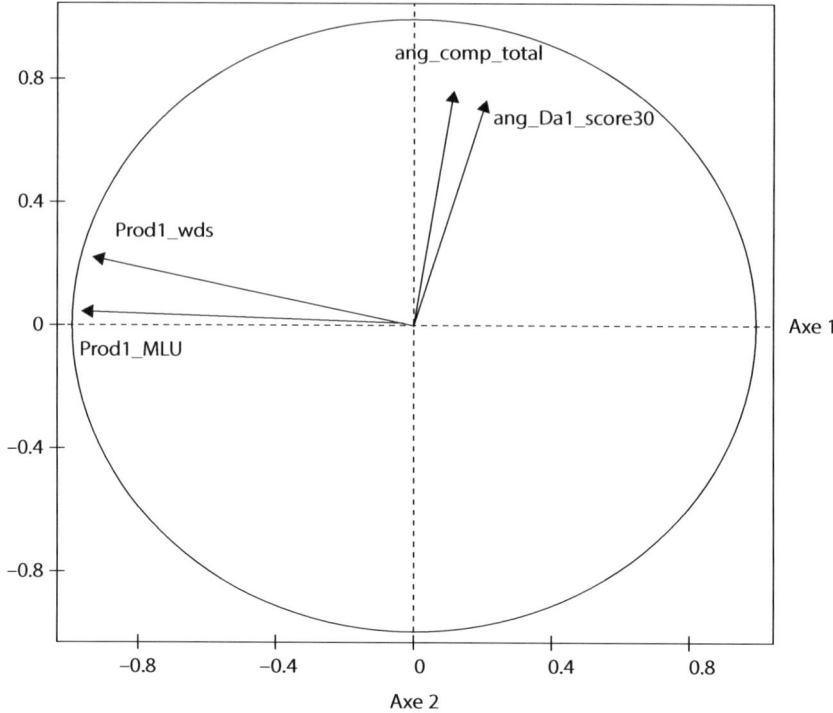

Figure 1. Axes described by performance on English tasks

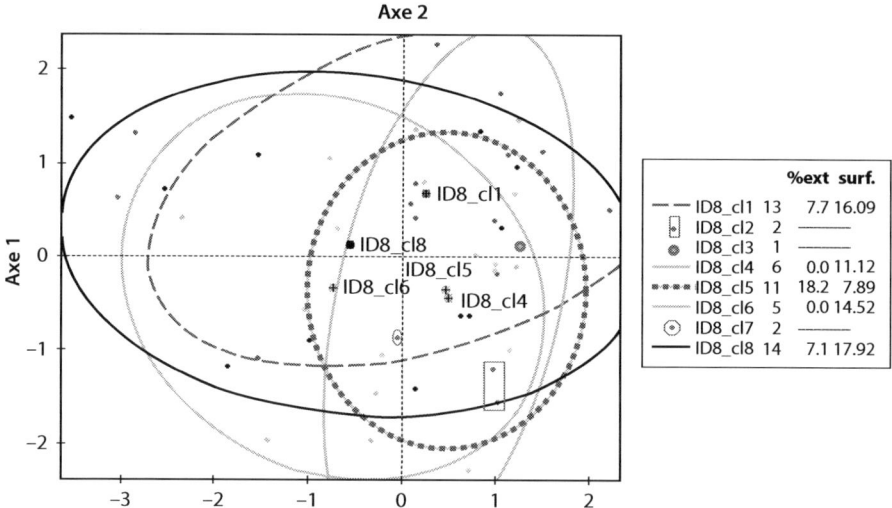

Figure 2. Clusters of learners situated in the geometric space defined by English task performance

metalinguistic skill), illustrates performance in English that is skewed towards the lower right quadrant of the English performance axes – more limited emerging L2 skill, for both production and reception. This is also the case for the two learners with lower attentional capacity in cluster 2 (situated inside the box in the lower right quadrant).

Methodological discussion: Considerations for L2 research on complexity

It is unusual, in the clusters presented in Table 3, to find six-year-olds and eight-year-olds grouped together (clusters 1, 5, and 8) on the basis of standardized cognitive and verbal measures that would normally show clear separation between learners at these two developmental stages. Of course, the effect in the language classroom of a cognitive trait (such as working memory capacity) can be offset by social variables (such as extraversion), and future analyses will incorporate data obtained through the social competence scale and the risk-aversion task. The inclusion of this data into a Geometric Analyses will, however, require restructuring the information obtained with the eight cognitive and verbal measures, so that no one set of components (cognitive, L1 verbal, social, or conative) artificially outweighs the others in PCA (Pardoux 2013). It is necessary to look at this larger set of variables, as we have done here, before any restructuring of this type.

Like all analytic methods, Geometric Analysis imposes its own set of imperatives on the data collection process, and therefore on project design. Since the Paris8 Primary project was not initially designed for CDS research, the analyses presented here are of an exploratory nature, useful for outlining ideas for future research within the complex systems paradigm. Since variability is the norm in classroom behavior and in language acquisition, individual characteristics must be an important part of the information we consider in our studies, and our observational tools should be able to reflect a large number of characteristics and the interactions between them. Despite the limitations of the static tests used here to measure individual differences, these are validated instruments (measuring a single characteristic), which are relatively quick to administer. Even so, these eleven individual tasks took a team of three trained psychometrists two days to administer in each school; this is already a hefty incursion into the French four-day primary school week, and it would have been difficult to ask for additional time for a more dynamic perspective on learner attributes. We must juggle between the types of optimal data collection that current theory dictates, and the practical challenges of classroom research. The meticulous collection of behavioral data in a dynamic perspective (reflecting change across time) requires sophisticated and costly recording techniques: multiple cameras, automatic recording and perhaps even automatic localization of voices and movements in the classroom. While we are waiting to find the technological solutions to methodological challenges of this type, researchers – as well as reviewers and journal editors – will need to accept that CDS research must start with small-scale or even individual studies, in which numerous qualitative and quantitative measurements are taken on very few learners at a time (Lowie & Verspoor 2013; Mackey 2013). We will have to build up slowly to "group" perspectives – where groups are defined in a data-driven way, and not necessarily by institutional level or age. The Paris8 project data turns up combinations of variables that give interesting results in the limited types of observations we carried out, and further studies could begin by identifying learners with similar characteristics in different language-learning contexts, in order to observe the effects of methodological and environmental variables. One of the more provocative findings suggested by the geometric configuration of our data in Figure 2 is the clustering of learners (and particularly of those with a strong cognitive and verbal profile) in the top right "receptive" quadrant of the geometrical space defined by the results on our English tasks. Does this suggest a trade-off between receptive and productive skill in the beginning stages of L2 learning by young learners ("listeners" are not "chatterboxes" and vice-versa)?

A final point, and one which is of paramount importance to SLA research in the complex dynamic systems paradigm, is the growing need for large, pluridisciplinary research teams, that include at least one full-time mathematician to carry out multivariate analyses (as well as technicians who can look into questions of automatic classroom recordings). Geometric Data Analysis is an interesting means of uncovering structure in data, and helping us to formulate qualitative interpretations of objectively-measured variables.

Acknowledgments

The Paris8 Primary English project was made possible by a grant for exploratory research by the Conseil Scientifique of the Université Paris 8. We wish to thank the parents, the children, the teachers, the school principals, and the members of the Seine-et-Marne *Inspection Académique*, whose collaboration made this study possible.

References

Abdi, H.W. and Lynne J. 2010. "Principal component analysis." *Wiley Interdisciplinary Reviews: Computational Statistics* 2 (4): 433–459. DOI: 10.1002/wics.101

Bates, E. and Goodman, J.C. 1999. "On the emergence of grammar from the lexicon." In *The Emergence of Language*, B. MacWhinney (ed.), 29–80. Mahwah NJ: Lawrence Erlbaum.

Bates, E. and MacWhinney, B. 1987. "Competition, variation, and language learning." In *Mechanisms of Language Acquisition*, B. MacWhinney (ed.), 157–193. Hillsdale NJ: Lawrence Erlbaum.

Benzécri, J.-P. 1973. *L'Analyse des Données. Volume II. L'Analyse des Correspondances*. Paris: Dunod.

Benzécri, J.-P. 1982. *L'analyse des données: leçons sur l'analyse factorielle et la reconnaissance des formes et travaux*. Paris: Dunod.

Beslon, G. 2012, 2 July. "Introduction to complex systems." Plenary lecture, *Sixth Annual Complex Systems Summer School*. Paris: Institut des Systèmes Complexes.

Carroll, J.B. 1993. "Abilities in the domain of language". In Chapter 5 of *Human Cognitive Abilities: A Survey of Factor-analytic Studies*, 145–195. Cambridge: Cambridge University Press. DOI: 10.1017/CBO9780511571312.006

de Bot, K. 2013, 8 April. "Language development at different time scales: Diachronic complexity." *Workshop on Dynamic Systems Analysis*. Paris: Groupe de Recherche ADYLOC.

de Bot, K., Lowie, W. and Verspoor, M. 2007. "A Dynamic Systems Theory Approach to Second Language Acquisition." *Bilingualism: Language and Cognition* 10 (1): 7–22. DOI: 10.1017/S1366728906002732

Dörnyei, Z. 2009. "Individual differences: Interplay of learner characteristics and learning environment." In *Language as a Complex Adaptive System*, N.C. Ellis and D. Larsen-Freeman (eds), 230–248. Oxford: Wiley-Blackwell.

Dumas, J.E., Lafrenière, P.J., Capuano, F. and Durning, P. 1997. *Profil socio-affectif*. Paris: ECPA.

Ellis, N.C. 1996. "Sequencing in SLA: Phonological memory, chunking, and points of order." *Studies in Second Language Acquisition* 18: 91–126. DOI: 10.1017/S0272263100014698

Ellis, N.C. 1998. Emergentism, connectionism and language learning. *Language Learning* 48 (4): 631–664. DOI: 10.1111/0023-8333.00063

Ellis, N.C. 2007. "Dynamic systems and SLA: The wood and the trees." *Bilingualism: Language and Cognition* 10 (1): 23–25. DOI: 10.1017/S1366728906002744

Enever, J. 2011. *ELLiE: Early Language Learning in Europe*. United Kingdom: British Council.

Hotelling, H. 1933. "Analysis of a complex of statistical variables into principal components." *Journal of Educational Psychology* 25: 417–441. DOI: 10.1037/h0071325

Larsen-Freeman, D. and Cameron, L. 2008. *Complex Systems and Applied Linguistics*. Oxford: Oxford University Press.

Le Roux, B. 2013, 25 June. *Analyse des données structurées*. Workshop on Analyse géométrique des données. Paris: Université Paris Descartes.

Le Roux, B. and Rouanet, H. 2010. *Multiple Correspondence Analysis*. Thousand Oaks: Sage.

Lowie, W. and Verspoor, M. 2013, 28 August. "DST & acquisition order." In *Language Learning Roundtable: Acquisition Orders in SLA: Perspectives from Emergentism and Dynamic Systems Theory, EUROSLA 23*, Amsterdam: Universiteit van Amsterdam.

Mackey, A. 2013, 29 August. "Methodology in SLA research: Past, present and future." Plenary lecture, *EUROSLA 23 Conference*. Amsterdam: Universiteit van Amsterdam.

MacWhinney, B. 1987. "The competition model." In *Mechanisms of Language Acquisition*, B. MacWhinney (ed.), 249–308. Hillsdale NJ: Lawrence Erlbaum.

MacWhinney, B. 1992. "Transfer and competition in second language learning." In *Cognitive Processing in Bilinguals*, R.J. Harris (ed.), 371–390. Amsterdam: Elsevier. DOI: 10.1016/S0166-4115(08)61506-X

MacWhinney, B. 1997a. "Second language acquisition and the competition model." In *Tutorials in Bilingualism: Psycholinguistic Perspectives*, A.M.B. de Groot and J.F. Kroll (eds), 113–142. Mahwah, NJ: Lawrence Erlbaum.
MacWhinney, B. 1997b. "Models of the emergence of language." *Annual Review of Psychology* 49: 199–227. DOI: 10.1146/annurev.psych.49.1.199
MacWhinney, B. 1999. "The Emergence of language from embodiment." In *The Emergence of Language*, B. MacWhinney (ed.), 213–246. Mahwah NJ: Lawrence Erlbaum.
MacWhinney, B. 2001. "Emergentist approaches to language." In *Frequency and the Emergence of Linguistic Structure*, J. Bybee and P. Hopper (eds.), 449–470. Amsterdam: John Benjamins. DOI: 10.1075/tsl.45.23mac
MacWhinney, B. and Bates, E. 1989. *The Cross-linguistic Study of Sentence Processing*. Cambridge: Cambridge University Press.
Martin, A. 2004. *L'analyse de données*. Course handout. Brest: École Nationale Supérieure de Techniques Avancées de Bretagne. www.arnaud.martin.free.fr/Doc/polyAD.pdf (25/07/2013)
McLaughlin, B. 1989. "The Three phases (faces?) of second-language research." In *Language Processing in Social Context*, R. Dietrich and C.F. Graumann (eds), 211–231. Amsterdam: North-Holland.
Papagno, C., Valentine, T. and Baddeley, A. 1991. "Phonological short-term memory and foreign-language vocabulary learning." *Journal of Memory and Language* 30: 331–347. DOI: 10.1016/0749-596X(91)90040-Q
Pardoux, C. 2013, 24 June. "Analyse en composantes principales." Workshop on *Analyse géométrique des données*. Paris: Université Paris Descartes.
Pearson, K. 1901. "On lines and planes of closest fit to systems of points in space. *Philosophical Magazine* 2: 559–572. DOI: 10.1080/14786440109462720
Robinson, P. (ed.). 2002. *Individual Differences and Instructed Language Learning*. Amsterdam: John Benjamins. DOI: 10.1075/lllt.2
Thelen, E. and Smith, L.B. 1994. *A Dynamic Systems Approach to the Development of Cognition and Action*. Cambridge MA: MIT Press.
van Geert, P. 1991. "A dynamic systems model of cognitive and language growth." *Psychological Review* 98: 3–53. DOI: 10.1037/0033-295X.98.1.3
van Geert, P. 2006, 24 January. "Dynamic systems methods in the study of language." *Apprentissage des langues premières et secondes Conference*. Paris: Ministère de la Recherche.
van Geert, P. 2007. "Dynamic systems in second language learning: Some general methodological reflections." *Bilingualism: Language and Cognition* 10 (1): 47–49. DOI: 10.1017/S136672890600280X
van Geert, P. 2010. "Dynamic systems methods in the study of language acquisition: Modeling and the search for trends, transitions and fluctuations." In M. Kail and M. Hickmann (eds), *Language Acquisition across Linguistic and Cognitive Systems*, 33–52. Amsterdam: John Benjamins. DOI: 10.1075/lald.52.04gee
van Geert, P. 2013, 8 April. "Modeling language development as a complex dynamic system: Concepts, principles and methods." Workshop on *Dynamic Systems Analysis*. Paris: Groupe de Recherche ADYLOC.

Aspect in L2 English
A longitudinal study of four Japanese child returnees

Neal Snape,[1] John Matthews,[2] Makiko Hirakawa,[3]
Yahiro Hirakawa[4] and Hironobu Hosoi[1]
[1] Gunma Prefectural Women's University / [2] Chuo University /
[3] Bunkyo University / [4] Tokyo Institute of Technology

Our study reports on data collected on three separate occasions over a period of 12 months from four Japanese child returnees who had lived in the U.S. between 8 and 12 years before returning to Japan. Their English proficiency was assessed by TOEIC and C-test scores, and they were each asked to complete an Acceptability Judgment Task (AJT). Results show very little change across Test sessions 1, 2 and 3. Initially, we expected to find differences over the course of 12 months as the returnees' exposure and daily use of English decreased substantially since returning to Japan. Some slight L2 attrition of English was found in the domain of aspect for one returnee. We believe our results overall indicate that rather than L2 language loss, the returnees have managed to maintain their competence in the L2 aspectual domain.

1. Introduction

In the current study we investigate second language (L2) acquisition of aspect in English by four Japanese child returnees. Specifically, we focus on the progressive aspectual form *-ing* (e.g., *Mary is walking*) and the present verb form (e.g., *Mary walks*) with the four basic verb classes (Vendler, 1967), i.e., activity, accomplishment, state, and achievement. Three of the returnees are sequential bilinguals, or child L2 learners, as they all started learning English after the age of 4 years, having already acquired their first language (L1), Japanese; one is a simultaneous bilingual (Montrul, 2008; Meisel, 2011).

The flip side of L2 acquisition is L2 attrition. This is not usually discussed in relation to L2 acquisition research since one generally assumes that once learners have reached a certain proficiency in the L2, they will retain that proficiency, but studies dating back to Cole (1929) have been concerned with the loss of foreign language skills by high school students during summer vacation after completing a language course. In more recent L2 attrition studies, researchers have been interested in returnees who have spent longer periods abroad (e.g., Yoshitomi, 1992, 1999; Tomiyama, 1999, 2009). Typically, people who stay a number of years in an L2-speaking environment gain a certain level of proficiency.[1] However, upon return to their country of origin, they may no longer have the opportunity to use the L2 in their daily lives; when this happens, attrition, or loss of the L2, is likely to take place. One domain where we might expect to find L2 attrition is in the lexicon (Weltens, de Bot, & van Els, 1986) and in the interlanguage grammars of returnees who use exclusively their L1 every day. Grammatical aspect is one area of grammar that may change over a period of time, especially when the aspectual semantics differ between the L1 and the L2, as is the case in Japanese and English. The aim of our study is simply to find out whether returnees' L2 grammatical knowledge attrites after their return from the L2-speaking environment.

L2 acquisition of aspect has been discussed cross-linguistically in terms of how certain types of predicate constructions in the target language are produced or interpreted by learners (e.g., Andersen & Shirai, 1996; Bardovi-Harlig, 1999; Gabriele, Maekawa & Alemán-Bañón, 2009; Slabakova, 2001, 2002; Slabakova & Montrul, 2002). However, we are unaware of any study that investigates the acquisition and/or attrition of aspect among child returnees. Previous studies have reported that adult Japanese-speaking learners of English have difficulty with certain forms in specific contexts such as accepting -*ing* in a sentence like *The plane is arriving at the airport* when the context describes a completed event, i.e., a picture shows that the plane is stationary at the airport (Gabriele, 2009). Other difficulties for Japanese L2 learners relate to an over acceptance of -*ing* with verbs like *know*, e.g., **He is knowing him for many years* (Al-Hamad et al., 2002; Hawkins et al., 2008). These studies suggest that difficulty results from influence of the -*te iru* form in Japanese, which superficially resembles the -*ing* form. An activity verb like *run* has an ongoing interpretation that describes an action with the property of duration and no specific endpoint as exemplified in (1a), but with an achievement verb such as *arrive*, the action is taking place in that particular moment with a specific endpoint, and it gives a perfective/resultative reading, as the example in (1b) shows.

---

1. In some cases, L2 learners may become fossilized in their L2 English (Lardiere, 1998).

(1) Activity
   a. Mari-ga   hasi-te-iru.
      Mari-NOM run-ASP-NON-PAST
      'Mary is running.'
   Achievement
   b. Mari-ga   tui-te-iru.
      Mari-NOM arrive-ASP-NON-PAST
      'Mari has arrived.' NOT 'Mari is arriving.'

The accomplishment verb/predicate in (2a) shows that Ken is in the process of making a chair, a process that specifies an inherent endpoint, illustrating a condition known as *telicity*; if the verb phrase encodes an endpoint, it is specified in the syntactic representation as [+telic]. Stative verb types as in (2b) differ from accomplishment verbs in that there is no process or stage of knowing John, and there is no endpoint; thus it is [–telic], or atelic.

(2) Accomplishment
   a. Ken-wa   isu-o   tsukut-te iru.
      Ken-TOP chair-ACC make-ASP-NON-PAST
      'Ken is making a chair.'
   Stative
   b. Ken-wa   John-o   shit-te-iru.
      Ken-TOP John-ACC know-ASP-NON-PAST
      'Ken knows John.' NOT 'Ken is knowing John.'

We will examine interpretations of lexical (the 4 verb classes) and grammatical (inflectional morphology) aspect in L2 English by the four child returnees. We met with each of them six months after their return from the U.S. – this we refer to as Time 1. We then met them again after 6-months (Time 2). Time 3 was the final data collection point for the current study (6-months after Time 2).

The paper is organized as follows. Section 2 outlines the theoretical approach we adopt to aspect. In section three, we briefly review previous studies of aspect, focusing mainly on Japanese learners of English. Section 4 provides details about child returnees. Section 5 examines L2 attrition studies of returnees. Section 6 provides details of our experimental study. Section 7 discusses the findings and concludes the paper.

2. Aspect in English

Aspect differs from tense in that tense places an event on a timeline, relevant to speech time (past, present, future) (Comrie, 1976; Chung & Timberlake, 1985). Aspect refers to how an event unfolds in time, focusing on the internal properties of the event, such as whether it is ongoing in time or whether it has already been completed (Smith, 1991). There are two types of aspect, *lexical aspect* and *grammatical aspect*. Lexical aspect (also referred to as *inherent aspect* and *situation aspect*) encodes the aspectual contribution of the verb phrase and usually refers to Vendler's (1967) four-way classification. Four basic verb classes can be grouped according to their inherent aspect: Semantic categories of verbs such as activity, accomplishment, achievement and stativity. Table 1 illustrates the differences between the four verb types.

The features [±dynamic], [±process] and [±telic] draw distinctions between the four verb types. For example, the feature [±dynamic] shows that statives are incompatible with a specification for [+dynamic]. A diagnostic test like the one used by Vendler (1967) and Dowty (1979) demonstrates the interaction of verb phrases with temporal adverbials and tense: The present progressive *be+V-ing* test is one such test that distinguishes statives from non-statives.

(3) a. Mari is running (Activity)
    b. Ken is making a chair (Accomplishment)
    c. Mari is arriving (Achievement)
    d. *Ken is knowing John (Stative)

In English, the stative verb *know* is incompatible with the present progressive, but the other verb types are compatible. Each of the four verb classes illustrated in (3) is discussed further in examples below.

Example (4) shows that the Japanese *-te iru* construction appears superficially to resemble *be+V-ing* because when the *-te* particle attaches to activity verbs, it specifies the process as 'ongoing', just like *-ing* in English. There are no differences in interpretation between English progressive marking *be+V-ing* and Japanese

Table 1. Properties that distinguish the four verb types

	[±dynamic]	[±process]	[±telic]
Activities	+	+	−
Accomplishments	+	+	+
Achievements	+	−	+
Statives	−	−	−

Based on Andersen (1991) and Rothstein (2004).

imperfective/duration grammatical marker -*te iru* for activity verbs as both indicate action-in-progress.

(4) Activity: Action in progress
    Ken-ga   utat-te iru.
    Ken-NOM sing-ASP-NON-PAST
    'Ken is singing.'

Example (5) illustrates the case of accomplishment verb types.[2] In English and Japanese the interpretation is one in which there is an action in progress with an endpoint.

(5) Accomplishment: Action with an endpoint
    Sam-wa   ichi-jikan-de / ? ichi-jikan   futa-tsu no   tegami-o
    Sam-TOP one hour in /   one hour for two-CL GEN letter-ACC
    kakimashita.
    write-PAST
    'Sam wrote two letters in an hour / ? for an hour.' (from Gabriele, 2010: 382)

Example (5) shows that the bare noun *tegami* (letter) in Japanese is not specified for number. The classifier *futa-tsu* (two) specifies a specific quantity and is compatible with the prepositional phrase *ichi-jikan-de* (in/for 1 hour): the interpretation is assigned the [+telic] feature. However, the prepositional phrase *ichi-jikan* (for 1 hour) is not compatible as it is [−telic]. A telic event is an event that has reached its inherent, built-in endpoint (see 6a and d); an atelic event has no endpoint (see 6b, c and e). The activity *run* is compatible with the prepositional phrase *for an hour* in (6a) but incompatible with *in an hour* in (6b). However, with achievement *arrive* in (6d) and accomplishment *make* in (6f) the reverse is true as only the prepositional phrase *in an hour* is compatible whereas *for an hour* in (6c–e) is incompatible.

(6) a. Mari ran for an hour.
    b. ?Mari ran in an hour.
       (? means that it is acceptable if previous discourse included discussion of Mari taking part in a marathon).
    c. ?Mari arrived for an hour.
       (? means that it is acceptable on an iterative reading where the arriving recurred repeatedly over the course of an hour).

---

2. Accomplishments like *Ken is making a chair* are ambiguous in Japanese as they can have a progressive reading or a perfective interpretation, e.g., *Kyonen / kako-ni isu-o tsukut-teiru* (last year / once in the past, he made a chair). It depends on the lexical semantics of the verb (e.g., Jacobsen, 1992).

d. Mari arrived in an hour.
e. ?Ken made a chair for an hour.
    (? means that it is acceptable if the context signifies that Ken was engaged in an activity in progress, but the event was not completed).
f. Ken made a chair in an hour.

Activities and accomplishments share the feature [±process] as they have a process component. States and achievements do not (see Table 1) and achievements are said to occur instantaneously. In (7) however, *-te iru* achievement verb types in Japanese do not allow a progressive interpretation, but rather entail a resultative interpretation instead. They can indicate the state of a subject resulting from the completion of the action of the verb, but not to a "process leading up to the endpoint" (Jacobsen, 1992; also Ogihara, 1998). In other words, in (7) the English interpretation is *the plane is still in mid air and has not yet reached its destination* but the Japanese interpretation is that *the plane has arrived and is no longer in flight*. It does not allow the reading *the plane is arriving at the airport* (Hirakawa, 2001).

(7) Achievement: Process leading up to an endpoint
    English   The plane is arriving.
    Resultative state
    Japanese   Hikōki-ga   kūkō   ni tui-te iru.
                    plane-NOM   airport   at arrive-ASP-NON-PAST
                    'The plane (has arrived and) is at the airport.'

Vendler (1967) groups accomplishments and achievements together for English on the basis that both specify inherent endpoints, while states and activities do not. With stative verb types English and Japanese are similar if the state is temporary, as in (8a), as one could be glancing out the window of a bullet train and get a passing glimpse of Mount Fuji. However, sometimes the same notion is lexicalized differently between the two languages. For example, in (8b), a situation is described using a stative verb in English, e.g., Ken *knows* John, but in Japanese it is typically described with an achievement verb like *shiru* (know).

(8) State:
    a. Vividness; temporariness
        English   John is thinking that he might be sick.
        Japanese   Fuji-san-ga   mie-te iru.
                     Mt. Fuji-NOM   be visible-ASP-NON-PAST
                     'We can see Mt. Fuji (at this moment).'

b. Incompatible
Stative
English   *Ken is knowing John.
Achievement
Japanese   Ken-wa   John-o   shit-te iru.
           Ken-TOP   John-ACC   know-ASP-NON-PAST
           'Ken knows John.'

We adopt a semantic account of aspect based on McClure (1993). The examples in (5)–(8) can be explained under McClure's account by positing differences in the aspectual operator PROG in English and Japanese. McClure (1993) argues that there are only three true stative verbs in Japanese (*iru* animate verb of existence, *aru* inanimate verb of existence, and a homophonous *iru* which means *to need* or *to want*). Many verbs that are classified as statives in English constitute activities, ('*ai-suru*' *to love*) or achievements ('*shiru*' *to know*, '*wakaru*' *to understand*) in Japanese (Sugita, 2008). McClure's semantic account manages to capture the differences in interpretation for the achievement and stative categories. For the purpose of our study, we are interested in whether or not the child returnees are able to make distinctions between lexical aspect and grammatical aspect in L2 English, as outlined above. As there are differences between English and Japanese in the aspectual domain, we may expect to find some L1 transfer effects. For example, we test the returnees on activity verb types in a present simple context and a present progressive context by asking them to make judgments about the appropriateness of verbs in each context. The activity verb type may be easier to judge accurately since English and Japanese overlap in interpretation, but the stative verb type like *know* in English has less similarity to the corresponding form in Japanese and thus the returnees may be unable to make a distinction between a present simple context and a present progressive context, i.e., they may judge both contexts to be appropriate.

3. Previous studies on aspect

L1 studies found that the English progressive aspect marker *be+V-ing* was one of the first grammatical morphemes to appear in child's speech (Brown, 1973). Early L2 studies by Bailey, Madden and Krashen (1974) and Dulay and Burt (1973) found that child and adult second language learners showed a similar pattern of acquisition where *be+V-ing* was acquired early on. However, a number of studies have shown that aspectual knowledge is difficult to acquire for L1 and L2 learners alike (e.g., De Villiers & De Villiers, 1973).

There is a range of studies that have looked at the role of the L1 in the L2 acquisition of tense-aspect systems (e.g., Izquierdo & Collins, 2008; Sugaya & Shirai, 2007). Studies that have specifically examined Japanese L2 learners of English include Al-Hamad et al. (2002), Gabriele (2005), Gabriele (2009), Hawkins et al. (2008), Okuwaki (2005), and Yamazaki-Hasegawa (2012). Al-Hamad et al. (2002) investigated the acquisition of present simple and present progressive *be+V-ing* verb forms by advanced adult L2 English learners with various L1 backgrounds, including French, Japanese and Chinese. The task instructed participants to judge the appropriateness of two potential continuations of a short context, as shown in example (9), by rating each continuation on a 5-point Likert scale; −2 represents completely inappropriate and +2 signifies completely appropriate.

(9) Whenever Mary and Alan meet …
    a. they talk about Linguistics until late.   −2 −1 0 +1 +2
    b. they are talking about Linguistics until late. −2 −1 0 +1 +2

The appropriate continuation in (9) is the habitual reading of the present simple form in (9a), not the event-in-progress reading of the present progressive form in (9b). The results of the Japanese L2 learners showed that they differed from native speakers on *be+V-ing* with present tense statives but did not accept *be+V-ing* with statives like (10) below:

(10) John has no desire to have a new car. He *is owning* an old car.

Okuwaki (2005) administered an interpretation acceptability task and a picture description production task with aspectual forms to intermediate and advanced Japanese learners of English. Both tasks are analysed in three aspectual contexts: event-in-progress, stative, and habitual. Examples are provided in (11).

(11)

Aspectual form	Example sentences
Event-in-progress (present progressive)	Bob cannot contact Julie at the moment. Apparently, she *is running* on the beach.
Habitual (present simple)	Twice every week, instead of taking his car, Bob *walks* from his house to the station.
Stative	The library *stands* by the lake.

The interpretation acceptability task is similar in its design to the task used by Al-Hamad et al. (2002). The overall results from the interpretation task showed that the Japanese L2 speakers had difficulty judging the *be+V-ing* construction correctly with achievements. In the picture description production task participants were asked to tell a detailed story about pictures that depict a scene where a lot of people are involved in various ongoing activities, such as swimming, playing with a ball, stealing valuables, cooking a meal, running away from a bull, and more. There were four types of pictures to elicit description, and the task was not timed. The description in (12) was provided by one of the intermediate Japanese learners.

(12) The people along the beach, along the coastline make a film. The cameraman take a film ... a film ... taking the man ... the man who is running to the sea. And ... the ... people who saw that scene try to taking a picture of them. But ... the man ... in the beach, a girl is drowning, so the lifeguard try to save her ... running to a beach. Many people on the left enjoy diving and swimming.

Often, simple verb forms were incorrectly used to express an event-in-progress, though in (12) the learner does self-correct herself with the verb *take* as she says *take a film* and changes to *taking the man* which means *filming the man*. A proficiency effect was found between the intermediate and advanced groups in the picture description production task, but this effect was not found in the interpretation acceptability task. Both proficiency groups had difficulty interpreting the aspectual form, and Okuwaki argues that L1 syntactic structure remains influential even at very late stages of L2 acquisition when interpreting aspectual forms. In other words, advanced adult Japanese learners have persistent difficulty with L2 aspect.

Most work has investigated the influence of L1 semantic properties by adopting a syntactic approach (e.g., Al-Hamad et al., 2002; Okuwaki, 2005; Yamazaki-Hasegawa, 2012). However, Gabriele (2009) and Gabriele and McClure (2011) have recently used McClure's (1993) framework on aspectual semantics. Gabriele (2009) examined the effects of L1 semantic transfer in a study that included Japanese learners of English and English learners of Japanese. Here we discuss the contexts and her findings in relation to the Japanese learners of English. In an interpretation task, Gabriele included contexts as outlined in (13) and (14). In (13), we see what Gabriele calls 'addition' because if Japanese learners of English incorrectly judge the progressive *be+V-ing* to mean the event has been completed (as is the case in Japanese with *-te iru*), they would rate it as inappropriate (rate as 1) since picture 2a clearly shows the plane is still in the air. They must *add* the interpretation that in English the progressive is used to show that it is an ongoing event. In (14), the term 'preemption' is used as it is effectively the reverse of addition; it is to rule out an interpretation that is available in the L1. Learners have to *preempt* the interpretation that the plane has arrived; if there is transfer from Japanese the learners will incorrectly judge *be+V-ing* to be appropriate (rate as 5).

(13) Incomplete story context (addition)
Picture 1: This is the plane to Tokyo. At 4:00 the plane is near the airport.
Picture 2a: There is a lot of wind. At 4:30 the plane is still in the air.
Present progressive: The plane is arriving at the airport.
(Expected rating – NSs: 5; L2 learners: 1)

(14) Complete story context (preemption)
Picture 2b: At 5:00 the passengers are at the airport.
Present progressive: The plane is arriving at the airport.
(Expected rating – NSs: 1; L2 learners: 5)

The results of the incomplete and complete contexts for achievements, in the present progressive, showed differences according to proficiency levels. While lower level learners demonstrated difficulty in correctly accepting the present progressive with an incomplete context, a more target-like interpretation emerged among participants with higher proficiency levels. These findings suggest that, as predicted, advanced learners perform more accurately when the acquisition task involves the addition of a new representation. The same pattern of development was not found with the preemption context: Individual analyses showed that even some advanced learners allowed the present progressive to refer to completed events.

Gabriele and Canales (2011) investigated how L2 learners would interpret a range of meanings or a 'shift' in meaning between present simple and present progressive verb forms. Their participants included L1 Japanese intermediate and advanced learners of English. They found that the Japanese intermediate L2 learners had difficulty with the present simple. That is, they incorrectly accepted present simple sentences as in (15a) for an ongoing context and they incorrectly rejected the same form, as in (16a), for a habitual context, suggesting that the learners had difficulty associating the -*ing* form with ongoing contexts and the present simple form with habitual contexts.

(15) Activity: Ongoing Context
Emily is a math student. She has never written a poem before in her life. However, she had to take an English class and by tomorrow, she has to write a 15-verse poem about love. At the moment, she is on verse 10. This is miserable!
a. ✘ Emily writes poetry.
b. ✓ Emily is writing poetry.

(16) Activity: Habitual Context
Sarah is a writer. Her job is to write poetry for children Monday through Friday. Today is Sunday, so she is at the movies with some friends.
a. ✓ Sarah writes poetry.
b. ✘ Sarah is writing poetry.

In addition, in English, the present simple and the *-ing* form can both encode future reference with achievement verbs in the presence of adverbials such as *next week*, as shown in (17).

(17) a. ✓ Tomoko returns to Japan next week.
  b. ✓ Tomoko is returning to Japan next week.

When such shifts in meaning were examined, it was observed that Japanese intermediate learners incorrectly rejected sentences like (17a) and (17b) over 50% of the time on a Grammaticality Judgment Task. Japanese advanced learners performed much better, especially in accepting the futurate with the *-ing* form. However, as Gabriele and Canales point out, examining grammaticality judgments for sentences in isolation does not allow one to examine semantics and discourse/pragmatics. Gabriele and Canales found that the Japanese learners performed much better on the Interpretation Task when the sentences were presented together with a context.

The authors discuss possible influence of the L1 versus the role of instruction and input. They suggest that instruction and input are more likely to take precedence over L1 transfer as learners can interpret sentences like (17a) even if they have limited exposure to such sentences. In sum, the studies by Al-Hamad et al. (2002), Hawkins et al. (2008), and Okuwaki (2005) show that adult Japanese intermediate and advanced learners of English do have problems with achievement and stative verb types when they are asked to make judgments on present simple continuations vs. present progressive continuations of short contexts. Gabriele (2009) and Gabriele and Canales (2011) found that advanced Japanese learners can make correct judgments when such continuations are presented to learners in a short story. In other words, learners are able to "integrate contextual information in the interpretation of aspectual forms" (Gabriele & Canales, 2011: 686).

4. Child returnees

Child returnees are children born and raised in one country who then move overseas typically because one of their parents works for a company that has an office abroad and then later return to their country of birth. Between 1992 and 1996 a total of 12,000 to 13,000 Japanese children spent time living abroad and subsequently returned to Japan (Reetz-Kurashige, 1999). Child returnees may spend a year outside of Japan or several years, as this depends largely on the parent's job and the length of time the parent is required to stay in his or her post. Child returnees, especially those children who return to their home country after many years, typically have started to learn a second language. For example, the Japanese returnees who are the focus of our study spent a number of years in the U.S. and though they had started learning English in Japan, they significantly increased their study and use of English on a daily basis whilst in the U.S. Thus, child returnees are a unique group of child L2 learners who have experienced, in some cases, a great deal of exposure to the L2. Given the prolonged exposure to L2 English, one might expect that child returnees are more target-like in the L2 than their adult L2 learner (non-returnee) counterparts.

English and Japanese aspectual systems are similar in many ways but there are some subtle differences in interpretation for both lexical and grammatical aspect between the two languages. Japanese child returnees are an interesting group to examine as there may have been changes over time in their L2 grammatical competence, whereby their knowledge of the English aspectual system has developed beyond that of L2 learners who have not received as much target input, i.e., EFL learners who have not lived abroad. However, for the child returnees, there is the risk that any potential gain in L2 knowledge while abroad may attrite over time after their return. The next section examines cases of L2 attrition.

5. L2 attrition

Yoshitomi (1992) and Reetz-Kurashige (1999) note that due to the drastic reduction in L2 input and interaction on a daily basis, there is a substantial risk of language loss among returnees. In our study, we are concerned with the loss of the L2 (English), not the L1 (Japanese). There are various hypotheses in the literature that predict what happens in language attrition. The critical threshold hypothesis (*best learned, last out*), proposed by Neisser (1984), claims that there are levels of attainment above which someone's linguistic system is immune to attrition. A slight variation on this hypothesis is known as "the more you know, the less you lose" (see Hansen, 1999:151). The regression hypothesis (Jakobson, 1941/1968), initially proposed as an account of language loss in aphasia but logically extended to attrition, is the idea that linguistic elements vulnerable to loss will follow an order opposite to the sequence seen in acquisition. According to the hypothesis attriters will follow a path of language loss that is the mirror image of the path seen in acquisition, with the last learned being the first forgotten, the first learned being the longest retained.

Some of the earliest studies (Cole, 1929, for French) in L2 attrition investigated the question of loss of foreign language proficiency by high school students over summer vacations. More recent studies have focused on children who have lived in an L2 environment for a number of years. The child and his or her family accompany a parent who is relocated to a foreign country for a short period of time, typically a few years, but in some cases longer. Such studies (e.g., Hansen-Strain, 1990) have shown that for siblings who grew up together in the same linguistic environment, younger children lost their L2 faster than older children. To our knowledge, there has been little attention paid to specific areas of grammar in previous L2 attrition studies of Japanese returnees. Tomiyama (1999) looked at Japanese child returnees' L2 attrition, but in a qualitative study. There was no focus on grammar per se. Yoshitomi (1999) examined article use by four child returnees, but this was only in spoken production. In session one, the older returnee produced only 63.6% of definite articles and 25% of indefinite articles. Yoshitomi (1999) found that two returnees who spent a longer time abroad were less accurate with articles compared to two who had spent less time abroad. She looked at possible L2 attrition of grammar in all four participants and found no evidence of attrition. However, crucially, it remains an open question as to whether the L2 grammar was ever fully acquired. It is furthermore unclear what the role of L1 transfer effects might be for returnees. Reetz-Kurashige (1999) examined 18 Japanese child returnees' verb usage through a storytelling exercise using Mayer's (1969) frog story picture book. Each returnee was tested two or three times within 12–19 months. The results showed that tense and agreement errors were common, including omission of morphology like past tense *-ed* and third person singular *-s*. Omission of auxiliary *be* verbs with the progressive was also found for six of the returnees, e.g., *and bees chasing the dog*, though at both Time 1 and Time 2 the same errors were made by four of the returnees.

6. Our study

6.1 Participants

The adult Japanese learners of English were originally recruited for another study on the acquisition of tense and aspect (Hirakawa et al., under revision). They are divided into 3 groups: low intermediate (n = 19), high intermediate (n = 20) and advanced (n = 10); a native speaker control group (n = 16) recruited at the University of Calgary was also included. These groups serve as comparisons to the four returnees despite their all being adult L2 learners or adult native English speakers, and not teenagers who had early exposure.[3] Data collection started in Japan six months after the child returnees had returned from the U.S. Ideally, the

---

3. We realize that the comparisons of the four returnees' development should be made with child L2 learners and child native speakers. However, the adult L2 learner groups are included

Table 2. Biographical and linguistic information about the four child returnees

	CS	YS	KS	TA
English proficiency level	TOEIC = 905	TOEIC = 785 ~ 990[4]	TOEIC = 785 ~ 990	TOEIC = 600
Age of first exposure to English (years)	12	7	5	3
Age at first testing	19	15	11	15
No. of years living in the U.S.	8	8	8	12
Parents' language – both Japanese	100%	100%	100%	100%
Language spoken at home (in the U.S. and Japan)				
Japanese	90%	90%	90%	100%
English	10%	10%	10%	0%
Primary language of schooling (in Japan)				
Japanese	90%	90%	90%	90%
English	10%	10%	10%	10%
Language used in other social situations				
Japanese	65%	65%	65%	80%
English	35%	35%	35%	20%
Dominant language				
Japanese	75%	70%	70%	80%
English	25%	30%	30%	20%
Speaks better				
Japanese	65%	50%	40%	75%
English	35%	50%	60%	25%
Understands better				
Japanese	70%	50%	25%	70%
English	30%	50%	75%	30%

Based on Montrul (2002).

administration of the tasks should have taken place much sooner after their return to Japan, but as they were busy reinstating themselves into Japanese schools etc., it was only convenient for them to meet us after they had settled back into their daily lives in Japan. The two returnees' families live close to each other and to the university where two of the authors are based, which made it easy for the returnees to meet with us every six months for data collection. Biographical and linguistic information such as age of acquisition, proficiency level in English, etc. for each returnee are presented in Table 2. All the information provided in Table 2

---

so the reader can see the typical types of judgments one might find from Japanese learners with little or no experience living in an English speaking environment.

4. YS and KS took a test equivalent to TOEIC called EIKEN, a test for practical English proficiency, and their scores were within the high corresponding TOEIC range.

is based on two background questionnaires (one in English; one in Japanese) and interviews with each of the returnees.

The background questionnaires revealed that the returnees, CS, YS, KS, and TA, have high levels of proficiency in English, based on Test of English for International Communication (TOEIC) scores. The maximum one can achieve on TOEIC is a score of 990. At the time of testing, KS was only 11 years old and had not taken the TOEIC test but she had passed the pre-first level (i.e., the second highest of seven degrees of difficulty) of the EIKEN, a Japan-based test for practical English proficiency (a TOEIC equivalent score between 605–780). For each session (Time 1, Time 2 and Time 3) we administered C-tests, a standard measure in L1 and L2 attrition studies.[5] The results of the C-tests show that each participant has a slightly higher score at Time 1 than at Time 2 and Time 3. TA scored the lowest on the C-tests for the testing sessions whilst CS scored the highest. The scores of YS and KS are between those of CS and TA. First exposure to English for CS began in Japan at senior high school from age 12. The other three returnees each started learning English in the U.S. All four returnees attended high schools while they lived in the U.S., and two of them attended kindergarten from age 4: It is conceivable that they all gained a high proficiency in English due to the schooling they received whilst in the U.S. On average, the four returnees received a substantial amount of exposure to English (roughly 30 hours a week) outside of their homes as they frequently socialized with friends. The parents of all four returnees spoke only Japanese to the children at home during their stay in the U.S. They did this first of all because they are Japanese and that is their first language but also because they wanted to maintain a 'one language at home policy' as they were concerned that their children might fall behind in their literacy skills once they returned to Japan, especially their knowledge of written Japanese, including hiragana and kanji characters. In addition, to bolster their children's level of kanji proficiency, the parents sent them once a week (usually on weekends) to a Japanese school in the U.S.

Table 2 shows that all four returnees spent a number of years living in the U.S. The returnee identified as TA spent the longest period of time abroad (12 years) in comparison to the three sisters, who all spent 8 years in the U.S. TA and KS are the only returnees to have started acquiring English from an early age. This is important to note as a child's age of acquisition may play a vital role in his or her L2 English competence. According to Meisel (2011) and Montrul (2008), children who acquire languages from an early age can be classified as either simultaneous bilingual or sequential bilingual. A simultaneous bilingual starts acquiring two

---

5. The C-tests were created by M. Schmid and are freely available online at http://www.let.rug.nl/languageattrition/

languages at approximately the same time. Thus, a child at age 3 years falls under this classification, as the child has not yet fully acquired the L1 grammar. Conversely, Meisel and Montrul claim that a child who starts to acquire his or her second language later than 4 years of age is described as a sequential bilingual (or child L2 learner). This distinction between the two types of bilinguals means that TA is the only returnee in our group who is a simultaneous bilingual: The other three returnees are best described as sequential bilinguals.[6] Two of the returnees (TA and YS) are the same age (15 years); one is older (CS; 19 years), and the youngest (KS) is 11 years old. Their levels of English education are likely to be different as they entered American high schools at different ages. The eldest of the four is likely to be more literate in L2 English as she would have started to receive classes regularly in reading and writing much sooner than the three younger returnees. Even though there are differences among the four returnees in their age at onset of acquisition, they all returned to Japan around the same time. Nevertheless, as discussed in Section 5, language attrition tends to occur faster in younger children.

Our research questions and predictions are provided in 6.2.

6.2 Research questions and predictions

Our research questions address whether the four returnees are able to make native-like judgments on the AJT when presented with present simple continuations of a context vs. present progressive continuations of a context with the four types of verb classes (activity, accomplishment, achievement and stative) (Vendler, 1967). We also address the role of the L1 performing this task since Japanese aspectual semantics differs from English aspectual semantics.

RQ1: Can the four returnees and the adult L2 learners provide target-like judgments for ongoing vs. habitual contexts for activity, achievement and stative verb types, or is L1 influence persistent?

Our second research question relates specifically to the accomplishment verb category.

---

6. One anonymous reviewer suggests that the simultaneous bilingual TA should be considered as a case study rather than trying to quantify all the returnees' performances together as they are not a homogenous group. We agree that in terms of L2 acquisition there are differences between the simultaneous bilingual and the sequential bilinguals but crucially they spent 8–12 years living in the U.S. and returned to Japan at the same time. Thus, in terms of investigating L2 attrition, we argue that all four returnees can be grouped together in order to compare their performances across the three test periods.

RQ2: Can the four returnees and the adult L2 learners provide target-like judgments for completed event contexts (telic) vs. incomplete event contexts (atelic) for the accomplishment verb category, or is L1 influence persistent?

The four returnees spent between 8 and 12 years living in the U.S where they attended high school. Our third research question addresses whether the four returnees differ from the adult L2 learners.

RQ3: Are the four returnees more target-like than the adult L2 learners on their judgments on each verb category?

There are differences in the ages at which the four returnees began to be immersed in an English-speaking environment such that TA qualifies as a simultaneous bilingual whereas the three sisters are sequential bilinguals. For CS, YS and KS, the Japanese aspectual system is already established as their L1 Japanese has already been fully acquired. L2 English was acquired later, so the aspectual semantics of the L2 compete with the existent L1 system. TA may be able to develop two separate (aspectual) systems (Genesee, 1989; Meisel, 1989), one for Japanese and the other for English. There are two possible predictions that apply to TA and KS. In terms of acquisition, we predict that TA will be more accurate in her judgments than the other returnees because we assume she has English native-like competence as both Japanese and English are effectively first languages for her. However, TA and KS are the two youngest returnees, and they started acquiring English from an early age. Regarding attrition, we can equally predict that TA (and KS) will undergo greater language loss because the attrition process occurs faster in young children (Hansen-Strain, 1990). Therefore, our predictions regarding TA are somewhat contradictory. On the one hand we expect TA to have more native-like competence in English, but because she was the youngest she may demonstrate more signs of L2 English loss over the 18-month time period since returning to Japan. Our fourth research question tackles the issue of whether L2 attrition in the aspectual domain takes place across the 12 months of testing.

RQ4: Are there any differences in AJT judgments between Time 1, Time 2 and Time 3 for the four returnees?

We expect there to be a decline in the returnees' judgments between Time 1, 2 and 3 if L2 attrition occurs.

6.3 Acceptability Judgment Task

The AJT used in our study is based on the task used by Al-Hamad et al. (2002) and Hawkins et al. (2008). Neither Al-Hamad et al. (2002) nor Hawkins et al. (2008) included the accomplishment category in their task however, so we created additional items in our task for that category. Each test item included an opening context followed by a pair of sentences presented at the same time for participants to judge. Participants were asked to judge the appropriateness of each sentence, involving either a present simple or present progressive verb form, in contexts favoring one kind of interpretation over the other. There are 52 test items in total. The numbers of items for each condition are as follows: Activity = 12, Achievement = 12, Accomplishment = 8 and Stative = 8. All test items were randomized and next to each sentence (a) and (b) there was a 4-point Likert scale: $-2, -1, +1, +2$. Participants were asked to judge the appropriateness of each sentence to the context by circling one of the numbers. They were told that -2 meant the sentence was 'completely inappropriate' in the context, that $+2$ meant it was 'completely appropriate', and -1, and $+1$ were gradations between the two extremes to be used if they thought the sentence was more or less appropriate to the context. Examples were given of the use of the scale, and the first two items of the test were practice items not scored for the purposes of data analysis. The native speaker control group's answers for all items on the task revealed a Cronbach's Alpha reliability score of 0.782. This score demonstrates that the items have relatively high internal consistency.

The pen and paper task was administered by one of the authors. Participants were not timed on the task but they were encouraged to give their judgments and then move on to the next item without going back to a previous item or changing their response. Two versions of the task were created to avoid ordering effects. The 52 items were randomized throughout version 1. There were 6 pages and for version 2, we reversed the order of pages, starting from page 6- 5- 4- 3- 2- 1. Page 1 in Version 1 is exactly the same in the order in Page 6 in Version 2; page 2 in Version 1 is page 5 in Version 2, etc. All items were renumbered for version 2. Each time we tested the participants we gave them a different version of the task, e.g., Time 1: 2 of the four participants received version 1 and the other 2 participants received version 2. Time 2: The 2 participants who completed version 1 for Time 1 received version 2 and the other 2 participants received version 1. Examples of each verb category are provided below.[7]

---

7. Note that task items appeared without a heading like habitual and without the labels present progressive / present simple / complete / incomplete.

Examples of the activity verb category items used in the task are shown in examples (18) and (19). The two examples are similar to the items used in Gabriele and Canales (2011). In example (18) the favored interpretation for the context is (a) because it is an ongoing event. In example (19) the favored interpretation for the context is (b) because it has a 'habitual/stative' reading.

(18) Activity: Ongoing context
 Bob cannot contact Julie at the moment. Apparently,
 a. ✓ Present progressive: she's running on the beach.
    (Expected ratings – NSs: +2; L2 English learners: +2)
 b. ✗ Present simple: she runs on the beach.
    (Expected ratings – NSs: –2; L2 English learners: –2)

(19) Activity: Habitual context
 Twice every week, instead of taking his car,
 a. ✗ Present progressive: Bob is walking from his house to the station.
    (Expected ratings – NSs: –2; L2 English learners: +2)
 b. ✓ Present simple: Bob walks from his house to the station.
    (Expected ratings – NSs: +2; L2 English learners: +2)

The returnees and adult L2 learners are predicted to judge the present simple in an ongoing context to be inappropriate (see 18b) but accept the present progressive in a habitual context (see 19b). They are not predicted to have difficulties in judging the present progressive continuation to be appropriate for ongoing contexts. However, for habitual events like *walk*, for example, there is a difference between English and Japanese. For a habitual reading the present simple form is required in English, but in Japanese the present simple and the present progressive are both possible, as shown in (20).

(20) Maishu ni kai, kuruma ni noru kawari ni …
 Week two times, car in ride instead of
 'Twice every week, instead of taking his car …'
 a. ✓ Ken wa   ie   kara eki   made aruku.
    Ken-TOP house from station to walk-NON-PAST
    'Ken walks from his house to the station.'
 b. ✓ Ken wa   ie   kara eki   made arui-te iru
    Ken-TOP house from station to walk-ASP-NON-PAST
    'Ken walks from his house to the station.'

Since the L1 may influence judgments, we predict that they will rate the present progressive as appropriate in English (see 19a).

Examples (21) and (22) are the accomplishment verb type.

(21) Accomplishment: Incomplete context (atelic)
Mary and Tom went to the library last Sunday.
a. ✘ They read books in 2 hours.
(Expected ratings – NSs: –2; L2 English learners: +2)
b. ✓ They read books for 2 hours.
(Expected ratings – NSs: +2; L2 English learners: +2)

(22) Accomplishment: Complete context (telic)
Tim got up very late this morning.
a. ✓ He ate an apple in 3 minutes.
(Expected ratings – NSs: +2; L2 English learners: +2)
b. ✘ He ate an apple for 3 minutes.
(Expected ratings – NSs: –2; L2 English learners: +2)

The sentence in (21a) is atelic as the verb phrase *read books* refers to an incomplete action. The prepositional phrase *in 2 hours* adds an endpoint to the event, thus (21a) is inappropriate as there is a clash between the verb phrase (incomplete) and the prepositional phrase (complete). Conversely, (21b) is appropriate as the verb phrase indicates an incomplete event and the prepositional phrase *for 2 hours* does not add an endpoint. Example (22a) with the verb phrase *ate an apple* plus the prepositional phrase *in 3 minutes* adds an endpoint to the event signifying a completed action. That is why (22a), but not (22b), is licit. In example (22b) the verb phrase *ate an apple* (telic) is combined with the prepositional phrase *for 3 minutes* (atelic), which creates an inappropriate continuation.

We predict L1 transfer as the returnees and adult L2 learners may be unable to make a distinction between bare plural noun phrases like *eat apples* (incomplete) and indefinite singular noun phrases such as *eat an apple* (complete) because Japanese lacks plurals altogether and indefinites (see example (5) above). Furthermore, they may not know that *in*-initial prepositional phrases are compatible with telic continuations but not with atelic continuations, and *for*-initial prepositional phrases are compatible with atelic continuations but not telic ones.

Examples of the achievement verb type are given in (23) and (24). If learners incorrectly interpret *The train is already arriving at the platform* to mean *The train has already arrived at the platform* in (23a) due to the resultant state reading of the equivalent in Japanese, they will incorrectly rate the present progressive as inappropriate with the ongoing context.[8] If learners interpret (23b) as a futurate,

---

8. Gabriele (*p.c.*) suggests that learners may find it difficult to judge whether the present progressive is appropriate or not because the window between 'is arriving' and 'has arrived' is so small that it is not really easy to make a distinction in this context. The L2 learners may have no idea whether the train arrived or not (*Maybe Simon missed the train*) so the learners could accept this and do well on either interpretation.

i.e., an event that happens upon Simon's arrival at the station, they are likely to rate it as appropriate. In (24), if the returnees map the truth conditions[9] for the imperfective marker *-te iru* onto the progressive *be+V-ing*, they are expected to interpret the present progressive sentence *She is leaving before the end* incorrectly to mean *She leaves before the end*, thus rating it as +2, appropriate.

(23) Achievement: Ongoing context
As Simon drives into the parking lot at the station…
a. ✓ Present progressive: the train is already arriving at the platform.
(Expected ratings – NSs: +2; L2 English learners: +2 or −2)
b. ✗ Present simple: the train already arrives at the platform.
(Expected ratings – NSs: −2; L2 English learners: +2)

(24) Achievement: Habitual context (a process leading up to an endpoint)
Susan often goes to the cinema, but she doesn't like unhappy endings, so quite often…
a. ✗ Present progressive: she is leaving before the end.
(Expected ratings – NSs: −2; L2 English learners: +2)
b. ✓ Present simple: she leaves before the end.
(Expected ratings – NSs: +2; L2 English learners: +2)

Under McClure's (1993) account, statives like *love* and *understand* do not have stative counterparts in Japanese. Only verbs that do not allow the *-te iru* construction are claimed by McClure to be true statives in Japanese. McClure argues that verbs like *love, understand, resemble, know*, etc. are not statives in Japanese but rather they are achievements that all allow the *-te iru* construction. In our study, if the returnees treat stative verbs like *know, own, belong, mean*, as they are in Japanese, they are predicted to judge the progressive *be+V-ing* as 'has come to know', as in (25b). The continuations of the context in (25a) and (25b) target whether certain verbs like *know* can be combined with the present simple and/or the present progressive *be+V-ing*.

(25) Stative
They say that treasure is buried in those woods. Bill says that …
a. ✓ Present simple: *he knows where it is.*
(Expected ratings – NSs: +2; L2 English learners: +2)
b. ✗ Present progressive: *he is knowing where it is.*
(Expected ratings – NSs: −2; L2 English learners: +2)

---

9. Gabriele (*p.c.*) points out that adverbials are also likely to influence L2 learners' judgments in these contexts.

6.4 Results

The first set of AJT results in Figures 1a–d come from the native speaker controls and adult L2 learners (see examples (18) and (19) above). All inappropriate continuations for each verb class are marked with an asterisk in Figures 1–5 below.

A series of one-way ANOVAs was performed between groups on all appropriate continuations and inappropriate continuations for each verb class. The results show no statistical differences for appropriate continuations among the four groups for activity ($F_{(3, 23)} = 1.554$, $p > 0.05$), but there are differences for inappropriate continuations ($F_{(3, 19)} = 5.062$, $p < 0.05$). Bonferroni post-hoc tests reveal that the low intermediate group differs significantly from the native controls ($p = 0.010$). The native controls clearly reject the inappropriate continuations, but the low intermediate participants are on the borderline between rejection and acceptance (0.04 and –0.09) of inappropriate continuations (see Figure 1). We predicted there might be L1 transfer as the present progressive may sometimes be appropriate in Japanese for habitual contexts but not in English. However, despite

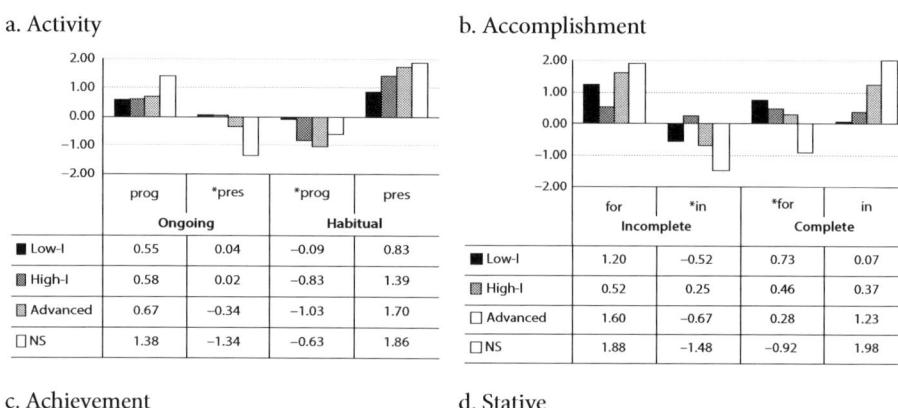

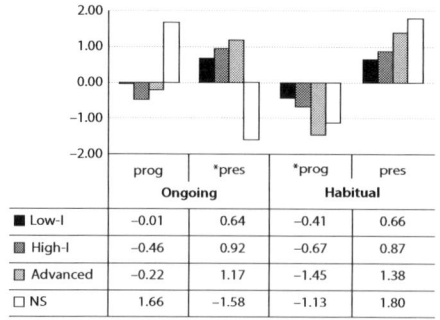

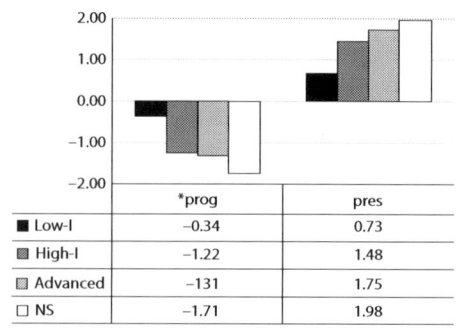

* Means it is inappropriate for the context.

Figure 1. Results of native English speakers and L2 learners for all four verb types

a statistical difference between the low intermediate group and native controls, the low intermediate participants do nevertheless rate the present progressive as inappropriate (–0.09). For accomplishment predicates, we predicted there might be L1 transfer due to differences between English and Japanese telic and atelic continuations (see examples (21) and (22) above). We found there to be statistical differences between the groups ($F_{(3, 11)}$ 7.477, $p < 0.05$) for appropriate continuations. Bonferroni post-hoc tests show the differences lie between the native controls and high intermediate group ($p = 0.024$) and between the native controls and the low intermediate group ($p = 0.019$). There are no statistical differences between the groups for inappropriate continuations ($F_{(3, 7)}$ 2679, $p > 0.05$). Statistical differences were found for achievement verbs in appropriate continuations ($F_{(3, 27)}$ 7.444, $p < 0.05$). Bonferroni post-hoc tests indicate that each L2 learner group differs significantly from the native controls (advanced: $p = 0.035$; high intermediate: $p = 0.002$; low intermediate: $p = 0.003$). With differences between English and Japanese in aspectual semantics for achievement verbs, we predicted that learners might transfer their L1 interpretation (see examples (23) and (24)). Figure 1c clearly shows the differences between the groups as the learners failed to judge the present progressive as appropriate in ongoing contexts. Learners performed much better on habitual contexts. No statistical differences were found for inappropriate continuations ($F_{(3, 15)}$ 2.061, $p > 0.05$). Finally, for stative verbs, we predicted that learners might not be target-like if there is L1 influence (see example (25)). Results revealed statistical differences for appropriate continuations ($F_{(3, 8)}$ 14.691, $p < 0.05$), and Bonferroni post-hoc tests show that the significant differences lie between the low intermediate group and the three other groups (native controls: $p = 0.001$; advanced: $p = 0.006$; high intermediate: $p = 0.041$). For inappropriate continuations, no statistical differences were found ($F_{(3, 11)}$ 2.923, $p > 0.05$) among the four groups. All groups correctly rate the present progressive as inappropriate continuations.

The results that follow are organized by each individual returnee and by time of testing. The first set of results for the returnees is illustrated in Figures 2a–d for the activity verb category.

Figures 2a–d reveal that there are no differences between KS, YS and CS as they performed similarly on the activity verb type (see examples (18) and (19)); with the exception of TA, they correctly judged present progressive to be appropriate for ongoing contexts and the present simple to be appropriate for habitual contexts. They correctly identified and judged the present simple to be inappropriate for ongoing contexts and the present progressive to be inappropriate for habitual contexts. TA's judgments at Time 3 for appropriate present simple and inappropriate present progressive changed as she started to reject the appropriate present simple as a continuation of habitual contexts and started to accept

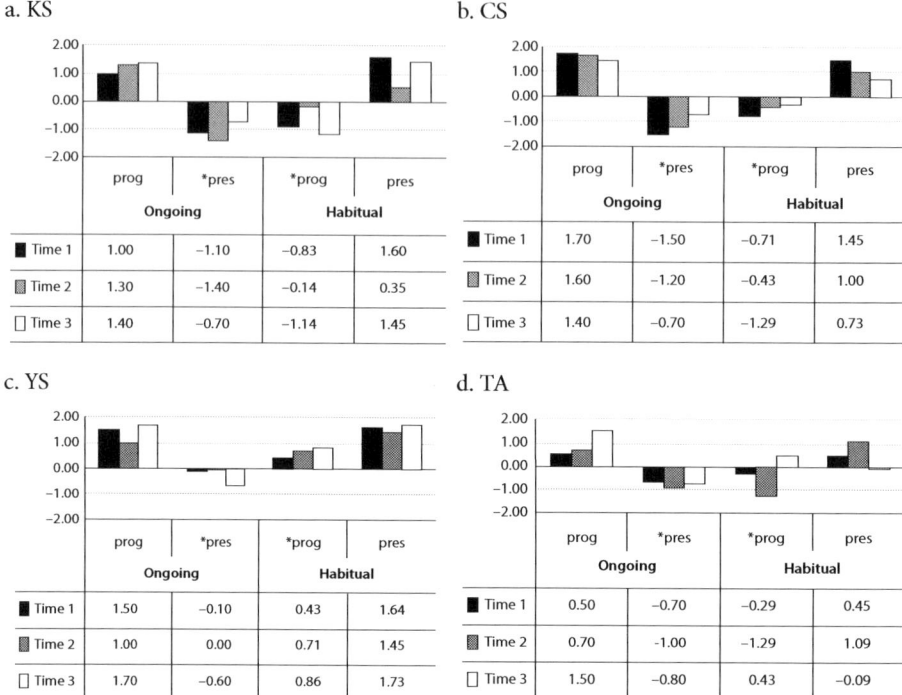

* Means it is inappropriate for the context.

Figure 2. Activity verb type

the inappropriate present progressive. All the returnees performed better than we had predicted in their judgments for ongoing and habitual continuations. A Wilcoxon Signed Ranks non-parametric test was performed on appropriate continuations and inappropriate continuations to find out whether there were any statistical differences between the four returnees across the three test times on the activity verb type. No statistical differences are observed for appropriate continuations between Time 1 and Time 2 ($Z = -0.546$, $p = 0.585$), Time 2 and Time 3 ($Z = -0.735$, $p = 0.462$) or Time 1 and Time 3 ($Z = -0.484$, $p = 0.629$). For the inappropriate continuations, no differences between the times were found (Time 1 and Time 2: $Z = -0.085$, $p = 0.932$; Time 2 and Time 3: $Z = -0.589$, $p = 0.556$; Time 1 and Time 3: $Z = -1.004$, $p = 0.315$).

The second set of results for the returnees is shown in Figures 3a–d for the accomplishment verb category (see examples (21) and (22) above).

For the accomplishment verb type, the results show that the returnees are target-like in their judgments overall on telic and atelic continuations as their judgments are similar to those of the native controls in Figure 1. However, by

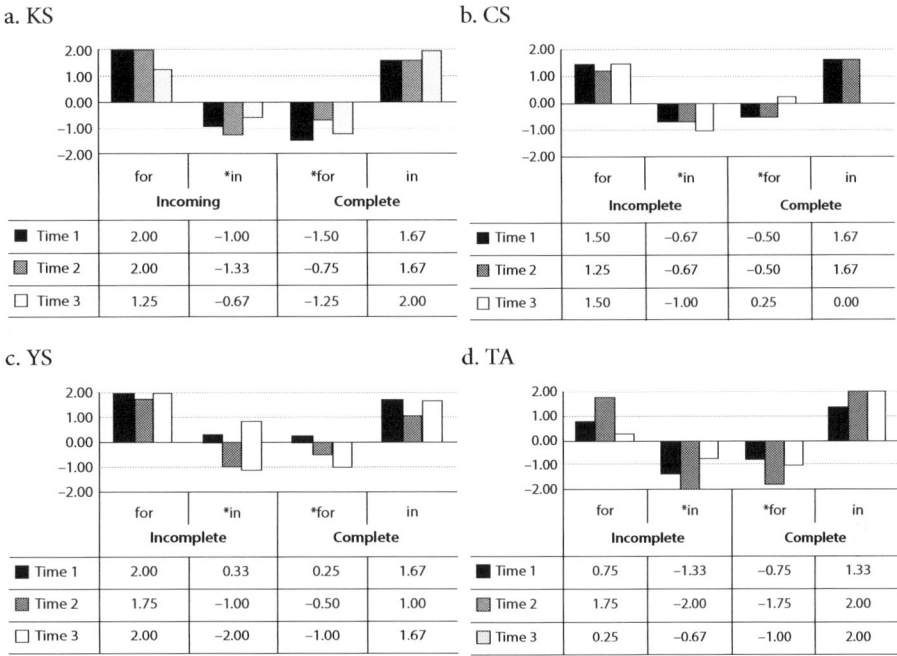

* Means it is inappropriate for the context.

Figure 3. Accomplishment verb type

Time 3, CS started to accept the inappropriate telic *for* verb phrase items. YS's judgments from Time 1 to Time 3 changed in cases with an inappropriate telic *in* verb phrase across all items, from a positive 0.33 rating to a negative –2.00 rating. For the inappropriate atelic *for* verb phrases YS started out at Time 1 with a positive rating of 0.25 and by Time 3 she was correctly rating the items as –1.00. At first, she was accepting the inappropriate versions at Time 1 but by Time 3 she was firmly rejecting them. A Wilcoxon Signed Ranks test for appropriate continuations indicates that there are no statistical differences between Time 1 and Time 2 ($Z = -0.138$, $p = 0.890$), Time 2 and Time 3 ($Z = -0.681$, $p = 0.496$), or Time 1 and Time 3 ($Z = -1.084$, $p = 0.279$). The results for inappropriate continuations show no statistical differences between the four returnees across the three test periods: (Time 1 and Time 2: $Z = -1.472$, $p = 0.141$; Time 2 and Time 3: $Z = -0.702$, $p = 0.483$; Time 1 and Time 3: $Z = -0.281$, $p = 0.779$).

The third set of results provides the judgments for the achievement verb category in Figures 4a–d.

The achievement verb category shows that TA differs in her judgments compared to the other three returnees in appropriate present progressive contexts,

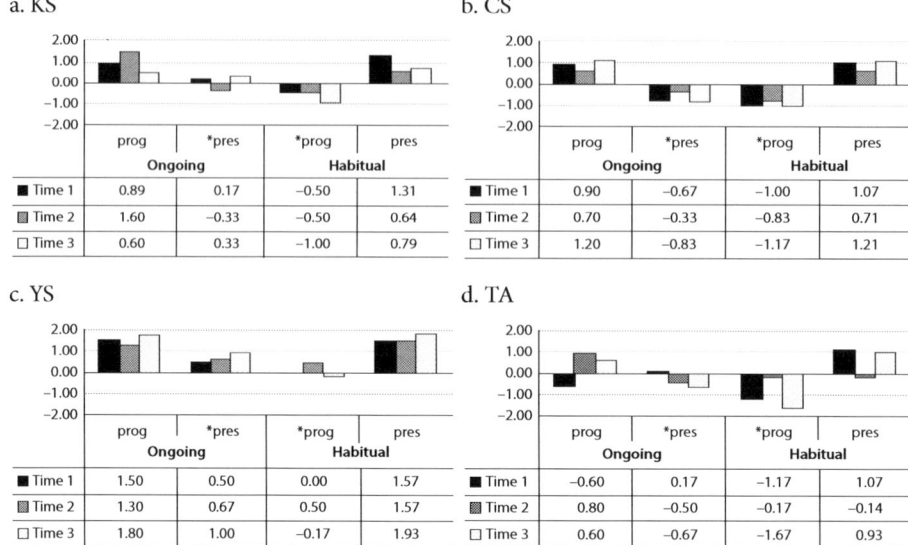

* Means it is inappropriate for the context.

Figure 4. Achievement verb type

inappropriate present and appropriate present contexts. At Time 1 TA incorrectly rejects the appropriate progressive but then at Time 2 and 3 correctly accepts the appropriate progressive. For the inappropriate present, both TA and KS incorrectly accepted such items at Time 1, though marginally, as they gave all the inappropriate items an average rating of 0.15. For Times 2 and 3 TA correctly rejected the inappropriate present, but KS rejected such items at Time 2 but then reverted back to accepting them again at Time 3. The appropriate present was correctly accepted by TA at Time 1 and Time 3 but incorrectly rejected at Time 2. YS was the only one who found the inappropriate progressive difficult to reject at Times 1 and 2. By Time 3 she correctly rejects it, though it is not a strong rejection (around −0.15). A Wilcoxon Signed Ranks test was performed for the appropriate continuations. No statistical differences are observed across the times of testing for Time 1 and Time 2 ($Z = -0.522$, $p = 0.602$) or Time 2 and Time 3 ($Z = -1.664$, $p = 0.096$), but a significant difference arises between Time 1 and Time 3 ($Z = -2.053$, $p = 0.040$). The difference between Time 1 and Time 3 is largely due to the performance by TA. No statistical differences are found for the inappropriate continuations (Time 1 and Time 2: $Z = -1.098$, $p = 0.272$; Time 2 and Time 3: $Z = -1.256$, $p = 0.209$; Time 1 and Time 3: $Z = -1.105$, $p = 0.269$).

The final set of results is provided in Figures 5a–b for the stative verb category.

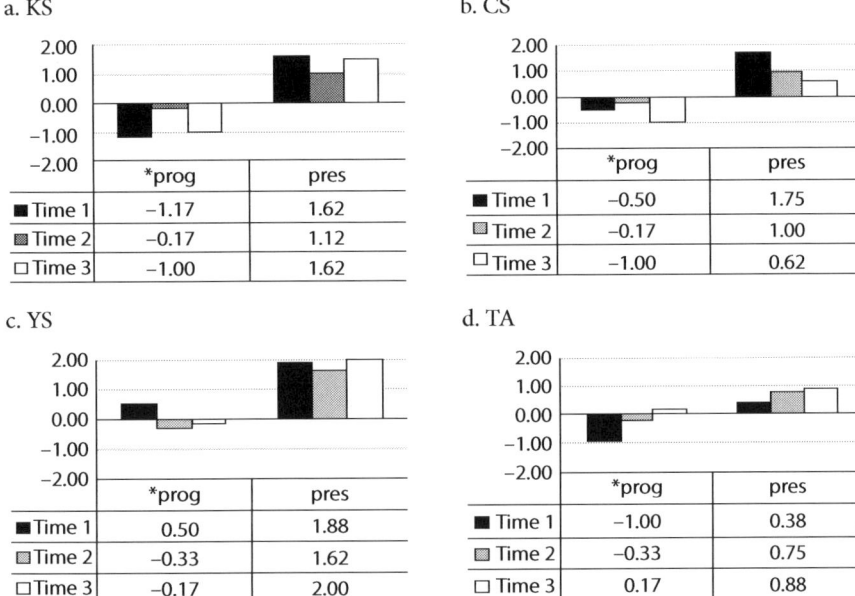

* Means it is inappropriate for the context.

Figure 5. Stative verb type

Figures 5c and 5d reveal that both YS and TA have difficulties with inappropriate present progressives. At Time 1 YS accepted the inappropriate present progressive but at Time 2 and 3 started to correctly reject it. TA's responses were the opposite of YS's as she started out by correctly rejecting the inappropriate present progressive but by Time 3 she was starting to accept it. For YS, inappropriate present progressive was a problematic condition. CS started correctly rejecting inappropriate present at Time 1 but at Time 2 she was accepting the present with an average rating of 1.00, but then by Time 3 the mean rating drops to 0.62. A Wilcoxon Signed Ranks test for the appropriate continuations reveals that there are no statistical differences (Time 1 and Time 2: $Z = -1.063$, $p = 0.288$; Time 2 and Time 3: $Z = -0.647$, $p = 0.518$; Time 1 and Time 3: $Z = -0.531$, $p = 0.595$). The inappropriate continuations show no statistical differences (Time 1 and Time 2: $Z = -0.511$, $p = 0.610$; Time 2 and Time 3: $Z = -0.949$, $p = 0.343$; Time 1 and Time 3: $Z = -0.639$, $p = 0.523$).

All the judgments given by the returnees were compared with those from the adult L2 learners and the adult native controls to see whether there were any differences in their judgments for each verb type. The returnees performed similarly to the adult L2 learners with most of the verb categories. There are only minor observable differences from Time 1 to Time 3 for each returnee.

7. Discussion and conclusion

The goal of our study was twofold: to examine judgments given by adult L2 learners and four Japanese returnees on lexical and grammatical aspect in English and to find out whether any L2 attrition was taking place in the four returnees' L2 English across the span of 12 months.

Our first and second research questions asked whether the returnees would provide target-like judgments for each of the verb types, and we predicted that if there is L1 influence they would be less target-like in their judgments of appropriate and inappropriate continuations compared with native controls. Our prediction was partially confirmed as the four returnees had little difficulty (except TA) with the activity verb type across the three test sessions, but accomplishment, achievement and stative types revealed judgments that were not so stable. Our third research question specifically focused on whether the returnees would be more target-like than adult L2 learners in their judgments on the AJT. The findings show that on the whole, the four returnees do not differ greatly from the advanced adult L2 learners except for the achievement category with present progressive continuations. Our fourth research question addressed whether there would be differences between each of the four returnees or differences across the three times of testing, and we predicted that there would be. We found that overall TA differed the most compared with the other returnees. TA had the greatest difficulty with the achievement verb type across the three times we met with her. TA changed her rating for the activity habitual type during the 12 months for inappropriate progressive and appropriate present (see 19 above). For the present progressive, she had rated it at Time 1 as −0.29 and Time 2 as −1.29, but at Time 3 she rated it positively as +0.43. For the present simple, she rated it at Time 1 and Time 2 as +0.45 and +1.09, respectively. However, at Time 3 she rated it as −0.09.

The change between the ratings for the habitual form may be due to some attrition in the aspectual domain. In other words, TA was able to distinguish between English and Japanese in regard to the use of the habitual present form in English and the *-te iru* form in Japanese, but by Time 3 she could no longer make this distinction.

The findings from our study suggest that there is not much L2 attrition of English in the domain of aspectual semantics. The performance of these returnees on the AJT shows that generally they are no worse in their judgments at Time 3 than when they started at Time 1. Age does seem to be a factor, as has been found in previous L2 attrition studies (e.g., Hansen-Strain, 1990); it is clear that the youngest returnee, TA (at the time she started acquiring English), was a little less confident in some of her judgments on three of the four verb categories (activity, achievement and stative). We argue that the returnees have managed to maintain their knowledge (i.e., competence) of the English aspectual domain, and we next explore how they have managed to achieve that given that they no longer live in an L2 environment.

We started out by assuming that the four returnees in our study would naturally start to lose the L2 in an exclusively L1 Japanese-speaking environment. But, the results show that far from a steady decline in grammaticality judgments, the returnees performed target-like most of the time. There are a number of possible factors for why the returnees maintained their L2 competence. The first explanation is that in Japan high school students regularly attend compulsory English classes. Though they are unlikely to receive explicit instruction in English aspectual semantics, they do study grammar. In other words, they do receive positive input in an educational setting of what structures are grammatical.[10] The second reason is due to the use of English in the home. The three sisters (CS, YS, KS) sometimes speak to one another at home in English because they want to be able to maintain their speaking skills. They are aware that if they do not use English, they will likely become less fluent in their L2. The third way they may have maintained their English is through the use of social media sites like Facebook and Twitter, as well as online phone and text conversations (e.g., Skype) to keep in contact with friends in the U.S.

We acknowledge that there are some limitations with our study: we met with the returnees three times in a one year period. This length of time is not long enough to see any decline in linguistic knowledge. Ideally, we would need to track any possible decline over the course of several years. The use of explicit knowledge could have been brought to bear on the AJT (e.g., Ellis, 1989; Krashen, 1982; Long, 1983 and others) as we did not set a time limit for the returnees. They had time to consider their responses to each context presented to them in the AJT. Furthermore, temporal adverbials may have played a larger role than we had expected in the AJT as learners may have based some of their judgments on continuations like *every day*, etc.

Perhaps reaction times to a self-paced reading task, as reported in Roberts and Liszka (2013), could have revealed more subtle differences in our study of the returnees' judgments on aspect across the four verb types at Times 1, 2 and 3 as they would have less time to consider each continuation in a story context.

---

10. The input the returnees receive at school has not been quantified in any systematic way. We agree with Montrul (2002) that we need to "examine in greater detail how the changing patterns in the input during bilingual development in addition to how language use affect the form of the emerging grammars, particularly from the age of early syntax and extending to at least the years of early schooling" (2002:61).

References

Al-Hamad, M., Al-Malki, E., Casillas, G., Franceschina, F., Hawkins, R., Hawthorne, J., Karadzovska, D., Kato, K., Liszka, S., Lozano, C., Ojima, S., Okuwaki, N. and Thomas, E. 2002. "Interpretation of English tense morphology by advanced L2 speakers". In *EUROSLA Yearbook* 2: 49–69. Amsterdam: John Benjamins. DOI: 10.1075/eurosla.2.06alh

Andersen, R.W. 1991. "Developmental sequences: The emergence of aspect marking in Second language acquisition." In *Crosscurrents in Second Language Acquisition and Linguistic Theories*, T. Huebner and C.A. Ferguson (eds), 305–324. Amsterdam: John Benjamins.

Andersen, R.W. and Shirai, Y. 1996. "Primacy of aspect in first and second language acquisition: The pidgin/creole connection." In *Handbook of Second Language Acquisition*, W.C. Ritchie and T.K. Bhatia (eds), 527–570. San Diego, CA: Academic Press.

Bailey, N., Madden, C. and Krashen, S. 1974. "Is there a "natural sequence" in adult second language learning?" *Language Learning* 21: 235–243. DOI: 10.1111/j.1467-1770.1974.tb00505.x

Bardovi-Harlig, K. 1999. "From morpheme studies to temporal semantics tense-aspect research in SLA." *Studies in Second Language Acquisition* 21: 341–382. DOI: 10.1017/S0272263199003010

Brown, R. 1973. *A First Language*. Cambridge: Harvard University Press. DOI: 10.4159/harvard.9780674732469

Chung, S. and Timberlake, A. 1985. "Tense, aspect and mood." In *Language Typology and Syntactic Description, Volume 3: Grammatical Categories and the Lexicon*, T. Schopen (ed.), 202–258. Cambridge, UK: Cambridge University Press.

Cole, R. D. 1929. "The effect of a summer vacation on students' knowledge of French." *Modern Language Journal* 14: 117–121. DOI: 10.1111/j.1540-4781.1929.tb00029.x

Comrie, B. 1976. *Aspect*. New York: Cambridge University Press.

De Villiers, J. and de Villiers, P. 1973. "A cross-sectional study of the acquisition of grammatical morphemes". *Journal of Psycholinguistic Research* 2: 267–278. DOI: 10.1007/BF01067106

Dowty, D. 1979. *Word meaning and Montague grammar*. Dordrecht and Boston: D. Reidel Publishing Co.

Dulay, H. and M. Burt. 1973. "Should we teach children syntax?" *Language Learning* 23: 245–258. DOI: 10.1111/j.1467-1770.1973.tb00659.x

Ellis, R. 1989. "Are classroom and naturalistic acquisition the same? A study of the classroom acquisition of German word order rules." *Studies in Second Language Acquisition* 11: 305–328. DOI: 10.1017/S0272263100008159

Gabriele, A. 2005. *The Acquisition of Aspect in a Second Language: A Bidirectional Study of Learners of English and Japanese*. Unpublished doctoral thesis, City University of New York Graduate Center.

Gabriele, A. 2009. "Transfer and transition in the SLA of aspect." *Studies in Second Language Acquisition* 31: 371–402. DOI: 10.1017/S0272263109090342

Gabriele, A. 2010. "Deriving meaning through context: The interpretation of bare nominals in L2 Japanese." *Second Language Research* 26. 379–405. DOI: 10.1177/0267658310365783

Gabriele, A. and Canales, A. 2011. "No time like the present: Examining transfer at the interfaces in second language acquisition." *Lingua* 21: 670–687. DOI: 10.1016/j.lingua.2010.07.010

Gabriele, A., Maekawa, J. and Alemán-Bañón, J. 2009. "Can we predict when *dying* will be difficult: Progressive achievements in L2 English." In *Proceedings of the 33rd Annual Boston University Conference on Language Development*, J. Chandlee, M. Franchini, S. Lord and G.M. Rheiner (eds), 175–186. Somerville, MA: Cascadilla Press.

Genesee, F. 1989. "Early bilingual development: One language or two?" *Journal of Child Language* 16: 161–179. DOI: 10.1017/S0305000900013490

Hansen-Strain, L. 1990. "The attrition of Japanese by English-speaking children: An interim report." *Language Sciences* 12 (4): 367–377. DOI: 10.1016/0388-0001(90)90004-Z

Hansen, L. 1999. "Not a total loss: The attrition of Japanese negation over three decades." In *Second Language attrition in Japanese Contexts*, L. Hansen (ed.), 142–153. Oxford: Oxford University Press.

Hawkins, R., Casillas, G., Hattori, H., Hawthorne, J., Husted, R., Lozano, C., Okamoto, A., Thomas, E. and Yamada, K. 2008. "The semantic effects of verb raising and its consequences in second language grammars." In *The Role of Formal Features in Second Language Acquisition*, J. Liceras, H. Zobl and H. Goodluck (eds), 328–351. Mahwah, New Jersey: Lawrence Erlbaum.

Hirakawa, M. 2001. "L2 acquisition of Japanese unaccusative verbs." *Studies in Second Language Acquisition*, 23: 221–245. DOI: 10.1017/S0272263101002054

Hirakawa, M., Hirakawa, Y., Snape, N. and Hosoi, H., Matthews, J. under revision. "Interpretations of the *-ing* vs. simple forms in L2 English by Japanese learners". Paper submitted to *Second Language*.

Izquierdo, J. and Collins, L. 2008. "The facilitative role of L1 influence in L2 tense-aspect marking: A comparison of Hispanophone and Anglophone learners of French." *The Modern Language Journal* 92 (3): 349–367. DOI: 10.1111/j.1540-4781.2008.00751.x

Jacobsen, W. 1992. *The Transitive Structure of Events in Japanese*. Tokyo: Kurosio.

Jakobson, R. 1941/1968. *Child Language, Aphasia and Phonological Universals*. (A.R. Keiler, Trans.) The Hague: Mouton.

Krashen, S.D. 1982. *Principles and Practice in Second Language Acquisition*. Oxford: Pergamon Press.

Lardiere, D. 1998. "Case and tense in fossilized steady state grammar." *Second Language Research* 14: 1–26. DOI: 10.1191/026765898674105303

Long, M. H. 1983. "Does second language instruction make a difference?" *A review of research*. TESOL Quarterly 17: 359–382. DOI: 10.2307/3586253

Mayer, M. 1969. *Frog, Where are you?* New York: Dial Press.

McClure, W. 1993. "A semantic parameter: The progressive in Japanese and English." In *Japanese/Korean Linguistics*, Vol. 3, S. Choi (ed.), 254–270. Stanford, CA: CSLI.

Meisel, J.M. 1989. "Early differentiation of languages in bilingual children." In *Bilingualism Across the Lifespan: Aspects of Acquisition, Maturity and Loss*, K. Hyltenstam and L.K. Obler (eds), 13–40. Cambridge: Cambridge University Press. DOI: 10.1017/CBO9780511611780.003

Meisel, J.M. 2011. *First and Second Language Acquisition: Parallels and Differences*. Cambridge: Cambridge University Press. DOI: 10.1017/CBO9780511862694

Montrul, S. 2002. "Incomplete acquisition and attrition of Spanish tense/aspect distinctions in adult bilinguals." *Bilingualism: Language and Cognition* 5 (1): 39–68. DOI: 10.1017/S1366728902000135

Montrul, S. 2008. *Incomplete Acquisition in Bilingualism: Re-examining the Age Factor*. Amsterdam: John Benjamins. DOI: 10.1075/sibil.39

Neisser, U. 1984. "Interpreting Harry Bahrick's discovery: What confers immunity against forgetting?" *Journal of Experimental Psychology: General* 113: 32–35. DOI: 10.1037/0096-3445.113.1.32

Ogihara, T. 1998. "The ambiguity of the –te iru form in Japanese." *Journal of East Asian Linguistics* 7: 87–120. DOI: 10.1023/A:1008208219882

Okuwaki, N. 2005. *Acquisition of Tense and Aspect in L2 English*. Unpublished doctoral thesis, University of Essex, UK.

Reetz-Kurashige, A. 1999. "Japanese returnees' retention of English-speaking skills: Changes in verb usage over time." In *Second Language Attrition in Japanese Contexts*, L. Hansen (ed.), 21–58. Oxford: Oxford University Press.

Roberts, L. and Liszka, S. 2013. "Processing tense/aspect- agreement violations on-line in the second language: A self-paced reading study with French and German L2 learners of English." *Second Language Research* 29 (4): 413–439. DOI: 10.1177/0267658313503171

Rothstein, S. 2004. *Structuring Events: A Study in the Semantics of Aspect*. Malden, MA & Oxford: Blackwell.

Slabakova, R. 2001. *Telicity in the Second Language* [Language Acquisition and Language Disorders, 26]. Amsterdam: John Benjamins. DOI: 10.1075/lald.26

Slabakova, R. 2002. "Recent research on the acquisition of aspect: an embarrassment of riches?" *Second Language Research* 18: 172–188. DOI: 10.1191/0267658302sr202ra

Slabakova, R. and Montrul, S. 2002. "Aspectual tenses in Spanish L2 acquisition: A UG perspective." In *Tense-aspect Morphology in L2 Acquisition*, Y. Shirai and R. Salaberry (eds), 363–396. Amsterdam: John Benjamins. DOI: 10.1075/lald.27.15sla

Smith, C. 1991. *The Parameter of Aspect*. Dordrecht: Kluwer. DOI: 10.1007/978-94-015-7911-7

Sugaya, N. and Shirai, Y. 2007. "The acquisition of progressive and resultative meanings of the imperfective aspect marker by L2 learners of Japanese." *Studies in Second Language Acquisition* 29: 1–38. DOI: 10.1017/S0272263107070015

Sugita, M. 2008. "Japanese experiential -te iru as an individual-level construction." *Kansas Working Papers in Linguistics* 30: 344–358.

Tomiyama, M. 1999. "The first stage of second language attrition: A case study of a Japanese returnee." In *Second Language in Japanese Contexts*, L. Hansen (ed.), 59–79. Oxford: Oxford University Press.

Tomiyama, M. 2009. "Age and proficiency in L2 attrition: Data from two siblings." *Applied Linguistics* 30 (2): 253–275. DOI: 10.1093/applin/amn038

Vendler, Z. 1967. "Verbs and times." In *Linguistics in Philosophy*, Z. Vendler (ed.), 97–121. Ithaca: Cornell University Press.

Weltens, B., de Bot, K. and van Els, T. 1986. *Language Attrition in Progress*. Dordrecht: Foris.

Yamazaki-Hasegawa, T. 2012. *Second Language Acquisition of Aspectual and Temporal Interpretation in English and Japanese*. Unpublished doctoral thesis, University of Cambridge.

Yoshitomi, A. 1992. "Towards a model of language attrition: Neurobiological and psychological contributions." *Issues in Applied Linguistics* 3: 293–318.

Yoshitomi, A. 1999. "On the loss of English as a second language by Japanese returnee children." In *Second Language Attrition in Japanese Contexts*, L. Hansen (ed.), 80–113. Oxford: Oxford University Press.

Effectiveness of implicit negative feedback in a foreign language classroom
The role of input, frequency and saliency

Nadia Mifka Profozic
University of Zadar, Croatia

This paper reports on a study that investigated the effectiveness of recasts and clarification requests in a French as a foreign language classroom. The target structures were French past tense structures the *passé composé* and the *imparfait*. The study was carried out with three intact classes of high school students in New Zealand, comprising in total 52 participants. A quasi-experimental design was employed, with a pre-test, treatment, immediate post-test and a delayed post-test. The treatment tasks were picture-based, designed to encourage communication and to elicit the use of past tense. The tests were also picture-based, written narrative tasks. The control group did not receive any treatment. Mixed design Repeated measures ANOVAs, followed by ANCOVAs, were computed to examine the effects of the treatment. Overall, results indicate that recasts were more effective for acquisition of the *passé composé* whereas both recasts and clarification requests proved beneficial for acquisition of the *imparfait* at this early stage of learning. However, non-parametric tests comparing more advanced and less advanced learners suggest that only the 'low proficiency' learners benefited from clarification requests.

Introduction

Negative, or corrective, feedback has been a largely researched topic in SLA over the past decades: as a hot issue it has received attention from several theoretical positions including linguistic theories and approaches based on cognitive psychology. In her seminal paper on corrective feedback in historical perspective Schachter (1991) pointed out that "one of the most important questions in the field of second language acquisition today is: Do second language learners adults and older children, need and/or make use of negative data" (1991: 96). Research so far has provided substantial evidence for the effectiveness of CF but the findings have not been in unison, in particular where classroom research is concerned. Much of the classroom research, for example, has indicated that output-prompting and explicit types of feedback by classroom teachers are more beneficial than input-providing implicit recasts, although recasts are the most frequently used type of feedback in classrooms (e.g. Ammar 2008; Ammar & Spada 2006; Ellis 2007; Ellis, Loewen & Erlam 2006; Havranek 2002; Lyster & Ranta 1997; Lyster 1998; Lyster 2004; Panova & Lyster 2002; Sheen 2007, 2008; Yang & Lyster 2010). Experimental one-on-one studies, in contrast, have been in favour of recasts, demonstrating their effects in laboratory conditions (e.g. Braidi 2002; Egi 2007; Ishida 2004; Iwashita 2003; Leeman 2003; Long, Inagaki & Ortega 1998; Mackey & Philp 1998; Philp 2003). A recent meta-analysis (Li 2010) also pointed to significantly different results obtained in classroom and laboratory studies. However, recent classroom research (Goo 2012; Révész 2009, 2012; Révész & Han 2006) has provided strong evidence for the effectiveness of recasts, thus lending support to only few earlier studies (Doughty & Varela 1998; Muranoi 2000) which found recasts in classroom as effective as those in tightly controlled laboratory conditions. Such mixed, even contradictory results call for more research in this area. In particular, it may be worthwhile to undertake further investigation of recasts and clarification requests as two types of implicit negative feedback, and examine their effectiveness in intact classrooms to see whether learning occurs in teacher-fronted communicative language lessons when CF is used as a focus-on-form (Long 1983, 1996).

An additional challenge might be the choice of language structures on which the effectiveness of CF is tested: two grammatical structures in French (the *passé composé* and the *imparfait*) that are considered as particularly difficult for Anglophone L2 learners. Clarification requests have so far been examined as part of a group of prompting techniques in classroom instruction but not as an isolated type of negative feedback. To the best of my knowledge only one study has looked at the differential effects of recasts and clarification requests in one-on-one condition (McDonough 2007) and only one study, of very short duration and with only few participants, attempted to compare the effectiveness of recasts, clarification requests and metalinguistic feedback in a classroom setting (Loewen & Nabei 2007). There is no record of a similar classroom study in the context of French FL. It is worth mentioning though, that the *passé composé* and the *imparfait* were the focus of recasts treatment in Ayoun's studies (2001, 2004) which were conducted in entirely different experimental conditions, using written recasts delivered via computer, so a direct comparison is not possible.

The paper is organized as follows: First, I discuss the characteristics of recasts and clarification requests as implicit types of negative feedback viewed as a focus-on-form in the framework of the Interaction Hypothesis. Then I briefly review the factors that have been found to influence the effectiveness of implicit CF in classrooms. This is followed by the description of the two French structures in focus and a presentation of the data collection methodology. The results of the study are then presented and discussed with reference to previous research.

Recasts and clarification requests

In the framework of the Interaction Hypothesis (Long 1983, 1996) recasts and clarification requests are seen as implicit types of negative feedback used by more competent speakers in communication with second or foreign language learners. While clarification requests are most often used as a strategy to negotiate meaning (Long 1983; Pica 1991, 1994; Pica, Holliday, Lewis & Morgenthaler 1989; Mackey 2006; Mackey, Oliver & Leeman 2003; Oliver 1995, 1998), recasts can have a purely corrective function (Doughty & Varela 1998; Farrar 1992; Long 2007; Long, Inagaki & Ortega 1998) as a focus-on-form in a communicative task. Below are the examples of a recast (1) and a clarification request (2) in the present study.

(1) Recast
T: alors seulement un garçon avait   de l'argent?   je ne sais
    so   only   one boy   have(IMP) of the money(GEN)? I no know
    pas
    not(PRES-NEG)
    'so only one boy had money? I don't know'
S2: er um un garçon devient   devient   jalous
    er um one boy   become(PRES) become(PRES) jealous
    'er um one boy becomes becomes jealous'
T: oh, il est   devenu   jalous?   – (Recast)
    oh he is(AUX) become(PP) jealous
    'oh, he became jealous?'

(2) Clarification request
S34: il faisait   très chaud donc ils   ont   très soif
     it make(IMP) very hot   so   they have(PRES) very thirst
     'it was very hot so they are very thirsty'
T: comment? tu peux   répéter?   – (Clarification request)
     how?   you be able(PRES) repeat (INF)?
     'how? can you repeat?'

As can be seen, both recasts and clarification requests only imply that a change in the utterance is needed, hence they both provide implicit negative feedback.

However, they differ in terms of input vs. output. In other words, recasts provide the target-like input whereas clarification requests require the learner to produce more output in order to make the utterance more target-like. Both recasts and clarification requests have been found to promote language development (e.g. Braidi 2002; Iwashita 2003; Leeman 2003; Lyster 2004; Lyster & Izquierdo 2009; Mackey 1999; Mackey & Philp 1998; Philp 2003; McDonough 2005; McDonough 2007; Pica et al. 1991; Yang & Lyster 2010). Research provided evidence of their use by adults (e.g. Long 1981, 1983) and children (Oliver 1995, 1998) in both naturalistic and instructional settings.

As numerous experimental studies have shown, the contribution of implicit negative feedback leading to negative evidence might be invaluable in promoting language learning. It is less clear however, whether the results obtained in laboratory studies can be easily projected to classrooms where most of the foreign or second language learning takes place. For example, a series of descriptive classroom studies indicated that recasts are the type of feedback which is most frequently used in language classrooms (Ellis, Loewen & Basturkmen 2001; Havranek 2002; Loewen & Philp 2006; Lyster 1998a, 1998b; Lyster & Ranta 1997; Panova & Lyster 2002) but in terms of immediate uptake recasts have been found the least effective type of feedback (Havranek 2002; Havranek & Cesnik 2001; Lyster 1998a, 1998b; Lyster & Ranta 1997; Panova & Lyster 2002), but see Ellis, Loewen and Basturkmen (2001) for different findings. According to Lyster and Ranta (1997) and Lyster (1998a, 1998b) recasts are the most ambiguous type of CF, not perceived as corrective by learners and therefore, of "questionable effectiveness as corrective feedback" (1998b: 75). These researchers argued that prompting strategies (which usually include elicitation, clarification requests and metalinguistic explanation) are significantly more useful than recasts because they encourage self-repair and hence promote so called 'discovery approach' (Chaudron 1977) to learning. However, the problem with Lyster and Ranta's (1997) and Lyster's (1998a, 1998b) widely cited and influential descriptive studies is that they have established a direct causal link between uptake and learning, hypothesizing that only the types of corrective feedback followed by uptake can lead to learning.[1]

---

1. Long (2007) critically examined this view and argued, providing relevant arguments, that uptake cannot be taken as an indication of learning and effectiveness of corrective feedback. Some studies, in particular, Philp (2003) have provided clear evidence that immediate uptake can be *red herrings*.

Salience and implicitness of recasts

A thorough investigation of contextual and prosodic characteristics of recasts (e.g. Egi 2007; Han 2002; Loewen & Philp 2006; Sheen 2006; Ellis & Sheen 2006) has led some researchers (Ellis 2006; Ellis & Sheen 2006; Lyster & Saito 2010) to propose a view which places recasts on a continuum from implicit to explicit so that, as they explain, in certain situations recasts can be more implicit and in other situations more explicit. However, it is noteworthy that both recasts and clarification requests used as negative or corrective feedback are implicit by definition (Long 2007), i.e. they only implicitly provide negative feedback since they do not state overtly that an error has been committed. It seems that the lack of saliency, more than the implicitness of negative feedback, could explain why recasts in certain situations may be difficult to notice. Specifically, morpho-syntactic corrections in recasts may not be as easy to notice as recasts containing lexical, or phonological corrections (Oliver & Mackey 2003; Mackey & Goo 2007). Salience, as N. Ellis and Collins (2009) put it, is "the perceived strength of stimuli" (2009: 331). Talmy (2008) posits that closed-class (functional) categories are less salient than open-class (lexical) categories. Among open-class categories, "nouns lend more salience than verb forms,[2] and within closed-class categories forms with phonological substance will outrank forms lacking such phonological substance" (2008: 29). Therefore, it is not surprising that lexical corrections in recasts may be easier to notice.

Proficiency and learner readiness

Other factors have also been identified as those influencing the effectiveness of corrective recasts in classrooms, so these factors may have also contributed to different findings thus far. Instructional setting, learning context, age, proficiency level and appropriate stage of interlanguage development are some of the most frequently emphasized and discussed such factors. For example, Ammar and Spada (2006) found that students of higher proficiency benefited from recasts more than those of lower proficiency whereas prompts in their study (including elicitations, clarification requests and metalinguistic feedback) equally benefited both lower and higher proficiency learners. Furthermore, studies have suggested that only if language corrections in recasts are "within the learnability range"

---

2. One reviewer has indicated that this is not always the case, since in some Asian languages, such as Korean, verbs are more or equally salient as nouns – there are frequent utterances containing only verbs in discourse.

(Oliver 1995: 476) of the learner, he or she will be ready to acquire a certain structure (Farrar 1990, 1992; Iwashita 2003; Mackey & Philp 1998; Oliver 1995). From a different perspective, involving both syntax and semantics, this actually means that learners who are to benefit from recasts should be able to understand the meaning of the utterance in order to notice the recast. If learners are not yet at the level of interlanguage at which they are able to grasp the general meaning of the utterance they are probably not ready yet to acquire the structure and not able to notice the recast either. Doughty (2001) argued that in order to notice the recast and in order for "cognitive comparison" (Nelson 1987) to take place, the meaning of the utterance should be known to the learner. According to Long and Robinson (1998), the positive impact of recasts in conversation is the consequence of a particular process that implicit negative feedback can induce while creating connections among input, selective attention and output. As N. Ellis (2005) explained, recasts can present learners with "psycholinguistic data that are optimized for acquisition" (2005: 332). This happens in the contrast between the learner's own non-target-like utterance and the corrective recast, when the relevant (corrected) element of the form that potentially can be acquired is highlighted, and simultaneously linked to the meaning which is to be expressed.

Summary

To summarise, recasts have been identified as the most frequent type of CF used in classrooms but their effectiveness has been questioned on the grounds of low rates of uptake. However, a positive impact of recasts, involving their psycholinguistic effects, has been associated primarily with the salience of linguistic features triggering CF, the learners' readiness to acquire a particular feature and also, the learners' proficiency level. Clarification requests, in comparison, have been found to be more conducive to uptake, although the uptake itself cannot guarantee target-like repair and subsequent learning.

Target structures

The difficulties in the acquisition of the *passé composé* (PC) and the *imparfait* (IMP) in French L2 arise from both their formal and functional complexity involving multiple discourse functions. The formal complexity of the PC lies in the nature of the rules governing its form. It employs two different auxiliaries (*avoir* and être) in a structure consisting of an auxiliary and a past participle which requires agreement with the subject according to relatively fixed grammatical rules. The PC has one basic meaning: perfective or completed action. On the other hand,

IMP has three semantic meanings: (a) imperfective (ongoing action in the past with out-of-focus endpoints), (b) iterative (habitual events and repeated events in the past), and (c) durative (states of being in the past), therefore it is functionally complex.

While the tense distinctions usually do not present particular problems to English speakers learning French, the aspectual distinction between English and French is much less transparent since French and English aspectual systems display some similarities but also some major differences (Ayoun & Salaberry 2005). The French language has perfective and imperfective grammatical aspect, whereas English distinguishes simple and progressive. Thus the particular difficulty for English learners of French is the fact that the strategy of matching an English form to a French form may sometimes result in a correct use of the target structure but can also lead to an overgeneralisation and erroneous equation of the English simple past tense with the French *passé composé*.

Following the classification proposed by Vendler (1967) and Comrie (1976), linguists also identify four different classes of verbs according to their lexical aspect. The four classes denote (a) states, (b) activities, (c) accomplishments and (d) achievements. It has been found that there is a strong correlation between lexical aspect and grammatical aspect so that the verbs encoding states and activities typically involve the use of the imperfective aspect (IMP) whereas the verbs encoding accomplishments and achievements typically involve the use of perfective aspect (PC). Bardovi-Harlig (2000: 112) proposed four principles based on longitudinal research into the acquisition of tense-aspect morphology: (1) the development of temporal expression is slow and gradual, (2) the acquisition of form often precedes the function, (3) irregular morphology precedes regular morphology and (4) learners tend to avoid discontinuous marking such as aux. + V-tense inflection and instead use only suffixed inflections. Research into French L2 has suggested (e.g. Harley 1989) that learners first begin to use the PC, in certain cases not yet entirely productive and then the IMP but only with être, avoir and the modals. It has been established in literature, according to the Lexical Aspect Hypothesis (Andersen & Shirai 1994; Shirai & Andresen 1995) that the acquisition of French IMP starts with verbs with inherent state lexical aspect and this is followed by verbs denoting activities, then accomplishments and finally achievements (punctual events). The acquisition of PC follows the opposite direction: it is first acquired with the verbs of achievement and then accomplishments, followed by activities and finally by the verbs of state lexical aspect. Kaplan (1987) conducted a study with 16 English speakers learning French, based on a semi-structured interview and found that, for example, first year students had more difficulty with the accuracy of PC forms than with the IMP forms. It is worth noting, however, that IMP at this level is used with a very limited number of verbs, involving state and some verbs of activity lexical aspect. Second year students in Kaplan's study, on the other hand, manifested errors in distribution of IMP. For these, more advanced learners, the use of IMP made 82% of all errors.

The study

The present study attempted to answer two questions, the first one being: Does oral corrective feedback in the form of (a) recasts and (b) clarification requests have an effect on L2 learners' acquisition of French *passé composé* and *imparfait*? Since it has been reported in some studies (Ammar & Spada 2006) that recasts are more effective for learners of higher proficiency, the second question asked: Does the learners' starting proficiency level mediate the effect of oral corrective feedback on the acquisition of the two past tense structures?

The study used a pre-test, treatment, post-test and a delayed post-test experimental design. As the participants could not be chosen randomly but were part of intact classes, this was a quasi-experimental study. Two treatment groups were involved whereas the third class served as a control group. One of the experimental groups received recasts (RE) and the other received clarification requests (CR) as corrective feedback while the students worked on three communicative tasks over two weeks. The learners in the control (CN) group did not undergo any treatment and did not perform the tasks the other two groups did.

Recasts were operationalised, following Long's definition of corrective recasts, as the teacher's "reformulation of all or part of a learner's utterance in which one or more non-target-like grammatical items is/are replaced by the corresponding target language form and where, throughout the exchange the focus of the interlocutors is on meaning" (2007:77). The mode of the recasts was interrogative. The definition of clarification requests has been adopted from Lyster and Ranta (1997:47) who borrowed the term from Spada and Fröhlich (1995) to indicate the feedback which shows students "that their utterance has been misunderstood by the teacher or that the utterance is ill-formed in some way that a repetition or a reformulation is required". Uptake with repair was operationalised as a learner's utterance that immediately follows the teacher's feedback and contains repair of the error which initially triggered the teacher's feedback. The following are the examples of (a) a recast, and (b) a clarification request, followed by uptake with repair:

(a) A recast
L2:   ummm les deux garçons un garçon <u>acheté</u> et ...   (trigger)
T: uh ils ont acheté ?   (recast)
L2:   ils <u>ont acheté</u> une coca   (uptake with repair)

(b) A clarification request
L36:   *er er il <u>téléphoné/er/ait</u>...*   (trigger)
T: *pardon? tu peux répéter?*   (clarification request)
L36:   *Paul <u>a téléphoné</u> à l'hôpital*   (uptake with repair)

Participants

The participants were high school students learning French as a foreign language. Both treatment groups consisted of classes from the same school whilst the CN group students were from another school.[3] Both treatment groups were taught by the same teacher. Altogether 52 students were involved: 18 in each of the treatment groups and 16 in the control group. The average age was 16 (15.76). In the RE (Recasts) group there were 9 males and 9 females, in the CR (Clarification Requests) group there were 5 males and 13 females and in the CN (Control) group 5 males and 11 females. All three groups involved speakers whose native language was not English, however, they all reported English native or near-native competency since all their schooling or most part of it had been in an English speaking environment. In the RE group 11 students were English native speakers, one was bilingual native English/German, two were German native speakers, two Korean, one Chinese and one a Filipino Tagalog native speaker. In the CR group there were ten English native speakers, four Chinese, two Korean, one German and one Romanian native speaker. In the CN group 14 participants were English native speakers, one was German and one was a native speaker of Serbian.

On average each class had had around 500 hours of French instruction to date. The school from which the treatment groups were recruited is a large multicultural school with a roll of around 3100 students. The CN group was also from a large multicultural school with a roll of around 2500 students. At both schools students sit the National Certificate of Educational Achievement (NCEA) exams. French is an optional subject and the French curriculum is driven by the NCEA assessments. It is based on a functional syllabus. The teachers at both schools claimed that their teaching practices favoured the communicative approach, but there was also an emphasis on grammar and accuracy. Apart from their daily French language classes, the students at the school from which the treatment

---

3. The three groups were comparable although there might have been slight differences in the process of language instruction at the two schools. The main difference was the opportunity that the students at one school had, to develop fluency in conversation with a French native speaker. However, in the class from the other school (i.e. the Control group), there was a French-English bilingual native speaker (who was excluded from the research) so presumably her peers in the same class also had opportunities to interact in French and develop fluency.

groups were recruited meet every week individually, or in small groups of 2–4, with a French native speaker assistant, in order to improve their fluency. Generally, at both participating schools flexibility in taking classes at different levels (depending on students' abilities and preferences) is one of the characteristics of their curriculum.

The target structures – the *passé composé* and the *imparfait* of (mainly) auxiliaries, modals and some verbs belonging to the first group of French conjugation (verbs ending in -*er*) had been introduced about a year earlier in both schools, so the participants had already received some instruction and metalinguistic information about the target structures, and presumably were also able to use both structures at their level of interlanguage.

Instruments for data collection

Three picture-based tasks were designed to elicit the use of the two past tense structures so that each story was introduced by a sentence indicating that it happened in the past. Prior to the study a number of similar tasks were trialed and piloted with different groups of students. Moreover, two independent French native speakers were asked to retell the stories, to establish that the tasks would elicit a sufficient number of the PC and the IMP forms. These tasks were two-way focused information gap tasks (Ellis 2003). In order to complete them, i.e. to retell the story shown in a series of six pictures, the participants first had to find out information that was missing from their set of pictures. The sheets they were given contained three pictures showing what happened in the story, presented in the form of a jig-saw. The teacher provided information about the other three pictures. Once the students obtained all information needed, they had to retell the whole story on their own, taking turns on a voluntary basis. New vocabulary related to each of the picture-based tasks was introduced at the beginning and put on the whiteboard for reference. The students were also allowed to ask for the meaning of any French word they did not know. Each treatment task lasted for about 20–25 minutes. During the performance of the tasks participants in one class received feedback in the form of recasts and in the other class in the form of clarification requests. All other errors were ignored. If the corrective feedback move did not result in uptake with repair it was repeated (see Apendix) but if there was no repair after the second CF move, the topic continued either by teacher or by the student.[4] The tasks were audio recorded by a digital voice recorder.

---

4. Repetition (once) of the CF move was part of the study design, aiming at increasing the salience of CF. However, the participants very quickly learnt what they were expected to do,

A student who was absent from pre-test (so could not take part in the study) or a relieving teacher, double-checked the order of participants taking part in conversation by using a seating plan and recording the order of each student turn in conversational exchange.

The tests also consisted of six pictures, requiring the learners to write up[5] a story based on the pictures. The students were asked to write a report for their school magazine. Even though this type of task was novel to students learning French as a FL, they were used to working with similar tasks in English, in order to practice their writing skills. From the pictures it was possible to make up a story involving the plot and the foreground, as well as the background information. In order to account for possible differences in the difficulty of the pre-test, immediate post-test (on the day following the treatment), and a delayed post-test (four to five weeks later), the tests were counter-balanced using a three-split block design. Thus on each occasion of testing participants were split into three groups (A, B, and C) and each group used a different story of the same format, so that those participants who had story A on the pre-test had story B on the immediate post-test and story C on the delayed post-test whereas those who had story B on the pre-test, later had story C on the immediate post-test and story A on the delayed post-test, etc. Obligatory occasions were then determined for each structure taking into consideration the context and the adverbs or connectives between two or more verbs or phrases. The following are the examples of the use of the IMP (1) and the PC (2), depending on the given context. As noted above, the PC is used when referring to a completed action whereas the IMP may refer to an ongoing action with out-of-focus endpoints:

(1) *Les garçons ont   vu*(PC) *une dame qui se faisait*
    the boys   have(AUX) see(PP) a   lady who make(IMP-REFL)
    bronzer(IMP)
    sunbathe(INF)
    "The boys saw a lady who was sunbathing"

or:

---

and started to produce uptake with repair immediately after the first CF move. In this regard it is possible to say that CF in the present study (both recasts and clarification requests) had an 'output-pushing' element.

5. This paper reports on the written tests results because only in written production of verbs ending in -*er* (1st group of French conjugation) it is possible to see if the imparfait has been used, whereas in oral production of these verbs the forms of the infinitive, the imparfait, and the past participle sound the same, e.g. *manger* (infinitive); *je mangais* (imparfait); *mangé* (past participle).

(2) Elle s'est   fait(PC)   bronzer   hier   après-midi.
     she is(AUX) make(PP-REFL) sunbathe(INF) yesterday afternoon
     'She sunbathed/was sunbathing yesterday afternoon'.

Coding and scoring of tests

All tests were coded and scored separately for each of the two target structures. The number of obligatory use contexts was established for each structure separately and instances of overuse of the two structures were identified. The tests used in written production elicited a range of 3 to 15 obligatory occasions for PC with an average of 8 per test per student whereas 3 to 11 obligatory occasions were elicited for IMP, with an average of 6 per student per test. In order to ensure the reliability of coding and scoring, 15% of each set of tests were coded and scored for obligatory use of the PC and the IMP by a French teacher native speaker. Agreement percentage on the three tests for the PC (pre-test, post-test 1, post-test 2) was 96%, and for the IMP 98%.

Scores were calculated using the target-like use analysis (Pica 1983) which takes into consideration the overuse of the target form. For each correct supply in obligatory context including the correct target-like form participants were given 2 points: one point was given for the correct use of the verb tense and one point was given for the correct form. For example, (a) if a particular context required the tense which was actually used and it was formed correctly participants were given 2 points, (b) if a particular context required the tense which was used but did not contain the fully correct form participants were given 1 point and (c) if a particular context did not require the tense which was actually used the score was 0. The number of obligatory occasions was then doubled to allow for the fact that two points were available for each obligatory occasion. Also, the number of overuses of the two structures was doubled so that these were weighted similarly to the number of obligatory occasions. The formula below calculates the percentage of target-like use for each structure:

$$\frac{\text{n correct supply in contexts (including correct form)}}{(\text{n obligatory contexts} \times 2) + (\text{n supply in non-obligatory contexts} \times 2)} \times 100 = \text{percent (\%) accuracy}$$

Since for the PC the target form consists of an auxiliary and the past participle, 2 points were given for the use of the correct auxiliary and a verb form (past participle), whereas 1 point was given for the use of an incorrect auxiliary and a verb form (past participle). If no auxiliary was used, the structure was not identified as the PC, 0 point was given. Such a decision was taken because certain frequently used verbs (e. g. *faire, écrire, dire*) have the same form in the present (third person singular) and past participle (*fait, écrit, dit*) so it would not be possible to make a distinction between the two, i.e. to see whether the student has used the present tense or has started to develop the PC by using the bare past participle without an auxiliary. Possible incorrect forms of the past participle were ignored because the learning of past participle forms is considered to be entirely lexical in nature: it cannot be learned but by memorization of individual items. The characteristic IMP inflections (for example *-ais, -ait, -aient*) were taken as indication of the use of the IMP in verbs. Possible spelling mistakes (e. g. *-ais* instead of *-ait* or *-aient*) were ignored.

Data analysis

The Statistical package for social sciences (SPSS) was used to perform the statistical analyses.

Descriptive statistics for each structure were first calculated and a one-way ANOVA was computed to test if the groups were comparable. The level of significance was set at .05.

(a) In order to answer first research question, a mixed design ANOVA with repeated measures, using the Bonferroni adjustments for multiple comparisons, was calculated to examine the change that occurred in each group after the pretest (within-group comparisons). Effect sizes were calculated at each level of testing for within-group comparison. Effect size was calculated and interpreted using Cohen's recommendation (Norris & Ortega 2000) so that an effect size lower than 0.50 was considered a small size, above 0.50 a medium effect size and above 0.80 a large effect size The following formula was used, based on the difference of mean scores, and taking into account standard deviations and the sample size:

$$\text{Cohen's } d = \frac{M1 - M2}{S \text{ (pooled)}} \qquad S \text{ (pooled)} = \frac{(N1 - 1)\, S1 + (N2 - 1)\, S2}{(N1 - 1) + (N2 - 1)}$$

Separate Repeated measures ANOVAs were calculated for the PC and for the IMP.

(b) Between-group differences were examined using an ANCOVA with the pre-test scores as a covariate because, even though there were no statistical differences between the groups on the pre-test, some variation was evident and it is recommended it be accounted for (Field 2009; Miller & Chapman 2001; Ammar & Spada 2006).[6] Testing for the homogeneity of regression slopes showed that all the assumptions for an ANCOVA were met.

---

6. As Miller and Chapman (2001) explain, this is a valid and recommended procedure to account for the differences on pre-test which are not significant (such differences often occur

(c) In order to answer the second question, the participants in each group were first divided into 'high' and 'low' based on their pre-test scores. The values of standard deviation in each group indicated that there were considerable differences between the lower and the higher proficiency learners in each class. For PC the median score for the whole sample on pre-test was 45.77. So, for each group, all learners above the median were placed in the 'high proficiency'[7] sub-group and all those below into the 'low proficiency' sub-group. For IMP the median score for the whole sample was 20.00. Once the 'low' and 'high' sub-groups were formed the Kruskal-Wallis non-parametric test, equivalent to one-way independent ANOVA, was computed using the participants' gain scores from pre-test to the immediate posttest and from pre-test to the delayed posttest (gain 1 and gain 2). The non-parametric tests were preferred because of the small sample size in lower and higher proficiency sub-groups. Where the Kruskal-Wallis test produced an overall statistically significant result, the Mann-Whitney Test, a non-parametric equivalent to the Independent samples t-test, was used to examine whether there were statistically significant differences between any two of the 'high' and 'low proficiency' sub-groups.

Results

Results: *passé composé*

Table 1 displays the descriptive data for the use of PC. A one-way ANOVA showed no statistically significant differences among the three groups at the time of pre-testing: $F(2, 47) = .681$, $p = .511$ ($p > .05$).

As shown in Table 2 and Figure 1, the analysis of repeated measures ANOVA revealed a significant group over time effect indicating that the three groups demonstrated different behaviour over time: $F(4, 94) = 3.64$, $p = .008$. The post-hoc tests using Bonferroni adjustments for multiple comparisons show that for the RE group there is a statistically significant difference between the pre-test and the immediate post-test ($p = .038$)'with a small to medium effect size ($d = 0.46$),

---

when the test results are expressed in percentage, in a span between 1 and 100). However, Miller and Chapman emphasize that it is not valid and not allowed to use an ANCOVA with the pre-test scores as a covariate in situations where there is a significant difference on the pre-test. Studies with such groups should not be conducted since such groups are not comparable at all.

7. It should be noted that the term *proficiency* is used here only to indicate the different levels of ability in using the French past tense structures, and does not refer to overall language proficiency.

Table 1. Descriptive statistics for *passé composé* in written production

Group	Pre-test		Post-test 1		Post-test 2	
	Mean	SD	Mean	SD	Mean	SD
RE (N = 17)	35.02	30.05	50.18	35.67	61.88	30.31
CR (N = 17)	45.51	28.08	47.02	33.74	49.80	32.12
CN (N = 16)	36.55	26.33	34.19	24.65	34.13	27.98

Table 2. PC: Repeated measures ANOVA – within group differences

	RE	CR	CN
Pre-test – Post-test 1	p = .038*	p > .05	p > .05
Pre-test – Post-test 2	p = .000*	p > .05	p > .05
Post-test 1 – Post-test 2	p = .061	p > .05	p > .05
	df = 16	df = 16	df = 15

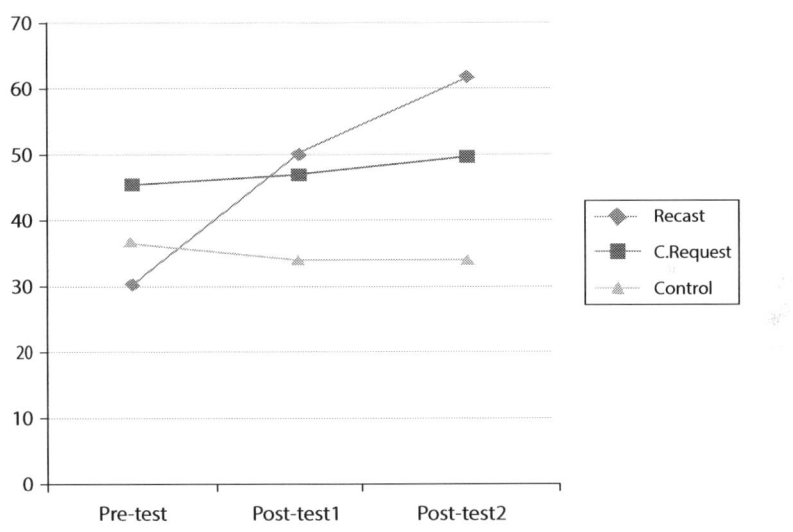

Figure 1. Performance of the three groups over time: PC

and between the pre-test and the delayed post-test (p = .000) with a large effect size (d= 0.89). In the CR group there is no evidence of statistically significant differences between any of the post-tests compared with the pre-test, neither between the post-tests themselves. Effect sizes between each post-test and the pre-test are small. Similar results, showing no statistically significant differences between any of the tests, are evident for the CN group.

Table 3. PC: Effect sizes for experimental groups

RE	ES	CR	ES
Pre-test < Post-test 1	0.46	Pre-test = Post-test 1	0.05
Pre-test < Post-test 2	0.89	Pre-test = Post-test 2	0.14
Post-test 1 = Post-test 2	0.35	Post-test 1 = Post-test 2	0.08

Since the main interaction effect (group over time) was significant, further analyses were needed to see whether there were any statistically significant group differences in post-test 1 and post-test 2. In an ANCOVA, using the pre-test scores as a covariate, the tests of between subjects effects on the immediate post-test failed to reveal any significant difference among the three groups: F (2, 46) = 2.28, p = .113, ns, but on the delayed post-test the group difference was statistically significant: F (2, 46) = 6.15, p = .004 (p < .05).

Post-hoc tests using pair-wise comparisons among the three groups on the delayed post-test for PC revealed a statistically significant difference between the RE and the CN Group (p =. 001, p < .05) and between the RE and the CR group (p = .027, p <. 05) while there was no significant difference between the CR and the CN group (p > .05).

In short, the results for PC indicate that only the RE group significantly improved over time, both between the pre-test and the immediate post-test and between the pre-test and the delayed post-test. Significant between-group differences were detected on the delayed post-test, pointing to the superiority of the treatment with recasts.

Results: *imparfait*

Table 4 presents the descriptive data for the IMP. A one-way ANOVA, performed for the three pre-tests, indicated no statistically significant differences among the three groups at the time of pre-testing: F (2, 47) = 1.056, p = .356 (p > .05).

Table 4. Descriptive statistics for imparfait in written production

Group	Pre-test		Post-test 1		Post-test 2	
	Mean	SD	Mean	SD	Mean	SD
RE (N = 17)	25.52	26.17	54.28	35.67	64.99	26.94
CR (N = 17)	16.01	20.72	29.20	23.44	37.84	26.02
CN (N = 16)	27.41	25.77	22.71	27.57	20.65	25.10

Table 5. IMP: Repeated measures ANOVA – within group differences

	RE	CR	CN
Pre-test – Post-test 1	p = .000*	p > .05	p > .05
Pre-test – Post-test 2	p = .000*	p = .003*	p > .05
Post-test 1 – Post-test 2	p > .05	p > .05	p > .05
	df = 16	df = 16	df = 15

Table 6. IMP: Effect sizes for each treatment group

Recast Group	ES	Cl. Request Group	ES
Pre-test < Post-test 1	0.93	Pre-test = Post-test 1	0.59
Pre-test < Post-test 2	1.49	Pre-test < Post-test 2	0.93
Post-test 1 < Post-test 2	0.34	Post-test 1 = Post-test 2	0.37

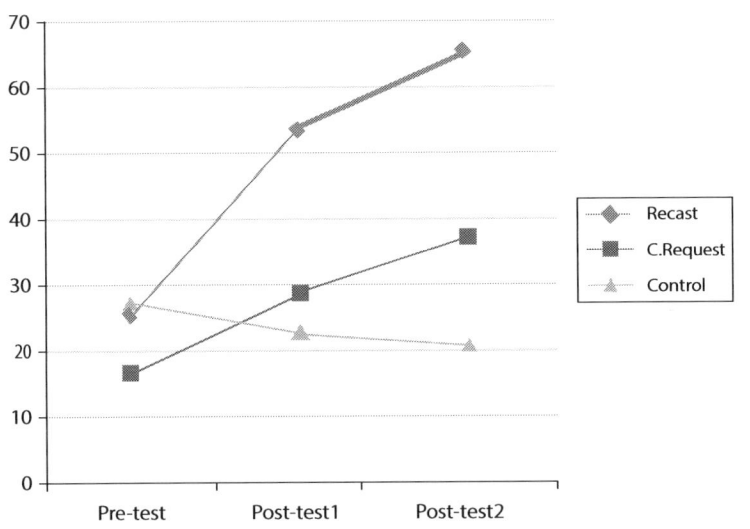

Figure 2. Performance of the three groups over time: IMP

Table 5 and Figure 2 show the results of a Repeated measures ANOVA, used to examine the change over time in each of the three groups. Table 6 displays the values of effect sizes for each of the treatment groups.

The results of a Repeated measures ANOVA, using Bonferroni adjustments for multiple comparisons, reveal the following: for the RE group there is a statistically significant difference between the pre-test and the immediate post-test (p = .000) with a large effect size (d = 0.93), and between the pre-test and the delayed post-test (p = .000), also with a large effect size (d = 1.49). In the CR group there is no evidence of a statistically significant difference between the pre-test and the immediate post-test (p > .05), but the effect size is medium (d = 0.59). Furthermore, there is a significant improvement between the pre-test and the delayed post-test (p = .003) with a large effect size (d = 0.93). The CN group did not show any significant improvement between any of the post-tests and the pre-test, neither between the two post-tests.

A mixed design ANOVA with repeated measures revealed a significant effect for time $F(2, 47) = 12.8$, $p = .000$ and a significant group over time interaction, $F(4, 94) = 7.09$, $p = .000$. An ANCOVA using the pre-test scores as a covariate on the immediate post-test showed a statistically significant group difference for IMP: $F(2, 46) = 7.58$, $p = .001$ ($p < .05$). The delayed post-test also revealed an overall statistically significant difference among the three groups: $F(2, 46) = 15.75$, $p = .000$. Post-hoc tests using pair-wise comparisons on post-test 1 and post-test 2 showed that on the immediate post-test there was a statistically significant difference between the RE and the CN group ($p = .001$), but the difference between the RE and the CR group was not significant. On the delayed post-test, pair-wise comparisons revealed a statistically significant difference between the RE and the CN group ($p =. 000$), between the RE and CR group ($p = .024$) and between the CR and the CN group ($p = .022$).

To sum up, the results for IMP indicate that both the RE group and the CR group, but not the CN group, significantly improved over time: both treatment groups showed significant gains from pre-test to the delayed post-test, and the RE group also from pre-test to the immediate post-test. Between-group differences were observable on the immediate post-test only between the RE and the CN group, whereas on the delayed post-test both recasts and clarification requests showed their superiority over no feedback (CN group).

Comparison of 'low' and 'high' sub-groups

Passé composé
Table 7 displays the descriptive data for written production of PC 'low' and 'high' sub-groups and Table 8 shows the descriptive data for gain scores with the PC.

The Kruskal-Wallis non-parametric test using gain scores was computed for the three "low" sub-groups (RE, CR and CN "low") and the three "high" sub groups (RE, CR and CN 'high'). While the test for the three "low" sub-groups did not show any significant results (p value set at .05), the test performed for the three "high" sub-groups revealed a statistically significant difference for both gain 1 (pre-test scores deducted from post-test 1) and gain 2 (pre-test scores deducted from post-test 2 scores):

Table 7. Descriptive statistics for 'low' and 'high' proficiency sub-groups: PC

Sub-group	Pre-test		Post-test 1		Post-test 2	
	Mean	SD	Mean	SD	Mean	SD
RE 'low' (N = 9)	10.00	13.64	23.47	23.76	42.78	29.08
RE 'high' (N = 8)	63.18	11.83	80.24	17.71	83.36	11.70
CR 'low' (N = 7)	19.20	23.98	36.59	37.07	34.49	37.70
CR 'high' (N = 10)	63.93	10.15	54.32	31.06	57.71	26.79
CN 'low' (N = 10)	18.84	12.50	22.59	18.38	24.34	18.83
CN 'high' (N = 6)	66.07	11.27	53.53	22.28	50.45	34.62

Table 8. Descriptive statistics: PC gain scores for six sub-groups

Sub-group	Gain 1		Gain 2	
	Mean	SD	Mean	SD
RE 'low' (N = 9)	13.47	21.47	32.78	33.20
RE 'high' (N = 8)	17.06	14.28	20.19	11.45
CR 'low' (N = 7)	17.39	30.23	19.29	29.25
CR 'high' (N = 10)	−9.62	30.55	−6.22	27.08
CN 'low' (N = 10)	3.75	19.56	5.50	12.03
CN 'high' (N = 6)	−12.54	12.88	−15.63	24.25

Gain 1: H (2) = 8.12, p = .017
Gain 2: H (2) = 7.83, p = .02

These results suggested that there was an effect for the type of corrective feedback in "high" sub-groups, so further analyses were carried out using the Mann-Whitney U test. Because some information may be lost when multiple Mann-Whitney U tests are performed, the p-value of .05 was divided by the number of tests (Field 2009). Since in the present study three Mann-Whitney U tests were computed at each level, p-value was set at .016 (.05 divided by 3). As presented in Table 9, the analyses on the immediate post-test resulted in a statistically significant difference between the gains of the RE 'high' and CN 'high' sub-group (U = 2.000, p = .003) and close to significant between the RE 'high' and CR 'high' (U = 16.000, p = 0.34). On the delayed post-test a statistically significant result was revealed again between the RE 'high' and the CN 'high' sub-group (U = 4.000, p = .008). The difference between the RE 'high' and the CR 'high' sub-group was only close to significant (U = 16.500, p = .034).

Table 9. PC: Mann-Whitney U tests for six sub-groups

Sub-groups	Gain 1		Gain 2	
	U	Asymp. Sig.	U	Asymp. Sig.
RE 'low' – CR 'low'		ns		ns
RE 'high' – CN 'high'		ns		ns
CR 'low' – CN 'low'		ns		ns
RE 'high' – CR 'high'	16.000	.034	16.500	.034
RE 'high' – CN 'high'	2.000	.003	4.000	.008
CR 'high' – CN 'high'		ns		ns

Imparfait

Table 10 displays the descriptive data for the production of the IMP 'low' and 'high' sub-groups and Table 11 shows the descriptive data for each group's gains in accurate use of the IMP.

The Kruskal-Wallis test performed for the three 'low' sub-groups indicated a statistically significant difference only on the delayed post-test: H (2) = 10.59, p = .005, whereas the same test computed for three 'high' sub-groups showed a

Table 10. Descriptive statistics for 'low' and 'high' sub-groups: IMP

Sub-group	Pre-test		Post-test 1		Post-test 2	
	Mean	SD	Mean	SD	Mean	SD
RE 'low' (N = 9)	4.31	8.55	36.24	29.77	52.82	30.79
RE 'high' (N = 8)	49.39	15.86	74.58	31.71	78.68	13.10
CR 'low' (N = 10)	1.25	3.95	23.88	23.66	32.17	28.24
CR 'high' (N = 7)	37.11	15.45	36.80	22.60	45.94	21.88
CN 'low' (N = 7)	4.90	8.52	9.18	18.77	5.95	10.45
CN 'high' (N = 9)	44.92	20.07	33.23	29.60	32.08	27.63

Table 11. Descriptive statistics: IMP gain scores for six sub-groups

Sub-group	Gain 1		Gain 2	
	Mean	SD	Mean	SD
RE 'low' (N = 9)	31.94	31.26	48.52	32.38
RE 'high' (N = 8)	25.19	27.21	29.29	24.22
CR 'low' (N = 10)	22.63	25.07	30.92	28.62
CR 'high' (N = 7)	−0.31	24.37	8.83	23.53
CN 'low' (N = 7)	4.28	20.85	1.06	11.78
CN 'high' (N = 9)	−11.69	14.68	−12.84	19.44

Table 12. IMP: Mann-Whitney U tests for six sub-groups

Sub-groups	Gain 1		Gain 2	
	U	Asymp. Sig.	U	Asymp. Sig.
RE 'low' – CR 'low'		ns		ns
RE 'high' – CN 'high'		ns	3.500	.001*
CR 'low' – CN 'low'		ns	10.500	.014*
RE 'high' – CR 'high'		ns		ns
RE 'high' – CN 'high'	7.000	.004*	6.000	.002*
CR 'high' – CN 'high'		ns		ns

significant difference on both the immediate post-test: $H(2) = 8.24$, $p = .016$ and on the delayed post-test: $H(2) = 10.39$, $p = .006$.

As shown in Table 12, both RE "low" and CR "low" sub-groups outperformed the CN sub-group ($U = 3.500$, $p = .001$, and $U = 10.500$, $p = .014$, respectively). For 'high' sub-groups the Mann-Whitney tests indicated there was a statistically significant difference between the RE 'high' and the CN 'high' sub-group on both the immediate post-test ($U = 7.000$, $p = .004$) and the delayed post-test ($U = 6.000$, $p = .002$), but the gains of the CR "high" sub-group were not significantly different from the CN "high" sub-group.

To summarise, when the three groups are divided into 'low' and 'high' based on their pre-test scores, the results of the analyses indicate a clear advantage for recasts only with the PC among the 'high proficiency'[8] sub-groups, whereas the 'low' sub-groups did not differ significantly with regard to the PC. Somewhat different results for the IMP showed the superiority of both the RE 'low' and the CR 'low' sub-groups over the CN 'low' sub-group. However, only RE 'high' group proved as significantly more effective than the CN 'high' sub-group.

Summary of overall results

Overall, the presented results suggest that the acquisition of PC was facilitated by the use of recasts, which were superior to both clarification requests and no feedback in the CN group. The results for the IMP, on the other hand, indicate that clarification requests can be as effective as recasts, particularly in longer term.

---

8. In the current study the level of uptake was rather high. It was notably larger in the RE group: 78.8% for PC and 71.4% for IMP. In the CR group it was 41.2% for PC and 34.8% for IMP. In the RE group 11 students participated in interaction, in the CR group 10 students took part. Participation was voluntary. Other students only listened. Although they did not participate in interaction they seemed to be engaged with the tasks.

However, when the groups are divided into 'low' and 'high' according to their pretest score, recasts proved their superiority for the acquisition of PC when 'high' proficiency groups are compared (although the gains of more and less advanced learners in the RE group were similar). Clarification requests, as the results indicate, benefited only the learners of 'lower proficiency' whereas those of 'higher proficiency' did not show any gains.

Discussion

The first research question was concerned with the effects of recasts and clarification requests on the acquisition of the French *passé composé* and *imparfait*, measured by semi-constrained written production tasks. This study was not designed to examine L2 development in terms of progress towards the next stage in learner interlanguage according to the Lexical Aspect Hypothesis (Andersen & Shirai 1994; Shirai & Andersen 1995) but rather in terms of increased accuracy in the use of the two past tense structures. As far as the IMP is concerned, it should be noted that the complex system of French past aspectual distinctions could not be captured in this study due to the participants' level of interlanguage. The use of the IMP was limited to verbs with inherent lexical aspects of state and some activities (Vendler 1967), for example être, avoir, pouvoir, devoir, savoir, pleuvoir, faire, parler, jouer, etc. This is consistent with the research showing that some of the state verbs are usually learnt early as "lexically bound chunks" (Harley 1989; Harley & King 1989). The results in the current study suggest that both recasts and clarification requests facilitate the acquisition of IMP at pre-intermediate stages of learner interlanguage, when the use of IMP is reduced to lexically determined group of verbs, some of them frequently used in a range of formulaic expressions and learnt as chunks, e.g. '*il avait soif*', '*il avait faim*', '*il y avait du soleil*, '*il faisait chaud*', etc. The semantic meaning of these and similar formulaic expressions is encoded in the noun or adjective part of the expression but not in the verb. So, if lexical categories are perceived as more salient than the functional ones, and if nouns lend more salience than verbs (Talmy 2008), this may explain why the IMP verb forms are easier to notice and acquire at this stage. Frequent appearance of these expressions and verbs in input can just multiply the opportunities for noticing and acquisition. As evidenced, both recasts and clarification requests proved beneficial for learning such verb structures, or consolidating the already existing knowledge of them.

On the other hand, the acquisition of the PC seems to be better facilitated by the use of recasts. Only the group that received recasts demonstrated significant gains over time, and outperformed the other two groups in between-group comparisons. A contributing factor to such results may be the frequency of the target structures in input, resulting from a higher level of uptake with repair in the RE group, and from the nature of recasts too. The transcript in the Appendix shows two corresponding sequences – excerpts from the treatment tasks in the two experimental groups, and how the different nature of recasts and clarification requests affected the frequency of the target structures in input. For example, in the 'whole' class environment where all learners are exposed to corrective feedback, a target-like form in the recast followed by uptake with repair is available as input to the whole class two times, but only once if a clarification request is followed by repair. If CF is not followed by uptake with repair, then at least some learners in the classroom have an opportunity to notice the target-like form in the recast; but they do not have this opportunity if clarification requests have been used as CF. Additionally, the current study used a repetition of CF move if either the recast or the clarification request did not result in uptake with repair after the first CF move. It seems that this very clearly indicated to the students in the RE group that they were expected to repeat the teacher's recast, so very soon they started producing uptake with repair immediately after the first CF move.[9] All in all, a non-parametric Mann-Whitney test, computed to examine the difference between the frequency of target forms in the input in the two experimental groups, showed a statistically significant difference: Asymp. sig = .008 for PC and Asymp. sig = .007 for IMP. This indicates that the learners in the RE group on the whole were exposed to a significantly larger number of target forms in the input than the learners in the CR group. Receiving an increased amount of input may be particularly important for acquisition of formally more complex structures such as the PC, which consists of an auxiliary and a past participle, and the choice of the auxiliary (être and *avoir*) depends on the semantic aspect of the main verb while the past participle can be either regular or irregular.

Even though uptake of corrective recasts in this study was relatively high it is not possible to claim that the post-test results and gains in the RE group were directly influenced by 'pushed' or modified output. Rather, it seems that these results were more related to the input to which the whole class was exposed. Specifically, as the analyses carried out elsewhere showed (Mifka Profozic 2013), the learners in the RE group who did not participate in interaction but only listened to their peers outperformed those learners who actually produced modified output and repair. The analysis of written narrative tasks reveals a significant difference between the gain scores in these two groups of students in the class who received treatment with recasts. Based on such a finding, the current study provides further

---

9. Very similar students' reactions were observed in Doughty and Varela (1998) study in which repetition of error was used to increase the saliency of corrective feedback.

evidence for claims that, focusing only on uptake in language classrooms is not sufficient to draw relevant conclusions about language acquisition. Therefore it is not surprising that the current findings, similar to Doughty and Varela's (1998), Révész and Han (2006), Révész (2009, 2012), and Goo (2012) contradict those of Lyster and Ranta (1997), Lyster (1998a, 1998b), and Panova and Lyster (2002), in which recasts were seen as ambiguous and ineffective.

Clarification requests, on the other hand, may be facilitative of learning only if they are followed by repair or modified output, as McDonough's study (2005) has shown, i.e. when learners are able to retrieve and deploy their already existing knowledge (Long 2007). By answering the second research question the current study points to the fact that clarification requests can only assist to retrieve and consolidate the existing knowledge but not to acquire new structures. Namely, the results demonstrate that only the learners of lower proficiency benefited from clarification requests whereas the more advanced ones did not move on because there was no available input that would provide them with new linguistic knowledge. Thus the advantage on the part of recasts became clearly evident when 'higher proficiency' groups are compared – not because recasts benefited only the more advanced learners, but because clarification requests benefited only the learners of 'lower proficiency' whereas the more advanced learners were disadvantaged by the use of clarification requests. Recasts, as the analyses show, benefited similarly the more advanced and the less advanced students.

Finally, it should be underscored that the tasks in this study were communicative and meaning oriented. It was vital that the feedback occurred while the learners were engaged with meaning. Long (1996) and Long & Robinson (1998) claim that recasts may be an ideal type of focus-on-form because they do not interrupt the "predominant focus on meaning" (1998: 26), although they do interrupt learners' processing at the moment when their attention briefly shifts from meaning to form. This claim has a special value for communicative language teaching in foreign language classrooms where focus on isolated forms has for long been the prevalent method of instruction, actually preventing learners from achieving higher levels in fluency. Equally, this claim holds value for immersion classes as well, where communicative ability has often been developed at the expense of accuracy and students failed to achieve higher levels of grammatical and linguisitic competence.

Limitations

The obvious limitation to this study is the number of participants, in particular the 'low' and 'high' sub-groups formed to examine the possible mediating role of learners' starting proficiency level. Because of the small sample size in the subgroups, non-parametric tests were used for analysis, although the Kolmogorov-Smirnov test performed on these data was not significant. Since the participants were recruited from intact high school classes, their distribution reflected the real-life situation in FL learning. One reviewer suggested that the Control group should be better excluded because the learners in this group came from a different school. It is true that there might have been slight differences in the instructional processes of the two schools but, in general, they followed the same curriculum, had very similar syllabi, had the same internal and external standard assessments, used the same text-books, their teachers attended the same professional development sessions, and importantly, there were no significant differences among the three groups on the pre-test. Another reviewer commented that the Control group should have been working on the same tasks except for receiving CF. This may be a limitation to the study, but in Norris and Ortega (2000) seminal study the authors state that "a true control group" is "a group receiving neither instruction nor exposure related to the target structure except in pre- and post-tests". A group receiving "non-focused exposure to the structure being taught in the experimental condition" would be a comparison group (2000: 445).

Concluding comments and suggestions for future research

The present findings are consistent with the line of research that has provided evidence of the effectiveness of recasts not only in laboratory conditions but also in language classrooms. Although the effects of clarification requests have been found too, the results have not confirmed the claims (Lyster & Ranta 1997; Lyster 2004; Yang & Lyster 2010) that output-prompting and 'pushing' learners to self-correct is superior to recasting. Uptake with repair has not emerged as a significant factor contributing to acquisition although it has played an important role in increasing the frequency of the target structures in input for the whole class. Furthermore, this study has not confirmed Ammar and Spada's (2006) claim that recasts are effective only for learners of higher proficiency. In contrast, recasts have been found facilitative of learning for both more and less advanced learners, but clarification requests apparently benefited only the learners of 'lower proficiency', and only for acquisition of morphologically simpler verb forms which could be easily retrieved from memory. More advanced learners in the CR group were disadvantaged by the use of clarification requests because corrective feedback did not provide them with any positive evidence. In comparison, recasts benefited the learners not only because of their psycholinguistic characteristics resulting from the simultaneous provision of negative feedback and positive evidence, but also because of their contribution to the frequency of target structures in the input. This seems to be particularly important when morphologically more complex structures such as the French *passé composé* are concerned.

The current study has clearly pointed to the differential effects of corrective feedback relative to the different target structures. Therefore, in future research it would be worthwhile to expand this line of investigation and further examine the effectiveness of implicit negative feedback on the acquisition of a variety of language structures. Further to this, different age groups should be also involved. The current study has only touched on the issue of negative feedback in relation to the different proficiency levels, so future studies should further examine this issue, involving larger groups of participants. Last but not least, the effectiveness of corrective feedback, in particular recasts, should be also examined in relation to acquisition operationalised not only as increase in accuracy but as a change in developmental stages. Such an operationalization of L2 acquisition has been employed in a number of studies investigating the development of English question formation (e.g. Mackey 1999; Mackey & Philp 1998; McDonough 2005; McDonough & Mackey 2006), but it would be worthwhile to focus on other language structures as well. One of the priorities, undoubtedly, should be the investigation of the effects of corrective feedback on the development of tense-aspect verbal morphology through the established stages of acquisition on the basis of Lexical Aspect Hypothesis.

References

Ammar, A. 2008. "Prompts and recasts: Differential effects on second language morphosyntax." *Language Teaching Research* 12 (2): 183–210. DOI: 10.1177/1362168807086287

Ammar, A. and Spada, N. 2006. "One size fits all? Recasts, prompts, and L2 learning." *Studies in Second Language Acquisition* 28 (4): 543–574. DOI: 10.1017/S0272263106060268

Andersen, R.W. and Shirai, Y. 1994. "Discourse motivations for some cognitive acquisition principles." *Studies in Second Language Acquisition* 16 (02): 133–156. DOI: 10.1017/S0272263100012845

Ayoun, D. 2001. "The role of negative and positive feedback in the second language acquisition of the passe compose and the imparfait." *The Modern Language Journal* 85 (2): 226–243. DOI: 10.1111/0026-7902.00106

Ayoun, D. 2004. "The effectiveness of written recasts in the second language acquisition of aspectual distinctions in French: A follow-up study." *The Modern Language Journal* 88 (1): 31–55. DOI: 10.1111/j.0026-7902.2004.00217.x

Ayoun, D. and Salaberry, M.R. 2005. *Tense and aspect in Romance Languages: Theoretical and Applied Perspectives*. Amsterdam : John Benjamins. DOI: 10.1075/sibil.29

Bardovi-Harlig, K. 2000. *Tense and Aspect in Second Language Acquisition: Form, Meaning and Use*. Oxford: Blackwel.

Braidi, S.M. 2002. "Reexamining the role of recasts in native-speaker/nonnative-speaker interactions." *Language Learning* 52 (1): 1–42. DOI: 10.1111/1467-9922.00176

Chaudron, C. 1977. "A descriptive model of discourse in the corrective treatment of learners' errors." *Language Learning* 27 (1): 29–46. DOI: 10.1111/j.1467-1770.1977.tb00290.x

Comrie, B. 1976. *Aspect: an Introduction to the Study of Verbal Aspect and Related Problems*. Cambridge: New York: Cambridge University Press.

Doughty, C. 2001. "Cognitive underpinnings of focus on form." In *Cognition and Second Language Instruction*, P. Robinson (ed.), 206–257. Cambridge: Cambridge University Press. DOI: 10.1017/CBO9781139524780.010

Doughty, C. and Varela, E. 1998. "Communicative Focus on Form." In *Focus on Form in Classroom Second Language Acquisition*, C. Doughty and J. Williams (eds), 114–138. Cambridge: Cambridge University Press.

Egi, T. 2007. "Interpreting recasts as linguistic evidence: The roles of linguistic target, length, and degree of change." *Studies in Second Language Acquisition* 29 (4): 511–537. DOI: 10.1017/S0272263107070416

Ellis, N.C. 2005. "At the interface: Dynamic interactions of explicit and Implicit language knowledge." *Studies in Second Language Acquisition* 27 (2): 305–352.

Ellis, N.C. and Collins, L. 2009. "Input and second language acquisition: The roles of frequency, form, and function." Introduction to the special issue. *The Modern Language Journal* 93 (3): 329–336. DOI: 10.1111/j.1540-4781.2009.00893.x

Ellis, R. 2003. *Task-based Language Learning and Teaching*. Oxford, U.K.: Oxford University Press.

Ellis, R. 2006. "Researching the effects of form-focussed instruction on L2 acquisition." *AILA Review* 19: 18–41. DOI: 10.1075/aila.19.04ell

Ellis, R. 2007. "The differential effects of corrective feedback on two grammatical structures." In *Conversational Interaction in Second Language Acquisition: A Collection of Empirical Studies*, A. Mackey (ed.). Oxford: Oxford University Press.

Ellis, R., Basturkmen, H. and Loewen, S. 2001. "Learner uptake in communicative ESL lessons." *Language Learning* 51 (2): 281–318. DOI: 10.1111/1467-9922.00156

Ellis, R., Loewen, S. and Erlam, R. 2006. "Implicit and explicit corrective feedback and the acquisition of L2 grammar." *Studies in Second Language Acquisition* 28 (2): 339–368.

Ellis, R. and Sheen, Y. 2006. "Reexamining the role of recasts in second language acquisition." *Studies in Second Language Acquisition* 28 (4): 575–600.

Farrar, M.J. 1990. "Discourse and the acquisition of grammatical morphemes." *Journal of Child Language* 17 (03): 607–624. DOI: 10.1017/S0305000900010904

Farrar, M.J. 1992. "Negative evidence and grammatical morpheme acquisition." *Developmental Psychology* 28 (1): 90–98. DOI: 10.1037/0012-1649.28.1.90

Field, A.P. 2009. *Discovering Statistics using SPSS: (and Sex, Drugs and Rock'n'roll)*, 3rd edition. London: SAGE.

Goo, J. 2012. "Corrective feedback and working memory capacity in interaction-driven L2 learning." *Studies in Second Language Acquisition* 34 (03): 445–474. DOI: 10.1017/S0272263112000149

Han, Z. 2002. "A study of the impact of recasts on tense consistency in L2 output." *TESOL Quarterly* 36 (4): 543–572. DOI: 10.2307/3588240

Harley, B. 1989. "Functional grammar in french immersion: A classroom experiment." *Applied Linguistics* 10 (3): 331–360. DOI: 10.1093/applin/10.3.331

Harley, B. and King, M.L. 1989. "Verb lexis in the written compositions of young L2 learners." *Studies in Second Language Acquisition* 11 (04): 415–439. DOI: 10.1017/S0272263100008421

Havranek, G. 2002. "When is corrective feedback most likely to succeed?" *International Journal of Educational Research* 37: 255–270. DOI: 10.1016/S0883-0355(03)00004-1

Havranek, G. and Cesnik, H. 2001. "Factors affecting the success of corrective feedback." *EUROSLA Yearbook* 1: 99–122. DOI: 10.1075/eurosla.1.10hav

Ishida, M. 2004. "Effects of recasts on the acquisition of the aspectual form -te i-(ru) by learners of Japanese as a foreign language." *Language Learning* 54 (2): 311–394.

Iwashita, N. 2003. "Negative feedback and positive evidence in task-based interaction: Differential effects on L2 development." *Studies in Second Language Acquisition* 25 (1): 1–36. DOI: 10.1017/S0272263103000019

Kaplan, M.A. 1987. "Developmental patterns of past tense acquisition among foreign language learners of French." In *Foreign Language Learning: A Research Perspective*, B. VanPatten, T. Dvorak and J.F. Lee (eds), 52–60. Cambridge [Cambridgeshire]; New York: Newbury House.

Leeman, J. 2003. "Recasts and second language development: Beyond negative evidence." *Studies in Second Language Acquisition* 25 (1): 37–63. DOI: 10.1017/S0272263103000020

Li, S. 2010. "The effectiveness of corrective feedback in SLA: A meta-analysis." *Language Learning* 60 (2): 309–365. DOI: 10.1111/j.1467-9922.2010.00561.x

Loewen, S. and Nabei, T. 2007. "Measuring the effects of oral corrective feedback on L2 knowledge." In *Conversational Interaction in Second Language Acquisition: A Collection of Empirical Studies*, A. Mackey (ed.). Oxford: Oxford University Press.

Loewen, S. and Philp, J. 2006. "Recasts in the adult English L2 classroom: Characteristics, explicitness, and effectiveness." *The Modern Language Journal* 90 (4): 536–556. DOI: 10.1111/j.1540-4781.2006.00465.x

Long, M.H. 1981. "Questions in foreigner talk discourse." *Language Learning* 31 (1): 135–157. DOI: 10.1111/j.1467-1770.1981.tb01376.x

Long, M.H. 1983. "Native speaker/non-native speaker conversation and the negotiation of comprehensible input1." *Applied Linguistics* 4 (2): 126–141. DOI: 10.1093/applin/4.2.126

Long, M.H. 1996. "The role of the linguistic environment in second language acquisition." In *Handbook of Second Language Acquisition*, W.C. Ritchie and T.K. Bhatia (eds), 413–468. San Diego: Academic Press.

Long, M.H. 2007. *Problems in SLA*. Mahwah, N.J.: Lawrence Erlbaum Associates.

Long, M.H., Inagaki, S. and Ortega, L. 1998. "The role of implicit negative feedback in SLA: Models and recasts in Japanese and Spanish." *The Modern Language Journal* 82 (3): 357–371. DOI: 10.1111/j.1540-4781.1998.tb01213.x

Long, M.H. and Robinson, P. 1998. "Focus on form: Theory, research, and practice." In *Focus on Form in Classroom : Second Language Acquisition*, C. Doughty and J. Williams (eds), 15–63. New York: Cambridge University Press.

Lyster, R. 1998a. "Negotiation of form, recasts, and explicit correction in relation to error types and learner repair in immersion classrooms." *Language Learning* 48 (2): 183–218. DOI: 10.1111/1467-9922.00039

Lyster, R. 1998b. "Recasts, repetition, and ambiguity in L2 classroom discourse." *Studies in Second Language Acquisition* 20 (1): 51–81. DOI: 10.1017/S027226319800103X

Lyster, R. 2004. "Differential effects of prompts and recasts in form-focused instruction." *Studies in Second Language Acquisition* 26 (3): 399–432. DOI: 10.1017/S0272263104263021

Lyster, R. and Izquierdo, J. 2009. "Prompts versus recasts in dyadic interaction." *Language Learning* 59 (2): 453–498. DOI: 10.1111/j.1467-9922.2009.00512.x

Lyster, R. and Ranta, L. 1997. "Corrective feedback and learner uptake: Negotiation of form in communicative classrooms." *Studies in Second Language Acquisition* 19 (1): 37–66. DOI: 10.1017/S0272263197001034

Lyster, R. and Saito, K. 2010. "Oral feedback in classroom SLA." *Studies in Second Language Acquisition* 32 (2): 265–302. DOI: 10.1017/S0272263109990520

Mackey, A. 1999. "Input, interaction, and second language development: An empirical study of question formation in ESL." *Studies in Second Language Acquisition* 21 (4): 557–587. DOI: 10.1017/S0272263199004027

Mackey, A. 2006. "Feedback, noticing and instructed second language learning." *Applied Linguistics* 27 (3): 405–430. DOI: 10.1093/applin/ami051

Mackey, A. and Goo, J. 2007. "Interaction research in SLA: A meta-analysis and research synthesis." *Conversational interaction in second language acquisition: A collection of empirical studies*. Oxford: Oxford University Press.

Mackey, A., Oliver, R. and Leeman, J. 2003. "Interactional input and the incorporation of feedback: An exploration of NS–NNS and NNS–NNS adult and child dyads." *Language Learning* 53 (1): 35–66. DOI: 10.1111/1467-9922.00210

Mackey, A. and Philp, J. 1998. "Conversational interaction and second language development: Recasts, responses, and red herrings?" *The Modern Language Journal* 82 (3): 338–356. DOI: 10.1111/j.1540-4781.1998.tb01211.x

McDonough, K. 2005. "Identifying the impact of negative feedback and learners' responses on ESL question development." *Studies in Second Language Acquisition* 27 (01): 79–103. DOI: 10.1017/S0272263105050047

McDonough, K. 2007. "Interactional feedback and the emergence of simple past activity verbs in L2 English." In *Conversational Interaction in Second Language Acquisition*, A. Mackey (ed.), 323–338. Oxford: Oxford University Press.

McDonough, K. and Mackey, A. 2006. "Responses to recasts: Repetitions, primed production, and linguistic development." *Language Learning* 56 (4): 693–720. DOI: 10.1111/j.1467-9922.2006.00393.x

Mifka Profozic, N. 2013. *The Effectiveness of Corrective Feedback and the Role of Individual Differences in Language Learning*. Frankfurt/Main: Peter Lang.

Miller, G.A. and Chapman, J.P. 2001. "Misunderstanding analysis of covariance." *Journal of Abnormal Psychology* 110 (1): 40–48. DOI: 10.1037/0021-843X.110.1.40

Muranoi, H. 2000. "Focus on form through interaction enhancement: Integrating formal instruction into a communicative task in EFL classrooms." *Language Learning* 50 (4): 617–673. DOI: 10.1111/0023-8333.00142

Nelson, K.E. 1987. "Some observations from the perspective of the rare event cognitive comparison theory of language acquisition." In *Children's Language*, Vol. 6, K.E. Nelson and A. Van Kleeck (eds), 289–231. Hillsdale, New Jersey: Lawrence Erlbaum Associates.

Nobuyoshi, J. and Ellis, R. 1993. "Focused communication tasks and second language acquisition." *ELT Journal* 47 (3): 203–210. DOI: 10.1093/elt/47.3.203

Norris, J.M. and Ortega, L. 2000. "Effectiveness of L2 instruction: A research synthesis and quantitative meta-analysis." *Language Learning* 50 (3): 417–528. DOI: 10.1111/0023-8333.00136

Oliver, R. 1995. "Negative feedback in child NS-NNS conversation." *Studies in Second Language Acquisition* 17 (4): 459–481. DOI: 10.1017/S0272263100014418

Oliver, R. 1998. "Negotiation of meaning in child interactions." *The Modern Language Journal* 82 (3): 372–386. DOI: 10.1111/j.1540-4781.1998.tb01215.x

Oliver, R. and Mackey, A. 2003. "Interactional context and feedback in child ESL classrooms." *The Modern Language Journal* 87 (4): 519–533. DOI: 10.1111/1540-4781.00205

Panova, I. and Lyster, R. 2002. "Patterns of corrective feedback and uptake in an adult ESL classroom." *TESOL Quarterly* 36 (4): 573–595. DOI: 10.2307/3588241

Philp, J. 2003. "Constraints on "Noticing the gap": Nonnative speakers' noticing of recasts in NS-NNS interaction." *Studies in Second Language Acquisition* 25 (1): 99–126. DOI: 10.1017/S0272263103000044

Pica, T. 1983. "Methods of morpheme quantification: Their effect on the interpretation of second language data." *Studies in Second Language Acquisition* 6 (01): 69–78. DOI: 10.1017/S0272263100000309

Pica, T. 1991. "Classroom interaction, negotiation, and comprehension: Redefining relationships." *System* 19 (4): 437–452. DOI: 10.1016/0346-251X(91)90024-J

Pica, T. 1994. "Research on negotiation: What does it reveal about second language learning conditions, processes, and outcomes?" *Language Learning* 44 (3): 493–527. DOI: 10.1111/j.1467-1770.1994.tb01115.x

Pica, T., Holliday, L., Lewis, N. and Morgenthaler, L. 1989. "Comprehensible output as an outcome of linguistic demands on the learner." *Studies in Second Language Acquisition* 11 (01): 63–90. DOI: 10.1017/S027226310000783X

Révész, A. and Han, Z. 2006. "Task content familiarity, task type and efficacy of recasts." *Language Awareness* 15 (3): 160–178. DOI: 10.2167/la401.0

Révész, A. 2009. "Task complexity, focus on form, and second language development." *Studies in Second Language Acquisition* 31 (3): 437–470. DOI: 10.1017/S0272263109090366

Révész, A. 2012. "Working memory and the observed effectiveness of recasts on different L2 outcome measures." *Language Learning* 62 (1): 93–132. DOI: 10.1111/j.1467-9922.2011.00690.x

Schachter, J. 1991. "Corrective Feedback in historical perspective." *Second Language Research* 7 (2): 89–102. DOI: 10.1177/026765839100700202

Sheen, Y. 2006. "Exploring the relationship between characteristics of recasts and learner uptake." *Language Teaching Research* 10 (4): 361–392. DOI: 10.1191/1362168806lr203oa

Sheen, Y. 2007. "The effects of corrective feedback, language aptitude, and learner attitude on the acquisition of English articles." In *Conversational Interaction in Second Language Acquisition: A Collection of Empirical Studies*, A. Mackey (ed.), 301–322. Oxford: Oxford University Press.

Sheen, Y. 2008. "Recasts, language anxiety, modified output, and L2 learning." *Language Learning* 58 (4): 835–874.

Shirai, Y. and Andersen, W.A. 1995. "The acquisition of tense-aspect morphology: A prototype account." *Language* 71 (4): 743–762. DOI: 10.2307/415743

Spada, N. and Fröhlich, M. 1995. *COLT. Communicative Orientation of Language Teaching observation Scheme:Coding Conventions and Applications*. Sydney, Australia: National Centre for English Language Teaching and Research.

Talmy, L. 2008. "Aspects of attention in language." In *Handbook of cognitive linguistics and second language acquisition*, P. Robinson and N.C. Ellis (eds), 27–38. London and New York: Routledge.

Vendler, Z. 1967. *Linguistics in Philosophy*. Ithaca, N.Y.: Cornell University Press.

Yang, Y. and Lyster, R. 2010. "Effects of form-focused practice and feedback on Chinese EFL learners' acquisition of regular and irregular past tense forms." *Studies in Second Language Acquisition* 32 (2): 235–263. DOI: 10.1017/S0272263109990519

Appendix

Transcript from the treatment task in the RE group

021 T: quelqu'un d'autre qui voudrait prendre part ? =
022   = dans la troisième image qu'est- ce qu'il y avait ? umm ?
023 L11: ils se sont ils sont arrivés au bord de la lac et umm ils ils *mange/ent* =
024   = ils *mange/ent* le déjeuner   (trigger)
025 T: tu peux les voir manger ? où ils ont déjà fini à manger ?
026 L11: um fini
027 T: alors ils *ont mangé* ?   (*recast*)
028 L11: ils *ont mangé* le déjeuner et umm umm la sœur la sœur a la sœur a la sœur a se =
029   = fait les bronzer
030 T: um elle *se faisait bronzer* ?   (*recast*)
031 L11: elle *se faisait* bronzer oui
032 T: et la mère …… la mère qu'est-ce qu'elle faisait ?
033 L11: elle *a se relaxer/é/ait* –   (trigger)
034 T: oh elle *se relaxait* ?   (*recast*)
035 L11: *se relaxait/é* oui
036 T: et le père ?

Transcript from the same treatment task in the CR group

036 T: et (name) qu'est –ce- qu' il s'est passé plus tard, quand ils sont arrivés à la =
037   = destination ?
038 L35: ils sont arrivés au camping um et ils sont installé la tente et er ils ont garé la voiture=
039   = derrière la tente
040 T: et la mère qu'est-ce qu'elle faisait ?
041 L35: je ne sais peut-être elle préparer/é/ait le dîner
042 T: tu peux la voir ? dans ton image elle préparait le dîner ?
043 L35: non …
044 T: alors qu'est-ce qu'elle faisait ?
045 L21: elle a vu les canards
046 T: bien … et les autres choses ?
047 L21: dans le lac
048 T: et qu'est-ce qu'elle faisait ?
049 L21: elle est ummm les pieds
050 T: où est-ce qu'elle a mis les pieds ?
051 L21: les pieds dans le lac
052 T: uh bien et les deux garçons qu'est-ce qu'ils ont fait ? les deux garçons les deux frères
053 L22: les garçons faisaient … *fait* umm ?   (trigger)

054 T: hein?   (*clarification request*)
055 L22: [giggling]
056 T: pardon, qu'est-ce qu'ils ont fait ? les garçons ?
057 L23: um *fait du feu* ?   (trigger)
058 T: est'ce que tu peux répéter ?   (*clarification request*)
059 L23: les garçons *fait* du feu

Adjectival modification in L2 Spanish Noun Phrases

Pedro Guijarro-Fuentes
Universidad de las Islas Baleares, Spain

The present paper investigates the grammar systems of Chinese learners of Spanish as a second language with the aim of contributing to current debates within contemporary generative second language (L2) acquisition theory: the extent to which adult learners are (un)able to acquire new functional features that result in a L2 grammar that is mentally structured like the native target language has led to recent accounts such as the *Interpretability Hypothesis* (Hawkins & Hattori 2006; Tsimpli & Dimitrakopoulou 2007) excluding L2A of non-L1 uninterpretable features, and more recently the *Feature Reassembly Hypothesis* (Lardiere 2009) claiming that L2 readjustment is an arduous acquisition task for [+/−] interpretable features. In evaluating both hypotheses, this study further explores L2A of uninterpretable and interpretable features by examining the development of certain Spanish features within the DP (i.e., [uGender]; [uNumber] and an interpretable Focus/Contrast feature) by L2 Chinese learners. Results of our two experimental tasks show that parametrically different uninterpretable and interpretable features are not totally accessible to adult L2 learners, but that proficiency level and individual differences figure largely in the implementation of them, causing competence target deviant patterns. Contrary to the *IH*, our results thus show initial underspecification of the [+/−] interpretable features in IL grammars and a gradual process which would first mimic L1-consistency before becoming native-like.

1. Introduction

Current research in L2 parameter re-setting (e.g., White 2003) has led to recent proposals such as the *Interpretability Hypothesis* (Hawkins & Hattori 2006; Tsimpli & Dimitrakopoulou 2007) excluding L2A of non-L1 uninterpretable features, and more recently *Feature Reassembly Hypothesis* (Lardiere 2009) maintaining that L2 readjustment is an arduous acquisition task for [+/−] interpretable features.

Under existing theoretical minimalist proposals (Chomsky 1995, 2007), parametric differences between grammars are connected with properties of the lexicon. The lexicon, for instance, comprises functional categories connected to number (Num), agreement (Agr), tense (T). These functional categories can differ from one language to another as to their configuration of related formal features and feature values. Furthermore, not all formal features have the same status whereby some are uninterpretable and others interpretable. Uninterpretable features have only formal syntactic properties; that is, these features are only relevant to the syntactic component, such as case, whereas interpretable features carry meaning and are also relevant to the semantic component such as specificity.[1] Bearing this in mind, languages can vary (a) as to the functional categories instantiated in their grammar and (b) the features associated with particular functional categories.

As to Second Language (L2) Acquisition, and in particular with regard to the availability of uninterpretable and interpretable features, there is a general consensus, amid researchers accepting in UG-compatible IL grammars, that interpretable features can be part of such developing grammars. However, there is certain disagreement as to whether L2 learners can have access to uninterpretable features; especially when these features have not been activated in the L1. Particularly, the *Interpretability Hypothesis* (IH) (Hawkins & Hattori 2006; Tsimpli & Dimitrakopoulou 2007) points to deficits with the pure uninterpretable features, but not with the interpretable ones. Namely, the IH claims that parameter (re-)setting is restricted to L1 interpretable feature values. Based on assumptions regarding the Critical Period hypothesis, the IH maintains that uninterpretable features such as case or others which may trigger overt and covert movement, are claimed to no longer be available to adults in SLA due to critical period constraints despite access to L2 input/lexicon that clearly exemplifies L2 features. Very simply put, while L1 parametric values associated with the uninterpretable features resist re-setting in L2 acquisition, LF-interpretable features are accessible to the L2 learner, even if L1 and L2 differ from each other and only those features (uninterpretable and interpretable alike) instantiated within the L1 and at most new interpretable features remain accessible to L2 learners. Tsimpli and Dimitrakopoulou (2007) are concerned with the use of the resumptive strategy in *wh-* subject and object extraction by intermediate (n = 21) and advanced (n = 27) Greek learners of English. It is proposed that the acceptability rate of pronouns in the extraction site is conditioned by the Logical Form (LF) interpretability of the features involved in the derivation. Therefore, the interpretable features

---

1. Namely, whereas the uninterpretable features are those whose role is restricted to formal syntactic derivations and possibly have PF-realization but no role at LF, LF-interpretable features have a semantic role.

of animacy and discourse-linking are evaluated as central elements which help the acquisition process in the analysis of English pronouns by Greek L2 learners, while the first language (L1) specification of resumptive pronouns as clusters of uninterpretable Case and Agreement features resists re-setting, and therefore their acquisition. A recent alternative account to the *Interpretability Hypothesis* is the *Feature Reassembly Hypothesis* (Lardiere 2009) that maintains that L2 readjustment is an arduous acquisition task for [+/−] interpretable features. According to Lardiere (2009), the main difficulty that L2 learners face then "[…] lies in assembling just the right combination of features into the right lexical items for each language, and in determining their appropriate conditioning environments for their expression" (p. 215). Such an assembly of features requires features to be checked, and the general learning task would then consist of appropriately reconfiguring or reassembling formal and semantic bundles in the L2 lexicon, and determining the specific conditions under which their properties may or may not be morphophonologically expressed. Thus, in addition to acquiring new features, the adult learner must redeploy the morphological expression of individual features from the way they are employed in the native language. For instance, two pairs of languages can select the same formal features such that a native speaker of language A acquiring language B would not need to 'reset' parameters in the target grammar. However, how a particular feature is assembled and the conditions of its expression in each of the two languages may be quite different.

The present study tests (a) whether uninterpretable features are (un-)problematic in L2 developing grammars and, at the same time, (b) assesses the role of interpretable features in the analysis of L2 properties. Specifically, the study investigates the development of both uninterpretable features (i.e., gender/number determiner-noun concord)[2] and interpretable features (i.e., adjectives can have an Focus/Contrast feature,[3] perhaps due to interface conditions, triggering movement to a FocusP in prenominal position), phenomena that do not exist in L1 (Chinese) language (see more on this in Section 2). This article is organized as follows: in Section 2 the differences between Spanish and Chinese in determiner noun phrases are presented, together with an analysis of the interpretable Focus/Contrast feature within the minimalist framework. An outline of previous L2A is then presented in Section 3, with the aim of formulating predictions of learnability and parameter-resetting. In Sections 4 and 5, the present study and its results

---

2. A note for clarification is in order here: whereas number feature is usually considered an interpretable feature of N's as it contributes to semantic interpretation, it is uninterpretable in D and A (we will come back to this issue in more detail in Section 2).

3. That is, this is an LF interpretable feature that is not realized in all adjectives, and that in turn makes certain adjectives to move; while nouns remain *in situ*.

are discussed; finally, in Section 6, the results of the study are viewed from the minimalist perspective on SLA suggested in Section 2 and in this Introduction.

2. Linguistic background assumptions

2.1 The syntax of gender and number within the DP

In this section, we present a concise description of the structural formal aspects of the Spanish determiner phrase (DP) compared to the structure of the Chinese DP. Spanish, unlike Chinese, has nominal agreement and the different elements of the Spanish DP (i.e. determiners, nouns and adjectives) concord with each other in both gender and number as illustrated in (1):

(1) La niña mexicana juega con
 The.FEM.SING. girl.FEM.SING. mexican.FEM.SING. play.PRES.3SG. with
 los perros.
 the.MASC.PL. dogs.MASC.PL.
 'The Mexican girl plays with the dogs.'

Gender and number in Spanish, masculine or feminine, singular or plural, are both morphologically marked on most nouns (Bernstein 1993; Harris 1991, 1995). As illustrated in (2), there is gender and number agreement of the head noun with all the constituents of the noun phrase including determiners and adjectives, which are also inflected for gender and number.

(2)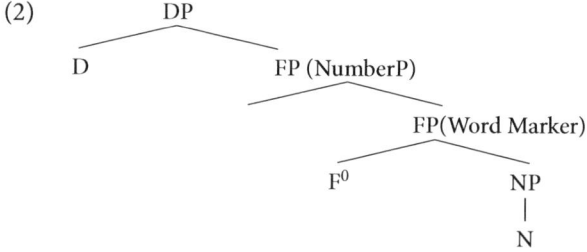

Conversely, Chinese does not possess nominal agreement. Namely, Chinese lacks both grammatical gender and number inflection, although it possesses a plural marker (i.e., -men) (Li 1999) as shown in (3a–b), (4a–b) and (5) respectively. In general, Chinese nouns remain *in situ* within the DP, a point to which we return in greater detail below.

No Gender:
(3) a. *yi-ge   kuailede   nanhai*
       one-CL   happy   boy
    b. *yi-ge   kuailede   nvhai*
       one-CL   happy   girl

No Number:
(4) a. *liang-ge kuailede   nanhai*
       two-CL   happy   boy
    b. *liang-ge kuailede   nvhai*
       two-CL   happy   girl

Possible Plural marker: *-men*
(5) *wo   kanjian   nanhai-men*
    I   see   boy-plural

Within the generative framework adopted in this paper, we adhere to Bernstein's (1993, 2001) analysis according to which the functional categories NumP and WMP (Word Marker Phrase) are located between DP and NP ([DP D [NumP Num [WMP WM [NP N]]]) where formal gender ([masc/fem]) and number ([±plural]) features are checked, valued and deleted. Features in the DP-internal functional categories are responsible for the differences or similarities in nominal word order amongst languages. In Romance languages including Spanish nominal movement (noun raising) is obligatory whereas in other languages, including Chinese, the noun remains *in situ* since there is no feature that attracts the noun to raise. If Number needs to be checked, it does so through AGREE without raising; while such feature checking happens via overt movement in Spanish, presumably due to an additional feature (of the EPP-type) that attracts the noun to raise (what exactly attracts the noun to raise in Spanish is inconsequential for our purposes here). Furthermore, the gender and number features found on nouns in Romance languages are interpretable. In contrast, those found on the articles and adjectives are uninterpretable.[4] The functional categories, NumP and WMP, are found

---

4. A word of clarification is needed here. As pointed out earlier and by one of the reviewers, for which I would like to thank, while grammatical number is obviously interpretable in N, it is quite plausible that grammatical gender may not be interpretable in the lexical N category (except for animate nouns). Nevertheless, Picallo (2008) amongst others puts forward that Gender is a formal exponent of an interpretable functional feature associated to classes and categorization. The same features, Num and G in A and D are by default uninterpretable. Following Chomsky (1995), they are deleted by Agree, after raising, in languages like Spanish, However, in recent linguistic analyses (Pesetsky & Torrego 2007, for instance), it is claimed that D and A have unvalued features, and they are part of a Probe that seeks for a Goal (the N) in order to be valued. Once valued, they must be deleted (interpretability and valuation are not always

between DP and NP. In languages like Spanish, the noun overtly raises to WMP to check its gender features and then to NumP to check its number features, yielding the commonly observed article-noun-adjective word order (Carstens 1991; Zagona 2002). In the derivation, uninterpretable gender and number features found on the article and adjective in Spanish are valued and deleted by the noun (and its interpretable features) in NumP (Carstens 2000) as shown in the structure in (6).

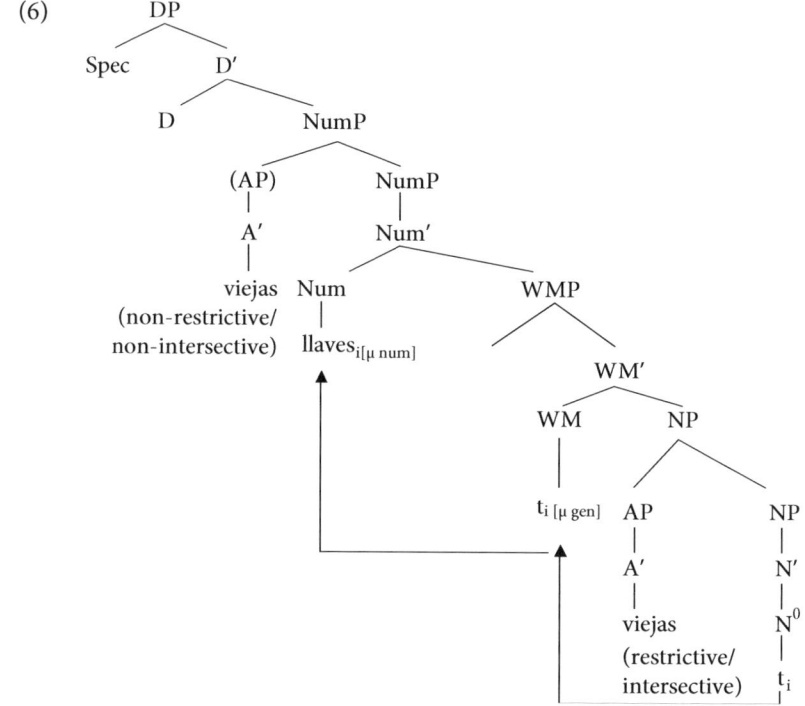

Following the DP structure for Chinese proposed by Pan and Hu (2003), there is a separation of classifier (ClP) and numerals (QP) in Chinese as shown in (7). The classifier phrase is very important in the language because it is always present in

---

totally correlated, but we leave this issue aside). Now, it should be noted that the i(nterpretable) feature Focus in A is located in a Goal which moves (perhaps) to value this feature; why does it move, and why optionally? As stipulated in the main text, the functional head attracting [focus] is optionally associated with an EPP feature. On the other hand, u(ninteptretable) features in A and D are Probe features. Considering this asymmetry among features in SLA, according to the *Interpretability Hypothesis* (IH) (Hawkins & Hattori 2006; Tsimpli & Dimitrakopoulou 2007), the *u*-features are more difficult to acquire. If, for instance, this is interpreted as referring to features in N, the IH would consequently predict that number is acquired faster than gender as the results from the present study suggest.

NPs except for bare NPs such as: *zuozhi* 'table', *shu* 'book' or demonstrative NPs, *zhe xie shu* 'these books'.

(7)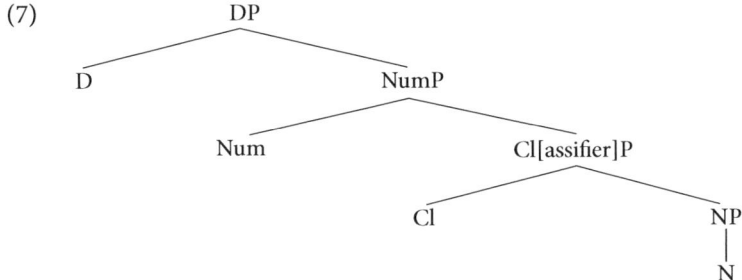

Our next task is to describe the ordering of nouns and adjectives. In particular, we describe different adjectival ordering restrictions depending on their semantics.

2.2 Adjectival ordering semantic restrictions

Although (adjectival) semantic interpretation is universal, languages vary syntactically in the way they calculate semantics. In this paper, we focus primarily on the category of *qualitative* adjectives (i.e., adjectives which specify a quality or property of a noun) which show different semantic construals with respect to whether they can appear in prenominal or postnominal positions as shown in (8a–b).

(8) a. una atractiva bailarina
'an attractive dancer (i.e., non-intersective/non-restrictive preferred: attractive as a dancer)'
b. una bailarina atractiva
'an attractive dancer (i.e., only intersective/restrictive: attractive person)'

We follow Demonte (1999, 2008) who claimed that specifically for prenominal adjectives a Focus/Contrast Interpretable Feature is responsible for the movement of the adjective to a prenominal position in Spanish. Demonte's analysis further induces the placement of the adjectives in terms of the existence of some extra functional categories besides the NP and the DP, that is, [nP] and [FocP] which will be positioned above the [nP] as the structure in (9) (which corresponds to (8a) above):

(9)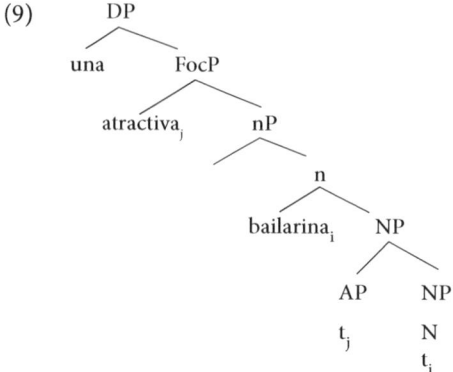

In Spanish N raises to NumP, so that any prenominal adjective must be non-intersective/non-restrictive, and any postnominal adjective must be intersective/restrictive (see Demonte 1999, 2008). Thus, in Spanish the syntactic position of the adjectives are conditioned by their Focus/Contrast interpretable feature. Namely, the semantic interpretations illustrated in examples (8) above are associated with two syntactic structures: (a) adjectives with a non-restrictive interpretation (that is, they refer to the whole set of properties on noun) occupy a prenominal position; (b) adjectives with a restrictive interpretation (that is, they refer to a subset of a class of objects denoted by the noun) tend to appear postnominally. Qualitative adjectives, both restrictive and non-restrictive, can also appear preceding the noun, in a focus position, if they receive a contrastive interpretation (fully fledged details of Demonte's analysis remain outside the scope of the present research and do not come to bear on what we investigate herein). There is, however, another large set of certain lexical categories of which are incompatible with this interpretable Focus/Contrast feature. For instance, adjectives such as *temporal modifiers, nationality, shape, colour, origin* or *relational* adjectives as shown in (10) do not bear an interpretable Focus/Contrast feature and that is why they are only allowed in one fixed syntactic position.

(10) a. *La mera necesidad*
'The mere necessity'
b. **La necesidad mera*
'The mere necessity'
c. *Las cortinas italianas*
'The Italian curtains'
d. **Las italianas cortinas*
'The Italian curtains'

In contrast, Chinese, exhibits covert movement at Logical Form (LF) only and adjectives can occur in between numerals and classifiers, as shown in (11a) or next to NP, as shown in (11b), but do not convey similar semantics as the one found in pre- and post-nominal adjectives in Spanish (i.e., taking the English equivalent 'a big book' is ambiguous because *big* can be underlyingly related either to the position in NumP (see (6) above) (which is taken as non-intersective/non-restrictive) or to the position in nP (see (9) above) (which is taken as intersective/restrictive)).

(11) a. yi da ben shu
      one big CL book
      'a big book'
   b. yi ben da shu
      one CL big book
      'a big book'

In sum, Spanish and Chinese differ with respect to the position attributive and other adjectives occupy and the meaning they express via the syntactic position. The two languages exhibit important parametric differences related to noun-movement, presumably because of differences (or lack thereof) in strength of Number feature. Table 1 summarizes the aspects of the nominal system that will need to be learned by Chinese learners of L2 Spanish.

Table 1. Spanish and Chinese noun phrases: parametric features

	Spanish	Chinese
Overt gender on the noun (interpretable gender features)	+	–
Overt number on the noun (interpretable number features)	+	–
Overt gender concord on the adjective (uninterpretable [*u*gender] features)	+	–
Overt number concord on the adjective (uninterpretable [*u*number] features)	+	–
Pre-nominal adjectives (via no movement in Chinese; n-movement in Spanish due to an interpretable Focus/Contrast feature)	+	+
Post-nominal adjectives (instantiation of WMP/NumP and obligatory noun raising in Spanish only)	+	–

3. Previous L2A studies[5]

In the nominal domain, evidence for underspecified representations has come, among others, from Hawkins (1998, 2001), Franceschina (2001, 2005) and Hawkins and Franceschina (2004) claiming that the mental representation of grammatical gender for L1 English adult learners of Spanish is necessarily different from that of native Spanish speakers. That is, such evidence is interpreted by them as *prima facie* support for the notion that L1/L2 disparities result from differences in accessibility to representation resources after a Critical Period failure of uninterpretable features, which is to say, learners of L2 after the Critical Period have more difficulties assigning gender to adjectives than to determiners. In contrast, others (e.g., Bruhn de Garavito & White 2002; Fernández 1999; White, Valenzuela, Koslowska-McGregor & Leung 2004; and Judy, Guijarro-Fuentes & Rothman 2008[6] amongst many others) questioned whether features absent from the first language (L1) are indeed not accessible in SLA. For instance, Fernández (1999) demonstrates that L2 learners have less difficulty with gender assignment with determiners than they do with adjectives. Bruhn de Garavito and White (2002) tested the acquisition of grammatical gender in French L2 learners of Spanish and were able to show that intermediate French learners had difficulty in assigning gender, especially to adjectives (less so with determiners), similar to Fernández's data for English L2 Spanish. However, they established that this difficulty virtually disappears by the advanced stages. White, Valenzuela, Kozlowska-Macgregor, and Leung (2004) also focused on gender and noun phrase (NP) ellipsis in Spanish and demonstrated that grammatical gender is acquired in L2 acquisition. Judy, Guijarro-Fuentes and Rothman (2008) recently reported on data which also prove that while the intermediate learners show native-like tendencies, adult English learners of L2 Spanish obtain a native-like command of gender and number as well as full knowledge of the semantics of adjective placement by the advanced proficiency level. They concluded that their main findings provide evidence contra IH hypothesis.

When it comes to the L2A research of noun placement with respect to adjectives within the generative grammar, it has attracted less attention. Although leaving aside semantic restrictions related to adjective placement, Gess and Herschensohn, (2001) and Parodi, Schwartz and Clahsen (2004) focus on the L2

---

5. Space limitations prevent us from going into more detail with each of the studies outlined in this section. However, interested readers are referred to them for more information.

6. Against one of the reviewers' requests, we are prevented to go into a more detailed treatment of this particular study whose results seem to be very similar to those of the present paper. We encourage the readers to review that study in detail.

acquisition of French by English-native speakers and on the L2 acquisition of German by Korean, Turkish, Italian and Spanish respectively. Both studies reported that target like order can be attained, with a potential L1 transfer effect at the start of the learning process. However, there are other studies conducted by Anderson (2001, 2007a,b, 2008) and Rothman, Judy, Guijarro-Fuentes and Pires (2010) respectively which specifically address the acquisition of semantic restrictions related to adjective placement. These studies on prenominal versus postnominal adjective noun placement showed that target knowledge of semantic consequences of adjective placement in French and in Spanish by L2 English non-native speakers can be attained. For instance, Rothman et al. (2010) investigated English-speaking intermediate (n = 21) and advanced (n = 24) learners of Spanish, as compared to a native-speaker control group (n = 15). Results of several elicited semantic production tasks show mixed results: whereas in some of the tasks the intermediate L2 learners appear to have acquired the syntactic properties of the Spanish determiner phrase; in other tasks, they showed some delay with respect to the semantic constraints of prenominal and postnominal adjectives. Crucially, however, the authors took their data as an indication of full convergence by all advanced learners and thus provide evidence in contra the predictions of representational syntactic deficit accounts (e.g., Hawkins & Franceschina 2004; Hawkins & Hattori 2006).

3.1 The task of the L2 learner: Hypotheses and predictions

In light of our linguistic background assumptions and some of the current L2 acquisition hypotheses, Chinese L2 learners of Spanish must learn that: (a) adjectives in Spanish can be either pre- or postnominal (which ultimately requires the acquisition of a new interpretable Focus/Contrast feature); (b) all nouns have grammatical gender and number features; and (c) there is number and gender agreement between nouns, determiners and adjectives (which requires the acquisition of new uninterpretable features, i.e., [uGender] and [uNumber]).

In particular, what L2 learners of Spanish need to acquire is: (i) the fact that Spanish has both grammatical gender and number (Chinese entirely lacks grammatical gender and number features and the functional category where they are checked). Essentially, Chinese speakers need to acquire the morpho-syntactic gender distinction of Spanish (namely, WMP where gender features are checked). However, Chinese speakers already have an agreement-like system in their classifier system. Therefore, their task may consist of changing from a classifier-mapping system to a gender-mapping system (instead of acquiring a feature-distinction system altogether). Even though Chinese lacks number features on Adjectives and NPs, speakers make a limited type of (interpretable) number distinction in the DP with numerals and definite demonstratives. Their task in learning Spanish is then to generalize the number marking to all NPs. (ii) the order of the noun and modifier(s), which syntactically varies in Spanish compared to Chinese (namely, the independent (interpretable) features associated with WMP and NumP that require raising in order to converge on the target syntax of the Spanish DP). Recall that there is no noun raising in Chinese, which thus accounts for its stringent determiner-adjective-noun word order. Crucially, Chinese speakers need to learn that gender and number features (on higher Agreement Projections, e.g. NumP) trigger obligatory N raising, yielding the order N-Adj that characterizes the intersective/restrictive interpretation.

This study thus attempts to test the following research questions and predictions:

i. Can native speakers of Chinese acquire new functional categories and associated (interpretable and uninterpretable) features such that they obligatorily raise nouns in L2 Spanish? According to the IH, the uninterpretable features are predicted to be problematic in L2 acquisition, but not the interpretable ones; even though the latter features may have not been activated in the L1. Their availability can be attained via access to interpretable features in general and be part of such developing grammar systems. L2 Chinese learners could show optionality/variability. According to the FRH, acquisition of interpretable and uninterpretable features should be possible, albeit they may be represented differently in both language grammars. Chinese learners of Spanish would need to tease apart the relevant features from the way they are employed in their L1, and re-employ them as required by the L2 (see above). This would involve processing the L2 input, identifying relevant features and reassembling these features from the way they are conditioned and realized in L1 Chinese to that of L2 Spanish. A further prediction made by the *Interpretability Hypothesis* concerns the developmental process. Although L1 transfer effects are expected at all stages of L2 acquisition, development is expected even in syntactic phenomena that involve formal uninterpretable features, thus:

ii. Are there group and individual differences among the L2 learners with different proficiency levels and with respect to the native speakers?

4. The study

Against this background, the current study sought to further discover if data from Chinese learners of Spanish could shed light on the investigation of interpretable and uninterpretable features in SLA and, more specifically, the acquisition of [*u*Gender], [*u*Number] together with an interpretable Focus/Contrast feature, serving as a testing ground of the different aforementioned hypotheses outlined.

4.1 Participants

The data for this study come from two groups of participants: a control group of 12 native speakers (NS) of Spanish whose ages ranged from 27 to 46 years, all from Spain; and a group of 32 Chinese learners of Spanish. All participants – natives and non-natives – completed one placement test in Spanish, which consisted of the vocabulary and cloze sections of a standardized Spanish proficiency test (*Oxford placement tests*) (Allan 2004). For the L2 learners, this was to determine their level of proficiency. Based on the results from the placement test, the L2 learners were divided into two proficiency levels, advanced and intermediate (see Table 2). The groups were divided according to their composite score.

Additionally, each participant completed a background questionnaire that sought information concerning their mother tongue, languages spoken and the frequency with which each language is spoken, age of first exposure to each

Table 2. Results from the placement test[7]

		Composite score (N = 50)
Spanish L1 controls [N = 12]	Mean	48.92
	SD	1.16
	Range	47–50
L2 Spanish Advanced [N = 12]	Mean	44.48
	SD	2.29
	Range	39–48
L2Spanish intermediate [N = 20]	Mean	32.08
	SD	3.32
	Range	26–37

---

7. As pointed out by one of the reviewers, the results and findings from the present study need to be taken with caution given the number of participants in the advanced and control groups. To that end, we are in the process of recruiting more participants, and collect more data, so that the statistical results become more reliable.

language, and any visit to countries where the language is spoken. The advanced speaker group (AS) consisted of 12 participants that had studied Spanish at the university level for a minimum of 5 years (7 years minimum of formal instruction including from high school to university) and had also had a period of study abroad in a Spanish-speaking country. Their ages ranged from 21–31. Lastly, the intermediate speaker group (IS) consisted of 20 undergraduate students that had completed the General Education program requirements (which consist of a series of four university-level modules) at Sichuan International Studies University (China). The age range for this group was 19–23. All non-natives were instructed learners of Spanish at the time of testing.

4.2 Methodology

Besides the linguistic background questionnaire and the proficiency test, all participants completed two linguistic tasks: a Grammaticality Judgment/Correction Task (GJCT) and a Context-based Collocation Task (CBCT).[8] The GJCT tested for knowledge of gender and number agreement between determiners and nouns and nouns and adjectives together with noun placement with respect to adjectives where the interpretable feature Focus/Contrast is absent as examples (10) above. Chinese lacks features of agreement of gender and number, although it does have classifiers for nouns, which may sensitize learners to the possibility of nouns having particular intrinsic distinctive features. The purpose of the CBCT was to specifically test for semantic restrictions of adjectives which are equipped with an interpretable Focus/Contrast feature which triggers movement to a prenominal position. Chinese also lacks this feature, with adjectives in the determiner phrase always being pre-nominal. It should be noted that vocabulary was controlled for and there was no time limit. Participants were also instructed to ask the investigator if the instructions or vocabulary were unclear. This was done in an attempt to reduce error based on misunderstanding. Given space limitations, we only provide examples of and report data on the relevant empirical sentence types, that is to say, not the fillers.

4.2.1 *Grammaticality Judgment/Correction (GJCT)*
The GJCT was made of a total of 80 items. Tokens containing ungrammatical determiner-noun gender agreement (n = 5) and ungrammatical determiner-noun

---

[8] A future study could include a production task which could test the acquisition of agreement in the DP dependency. We would like to thank to one of the reviewers for such valuable and useful suggestion for the future.

number agreement (n = 5) were counterbalanced by tokens containing grammatical determiner-noun gender and number agreement (n = 5 each). Tokens containing ungrammatical noun-adjective gender agreement (n = 5) and ungrammatical noun-adjective number agreement (n = 5) were counterbalanced by grammatical noun-adjective gender and number agreement (n = 5 each). It is important to note that the number of feminine vs. masculine and singular vs. plural tokens was controlled for across all item types. Ungrammatical prenominal (n = 5) and postnominal adjective tokens (n = 5) were counterbalanced by grammatical prenominal and postnominal adjective tokens (n = 5 each). Finally, fillers (n = 20) were included to disguise the purpose of the task. Participants were instructed to read each sentence and correct it if they judged it to be ungrammatical (see examples (12a–b) below[9]). Instructions to follow for this task were given in both Spanish and Chinese.

(12) **Knowledge of gender and number agreement**
　a.　*Iván necesita lavar   el   ropa.
　　　Iván   needs to wash the.MASC.SING. clothes.FEM.SING.
　　　(*ungrammatical Det-Noun gender agreement*)
　　　'Iván needs to wash the clothes.'
　b.　*Mis tíos   de Los Ángeles son famosas.[10]
　　　My uncles.MASC.PL. from L.A.   are famous.FEM.PL.
　　　(*ungrammatical Noun-Adj gender agreement – long distance*)
　　　'My uncles from L.A. are famous.'

As said previously, this task also tested for knowledge of syntactic positions of Spanish adjectives (e.g., *nationality, colour, origin* and so on) which lack an interpretable Focus/Contrast feature. Examples (13a) and (13b) are examples of grammatical prenominal and postnominal adjectives, respectively. Example (13c) is an example of an ungrammatical prenominal adjective. The noun and the adjective should be inverted. The adjectives used in this portion of the GJCT were of the

---

9. In describing both linguistic tasks, space limitations restrict ourselves from presenting the whole set of tokens.

10. Even though we agree with one of the reviewers that kinship names refer to a set formed by two members (one masculine and one feminine), we believe that the use of *tíos* 'uncles' in this item without being embedded in a context would not force the induction that the predicate *famosas* 'famous' is ungrammatical since the item is designed as such for the participant to focus on the formal features of gender at long distance and not on the semantic feature.

type that are strictly prenominal or strictly postnominal, corresponding to the types of adjectives exemplified in (10) of Section 2.2.[11]

(13) **Knowledge of syntactic placement of adjectives**
   a. *La policía está investigando el supuesto asesinato.*
      (*grammatical prenominal adjective*)
      'The police are investigating the alleged assassination.'
   b. *Quiero comprar los pantalones azules.*
      (*grammatical postnominal adjective*)
      'I want to buy the blue pants.'
   c. **Ellos compraron una japonesa mesa.*
      (*ungrammatical postnominal adjective in prenominal position*)
      *'They bought a Japanese table.'

4.2.2 *Context-based Collocation Task (CBCT)*

This second task was designed to examine if the L2 participant groups could accurately produce pre- and postnominal adjectives based on how adjectival meaning interacts with the noun in a particular given linguistic context. Particularly, this task tested whether or not participants prefer the overt syntactic position for the adjective that was compatible with the meaning the adjective would have over the head noun (intersective/restrictive vs. non-intersective/non-restrictive semantic interpretations). If so, this would inform us that noun-raising is obligatory in their Spanish grammar respectively and that further movement of the adjective (to get high attachment) has to take place in the case they attain the interpretable Focus/Contrast feature. The task was made up of 20 items in total and participants were confronted with a short linguistic context in Spanish and asked to write the adjective found in bold at the end of the sentence in either a pre- or postnominal blank. In the instructions given in the two languages, however, it also was indicated that participants were permitted to write the adjective in both spaces if they thought both choices were equally possible or they could leave it blank if they had no intuitions. All adjectives included in this task could be either pre-nominal or post-nominal. Hence, the collocation depended directly and entirely on the linguistic context.[12] In addition to 10 fillers testing other unrelated

---

11. On request by one of the reviewers, here is a list of adjectives included in this task: *mero* 'mere', *supuesto* 'alleged', *italiano* 'Italian', *japonés* 'Japanese', *azul* 'blue'.

12. That is, only adjectives that clearly maintain the same referential meaning irrespective of whether they appear pre- or postnominally were included. Alternating the syntactic position of such adjectives only restricts the set the DP refers to: namely, whether or not the adjective must refer to the noun head as a subset of all possible members of the set referred to by the noun (restrictive reading) or if it must be interpreted as pertaining to all possible members

phenomenon, there were five prenominal items and five postnominal items. The context in example (14) calls for a prenominal adjective whereas that of example (15) calls for a postnominal adjective.

(14) **Prenominal Adjective (non-intersective/non-restrictive interpretation)**
En general, la dinastía Ming era una de las más fuertes y exitosas en la historia del mundo. Los aventureros Ming _____ conquistaron muchas tierras.
(*aventurero*)
'In general, the Ming dynasty was one of the strongest and most successful dynasties in the history of the world. The adventurous Ming conquered many lands.'

(15) **Postnominal Adjective (intersective/restrictive interpretation)**
No todo chico en mi escuela es atlético, pero los _____ chicos fuertes corren 7 millas cada día. (*fuerte*)
'Not every boy at my school is athletic, but the athletic boys run 7 miles each day.'

5. Results: Group and individuals

The results of the experiments and the statistical analyses are presented below. Each of the analyses compares the performance of the participant groups presented above using a mixed-model ANOVA. Bonferroni post-hoc tests were conducted when necessary and all analyses used a significance level of $\alpha = 0.05$. For statistical purposes in both tasks, we assessed the number of correct responses by the L2 learners against the average number of answers provided by the native speaker groups (which for each paradigm showed agreement of 93% or higher) which was in line with our expectations. Any deviation from the average native control groups' answers was counted as incorrect.

5.1 Grammaticality Judgement Test

The first part of the GJCT examined the acquisition of L2 gender features, which are uninterpretable on determiners and adjectives and interpretable on nouns. Figure 1 below displays the average number of tokens accepted (n = 10) by

---

of the nominal set (non-restrictive reading). Here is a list of adjectives included in the tasks: *apasionado* 'impassioned', *aventurero* 'adventurous', *deshonesto* 'dishonest', *estudioso* 'studious', *fuerte* 'strong', *honesto* 'honest', *inteligente* 'intelligent', *influyente* 'influential', *orgulloso* 'proud' and *valiente* 'brave'.

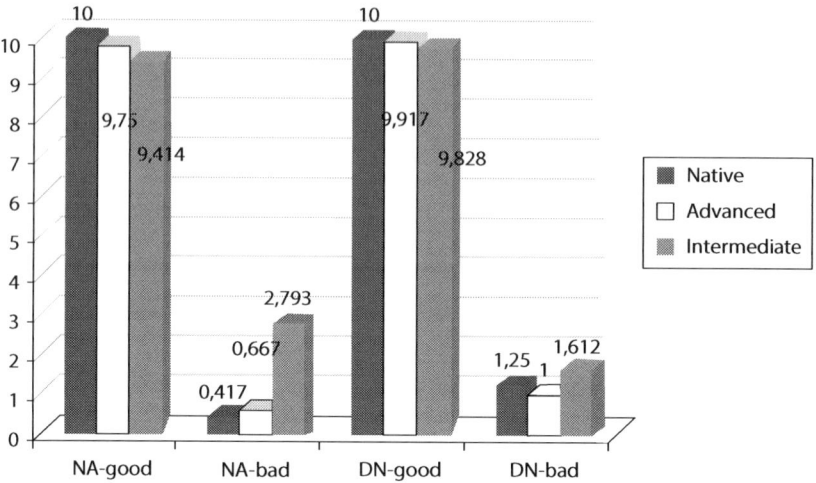

Note here and elsewhere below: NA-good = grammatical noun-adjective agreement;
NA-bad = ungrammatical noun-adjective agreement;
DN-good = grammatical determiner-noun agreement;
DN-bad = ungrammatical determiner-noun agreement.
The scale on the y-axis corresponds to the absolute number of tokens.

Figure 1. GJCT results (average group acceptance): gender/number features

each of the three groups for the following types of sentences (see Section 4.2.1 for examples): (a) grammatical noun-adjective agreement, (b) ungrammatical noun-adjective agreement, (c) grammatical determiner-noun agreement and (d) ungrammatical determiner-noun agreement. In this part of the GJCT, agreement with either pre- or postnominal adjectives was not tested in order to avoid any confoundedness as to know whether the participants were judging the items considering the agreement and/or the collocation.

As can be seen, the Spanish controls performed as expected, accepting all sentences in the grammatical conditions and rejecting sentences in the ungrammatical conditions. On the other hand, the Advanced (AS) group performed very similarly to the NS group with all four token types, distinguishing between the four different conditions. The same goes for the Intermediate (IS) group performance with respect to the grammatical tokens; nevertheless, the IS group accepted more ungrammatical noun-adjective tokens (2.793) and more ungrammatical determiner-noun tokens (1.621) than any of the other groups. In actual fact, the IS group accepted more tokens, whether grammatical or ungrammatical, than the AS group and the NS group did on average, showing certain degree of uncertainty, but at the same time a degree of gradual acquisition which would partly support some of the predictions made by some current L2 accounts (more on this

Table 3. GJCT (intergroup comparison)

	NA-good			NA-bad			DN-good			DN-bad		
	T	P	df	T	P	df	T	P	df	T	P	df
ANOVA	4.11	0.022	2	8.98	<0.001	2	0.73	0.485	2	0.78	0.463	2
NS vs. AS	1.91	0.082	0.452	0.68	0.501	21	*	*	*	*	*	*
NS vs. IS	4.05	<0.001	0.78	4.66	<0.001	37	*	*	*	*	*	*
AS vs. IS	1.72	0.094	34	3.96	<0.001	38	*	*	*	*	*	*

in the discussion section). Nevertheless, in order to determine if these differences were significant, further statistical analyses were conducted. Firstly, a one-way ANOVA that compared all three groups to each other was carried out. In the case of Noun-Adjective agreement, a statistically significant difference was found. Therefore, a two-sample t-test was conducted to pin down where the differences were. As can be seen from Table 3, upon comparing the AS group to the NS group, it was found that the AS group did not differ statistically from the NS group. However, the IS group results were statistically significantly different from the NS group in regard to the grammatical and ungrammatical noun-adjective items. The IS group also differed significantly from the AS group in regards to the ungrammatical noun-adjective tokens.

The second part of the GJCT tested for knowledge of fixed syntactic positions of Spanish adjectives (e.g., origin, colour and relational adjectives (see examples in (10)) that lack the interpretable Focus/Contrast feature. Recall that while there is only one fixed position for adjectives in Chinese (prenominal), adjectives in Spanish can be either prenominal or postnominal depending on their type (see Section 2.1, examples in (10)). Figure 2 below shows the average number of tokens accepted (n = 5) by the three groups for the following sentence types: (a) grammatical prenominal adjectives, (b) ungrammatical prenominal adjectives, (c) grammatical postnominal adjectives and (d) ungrammatical postnominal adjectives (see examples in (13) above).

Recall that the occurrence of any non-*qualitative* adjective is syntactically fixed: namely, for these adjectives a prenominal/postnominal position was deemed either grammatical or ungrammatical in Spanish. Figure 2 shows that the NS group distinguished between the grammatical and ungrammatical items. This can be seen by their high group average of acceptance for the grammatical tokens (4.917 for both pre- and postnominal position) and their very low group average of acceptance for the ungrammatical ones. We can safely say that the Spanish control group performed as expected in all items. Turning to the learners, we can observe that they gave different patterns of answers depending on their level of proficiency: whereas the Advanced (AS) also discriminated between the two to a

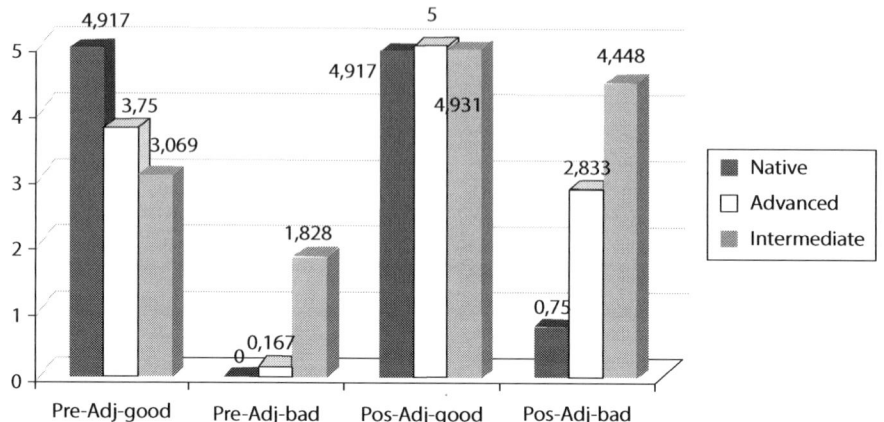

Note here and elsewhere: PreAdj-good = grammatical prenominal adjective;
PreAdj-bad = ungrammatical prenominal adjective;
PosAdj-good = grammatical postnominal adjective;
PosAdj-bad = ungrammatical postnominal adjective.
The scale on the y-axis corresponds to the absolute number of tokens.

Figure 2. GJCT results (average group acceptance): adjective placement

slightly lesser extent, the Intermediate (IS) group made virtually no distinction between grammatical and ungrammatical prenominal and postnominal adjectives. On the whole, learners are deemed to have a weaker judgment and variability is obtained again, and it is not always because of the L1. A certain gradual development can be detected moving towards the target pattern being the AS who performed more like the control group. To determine if the apparent differences were in fact significant, the same battery of statistical analyses discussed above were carried out. The one-way ANOVA showed that there were in fact statistically significant differences among the three groups. Thus, a two-sample t-test was conducted to determine where the differences were (see Table 4). The results of this test showed that the AS group performance differed from that of the NS group

Table 4. GJCT (intergroup comparison)

	PreAdj-good			PreAdj-bad			PosAdj-good			PosAdj-bad		
	T	P	df	T	P	df	T	P	df	T	P	df
ANOVA	7.67	0.001	2	13.97	<0.001	2	0.46	0.632	2	41.75	<0.001	2
NS v. AS	2.78	0.018	11	1.48	0.166	0.389	*	*	*	3.79	0.002	14
NS v. IS	5.98	<0.001	32	6.22	<0.001	1.583	*	*	*	12.63	<0.001	28
AS v. IS	1.34	0.192	23	5.28	<0.001	34	*	*	*	2.98	0.010	14

Table 5. GJCT (intragroup comparison)

	NA-good vs. NA-bad		DN-good vs. DN-bad		PreAdj-good vs. PreAdj bad		PosAdj-good vs. PosAdj-bad	
	T	P	T	P	T	P	T	P
NS	41.87	< 0.001	26.63	< 0.001	59.00	< 0.001	15.40	< 0.001
AS	22.82	< 0.001	38.95	< 0.001	8.25	< 0.001	4.29	0.001
IS	14.19	< 0.001	20.30	< 0.001	3.55	0.001	2.39	0.024

for two item types: grammatical prenominal adjectives and ungrammatical postnominal adjectives. Statistically significant differences were also found between the NS group and the IS group in all three categories in question.

While some of the AS and IS group averages were similar to those of the NS group, it was crucial to determine if the L2 learner groups differentiated between grammatical and ungrammatical tokens. This was done by comparing the average number of tokens accepted for each of two corresponding structures for all three groups. For example, the average number of grammatical noun-adjective tokens accepted by the AS group was compared to the average number of ungrammatical noun-adjective tokens accepted by the AS group to determine if the AS group differentiated between grammatical and ungrammatical gender on adjectives. A paired t-test was used to determine this. All three groups differentiated between the grammatical and ungrammatical structures in Task 1 as shown in Table 5.

Lastly, we calculated the number of participants and the conditions in which they performed above chance level in each group, as shown in Table 6. Following our calculation method, we found that all but one Spanish native performed as expected in all categories. The two L2 groups displayed interesting individual behaviours: some, but not all L2 learners' data reveal that they clearly demonstrate a trend towards native-like performance. That is, despite the difficulty of acquiring certain features, native-like grammars may be reached after having been exposed to the language for a considerable amount of time.

Table 6. GJCT – individual results

	NA-good (> 5)	NA-bad (< 5)	DN-good (> 5)	DN-bad (< 5)	Pre-Adj-good (> 2.5)	Pre-Adj-bad (< 2.5)	Pos-Adj-good (> 2.5)	Pos-Adj-bad (< 2.5)
NSSp (N = 12)	11	0	11	0	11	11	11	11
AdvL2Chinese (N = 12)	9	0	9	0	9	9	9	9
IntL2Chinese (N = 20)	9	0	9	0	6	6	9	9

5.2 Collocation based context task (CBCT)

The second task tested for knowledge of the adjectival ordering restrictions, by focusing exclusively on the semantic of *qualitative* adjectives which are equipped with an interpretable Focus/Contrast feature which triggers movement to a prenominal position by means of a production task. Figure 3 below displays the average number of correct collocations (n = 5) by each of the three groups for two types of sentences: (a) sentences that require a prenominal adjective and (b) sentences that require a postnominal adjective (see examples provided in Section 4.2.2).

As can be seen from Figure 3, the Spanish controls performed as expected. The mean answers are at least 3.083 and 4.833 out of 5 respectively. The AS groups also show evidence of having attained the target interpretable Focus/Contrast feature, approaching native-like performance. Less clear evidence of acquisition of the interpretable Focus/Contrast feature can be observed with the IS data group. On the whole, the IS and AS learners performed similarly in the sense that they performed much worse than the native speaker group, there being a main effect for language at a level of significance of p = .002, but there is also a main effect for adjectival position with post-positioned adjectives being the preferred option than pre-positioned adjectives $F(1, 26) = 52.7$, $p < .001$ for both groups, indicating they have failed to attain the very much needed interpretable Focus/Contrast feature, which triggers *qualitative* adjectives to a prenominal position. Particularly, the AS group average number of correct collocations is very similar to that of the NS group for both prenominal and postnominal adjectives (3.0 and 4.5 out of 5

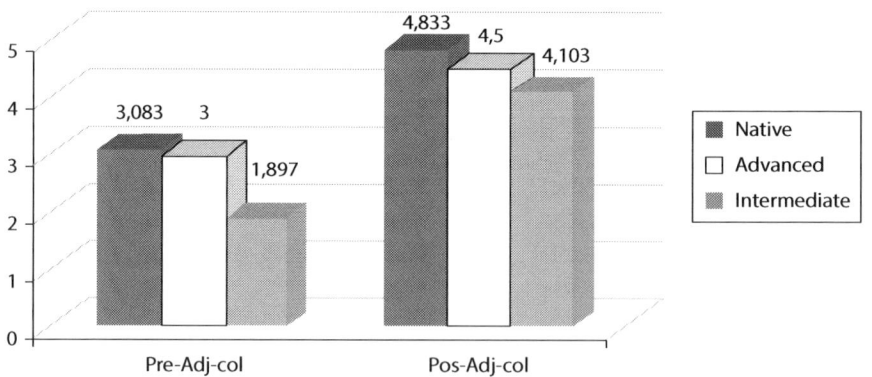

Note here and elsewhere: PreAdj-Col = grammatical prenominal adjective; PosAdj-Col = grammatical postnominal adjective.
The scale on the y-axis corresponds to the absolute number of tokens.

Figure 3. CBCT results (average group acceptance)

Table 7. CBCT (intergroup comparison)

	PreAdj-Col			PosAdj-Col		
	T	P	df	T	P	df
ANOVA	8.36	0.001	2	1.91	0.159	2
NS vs. AS	0.19	0.850	16	*	*	*
NS vs. IS	4.48	< 0.001	29	*	*	*
AS vs. IS	2.57	0.021	15	*	*	*

Table 8. CBCT (intragroup comparison)

	PreAdj-Col vs. PosAdj-Col	
	T	P
NS	8.04	< 0.001
AS	4.78	0.001
IS	8.07	< 0.001

respectively). However, the IS group average number of correct collocations was similar to the NS group for postnominal adjectives only (4.103). The IS group average number of correct collocations is below that of both AS and NS groups for prenominal adjectives (1.897). In order to determine if either the AS group or the IS group performed in a native-like manner, two additional statistical analyses were conducted. A one-way ANOVA was computed to compare all three groups to each other (see Table 7). The results of this test showed that there was a statistically significant difference among the groups with regard to the prenominal adjective tokens only. Therefore, a two-sample t-test was conducted to determine among which groups these differences were. The two-sample t-test revealed that the IS group differed statistically from the NS and AS groups. No statistically significant differences were found between the performance of the NS group and the AS group.

A paired t-test revealed that there was a statistically significant difference in the number of correct collocations for each of the three groups. This result was expected and is due to the significantly higher number of correct postnominal collocations as compared to the number of correct prenominal collocations for all participants (see Table 8).

In order to compute individual results, we calculated the number of participants and the conditions in which they performed above chance level in each group as we did for the GJCT. The individual results confirm the group results

Table 9. CBCT – Individual results

	PreAdj-Col (> 2.5)	PosAdj-Col (> 2.5)
NSSp (N = 12)	8	10
AdvL2Chinese (N = 12)	7	8
IntL2Chinese (N = 20)	11	13

reported earlier. Interestingly, there are some Chinese speakers who do as well as native speakers (see respondents in Table 9).

In sum, when the data from the *Grammaticality Judgment/Correction task (GJCT)* and the *Collocation Based Context task* (CBCT) are examined together, there appears to be a trend that indicates that the advanced learners perform according to what the norm in Spanish is. However, the representations that give rise to target-like outputs might be qualitatively different of those of the native speakers of the target language. In the next section, we discuss what these group and individual results of the study are telling us in relation to the minimalist perspective on SLA suggested in Section 2 and in the Introduction.

6. Discussion and general remarks

The present study was set up to investigate two research questions comparing two Chinese groups of L2 Spanish learners at two different proficiency levels to a monolingual control group with the help of two experimental linguistic tasks: a GJCT which tested for the acquisition of uninterpretable gender and number features (via their morphological reflexes) on determiners and adjectives as well as knowledge of the fixed syntactic positions of Spanish *nationality, origin, relational* adjectives and a CBCT which tested for knowledge of an interpretable Focus/Contrast feature that triggers movement of *qualitative* adjectives to a prenominal position, based on a specific linguistic context.

Our first research question was whether native speakers of Chinese can acquire new functional categories and associated (interpretable and uninterpretable) features such that they obligatorily raise nouns in L2 Spanish. Based on the results of our two experimental tasks, the NS performed as expected with regard to the uninterpretable and interpretable features, and regarding prenominalization of *qualitative* adjectives closely tied to intersectivity (see Section 2.1 above). This semantic interpretable feature distinguishes *qualitative* adjectives from other *colour, nationality, relational* adjectives which lack an interpretable Focus/Contrast feature (Demonte 1999, 2008). Considering the results from the GJCT, the illicit acceptance of ungrammatical forms in IS proficiency learners seems to suggest a failure of the current interlanguage grammar to license dependencies that rely on *u*Gender and *u*Number (see Lardiere's 2009, *Feature Reassembly Hypothesis*). In contrast, the native-like behavior of the advanced learners indicates eventual and gradual convergence on a Spanish-like grammar. When it comes to the acceptance or rejection of the fixed position of adjective placement, while no differences were obtained between the native and AS groups, IS group made little distinction between grammatical and ungrammatical prenominal and postnominal adjective items. Based on these results alone, L2 learners show to have weaker judgments and variability is obtained again, which cannot be attributable to their L1. Our results from the second task, CBCT, show that prenominal adjectives are a source of confusion for L2 learners of Spanish. The input may hinder the acquisition process since prenominal *qualitative* adjectives can also appear postnominally in Spanish. This fact would make it difficult for the learners to ascertain the presence of the Focus/Contrast feature on the relevant contexts/items. In turn, IS learners showed different type of behavior compared to the AS and NS group. There is variability, but it cannot always be attributable to the L1 as Chinese does have a very fixed prenominal Adj-Noun syntactic order. The all-inclusive picture, that emerges from conjoining all the data of both tasks favours the position that new uninterpretable and interpretable features not instantiated in the L1 cannot easily be (although they eventually are) acquired in adult SLA. The semantic interpretative optionality of prenominal adjectives in Spanish shown may indeed occur because the interpretability of formal and semantic features has not yet been acquired and L2ers make use of other preposing mechanisms to derive the target noun adjective word order. Thus, our results from both tasks are unexpected on a representational syntactic deficit account such as the *Interpretability Hypothesis* (e.g., Hawkins & Hattori 2006; Tsimpli & Dimitrakopoulou 2007), given that this account predicts difficulties with uninterpretable features, but acquisition of L2A of non-L1 interpretable features. That is, while interpretability can be intuitively considered a factor in second language acquisition, the availability of a syntactic resource is hard to accept.

On the other hand, our second research question concerned the group and individual differences among the L2 learners with different proficiency levels and with respect to the native speakers. In answering this question, across both tasks, the advanced Chinese group performed comparably to natives on the GJCT (i.e., gender and number features and fixed placement of adjectives), and on the collocation-based task (albeit differing from them with prenominal adjectives). The Intermediate Chinese group performed differently from the natives on almost all features including prenominal adjectives on the collocation task. Looking closer at the results from our GJCT, the intergroup comparisons carried out showed significant differences between the NS and IS group performance for grammatical and ungrammatical noun-adjective agreement as well as grammatical and ungrammatical prenominal adjectives and ungrammatical postnominal adjectives. Based on these results alone, we can safely say that at this point in their interlanguage development, the IS does not seem to have attained the narrow formal syntactic properties (i.e., uninterpretable features found on determiners and adjectives in Spanish) of the Spanish DP and thus acquired new L2 features (and instantiated a new functional category, WMP). These findings support previous findings of others with learners with other L1 backgrounds, suggesting that adjectival agreement is more problematic than determiner gender agreement (Fernández 1999; Bruhn de Garavito & White 2002; Rothman et al. 2010). Particularly when it comes to the acquisition of noun placement with respect to prenominal and postnominal adjectives, our Chinese learners perform very similarly to what has been shown at similar levels with L1 English and L1 German learners (e.g., Gess & Herschensohn 2000; Parodi et al. 2004, respectively). The learning task then is not all that different, regardless of the typological differences amongst language pairs (Guijarro-Fuentes in press, forthcoming). Although these results would ultimately support some of the claims made by the IH, we, nevertheless, claim that it may be a morphological and not a narrow syntax problem, since one would also expect equal variability with determiner-noun agreement, yet this is not observed. With others (Lardiere 1998a, b; Prévost & White 2000), we believe that morphological variability is a reflex of a feature mapping problem. We should note that Chinese language is a language with extremely impoverished morphology. This could be the deterministic factor in terms of time needed for convergence.

Overall, we observed variability amongst the IS group, and less so in the advanced learners. No significant differences were found between the AS group and the NS group when looking at the gender agreement between nouns and adjectives or determiners and nouns. AS group pattern, for the most features, like the native controls indicates that with continual exposure to the target language the IS group participants may also come to fully attain new DP-features and overcome morphological competence deficits. We should point out that variability may indeed be overcome, as certain respondents clearly displayed native-like intuitions (see Table 6 above for individuals who respond within the NS range). We nevertheless remain cautious as to any strong claims attached to our results given the overall number of the participants in the experiments as acknowledged earlier. A task for a future study together with a more fine-grained study of other external variables (i.e., amount and type of exposure to the target language (e.g., classroom vs. a combination of classroom and naturalistic)).

Moreover, in order to consider the results regarding adjective placement and the role of interpretable features in this present SLA scenario, let us look closely at the findings from our CBCT (Figure 3 above). The intergroup comparison carried out showed that no statistically significant differences were found between the two L2 groups and NS group when contrasting the number of correct collocations of postnominal adjectives, indicating that the syntax of adjectival placement in L2 Spanish is target-like even at the intermediate level. However, a statistically significant difference was found between the IS group's number of correct collocations of prenominal adjectives and that of the AS and NS groups. As alluded to above, when this result is considered, we are faced with a similar difficulty that was encountered in the acquisition of uninterpretable features found on determiners and adjectives in Spanish as tested in the GJCT. Namely, [+/− interpretable] features seem to be underspecified in intermediate interlanguage grammars (i.e., gradual feature specification process would first look like L1-uniform before becoming native-like). To a certain degree, it is reasonable to argue that IS learners have not yet acquired the interpretable Focus/Contrast feature and, hence, their delay with respect to the AS group. As no significant differences were found among the AS group and the NS with respect to both prenominal and postnominal collocation, it is clear that this interpretable feature can indeed be acquired in later stages of L2 interlanguage development. As it was the case in Task 1, some, but not all, learners show native-like intuitions (see Table 9 above for respondents within the NS range).

In sum, it was found that the majority of L2 learners' performance reflects native-like semantic reflexes and formal syntactic features, whereas the performance for those learners at a lower proficiency level appears to lag behind, putting into test some of the claims made by current L2 accounts, particularly the *Interpretability Hypothesis*. Our data is suggestive of feature valuation, morphological defaults, and spell-out process, which support a feature reassembly account (e.g., Lardiere 2009). The hypothesis (i.e., IH) that the Critical Period amounts to differences in L1/L2 accessibility to representational features (i.e. UG-features) is not a plausible one. However, such claims in no way seek to undermine the observation that native and non-native competences are qualitatively and quantitatively different. The claims simply suggest that accessibility to features, regardless of whether they are uninterpretable or interpretable, cannot be the only source of such divergences (Guijarro-Fuentes 2012; Guijarro-Fuentes & Larrañaga 2011). Comparing the results of our tasks with the results of other tasks would be an interesting area for further research. In oral production, processing loads are evidently much higher and perhaps the mental model needs to be more robust to translate into correct performance. Nevertheless, the individual profile data found in early (and more advanced) stages of acquisition suggests that L2 grammar acquisition is mediated by the universal grammar (White 2003), and that UG's features are eventually accessible to adult L2 learners and acquisition takes place after the alleged offset of the critical period.

References

Allan, D. 2004. *Oxford Placement Test 1 – Test Pack*. Oxford: Oxford University Press.

Anderson, B. 2001. "Adjective position and interpretation in L2 French." In *Romance Syntax, Semantics and L2 Acquisition*, J. Camps and C.R. Wiltshire (eds), 27–42. Amsterdam: John Benjamins. DOI: 10.1075/cilt.216.05and

Anderson, B. 2007a. "Learnability and parametric change in the nominal system of L2 French." *Language Acquisition* 14: 165–214. DOI: 10.1080/10489220701353842

Anderson, B. 2007b. "Pedagogical rules and their relationship to frequency in the input: Observational and empirical data from L2 French." *Applied Linguistics* 28: 286–308. DOI: 10.1093/applin/amm015

Anderson, B. 2008. "Forms of evidence and grammatical development in the acquisition of adjective position in L2 French." *Studies in Second Language Acquisition* 30: 1–29. DOI: 10.1017/S0272263108080017

Bernstein, J. 1993. *Topics in the Syntax of Nominal Structure across Romance*. Ph.D. Graduate Center, City University of New York.

Bernstein, J. 2001. "The DP hypothesis: identifying clausal properties in the nominal domain." In M. Baltin and C. Collins (eds), *The Handbook of Contemporary Syntactic Theory*, 536–561. Oxford: Blackwell. DOI: 10.1002/9780470756416.ch17

Bruhn de Garavito, J. and White, L. 2002. "The L2 acquisition of Spanish DPs. The status of grammatical features." In *The Acquisition of Spanish Morphosyntax: The L1/L2 Connection*, A.T. Pérez-Leroux and J. Liceras (eds), 151–176. Dordrecht: Kluwer.

Carstens, V. 1991. *The Morphology and Syntax of Determiner Phrase in Kiswahili*. Ph.D., University of California, LA.

Carstens, V. 2000. "Concord in minimalist theory." *Linguistic Inquiry* 31: 319–355. DOI: 10.1162/002438900554370

Chomsky, N. 1995. *The Minimalist Program*. Cambridge, MA: The MIT Press.

Chomsky, N. 2007. "Of minds and language." *Biolinguistics* 1: 9–27.

Demonte, V. 1999. "A minimal account of spanish adjective position and interpretation." In *Analyses in Basque and Romance Linguistics. Papers in Honor of Mario Saltarelli*, J.A. Franco, A. Landa and J. Martin (eds), 45–76. Amsterdam: John Benjamins. DOI: 10.1075/cilt.187.05dem

Demonte, V. 2008. "Meaning-form correlations and adjective position in Spanish." In C. Kennedy and L. Mcnally (eds), *The Semantics of Adjectives and Adverbs*, 71–100. Oxford University Press.

Fernández, M. 1999. "Patterns in gender agreement in the speech of second language learners." In *Advances in Hispanic Linguistics*, J. Gutiérrez-Rexach and F. Martínex-Gil (eds), 3–15. Sommerville MA: Cascadilla Press.

Franceschina, F. 2001. "Morphological or syntactic deficit in near-native speakers? An assessment of some current proposals." *Second Language Research* 17: 213–147. DOI: 10.1191/026765801680191497

Franceschina, F. 2005. *Fossilized Second Language Grammars: The Acquisition of Grammatical Gender*. Amsterdam: John Benjamins. DOI: 10.1075/lald.38

Gess, R. and Herschensohn, J. 2000. "Shifting the DP parameter: A study of Anglophone French L2ers." In *Romance Syntax, Semantics and their L2 Acquisition*, J. Camps and C.R. Wiltshire (eds), 105–119. Amsterdam: John Benjamins.

Guijarro-Fuentes, P. 2012. "The acquisition of interpretable features in L2 Spanish: Personal *a*." *Bilingualism: Language and Cognition* 15: 701–720. DOI: 10.1017/S1366728912000144

Guijarro-Fuentes, P. in press. "Features and (re-)assembly in L2 Spanish: Evidence from the syntax and semantics of adjectives." In *The Acquisition of Romance Languages*, J. Costa et al. (eds). Cambridge Scholars Publishing.

Guijarro-Fuentes, P. forthcoming. "A bidirectional study: Is there any role for transfer in adjective placement?." In *Acquisition of French in its Different Constellations*, P. Guijarro-Fuentes et al. (eds). Multilingual Matters.

Guijarro-Fuentes, P. and Larrañaga, P. 2011. "Evidence of V to I raising in L2 Spanish." *International Journal of Bilingualism* 15: 486–520. DOI: 10.1177/1367006911425631

Hawkins, R. 1998. "Explaining the difficulty of gender attribution for speakers of English." Paper presented at *EUROSLA*, Paris.

Hawkins, R. 2001. *Second Language Syntax*. Malden NJ: Blackwell.

Hawkins, R. and Franceschina, F. 2004. "Explaining the acquisition and non-acquisition of determiner-noun concord in French and Spanish." In *The Acquisition of French in Different Contexts: Focus on Functional Categories*, P. Prévost and J. Paradis (eds), 175–205. Amsterdam: John Benjamins. DOI: 10.1075/lald.32.10haw

Hawkins, R. and Hattori, H. 2006. "Interpretation of English multiple wh-questions by Japanese Speakers, a missing uninterpretable feature account." *Second Language Research* 22: 269–301. DOI: 10.1191/0267658306sr269oa

Harris, J. 1991. "The exponence of gender in Spanish." *Linguistic Inquiry* 22: 27–67.

Harris, J. 1995. *The Syntax and Morphology of Class Marker Suppression in Spanish*. Ms. MIT.

Judy, T., Guijarro-Fuentes, P. and Rothman, J. 2008. "Adult accessibility to L2 representational features: Evidence from the Spanish DP." In M. Bowles, R. Foote, S. Perpiñán and R. Bhatt (eds), *Selected Proceedings of Second Language Research Forum 2007*, 1–21. Somerville, MA: Cascadilla Press.

Lardiere, D. 1998a. "Case and tense in the 'fossilized' steady state." *Second Language Research* 14: 1–26. DOI: 10.1191/026765898674105303

Lardiere, D. 1998b. "Dissociating syntax from morphology in a divergent L2 end-state grammar." *Second Language Research* 14: 359–375. DOI: 10.1191/026765898674105303

Lardiere, D. 2009. "Some thoughts on the contrastive analysis of features in second language acquisition." *Second Language Research* 25: 173–227. DOI: 10.1177/0267658308100283

Li, Yen-Hui A. 1999. "Plurality in a classifier language." *Journal of East Asian Linguistics* 8: 75–99. DOI: 10.1023/A:1008306431442

Pan, H. and Hu, J.H. 2003. "Head noun movement, focus, and topicalization in Mandarin Chinese". In J. Xu, J. Donghong, and K. Teng Lau (eds), *Chinese Syntax and Semantics*, 119–156. Singapure.

Parodi, T., Schwartz, B. and Clashen, H. 2004. "On the L2 acquisition of the morphosyntax of German nominal." *Journal of Linguistics* 42: 669–705.

Pesetsky, D. and Torrego, E. 2007. "The syntax of valuation and the interpretability of features." In *Phrasal Clausal Architecture*, S. Karimi, V. Samiian and W.K. Wilkins (eds), 262–294. Amsterdam: John Benjamins. DOI: 10.1075/la.101.14pes

Picallo, C. 2008. "Gender and number in Romance." *Lingue e Linguaggio* 7: 47–66.

Prévost, P. and White, L. 2000. "Missing surface inflection hypothesis or impairment in second language acquisition? Evidence from tense and agreement." *Second Language Research* 16: 103–133. DOI: 10.1191/026765800677556046

Rothman, J., Judy, T., Guijarro-Fuentes, P. and Pires, A. 2010. "On the (un)-ambiguity of Adjectival interpretations in L2 Spanish: Informing debates on the mental representations of L2 syntax." *Studies in Second Language Acquisition* 32: 47–77.
DOI: 10.1017/S0272263109990258

Tsimpli, I.M. and Dimitrakopoulou, M. 2007. "The interpretability hypothesis: Evidence from wh-interrogatives in second language acquisition." *Second Language Research* 23: 215–242.
DOI: 10.1177/0267658307076546

White, L. 2003. *Second Language Acquisition and Universal Grammar*. New York: Cambridge University Press. DOI: 10.1017/CBO9780511815065

White, L., Valenzuela, E., Koslowska-MacGregor, M. and Yan–Kit Ingrid, L. 2004. "Gender and number agreement in nonnative Spanish." *Applied Psycholinguistics* 25: 105–133.
DOI: 10.1017/S0142716404001067

Zagona, K. 2002. *The Syntax of Spanish*. Cambridge: CUP.

Interfaces in the interpretation of mood alternation in L2 Spanish
Morpho-phonology, semantics and pragmatics*

Aoife Ahern, José Amenos-Pons and Pedro Guijarro-Fuentes
Universidad Complutense de Madrid / UNED, Madrid / Universidad de las Islas Baleares, Spain

In this paper, we present the results of one written task testing the interpretation of mood choice in *if*-conditional constructions in L2 Spanish: a linguistic task of conditional utterances containing both regular and irregular indicative and subjunctive forms was completed by 48 L1 French and 40 L1 English speakers, and by an L1 Spanish control group (n = 35). Results show a similar pattern in the answers of both experimental groups despite the varying degree of similarity and disparity among the languages. We adopt a cognitive pragmatic perspective for the analysis of the results in connection with the various kinds of effects created by mood alternation in the constructions studied. Furthermore, in relation to current SLA debates (Lardiere 2008, 2009), our findings demonstrate that feature re-assembly in L2 Spanish is not trouble-free, as simple current feature accounts would advocate, even if those features exist in the learners' L1.

1. Introduction

This paper discusses the ability of a group of adult French and English advanced L2 learners of Spanish to detect and interpret variation in sentence meaning

---

* This study was made possible thanks to a large number of generous collaborators: students and academic staff at the Instituto Cervantes in Albuquerque, Bordeaux, Dublin, London, Manchester, Paris, Toulouse and Sydney, students of the UCM Faculty of Education and Trainee Teachers of Instituto Cervantes in Alcala de Henares, friends and colleagues, whose help we are very grateful for. We also thank Susana Olmos for revising the linguistic task. Financial support was provided by the Ministerio de Economía y Competitivad, Spain, through the project SPYCE II, reference FFI2009-07456. Finally, we wish to thank the two anonymous reviewers who have offered their time and energy to provide constructive and useful criticism and suggestions to a previous draft of this paper.

linked to indicative / subjunctive mood alternation in Spanish, in *if*-conditional sentences.

The starting point for our study is a perspective on linguistic communication based on cognitive pragmatics, more specifically, on Relevance Theory (henceforth, RT) (Sperber & Wilson 1986/1995). RT adopts a particular conception of "relevance", which consists of a relationship by which cognitive effort and cognitive effect in utterance interpretation are interconnected: other things being equal, an utterance achieves relevance by creating a relatively large set of cognitive effects from a relatively small amount of processing effort. The interpretation of utterances is limited by the human mind's tendency to strive to obtain "benefits" (*positive cognitive effects*, which contribute to the fulfillment of cognitive functions or goals) and to avoid expending more effort than necessary to do so. By the same token, an increase in the effort required to interpret an utterance leads to expectations of an increase in positive cognitive effects.

In this framework, context is a cognitive construct, consisting of the set of assumptions that are accessible to the participants in a given communicative situation. Contextual assumptions, including those arising from the discourse, from the interpreter's perceptual awareness, memory, or other sources, are selected based on a presumption of optimal relevance (Sperber & Wilson 1986/1995), and integrated into inferential processes of utterance interpretation directed at identifying the speaker's meaning, i.e., the meaning the speaker intends to convey by means of an utterance. This notion of context constitutes an appropriate framework for analyzing the complexity of utterance interpretation in terms of the degree to which the integration of linguistic and non-linguistic data is required.

Pragmatic enrichment of linguistic information has been seen as an inherent source of complexity in utterance interpretation in general, and particularly in L2 (Foster-Cohen 2002). However, little has been said in SLA theories about exactly what pragmatic enrichment consists of and how it operates, an area in which RT may contribute valuable insights.

According to RT, linguistic items can encode concepts or instructions. Concepts are representational, linked to encyclopedic knowledge, while instructions are operational, functioning at two different levels: syntactic computations and interpretation. Items encoding instructional content are known as 'procedural' expressions. Escandell-Vidal and Leonetti (2011: 84) claim that "a strong connection can be established between the 'lexical/functional' distinction in grammatical theory and the conceptual/procedural distinction". Lexical categories can encode conceptual and/or procedural meaning, but functional categories are always procedural. The term 'procedural' can be understood, within this framework, "as a shorthand term to refer to functional categories that encode interpretive instructions" (Escandell-Vidal & Leonetti 2011: 85).

Tense and mood, as functional categories, encode procedural meaning. Tense imposes restrictions on the determination of temporal reference, as well as on the inferential processing of conceptual representations of states and events (Nicolle 1997; Moeschler 1998; Saussure 2003). Mood enables the hearer to infer speaker attitude, intention and mental state information (Rouchota 1994; Jary 2009; Ahern 2004, 2006 and 2010).

Thus, we investigate whether the acquisition of mood semantic features, which can be argued to be interpretable features, raise problems for adult L2 learners at different proficiency levels, in comparison to adult monolinguals, by analyzing data related to their knowledge of *if*-conditional constructions. We further explore whether, even at advanced stages of L2 acquisition, procedural expressions are among the most problematic areas for learners, regardless of whether the same expressions are present in the L1.

Regarding the SLA theoretical implications of our object of study, it should be pointed out that different Universal Grammar (UG) accounts of SLA hold dissimilar views of parameter resetting, depending on the capacity attributed to interlanguage grammars to attain new values for interpretable and uninterpretable features. Recall that under current minimalist proposals (Chomsky 1995, 2007), parametric variation among adult grammars is associated with properties of the lexicon. The lexicon, for example, comprises functional categories connected to number (Num), agreement (Agr) and tense (T). These functional categories can be different from one language to another as to their configuration of associated formal features and feature values. Moreover, not all formal features have the same status: some are uninterpretable and others interpretable. Uninterpretable features have only formal syntactic properties; that is, they are relevant to the syntactic component, whereas interpretable features carry meaning and are relevant to the semantic component. More specifically, for our purposes we assume the distinction between uninterpretable features such as person and number (which are irrelevant for semantic interpretation) and interpretable features such as tense and mood (which contribute to sentence interpretation) (see Section 2 below).

Our study may be related, in particular, to the claims of the *Feature Reassembly* Hypothesis (henceforth, FRH). Lardiere's (2008, 2009) FRH maintains that acquiring an L2 grammar is not a question of whether features are still available for selection from a universal inventory. The pertinent question is how features are assembled and mapped to lexical items taking into consideration particular language-specific conditions under which they are phonologically realized. Thus, two languages can select the same formal features such that a native speaker of language A acquiring language B would not need to 'reset' the parameter in question. Nevertheless, how a particular feature is assembled and the conditions of its expression in each of the two languages may be quite different. The learning task would then consist of appropriately re-configuring or re-assembling formal and semantic bundles in the L2 lexicon, and determining the specific conditions under which their properties may or may not be morpho-phonologically expressed. Thus, in addition to acquiring new features, the adult learner must redeploy the morphological expression of individual features from the way they are employed in the native language.

Alternative accounts, however, have asserted that long-term L2 variability emerges from interface vulnerabilities, namely interpretable features relevant to the syntax-semantics or syntax-pragmatics interface (e.g., Belletti et al. 2007; Sorace & Filiaci 2006; Tsimpli & Sorace 2006; White 2009, *inter alia*). That is, it is argued that linguistic features which are interface-conditioned (e.g., Chomsky 2007) may be universally more difficult to acquire, and interface-conditioned features can similarly be expected to pose acquisition or learnability problems for L1, L2 and bilingual speakers.

Still, in Sorace's (2011) *Interface Hypothesis* (henceforth, IH) predictions are made not for all interfaces, but specifically for external ones (that is, the ones related to pragmatics) and furthermore, IH is specifically focused on bilinguals. It is claimed that, even when the L1 and the target L2 are very similar for a given relevant property (even when those languages are genetically related, as is the case for one of the pair of languages investigated in this paper) there should still be evidence of interface integration problems, precisely because the processing issues appealed to in order to explain this effect are true for all bilinguals. It should be emphasised, however, that the IH is not intended to be applied to developing L2s, but as a theory of ultimate attainment (Sorace 2011, 2012). It is not the case, then, that interface conditioned properties should be harder to obtain; however, it should be the case that advanced L2 learners show some level of residual optionality.[1]

The paper is organized as follows. In Section 2, we present the linguistic assumptions made about the underlying structure of the target sentences together with the review of previous studies. In Section 3, we describe the study design. In Section 4, group and individual results are presented. Section 5 contains the discussion and conclusions.

---

1. See Rothman (2009), Rothman & Slabakova (2011) and White (2011) for alternative accounts.

2. If-conditional constructions with Imperfect indicative / subjunctive

2.1 Spanish

Spanish has a complex system of morphologically encoded mood. Some types of Spanish *if*-conditional constructions allow mood alternation, linked to substantial differences in utterance interpretation.

Conditionals introduced by the conjunction *si* 'if' never accept present/perfect subjunctive forms. In the antecedent of factual conditionals, such as (1) below, the indicative mood is used; the consequent of factual conditionals takes either indicative (as in (1)) or imperative. Conversely, in irrealis conditionals, like (2), Imperfect Subjunctive (IMP-SUBJ) is the standard tense in the antecedent and Conditional (COND) is the most frequent tense in the consequent:

(1) **Si llego tarde, mi padre me lleva al colegio.**
If I am late, my father takes me to school.

(2) **Si pudiera, me iría al Caribe.** Las playas, el sol… ¡Qué rico! ¡Qué ganas tengo de que lleguen las vacaciones!
If I could, I'd go to the Caribbean. The beaches, the sun … how luxurious! I'm just dying for the holidays!

In the consequent of irrealis conditionals, imperfect indicative (IMP-IND) can also be found, instead of COND. Use of IMP-IND in the consequent is typical of informal oral language and is normally related to the speaker's attitude: IMP-IND adds an effect of emotional closeness (with varying nuances depending on the context), due to the absence of the [+posteriority] feature that is linked to the meaning of COND (Amenos-Pons 2014).

On the other hand, IMP-IND may appear in the antecedent of *if*-conditionals, with two different types of interpretation: habitual and quotative-echoic. The choice between the two interpretations (illustrated below in (3) and (4)) is related to the tense used in the consequent (IMP or COND), but it also (and crucially) depends on the predicate type and contextual assumptions:

(3) If + IMP-IND + IMD-IND → Habitual interpretation.
Yo siempre tenía vértigo… **Si me trataban con medicina natural, yo creo que era una medicina equivocada.**
I always had vertigo… If they treated me with natural medicine, I think it was the wrong medicine.

(4) If + IMP-IND + COND (or IMP-IND) → Quotative-echoic interpretation.
El programa electoral del Partido Ecologista establecía que **si llegaba al gobierno acabaría (acababa) con la energía nuclear** en menos de 20 años.
*The electoral programme of the Ecologist Party established that **if they got into government they would put (*put) an end to nuclear energy** in less than 20 years.*

Habitual conditionals represent iterated past events; they are generally described as factual conditionals (Montolío 1999). The IMP-IND is a past tense, and its imperfective nature is fully compatible with iterativity. Besides, iterative readings involve unboundedness, and atelic events (states and activities) are inherently associated with imperfective tenses.[2] Therefore, habitual readings of the IMP-IND such as (2) are the most frequent type found in the antecedent of *if*-conditionals, provided a past frame is available to establish temporal reference and that there is no contextual obstacle to the iteration of the eventuality being depicted.

On the contrary, in quotative or echoic interpretations, IMP-IND refers to unique situations that were not (yet) accomplished at some specific point in the past: the state of affairs at that time was different from the one at speech time; at speech time, the condition may have been accomplished or not. Quotative or echoic interpretations of IMP-IND may appear only when an eventuality (contextually seen as unique) lacks an available past reference frame: to preserve the interpretability of the IMP-IND, the hearer is obliged to mentally represent a perceiving subject located in the past (De Saussure 2003, 2013). In that case, it is the utterance act that is located in the past, and not (necessarily) the eventuality itself. More precisely, the antecedent of (4) conveys a set of possibilities not represented as actual facts, but as metarepresentations: as attributional thoughts entertained in the past. Hence, the antecedent of (4) is understood as echoic, even though no reporting verb is provided. This type of reading has formal restrictions. Linguistic environments that favour echoic readings of antecedents in the IMP-IND have many similarities with other quotative uses of IMP-IND (Leonetti & Escandell-Vidal 2003). Typically, (a) the antecedent involves a unique telic event in IMP-IND, (b) the tense receives a prospective interpretation, (c) the utterances contain events that can be planned, and (d) the IMP-IND is not in the first or in the second person.

In the consequent of quotative *if*-constructions, use of IMP-IND instead of COND is a frequent option in oral language, and it has the same effect of emotional closeness found in plain irrealis cases (with IMP-SUBJ in the antecedent).

---

2. However, unboundedness is not exclusive of atelic predicates: it can also be achieved by iterating telic events, which are seen as parts of an embedding atelic macroevent.

By contrast, IMP-IND is compulsory in the consequent of habitual *if*-conditionals. Thus, in irrealis and quotative environments, the IMP-IND of the consequent brings about a supplementary effect related to the attitude of the speaker. Conversely, in habitual conditionals, the use of IMP-IND in the consequent does not add any effect, because there is no possibility of alternation.

2.2 French and English

French, like Spanish, has morphological mood, and the systems of both languages are analogous in many respects. Still, in contemporary French the choice of subjunctive tenses is reduced to present and perfect forms. Therefore, alternation of indicative and subjunctive is not available in conditional environments: if utterances (2), (3) and (4) above are translated into French, IMP-IND is required. Unavailability of mood alternation in the antecedent undermines the possibility of using IMP-IND in the consequent when a habitual interpretation is not intended: if only IMP-IND (and not IMP-SUBJ) is available in the antecedent of French conditionals, the tense of the consequent (COND or IMP-IND) is essential for distinguishing habitual readings (with IMP-IND) from irrealis (with COND).

Yet, in French, IMP-IND may be used in the consequent of conditional and pseudo-conditional constructions, when there is no ambiguity about the counterfactuality of the antecedent (Bres 2006, 2007, 2009; Corminboeuf 2009):[3]

(5) (TV, lors d'un concours de saut en hauteur) y avait un centimètre de plus, si y avait eu un mètre huitante neuf **elle la passait pas** cette barre. (Corminboeuf 2009)
*(TV broadcaster, high jump competition) if there'd been just one more centimeter, **she wouldn't have passed** (*passed-IMP) over that bar*

(6) Mon sang se glace, dit Madeleine, quand je songe *qu'une minute de plus et* **vous n'étiez** *(IMP-IND) qu'un froid cadavre.*
*My blood freezes, Madeleine said, when I realize that (if the situation had lasted) one more minute, **you would be** (*were-IMP) dead by now*

As in Spanish, use of IMP-IND instead of COND in French produces a pragmatic effect of emotional closeness.[4] This suggests that the difference between both languages does not rely on the respective meanings of IMP-IND and COND

---

3. Thus, use of IMP-IND in the consequent (instead of COND) is more restricted in French than in Spanish: the former (but not the latter) allows it only with counterfactual antecedents.

4. Grevisse (2011) describes an effect of 'inevitability' linked to the used of IMP-IND instead of COND. An example of this effect, by 19th century writer Victor Hugo, is found in the

themselves, but on the availability of dissimilar sets of linguistic devices in each verbal system, taken as a whole (Amenos-Pons 2014); this variation between the two systems is at the heart of the cross-linguistic differences found in the distribution of IMP-IND and COND.

Compared to other Indo-European languages, modern-day English has a minimal inflectional system. Unlike Spanish and French, mood in English is not clearly signaled by specialized morphemes (Bergs & Heine 2010). Thus, English makes frequent use of analytic devices (Huddleston 1989; Palmer 2001) to signal nuances in meaning that Spanish and French would express through mood alternation or, more generally speaking, through synthetic devices (mood, tense and grammatical aspect markers).

Hence, as shown in the translations of (2), (3) and (4), in English only the Simple Past tense (SP) is available in the antecedent, and COND is required in the consequent. Still, when the verb *to be* is used in the antecedent of irrealis conditional clauses, subjunctive *were* has traditionally been considered the standard form, as in Spanish. Additionally, with other verbs in the antecedent, irreality and prospectivity may be emphasized with *were to + infinitive*:

(7) If **I were to lose** my job next year, I probably would not find a new one quickly.

Iterativity and habituality may be expressed in English with '*if* + Simple Past + Simple Past', although other (analytic) devices, such as '*would* + infinitive' may alternatively be used in the consequent in order to make these interpretations more explicit.

Taken together, all these facts suggest a remarkable paradox, whose effects on L2 acquisition have yet to be clarified. On the one hand, unlike English, both French and Spanish make extensive use of synthetic devices attached to the verb, and have interpretive effects linked to mood alternation. If transfer is assumed, this would suggest a possible advantage for L1 French (over L1 English) speakers when acquiring L2 Spanish mood contrasts. On the other hand, when *if*-conditionals are considered in isolation, it turns out that, although the mood systems of French and English are typologically different, both languages have parallel possibilities (i.e., no mood alternation in the antecedent of if-conditional sentences and severe restrictions regarding the substitution of COND in the consequent of those constructions), which in turn are different from those existing in Spanish. This casts doubt upon the alleged advantage of L1 French speakers for L2 Spanish acquisition, as far as *if*-conditionals are concerned.

---

dictionary *Trésor de la Langue Française*. Indeed, inevitability is not an objective property of events, but a subjective representation.

2.3 Mood in SLA: Previous studies and background

Iterative readings of the IMP-IND have been described extensively in the literature (RAE/AALE 2009), though little attention has been paid so far to quotative interpretations of IMP-IND in Spanish. However, it has been convincingly shown (Escandell-Vidal & Leonetti 2003) that quotative readings tend to arise as a last-resort pragmatic inference: when no past situation is contextually salient for referential purposes, a metalinguistic representation is built to establish the temporal reference of the tense. Therefore, quotative or echoic interpretations are pragmatically marked uses of IMP-IND, based on aspectual coercion.[5]

Habitual readings of IMP-IND have also been analyzed as coercion (Montrul & Slabakova 2002, 2003; Bott 2010), because they force iterative interpretations of single events to make them compatible with a broad timespan, contextually acting as referential framework. Still, the interpretive requirements of habituality are comparatively less demanding: unlike quotativity, habituality always preserves the factuality and pastness of the event, and (unlike in quotative cases) there is no need to contextually access a metalinguistic perspective to ensure interpretability. Therefore, the cognitive burden of quotative readings of IMP-IND is heavier (Escandell-Vidal & Leonetti 2003; De Saussure 2013).

Generally speaking, coerced interpretations of IMP-IND have been described as a potential source of variability in Spanish L2 acquisition (Montrul & Slabakova 2002, 2003; Perez-Leroux et al. 2007). By analysing data of utterance interpretation tasks (L1 English speakers), Montrul and Slabakova (2002, 2003) conclude that interpreting coerced readings of IMP-IND is particularly demanding (compared to non-coerced readings), because integration of information from different cognitive modules (linguistic and pragmatic) is at stake.

Coercion is not explicitly mentioned in the well-known Aspect Hypothesis (Andersen & Shirai 1994), but it is nevertheless implied that reconciling contradictory features (such as imperfectivity and telicity) is particularly challenging and has a hindering effect on the full acquisition of IMP-IND in L2 Spanish, at least for speakers of languages lacking the contrast between perfectivity and imperfectivity. Other studies (Amenos-Pons 2010) suggest that interpretation and use of IMP-IND with telic predicates is difficult also for speakers of languages like French, despite having this contrast in their L1. This has been considered a consequence of the inherently heavier processing burden described by Leonetti & Escandell-Vidal (2003) and De Saussure (2013).

---

5. As mentioned in Section 2.1, quotative readings of IMP-IND tend to appear with telic predicates. Being aspectually imperfective, IMP-IND systematically forces an unbounded reading of telic predicates, which is one type of aspectual coercion.

The idea that not all types of coercion are equally difficult to interpret is not a mere hypothesis. Summarising psycholinguistic research on aspectual coercion, Bott (2010: 261) concludes that when coercion involves reinterpretation at the lexical level, its resolution is faster and more efficient than in other types of coercion, where linguistic processing interacts with social cognition. As stated above, iterative IMP-IND belongs to the former type of coercion, whereas quotative IMP-IND belongs to the latter type.

Generally speaking, the indicative and the subjunctive have different functions because they have a different "meaning", i.e. semantic content. We assume that the grammatical distinction between indicative and subjunctive is yielded by an [*i*mood] semantic feature (cf. Giorgi & Pianesi 1997). As for the semantics of the subjunctive mood (SUBJ), it has often been analysed as intrinsically non-assertive (Terrell & Hoopper 1974; Jary 2009; Ahern 2004, 2006), and leading to several kinds of complex metalinguistic and metarepresentational readings through its interaction with different sentential contexts. However, in conditionals, the interpretation of SUBJ is standardly seen as irrealis and, as far as IMP-SUBJ is concerned, unambiguously related to non-past situations (Montolío 1999). Thus, IMP-SUBJ in conditional contexts has a more restricted range of possible interpretations than IMP-IND, which in turn may be factual (in habitual readings) or non-factual (in quotative-echoic cases).

In the interpretation of Spanish SUBJ in concessive and polarity environments by L1 French advanced learners, optionality has been found, although it has been claimed that optionality can be overcome (Borgonovo & Prevost 2003; Borgonovo et al. 2008; Iverson, Kempchinsky & Rothman 2008). Polarity, concessive and *if*-conditional environments have in common that mood is not lexically selected in any of them; instead, mood choice is allowed and each mood licenses a certain type of interpretation. Therefore, it has been argued that mood choice in these environments is not a purely grammatical matter, but an interface issue (Borgonovo et al. 2008). The fact that polarity SUBJ is nevertheless acquirable hypothetically suggests that *if*-conditional SUBJ could be as well.

To our knowledge, no research has been carried out on the acquisition of features related to *if*-conditional constructions. More importantly, nor has much research been conducted examining the acquisition of two languages which belong to the same family, with similar interpretable features, such as French and Spanish.

As for our present proposal, in addition to contributing data related to the two aspects just mentioned, it is relevant to various theoretical issues. Against the aforementioned linguistic background, we can assume that in L2 acquisition UG is available at all stages (i.e., access to the feature inventory and the computations is available in interlanguage grammars), and that parametric differences are at the level of lexical-feature specification, uninterpretable features (uF) being the locus of variation while interpretable features (iF) are universal and available. The prediction that would follow is that there should be no differences between L1 speakers of French and L1 speakers of English in the acquisition of L2 Spanish, even though French has mood selection while English does not. This prediction could also follow, although for different reasons, from the point of view of the FRH (Lardiere 2008, 2009): even if an L1 includes features that are also found in the L2 (as in mood for French learners of Spanish), feature acquisition may not be any simpler, since learning involves two different tasks as stated above: (1) feature re-assembly and (2) identifying the lexico-semantic restrictions placed upon the feature in the L2, differentiating these restrictions from those of the L1.

In sum, comparing L1 French and L1 English learners will provide not only empirical conclusions, but also information of theoretical import, as to how (and if) two groups of learners whose starting point is typologically different manage to acquire features that are either present or absent in their native language. The research questions we intend to address here are:

1. Do French and English L2 learners of Spanish differ in their semantic interpretation of native-like and non-native-like uses of Spanish *if*-conditional constructions?
2. Are there group and individual differences among the L2 learners with two different proficiency levels (i.e., advanced vs. upper intermediate) in the conditions underlying the mood selection interpretations?

3. Our study

3.1 Research predictions and design

As mentioned above, French and Spanish have morphological mood, but its features are differently assembled and mapped onto lexical items in each language; they also have dissimilar phonological realizations. Therefore, in order to parse the semantic interpretation of *if*-conditionals in Spanish, French speakers must (re-) acquire the corresponding interpretable features. In spite of this, some bootstrapping effects may be anticipated for these learners, given the overall similarities between French and Spanish (including lexical and syntactic cues). Conversely, for English speakers, their L1 does not provide the interpretable feature cues to the structures in the L2. Thus, difficulty in interpreting mood alternation is typically predicted for them. Still, for *if*-conditionals no direct equivalent of Spanish mood alternation is found in French (nor in English), so positive effects of L1 are dubious in both cases.

In the study, an interpretation task containing twenty *if*-conditional and ten *although*-concessive multiple choice items in randomized order was used. They were built on contextualised utterances adapted from a press corpus (*Corpus de Referencia del Español Actual*).[6] For every item, three answer options were given, each describing a different type of interpretation (quotative-echoic, habitual or irrealis). The *although*-concessive items were used as distractors; they also constituted a separate piece of research which will not be dealt with in this paper, due to lack of space. The linguistic task was preceded by an ethno-linguistic questionnaire which contained written questions related to information about the subjects' language learning experiences and about the approximate length of time they had studied Spanish.

The linguistic task and questionnaire were completed by adult learners of L2 Spanish at a relatively homogenous non-immersion formal setting: Instituto Cervantes,[7] either in France or in one of the following English speaking countries: the UK, Ireland, the USA or Australia. Online and paper versions of the material were used (subjects chose the most suitable format). Respective groups of L1 French (N = 48) and of L1 English (N = 40) were formed; all subjects had been independently assessed for language proficiency and placed at CEFR B2 level (L1 French, N = 16 / L1 English, N = 26) or C1/C1+ level (L1 French, N = 32 / L1 English, N = 14). A control group of native speakers of European Spanish (N = 35) also completed the task. All the subjects from the experimental and the control groups had at least completed high school education.

There was no strict time limitation, but the subjects were advised not to take more than forty minutes to complete the task; they were asked to self-report the amount of time devoted to the task (see Section 5.1). Table 1 shows the distribution of the conditional items in the linguistic task, according to their content, including an example of each item type.

3.2 Research hypotheses

Recall that two types of interpretation of the Spanish IMP-IND have been tested in our study: quotative-echoic and habitual. Among them, the former has

---

6. Examples of each of the item types are included here in an appendix.

7. The language courses offered at Instituto Cervantes centers around the world are primarily built on an extremely thorough, single CEFR-based curriculum, which is subsequently adapted to different areas, following cross-linguistic and cross-cultural criteria. Students are required to pass a placement test before enrolling; exams based on the institutional curriculum are performed at the end of each course.

Table 1. Conditional items

Items 1–4	If + IMP-IND + COND	
El programa electoral del Partido Ecologista establecía que, **si llegaba al gobierno, acabaría con la energía nuclear** en menos de 20 años. *The electoral programme of the Ecologist Party established that if they got into government they would put an end to nuclear energy in less than 20 years.*		Quotative / Echoic
Items 5–8	If + IMP-IND + IMP-IND	
Era una situación muy comprometida: **si aprobaba aquella ley se creaba un conflicto** con todos los demás países; si no la aprobaba, se creaba un conflicto con la extrema derecha republicana. *It was a no-win situation: if they approved that law, a conflict was created with all the other countries; if they didn't approve it, a conflict was created with the Republican far right.*		
Items 9–12	If + IMP-IND + IMP-IND	
Yo siempre tenía vértigo… **Si me trataban con medicina natural, yo creo que era una medicina equivocada.** *I always had vertigo… If they treated me with natural medicines, I think it was the wrong medicines.*		Habitual
Items 13–16	If + IMP-SUBJ + COND	
Me gusta mucho la política, tengo una gran vocación. Por eso, **si le dijera que me voy a retirar pronto, le engañaría.** *I like politics a lot, it's my vocation. That's why, if I said I'm going to retire soon, I'd be deceiving you.*		Irrealis
Items 17–20	If + IMP-SUBJ + IMP-IND	
Si pudiera, me iba al Caribe. Las playas, el sol… ¡Qué rico! ¡Qué ganas tengo de que lleguen las vacaciones. *If I could, I went to the Caribbean. The beaches, the sun… how luxurious! I'm just dying for the holidays!*		

been claimed to be particularly costly, requiring, as also argued above (following Amenos-Pons 2014) distinguishing these readings from the prototypical irrealis interpretation of IMP-SUBJ. In conditional constructions, the tense found in the consequent constitutes a clue for the temporal location of the whole sentence. Still, in Spanish, with quotative IMP-IND antecedents, and also with IMP-SUBJ antecedents, IMP-IND may be used in the consequent instead of the standard COND. When this happens, contextual, extralinguistic assumptions must come into play for an adequate interpretation to be identified. This may be expected to increase processing difficulties for L2 learners. More specifically, we predict for each item condition the following:

1. **High success rate is expected (especially in the C1/C1+ group) for items 9–12 (habitual IMP-IND) and 13–20 (IMP-SUBJ).** Antecedents in IMP-SUBJ are the most frequent, unmarked option in Spanish. They are part of the Instituto Cervantes B2 syllabus. Habitual IMP-IND is frequent in Spanish, not only in if-clauses, and is part of the institution's B1 syllabus.
2. **Difficulties are expected (even in the C1/C1+ group) for items 1–8 (quotative IMP-IND).** Quotative readings of the IMP-IND have many restrictions, both linguistic and pragmatic: they require events contextually represented as unique (i.e., not iterated), usually telic, and they tend to appear with events that can be planned. This type of IMP-IND is not found in the syllabus until C1 level.
3. **Use of IMP-IND in the consequent instead of COND in items 5–8 and 17–20 is expected to increase difficulty.** This is typical of informal and colloquial registers. Despite its relatively high frequency in oral Spanish, this use does not appear in the syllabus until C1 level either.
4. **L1 French will offer certain advantages over L1 English in ability to associate mood with effects on interpretation.** The use of the grammatical information of mood will be familiar to L1 French speakers and may bias their interpretations; besides, lexical processing will be easier for them (thanks to cognates). L1 English speakers lack grammatical cues; they will rely purely on context.

4. Analyses and results

For each L1 and proficiency level, individual results were collected and correlated. Item results were considered separately, then arranged in content-based groups (see Table 1 above). The mean and standard deviation for each L1 group were also obtained and correlated. T-tests (L1 French and L1 English), contingency tests, chi-square tests and one-way ANOVAs between groups (L1 French, L1 English and Control) were performed. However, due to space limitations, only the most relevant results will be analyzed and discussed here.

Results set by content-based groups of items and L1 are summarized in Figures 1 and 2 below.

Figure 1 displays the overall success rate of the learners grouped by L1, regardless of their general proficiency level. In the groups of items, no significant difference was found between the learners relating to their L1 ($p > 0.05$ in all cases). Figure 2 shows the percentage of learners of each proficiency group (B2 and

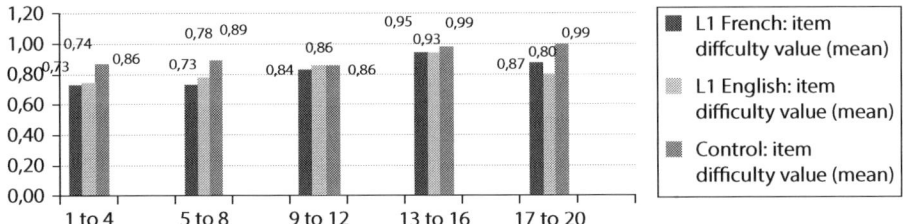

Figure 1. Results by groups of items

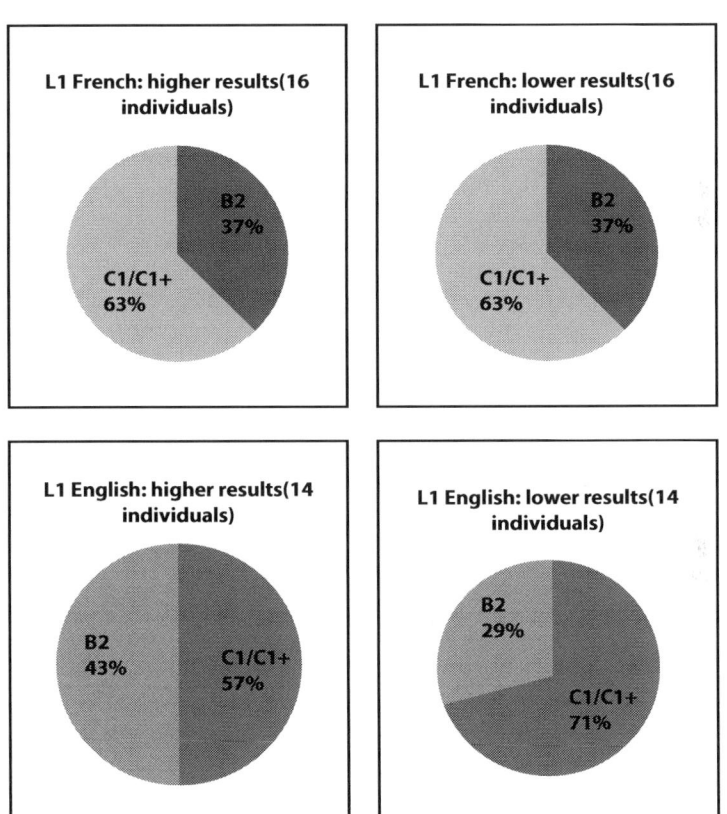

Figure 2. Relation between proficiency level and results

C1/C1+)[8] having achieved higher and lower success, measured in the amount of correct answers. This classification was developed, following Item Response Theory (Hambleton, Swaminathan & Rogers 1991), by putting all of the participants in order from highest to lowest scores obtained, dividing them into 3 groups of equal number and using the upper third as "higher success group", and the lower third as "lower success group" for each of the L1 groups. For the L1 French learners, equal percentages of B2 and C1/C1+ are found in higher and lower success groups; for the L1 English learners, there is a higher percentage of B2 in the lower success group. Still, in none of the L1 groups are the results clear-cut: overall proficiency level systematically underdetermines task performance. Thus, in Figure 1, we have chosen to represent the learners of each L1 group as a single entity.

As expected, items 1–4 and 5–8 (quotative uses of IMP-IND) were the most difficult for both L1 groups: in items 1–4, there is 73% of correct answers for the L1 French group and 74% for the L1 English group; in items 5–8, the percentage of correct answers is 73% for the French group and 78% for the English group. A one-way ANOVA was used to test for differences between both groups of learners and the control group, finding fully significant differences for items 1–8 ($F(2, 122) = 7.235$ (L1 French / Control, $p = 0.001$; L1 English / Control, $p = 0.020$). In contrast, items 13–16 were the easiest for both experimental groups, with 95% correct answers for the French group and 93% for the English group. Differences between the experimental groups and the control group are not significant ($F(2, 122) = 8.885$, $p > 0.05$).

The ability to interpret IMP-IND when used instead of COND in the consequent is found to be unsteady: in one type of construction (quotative IMP-IND), T-tests showed no significant difference for any of the experimental groups ($p > 0.05$); thus, comparing items 1–4 to 5–8, the utilization of IMP instead of COND does not significantly alter the accuracy of the answers. However for the constructions with irrealis IMP-SUBJ, consequents with IMP-IND instead of COND are harder for both groups; for the L1 French group, if items 13–16 are compared to items 17–20, $p = 0.046$, a difference that approaches significance; whereas for the L1 English group the difference is fully significant ($p = 0.005$).

In the control group, changing the tense of the consequent does not modify the accuracy of the answers. However, this does not mean that native speakers always give correct answers. Interestingly, 100% accuracy is only approached for items 13–20, that is, for the groups of items not involving any type of coercion.

---

8. As mentioned in 3.1, the participants had completed general proficiency tests at the Cervantes Institutes where they studied and were assessed to be at either B2, C1 or C1+ levels. Figure 2 shows the distribution of individuals in the upper and lower groups of results in the mood interpretation tasks in terms of their placements across the general proficiency levels.

This is hardly a surprise: when complex integration of pragmatics, semantics and morphosyntax is at stake, some degree of variability is predictable also for native speakers, as reported in the literature (Borgonovo & Prévost 2003; Borgonovo et al. 2008). However, for items 9–12, the performance of the control group literally equates that of the L2 learners, and this may seem odd: as hypothesized, those items were significantly less problematic for the learners than items 1–8 (L1 French, $p = 0.001$; L1 English, $p = 0.006$), and also significantly easier than items 13–20 (L1 French, $p < 0.001$; L1 English, $p = 0.007$). On the other hand, between items 1–8 and 9–12, the degree of accuracy in the control group does not significantly change, which creates a striking contrast. A closer look at the options chosen for individual items 9–12 reveals that our natives were prone to hesitate mainly between two linguistically possible interpretations of the IMP-IND (habitual and quotative); conversely, interpretations that would be typical of the IMP-SUBJ were normally discarded. Thus, it may be assumed, tentatively, that native speakers are not confused by the tenses themselves, but experience difficulty in the enrichment processes required to interpret coercion. However, more research is required to confirm this hypothesis.

On the other hand, the fact that both groups of learners have little difficulty with items 9–12 (which involve coercion) may be due of the type of coercion itself (as described in Section 2.3 above), but it may also be seen as a combined effect of input frequency (habitual uses of IMP-IND are much more frequent than quotative and echoic cases), instruction (habitual IMP-IND is studied at B1 level, whereas quotative IMP-IND does not appear until B2) and positive L1 transfer. Further research is also needed to disentangle all these factors.

Summing up the data provided so far, we can now make the following claims, related to our predictions for each set of items:

1. Full confirmation of hypotheses 1 and 2, for both L1 groups: items 1–8 (quotative/echoic IMP-IND) are the most difficult cases; items 9–12 (habitual IMP-IND) and items 13–20 (irrealis IMP-SUBJ) are easier. However, there are differences among the sub-groups of items (see discussion below on hypothesis 3).
2. Partial confirmation of hypothesis 3, regarding the increase in difficulty with the use of the IMP instead of COND: in one group of items (numbers 17–20) the percentage of correct answers with IMP-IND (used instead of COND) is lower;[9] still, there is no systematic effect in the other group of items (numbers 5–8). Thus, for L2 learners, the contribution of tense in the consequent

---

9. Still, it should be remembered that the difference is only fully significant for the L1 English group.

(COND / IMP-IND) is uncertain; this suggests inconsistent use of grammatical information for interpretation.
3. Hypothesis 4 is not clearly confirmed: an L1 effect was only detected for items 17–20. Overall, relatively stable tendencies are found in both L1 groups and at both proficiency levels.
4. Integration of semantics, morpho-syntax and pragmatics is a source of variability for L2 learners, regardless of their overall proficiency.
5. Native speakers are also sensitive to interface issues between different cognitive domains.

The general and theoretical implications of these empirical conclusions will be discussed in Section 6, after introducing further data on general tendencies found in the groups.

5. General tendencies: Task completion and L2 exposure times

Although the present study is focused on identifying the capacity to choose adequate interpretations of mood alternation by the different groups of participants, and it was not designed to identify relationships between time and accuracy, some information was gathered regarding how much time was used to complete the task by the participants. A brief overview of these findings may offer some interesting insights regarding an apparent lack of relationship between the amount of time used by the participants and the scores they obtained.

The L1 English speakers reported requiring the largest amount of time (mean 41 minutes), followed by the French L1 group (mean 38 minutes), using a slightly, though not significantly, shorter amount of time. Finally, the Spanish L1 control group used significantly less time (mean 26 minutes) than the groups of learners. These facts are in line with the hypotheses discussed in 3.2: L1 English speakers were not significantly different from French speakers with regards to the time used to complete the task. Nevertheless, as mentioned in 3.1, information regarding task completion time was reported by the participants themselves, so any tendencies suggested here cannot be seen as conclusive.

Among the data collected from all the L2 Spanish learner participants in this study, information about the language learning experiences and about the approximate length of time they had studied Spanish was obtained through the ethno-linguistic questionnaire previous to the linguistic task, which may contribute to further insights related to our research questions. As mentioned in Section 4, the analysis of the linguistic task results was used to distinguish two groups of L2 Spanish learner participants, those with a higher or lower task success rate, based on the number of items answered correctly. When the language learning experience and number of years of study data are quantified for each of the success rate groups, lower and higher, a few interesting tendencies are suggested.

As mentioned previously, all learners were students of Spanish language courses at the Instituto Cervantes in their countries of residence at the time they completed the tasks. In addition, they reported whether they had learnt Spanish by attending immersion courses and whether they had visited or resided in Spanish-speaking countries. Of the participants in the higher success rate group, 40% had attended immersion courses, two-thirds (66%) had visited, and 17% had resided, in Spanish-speaking countries. The frequency of such experiences were lower for the lower success rate group, in which 30% had attended immersion courses, just over half (53%) had visited Spanish-Speaking countries, and only 6% had resided in one of these countries. Furthermore, the participants in the higher success rate group had spent more years studying Spanish than those in the lower success rate group: almost half (47%) of the higher group reported they had spent more than 5 years studying, whereas in the lower group, only around a quarter (27%) reported having spent more than 5 years learning Spanish.

In contrast with the findings shown in Figure 2 (Section 3.2), where it was seen that in general, the overall proficiency level of the learners did not affect the likelihood that they belong to the higher or lower success-rate groups, the raw data related to the learners' experiences and time spent studying Spanish does appear to hold a clearer positive correlation with more accurate task completion. All this suggests that, independently of what may be detected in diagnostic tests of students' general command of L2 Spanish, such as those completed to place the students in the Instituto Cervantes' courses, the ability to identify the nuances expressed through verbal mood alternation – at least in the structures tested here – appears to be associated with plentiful exposure to the language over a relatively long-term period, although it is beyond the scope of our study to offer clear evidence of this relationship.

With regards to how these observations relate to our research predictions, the fact that the discourse-contextual factors impinging on the process of identifying the most appropriate interpretation for some of the items, in particular those obtaining quotative readings, are only included in the syllabus of the Instituto Cervantes' C1 courses entails that acquiring the ability to interpret mood alternation appropriately in such items is unlikely to be a result of explicit teaching and learning: the subjects of the higher success-rate groups, who were more efficient at interpreting the items, were more or less equally distributed among students of B2 and C1 course levels. In this sense, it seems that the data suggesting a connection between higher scores on the linguistic tasks and residence in a Spanish-speaking country as well as greater numbers of years of exposure to the language, rather than the overall proficiency level, is in line with our research hypotheses.

6. Concluding remarks

It has been seen that the linguistic task required integrating processing from several different domains. The syntactic and semantic information encoded in the utterances used had to be integrated with discourse knowledge in order to differentiate between the possible readings of the imperfect tense: quotative, habitual or irrealis. In accordance with our hypotheses (Section 3.2 above), the L2 learners encountered difficulty identifying the most adequate interpretation, especially in the more complex cases involving quotative readings of the IMP-IND, obtainable only under particular lexical and pragmatic conditions. Meanwhile, even native speakers of Spanish were found to present variability in their responses to the interpretation task, overall, and in particular in relation to certain items, including those obtaining echoic interpretations. It is thus worth bringing up some of the possible causes of the variability that we have identified in both L2 learners and the control group.

With respect to learners' responses, it has been observed that neither the L1, nor the overall level of proficiency in L2 Spanish, have been found to have a clear impact on the ability to interpret verbal mood alternation. Thus, putative advantages of similarity in the representation of morpho-syntactic properties between the L1 and L2 have not been identified in the data. In spite of the typological similarities between French and Spanish, most of the difficulties encountered by French L1 speakers were similar to those of the English-speaking group. Interpreting mood in Spanish is challenging, regardless of the L1, due to the fact that it involves integrating pragmatic (information from the communicative and discourse context), morpho-phonological (ability to detect imperfect indicative morpho-phonological features) and syntactic processing. As mentioned in the previous section, we have observed indications that the availability of long term, quality input has particularly positive effects on acquisition, perhaps because it leads to familiarity with the lexical, morphosyntactic and discourse conditions mood alternation involves.

Our findings point towards the idea that interface integration is an issue in L2 acquisition at upper intermediate and advanced levels. This can be seen as indirectly related to the claims of Sorace's Interface Hypothesis (Sorace 2011), although these claims are primarily related to ultimate attainment, not to developing L2 grammars.

As regards parameter re-setting, our findings are compatible with Lardiere's (2009) view that, regardless of the presence of similar formal features – morphological aspect, verbal mood – in the L1 for the French-speakers, differences in the way in which such features are assembled and the conditions for their expression entail that learners must re-configure sets of formal and semantic properties in order to acquire them in the L2. More specifically, the L1 French learners may rely on the functional opposition between indicative and subjunctive mood morphology, assuming that the category of mood is associated to the same features in the syntax of both their L1 and the L2. Nevertheless, in order to adequately interpret mood, these learners have to deal with the questions Lardiere (2009: 175) sums up as whether certain forms, in this case indicative or subjunctive, are optional or obligatory in certain contexts, and what constitutes an obligatory context for each mood.

Furthermore, L1 transfer did not seem to play a role in establishing the correct interpretations. Overall, our L2 Spanish speakers, regardless of their L1, show non-native like performance. In an account of SLA where interpretable features (selected, or not selected, during the course of L1 acquisition) are available for post-critical period L2 acquisition, the observed problems in both L2 groups cannot have their source in the (non-)availability of the mood feature in their L1s, and consequently in their interlanguages.

L2 speakers whose interpretations did not resemble those of the native speakers may have resorted to the use of a misanalysis strategy or mis-mapping between features and morpho-phonology, involving a wrong morphological 're-analysis' mechanism of the interpretable features in the target language by the assignment of (un-) available semantic features that regulate the distribution of these items. This may have encouraged optionality for the adult L2 speaker, justifying illegibility conditions at the interfaces. Along the previous lines, L2 speakers do not re-assign the values of (un-)available interpretable features to the parameterized interpretable ones. Thus, our findings suggested that in spite of long immersion and overt evidence of mood contrasts in the input, neither experimental group converged fully with the native speaker interpretations, regardless of whether there are cross-linguistic similarities or differences.

On the other hand, the variability found in the participants' responses to the items tested is likely to reflect, to a degree that cannot be clearly determined here due to the limitations of the present study, a lack of awareness of the presence of morphological mood marking, and hence of its effect on sentence meaning, in the test items. This line of reasoning would follow from hypotheses such as Clahsen and Felser's (2006) Shallow Structure Hypothesis (henceforth, SSH). L2 learners, on this view, pay limited attention to morpho-syntactic details during sentence processing, tending instead to allocate attentional resources to lexical-semantic cues. Thus, participants may have been less effective in distinguishing the most adequate interpretations because their processing resources were allocated to lexico-semantic analysis over and above identifying the relatively less salient details of the grammatical forms used, such as the mood in the conditional antecedents of the items tested.

In this respect, however, it was also seen in our study that certain interpretations were relatively challenging even for the control group. The SSH consists of a generalization related to L2 processing; therefore, an explanation of the variation found in the present study necessarily requires further consideration so as to be able to account not only for the learner groups but also for the control group.

As mentioned in 2.1, resolving aspectual coercion has been analysed as requiring complex cognitive processes of interpretation, since this phenomenon consists of a mismatch between the nature of an eventuality and the representation that the selection requirements imposed by grammatical elements in the sentential context require. The mismatch leads the addressee to recur to contextual assumptions which, introduced into the interpretation process, lead to identifying the speaker's meaning, according to the RT view of utterance interpretation (see introduction). However, the control group's responses showed variation not only in items involving quotativity; they also varied in their responses to items expected to give rise to habitual readings. Distinguishing these two kinds of readings requires enriching the tense and mood morphological cues with contextual assumption in order to reach an appropriate interpretation. The varied responses of the control group seem to indicate flexibility and spontaneity in accessing cognitive contexts that would facilitate one or another of the possible interpretations of the linguistic expressions.

According to the operation of pragmatic enrichment processes in utterance interpretation developed in RT, it was unsurprising that the control group responded irregularly, choosing interpretations other than those that were considered most appropriate, to the items that included instances of coercion. The range of possible contextual assumptions which are accessible to an addressee when interpreting utterances in the L1 can be expected to be much more ample than in an L2, as the overall processing effort can be expected to be less costly in the former case.

In sum, the results of our study can be seen as providing evidence of the differences between L1 and L2 processing in terms of the ability to access, manipulate and integrate information from diverse cognitive domains. Accessing contextual assumptions may be an interpretive advantage, but it is also a source of variability, related to the heuristic, inferential nature of utterance interpretation.

The framework offered by the cognitive pragmatics developed within RT provides a comprehensive and systematic perspective of how linguistic meaning interacts with context in human communication, thereby offering promising avenues of research into pragmatic phenomena in both language use and language acquisition. We hold that what this framework has to offer constitutes a necessary complement to theories of second language acquisition, considering the current state of the discipline and the recognition that linguistic interface areas constitute a focus for furthering current understanding of the principle challenges in SLA.

References

Ahern, A. 2004. *El subjuntivo: significado e inferencia. Un estudio basado en la Teoría de la Relevancia*. Ph.D. Dissertation, Madrid: UNED.
Ahern, A. 2006. "Spanish mood, metarrepresentation and propositional attitudes." In *Where Semantics Meets Pragmatics*, K. Turner and K. von Heusinger (eds), 445–471. Leiden: Brill.
Ahern, A. 2010. "Propositional attitudes in relevance theory: An overview." In *In the Mind and across Minds: A Relevance-Theoretic Perspective on Communication and Translation*, E. Wałaszewska, M. Kisielewska-Krysiuk and A. Piskorska (eds), 147–167. Cambridge: Cambridge Scholars.
Amenos-Pons, J. 2010. *Los tiempos de pasado del español y el francés: semántica, pragmática y aprendizaje de E/LE. Perspectivas desde la Teoría de la Relevancia*. Ph.D. Dissertation, Madrid: UNED.
Amenos-Pons, J. 2014. "Spanish 'Imperfecto' vs. French 'Imparfait' in hypothetical clauses: A procedural account." *Cahiers Chronos* 27: 243–271.
Andersen, R. and Shirai, Y. 1994. "Discourse motivations for some cognitive acquisition principles." *Studies in Second Language Acquisition* 16: 133–156.
DOI: 10.1017/S0272263100012845
Belletti, A., Bennati, E. and Sorace, A. 2007. "Theoretical and developmental issues in the syntax of subjects: Evidence from near-native Italian." *Natural Language and Linguistic Theory* 2: 657–689. DOI: 10.1007/s11049-007-9026-9
Bergs, A. and Heine, L. 2010. "Mood in English." In *Mood in the Languages of Europe*, B. Rothstein and R. Thieroff (eds), 103–116. Amsterdam: John Benjamins.
DOI: 10.1075/slcs.120.06ber
Borgonovo, C. and Prévost, P. 2003. "Knowledge of polarity subjunctive in L2 Spanish." In *Proceedings of the 27 Boston University Conference on Language Development*, B. Beachley, A. Brown and F. Conlin (eds), 150–161, Boston: Cascadilla Press.
Borgonovo, C. et al. 2008. "Methodological issues in the L2 acquisition of syntax/semantics phenomenon: How to assess L2 knowledge of mood in Spanish Relative Clauses." In *Proceedings of the Hispanic Linguistics Symposium*, J. Bruhn de Garavito and E. Valenzuela (eds), 13–24. Somerville, MA: Cascadilla Press.
Bott, O. 2010. *The Processing of Events*. Amsterdam: John Benjamins. DOI: 10.1075/la.162
Bres, J. 2006. "Encore un peu, et l'imparfait était un mode. L'imparfait et la valeur modale de contrefactualité." *Cahiers de Praxématique* 46: 149–176.
Bres, J. 2007. "Et plus si affinités… Des liaisons entre les instructions du plus-que-parfait et les relations d'ordre." *Cahiers Chronos* 18: 139–157.

Bres, J. 2009. "Sans l'imparfait, les vendanges tardives ne rentraient pas dans la jupe rhénane… Sur l'imparfait contrefactuel, pour avancer". *Syntaxe et Sémantique* 10: 33–50.

Chomsky, N. 2007. "Of minds and language." *Biolinguistics* 1: 9–27.

Chomsky, N. 1995. *The Minimalist Program*. Cambridge, MA: MIT Press.

Clahsen, H. and Felser, C. 2006. "Grammatical processing in language learners." *Applied Psycholinguistics* 27 (1): 3–42.

Corminboeuf, G. 2009. *L'expression de l'hypothèse en français. Entre hypotaxe et parataxe*. Bruxelles: De Boeck-Duculot.

De Mulder, W. 2010. "Mood in French". In *Mood in the Languages of Europe*, B. Rothstein and R. Thieroff (eds), 157–169. Amsterdam: John Benjamins.

De Saussure, L. 2003. *Temps et pertinence. Éléments de pragmatique cognitive du temps*. Bruxelles: De Boeck / Duculot.

De Saussure, L. 2013. "Perspectival interpretation of tenses." In *Time, Language, Cognition and Reality*, K.M. Jaszcolt and L. de Saussure (eds), 46–69. Oxford: Oxford University Press. DOI: 10.1093/acprof:oso/9780199589876.003.0004

Escandell-Vidal, V. and Leonetti, M. 2003. "On the quotative readings of Spanish imperfecto." *Cuadernos de Lingüística* X: 135–154.

Escandell-Vidal, V. and Leonetti, M. 2011. "On the rigidity of procedural meaning." In *Procedural Meaning: Problems and Perspectives*, V. Escandell-Vidal, M. Leonetti and A. Ahern (eds), 81–103. Bingley: Emerald.

Escandell-Vidal, V., Leonetti, M. and Ahern, A. (eds). 2011. *Procedural Meaning: Problems and Perspectives*. Bingley: Emerald.

Foster-Cohen, S. 2002. "The relevance of relevance theory to first and second language acquisition." In *Selected Papers on Theoretical and Applied Linguistics from the 14th International Symposium. Department of Theoretical and Applied Linguistics*, M. Makri-Tsilipaku (ed.), 9–23. Aristotle University of Thessaloniki, Greece.

Giorgi, A. and Pianesi, F. 1997. *Tense and Aspect. From Semantics to Morphosyntax*. New York / Oxford: Oxford University Press.

Grevisse. M. 2011. *Le bon usage de la langue française*, 15th Edition. Bruxelles: De Boeck-Duculot.

Hambleton, R.K., Swaminathan, H., & Rogers, H.J. 1991. *Fundamentals of Item Response Theory*. Newbury Park, CA: Sage Pres.

Huddleston, R. 1989. *An Introduction to English Transformational Syntax*. London: Longman.

Iverson, M., Kempchinsky, P. and Rothman, J. 2008. "Interface vulnerability and knowledge of the subjunctive/indicative distinction with negated epistemic predicates in L2 Spanish." *EUROSLA Yearbook* 8: 135–163. DOI: 10.1075/eurosla.8.09ive

Jary, M. 2009. "Relevance, assertion and possible worlds: A cognitive approach to the Spanish subjunctive." In *Utterance Interpretation and Cognitive Models*, P. de Brabantier and M. Kissine (eds), 235–277. Bingley: Emerald. DOI: 10.1163/9789004253148_010

Lardiere, D. 2008. "Feature assembly in second language in second language acquisition." In *Features in Second Language Acquisition*, J. Liceras et al. (eds), 106–140. New Jersey: Lawrence Erlbaum.

Lardiere, D. 2009. "Some thoughts on a contrastive analysis of feature in second language acquisition." *Second Language Research* 25 (2): 173–227. DOI: 10.1177/0267658308100283

Moeschler, J. 1998. "Pragmatique de la référence temporelle." In *Le temps des événements*, J. Moeschler (ed.), 157–180. Paris: Kimé.

Montolío, E. 1999. "Las construcciones condicionales." In *Gramática descriptiva de la lengua española. Vol. 3. Entre la oración y el discurso*, I. Bosque Morfología and V. Demonte (eds), 3643–3739. Madrid: Espasa-Calpe.

Montrul, S. and Slabakova, R. 2002. "On aspectual shifts in L2 Spanish." In *BUCLD 26 Proceedings*, B. Skarabela et al. (eds), 631–642. Somerville, MA: Cascadilla Press.

Montrul, S. and Slabakova, R. 2003. "Competence similarities between natives and near-native speakers: An investigation of the preterit/imperfect contrast in Spanish." *Studies in Second Language Acquisition* 25: 351–398. DOI: 10.1017/S0272263103000159

Nicolle, S. 1997. "A relevance-theoretic account of be going to." *Journal of Linguistics* 33: 355–377. DOI: 10.1017/S0022226797006567

Palmer, F.R. 2001. *Mood and Modality*, 2nd Edition. Cambridge: Cambridge University Press. DOI: 10.1017/CBO9781139167178

Perez-Leroux, A et al. 2007. "Non-native recognition of the iterative and habitual meanings of Spanish preterite and imperfect tenses." In *The Role of Formal Features in Second Language Acquisition*, J. Liceras, H. Zolb and H. Goodluck (eds), 432–451. London: Routledge.

Real Academia Española and Asociación de Academias de la Lengua Española. 2009. *Nueva gramática de la lengua española*. Madrid: Espasa.

Rothman, J. 2009. "Understanding the nature and outcomes of early bilingualism: Romance languages as heritage languages." *International Journal of Bilingualism* 13 (2): 145–155.

Rothman, J. and Slabakova, R. 2011. "The mind-context divide: On linguistic interfaces and language acquisition." *Lingua* 121 (4): 568–576 DOI: 10.1016/j.lingua.2011.01.003

Rouchota, V. 1994. "The subjunctive in modern Greek: Dividing the labour between semantics and pragmatics." *Journal of Modern Greek Studies* 12: 185–201. DOI: 10.1353/mgs.2010.0319

Serratrice, L., Sorace, A. and Paoli, S. 2004. "Transfer at the syntax-pragmatics interface: Subjects and objects in Italian-English bilingual and monolingual acquisition." *Bilingualism: Language and Cognition* 7: 183–205. DOI: 10.1017/S1366728904001610

Sorace, A. 2006. "Gradience and optionality in mature and developing grammars." In *Gradience in Grammars: Generative Perspectives*, G. Fanselow et al. (eds), 106–123. Oxford: Oxford University Press. DOI: 10.1093/acprof:oso/9780199274796.003.0006

Sorace, A. 2011. "Pinning down the concept of 'interface' in bilingualism." *Linguistic Approaches to Bilingualism* 1: 1–33. DOI: 10.1075/lab.1.1.01sor

Sperber, D. and Wilson, D. 1986/1995. *Relevance. Communication and Cognition*. Oxford: Blackwell.

Terrell, T.D. and Hooper, J. 1974. "A semantically based analysis of mood in Spanish." *Hispania* 57: 484–494. DOI: 10.2307/339187

Tsimpli, I.M. and Sorace, A. 2006. "Differentiating interfaces: L2 performance in syntax-semantics and syntax-discourse phenomena." In *Proceedings of the 30th Boston University Conference on Language Development*, D. Bamman, T. Magnitskaia and C. Zaller (eds), 653–664. Somerville, MA: Cascadilla Press.

Tsimpli, I.M., Sorace, A., Heycock, C. and Filiaci, F. 2004. "First language attrition and syntactic subjects: A study of Greek and Italian near-native speakers of English." *International Journal of Bilingualism* 8: 257–277. DOI: 10.1177/13670069040080030601

White, L. 2003. *Second Language Acquisition and Universal Grammar*. New York: Cambridge University Press. DOI: 10.1017/CBO9780511815065

White, L. 2009. "Grammatical theory: Interfaces and L2 knowledge." In *Handbook of Second Language Acquisition*, W. Ritchie and T.K. Bhatia (eds), 49–67. Bingley: Emerald.

Appendix: Examples from the task

Included here are the actual stimuli used in the interpretation task, including at least an example of each type of item, as discussed in Section 3.1 above.

> 1. (Fragmento de un artículo de prensa escrito después de unas elecciones)
> El programa electoral del Partido Ecologista establecía que **si llegaba al Gobierno acabaría con la energía nuclear en España en menos de 20 años** y la sustituiría por energías renovables.

Según la frase destacada, entendemos que…
a) ahora mismo, la llegada del Partido Ecologista al Gobierno es una posibilidad para el futuro.
b) cada vez que el Partido Ecologista llegaba al Gobierno, intentaba acabar con la energía nuclear.
c) **llegar al Gobierno era la intención del Partido Ecologista en el momento de preparar el programa electoral.**

> 6. (Conversación entre compañeros de trabajo acerca de otro compañero que tenía la intención de irse de la empresa)
> + Al final, ¿Pedro se va?
> – Pues sí, dice que sí. Hombre, parece que **si podía seguir en las mismas condiciones en que estaba no se iba**. Pero al final no le han dado permiso.

Según la persona que responde…
a) ahora mismo, aún es posible que Pedro pueda seguir en las mismas condiciones.
b) cada vez que Pedro era autorizado a seguir en las mismas condiciones, se quedaba en la empresa.
c) **Pedro quería quedarse, pero exigía seguir en las mismas condiciones.**

> 9. (Irene estaba en París con su novio, pero se enfadaron y él se fue; ella se quedó sola durante unos días)
> En París, Irene pasó más horas en el hotel que en ningún otro viaje en toda su vida. Y **si salía a la calle procuraba no mirar**. No quería ver París en esa situación.

Según la frase destacada, entendemos que…
a) **cada vez que Irene estaba en la calle, intentaba no ver nada.**
b) en aquel momento, Irene tenía la intención de salir a la calle, pero no quería mirar.
c) es posible que Irene salga a la calle ahora, pero es poco probable.

> 12. (Un paciente acaba de cambiar de médico y habla de sus experiencias con otros médicos)
> Yo siempre tenía vértigo… **Si me trataban con medicina natural, yo creo que era una medicina equivocada.**

Según el paciente…
a) él quiere ser tratado con medicina natural en el futuro.
b) **no sabe exactamente si el tratamiento que estaba recibiendo en el pasado era medicina natural o no.**
c) para él, en el pasado, ser tratado con medicina natural era una expectativa, un deseo.

> 13. (Fragmento de entrevista a un amante de los deportes de aventura)
> Saltar en paracaídas desde un globo es una experiencia muy distinta a saltar desde un avión. Caer desde un globo es una experiencia tan agradable que **si durara toda la vida no me importaría.**

Según el deportista entrevistado…
a) antes, cada vez que saltaba, le gustaba que la caída fuese muy larga.
b) en el pasado, tenía el proyecto de tener una caída muy larga.
c) **desearía que las caídas fuesen muy largas, porque son muy agradables.**

> 16. (Entrevista a un escritor que siempre lleva bufanda y fuma puros)
> + Para usted, ¿qué es más importante: el puro o la bufanda?
> − Mire usted: **si jugara a las cartas y perdiera, nunca dejaría ninguna de las dos cosas.** Antes me quitaría la corbata, por ejemplo.

Según el escritor…
a) en el pasado, cada vez que jugaba y perdía, se quitaba la corbata, pero no dejaba la bufanda ni el puro.
b) en el pasado, tuvo intención de jugar a las cartas, pero decidió no dejar la bufanda ni el puro.
c) **si, en el futuro, juega y pierde, se quitará la corbata, pero no dejará la bufanda ni el puro.**

> 19. (Luis le cuenta a Juan la disputa que ha tenido con un Antonio, un amigo común)
> ¿Qué si estoy enfadado? Enfadado es poco, estoy enfadadísimo. Mira, es que **si me lo encontrara de frente, por la calle, no sé qué le decía**, oye.

Luis dice que…
a) en el momento de hablar, tenía la intención de ver a Antonio, pero no podía prever su reacción.
b) en el pasado, cada vez que veía a Antonio, era difícil prever su reacción.
c) **si cen el futuro ve a Antonio, no sabe cómo va a reaccionar.**

> 20. (Luisa da consejos sentimentales a su amiga Ana)
> **Si yo estuviera en tu lugar, rompía con ese chico de una vez.** Después de lo que te ha hecho, es lo que se lo merece.

Según la frase destacada, entendemos que…
   a) cuando Luisa era novia de ese chico, cada vez que tenían problemas ella rompía con él.
   b) en el pasado, Ana tenía la intención de romper con ese chico, gracias al consejo de Luisa.
   c) **Luisa aconseja a Ana romper inmediatamente con ese chico.**

Word order and case in the comprehension of L2 German by L1 English speakers

Tom Rankin
Vienna University of Economics and Business

This paper replicates and extends experiments by Grüter (2006) and Grüter & Conradie (2006) to explore some of the learnability implications of Full Transfer at the initial state of L2A. L1 English-speaking learners' comprehension of L2 German questions and relative clauses is tested on the basis of a picture interpretation task. Patterns of (mis)interpretation of the German clauses suggest that lower-intermediate proficiency learners still access the L1 syntax in order to parse L2 input. This is taken to indicate that learners are influenced by L1 word order patterns in assigning thematic roles in L2 clauses. This is discussed in light of approaches to L2 parsing and processing which attribute different roles to L1 influence.

1. Introduction

Full Transfer (Schwartz & Sprouse 1994, 1996) as a model of the initial state in L2A has received a great deal of theoretical and empirical support, not least in the form of compelling evidence from comprehension studies by Grüter (2006) and Grüter & Conradie (2006). They studied the comprehension of L2 German wh-questions at the initial state and interpreted their results to mean that second language learners access the full L1 syntactic representation to parse L2 input. By replicating Grüter's methodology with L2 German learners beyond the initial state, the study presented below seeks to explore the learnability implications of Full Transfer/Full Access/Full Parse (to give the model its full name, but henceforth simply 'FT' for simplicity). This predicts that learners can assign "deep" syntactic parses to input and that the grammar is restructured when it cannot assign a parse to L2 input strings.

Studying how L2 German speakers parse input also touches upon contemporary controversies in L2 processing and parsing research, which VanPatten & Jegerski (2010: 8) observe are "reminiscent" of the earlier debates on the extent of syntactic transfer at the initial state. FT again constitutes one end of the theoretical spectrum on parsing and processing. Dekydtspotter, Schwartz & Sprouse (2006: 35) point out that differences between native and L2 processing may have a number of sources which do not involve fundamentally different parsing mechanisms. At the other extreme in the parsing/processing debate, the Shallow Structure Hypothesis (Clahsen & Felser 2006), at least in a strong form of the model, sees no role for the L1 in L2 processing. Rather than computing syntactic parses during L2 processing, learners over-rely on universal lexical and pragmatic strategies, unlike native speakers.

Existing work on online processing in L1 English-L2 German has found that intermediate and advanced learners tend to have similar subject-first parsing strategies as native speakers (Jackson 2008, 2010). Overall, these results seem to reflect target parsing strategies and so do not support the notion that L2 processing is generally "shallower" than native processing. However, the nature and role of the L1 syntax and the status of the L2 grammatical representation remain unclear. In order to assign target parses and interpretations to German clauses, L1 English-speaking learners need to have reset the grammatical properties of their initial state grammar to the target verb second (V2) and verb-final (OV) settings. A general subject-first parsing strategy may reflect target parsing preferences, but does not necessarily mean that learners also have target-like syntax underlying their parsing. A replication of Grüter's experiment with L1 English-L2 German learners beyond the initial state should shed light on any continued L1 syntactic influence in the comprehension of L2 input, and thus contribute to the debate on transfer in L2 processing and parsing, and, in turn, to our understanding of the development of L2 knowledge.

The paper is organized as follows: The linguistic background and the relevant syntactic properties of English and German are discussed in the next section. The following two sections then survey previous work on parsing at the initial state and processing at higher proficiencies in L1 English-L2 German acquisition. The predictions for the experiment are then discussed in light of these previous results. Presentation of the experimental task and discussion of the results conclude the paper.

2. Syntactic structure and surface order in English and German

German and English differ in their verb movement properties and the settings for headedness of VP and IP. German instantiates V-to-C movement (the V2 property) while English does not permit lexical verb movement (V3). VP and IP are head-final in German (OV property). English is head-initial and verbs precede their objects (VO). These differences give rise to a series of surface word order distinctions between the languages concerning the linearization of verbs with respect to arguments and adjuncts.

However, for the purposes of the experiment outlined below, the more interesting clauses are those where surface word order is identical in English and German, as is the case in some wh-questions and relative clauses. Such clauses are compatible with either a German V2/OV grammar or an English V3/VO grammar. Each grammar will, however, license different interpretations. The V3/VO properties of English mean that there are consistent word order asymmetries in subject versus object wh-questions and relative clauses. In wh-questions, the wh-phrase and auxiliaries raise to CP. Where there are no auxiliaries, the dummy auxiliary *do* raises to C. Subject wh-questions are an exception in that they require no movement of auxiliaries and no *do*-insertion. Mapping between word order and interpretation is always consistent, as illustrated in (1) and (2). (I leave aside a great deal of syntactic detail which is not relevant to the study, especially on the analysis of English subject-questions, see for example Agbayani 2000; Pesetsky & Torrego 2001).

(1) What$_{SUBJ}$ chased the cat$_{OBJ}$?

(2) What$_{OBJ}$ did the dog$_{SUBJ}$ chase?

In relative clauses, the relative pronoun moves to CP. The verb remains in situ. This gives rise again to word order asymmetries between subject and object clauses, as shown in (3) and (4).

(3) The animal which$_{SUBJ}$ chased the cat$_{OBJ}$.

(4) The animal which$_{OBJ}$ the dog$_{SUBJ}$ chased.

By contrast, German shows no word order asymmetries in subject versus object questions and relatives. In simple tense wh-questions, V2 means that the finite lexical verb appears in second position after the wh-phrase, giving rise to consistent Wh-V-DP order. In compound tenses, the finite auxiliary appears in second position and the participle occurs clause-finally, producing Wh-Aux-DP-V order. Interpretation is conditioned by case-marking on wh-phrases and DPs, as shown in (5) to (8).

(5) Wer   sieht   den   Hund?
    who.NOM   see.3PS   the.ACC   dog
    'Who sees the dog?'

(6) Wen   sieht   der   Hund?
     who.ACC see.3PS   the.NOM dog
     'Whom does the dog see?'

(7) Wer   hat   den   Hund gesehen?
     who.NOM have.3PS the.ACC dog   see
     'Who has seen the dog?'

(8) Wen   hat   der   Hund gesehen?
     who.ACC have.3PS the.NOM dog   see
     'Whom has the dog seen?'

Examples (9) and (10) show that simple tense relative clauses in German always display the order RelPro-DP-V, with thematic roles indicated by case marking on relative pronouns and DPs.

(9) Der Mann, den   der   Hund sieht.
     the man   who.ACC the.NOM dog   see.3PS
     'The man whom the dog sees.'

(10) Der Mann, der   den   Hund sieht.
     the man   who.NOM the.ACC dog   see.3PS
     'The man who sees the dog.'

However, only masculine DPs inflect for accusative case. So, in combination with the word order facts, nominative-accusative syncretism in singular feminine and neuter DPs produces a range of globally ambiguous clauses such as those in (11) and (12).

(11) Was   jagt   die   Katze?
     what.NOM/ACC   chase.3PS   the.NOM/ACC cat
     'What is the cat chasing?' **or** 'What is chasing the cat?'

(12) Das Tier,   das   die   Katze jagt.
     the animal,   which.NOM/ACC the.NOM/ACC cat   chases.3PS
     'The animal which the cat chases' **or** 'The animal which chases the cat.'

In sum, despite underlying differences in their phrase structures, English and German share identical surface word order in a range of clause types. German present tense questions have the same linear order as English simple present tense *subject* questions. German present tense relative clauses have the same linear order as English simple present tense *object* relative clauses. Thus for L1 English-speaking learners of L2 German, questions and relatives in the input will be formally compatible with an English V3/VO parse. Where a learner is influenced by English word order patterns in their parsing of German questions and relatives, this will also give rise to non-target patterns of interpretation (see discussion of Grüter 2006 below). In order to provide target interpretations of German questions and relatives, learners will need (i) to have acquired the V2/OV properties of German, and (ii) be able to process case-marking and use it is a cue to thematic role assignment. These issues are explored in the next two sections to set the scene for the study.

3. Parsing at the initial state in L1 English-L2 German

Grüter (2006) and Grüter & Conradie (2006) exploit the ambiguity of German wh-questions as in (13)–(14) to study the extent of L1 syntactic transfer at the initial state. Using a picture interpretation task, they test the comprehension of such questions by L1 English and Afrikaans speakers. (This experiment is replicated and therefore described in more detail in 'Method and Materials' section below.)

(13) Was$_{SUBJ/OBJ}$ beisst die Katze$_{SUBJ/OBJ}$?
'What is biting the cat?' / 'What is the cat biting?'

(14) Was $_{SUBJ/OBJ}$ hat die Katze$_{SUBJ/OBJ}$ gebissen?
'What has bitten the cat?' / 'What has the cat bitten?'

The main predictions they test are those of Full Transfer versus Minimal Trees (Vainnika & Young-Scholten 1996a, b). According to a model such as Minimal Trees, in which only lexical categories transfer, learners would not be able to assign a full parse to structures involving movement of wh-phrases to functional positions above the VP. For comprehension, this would mean that learners at the initial state would have to resort to a default non-syntactic strategy in interpreting wh-questions. In the absence of a syntactic parse, they may show evidence of guessing in their patterns of responses. Alternatively, a default preference for a linear order strategy, i.e. assigning the agent theta role to the first NP in the clause, would give rise to a preference for subject interpretations. Full Transfer, however, predicts that wh-questions will pose no parsing problem *per se* because the functional structure to license a full parse can be transferred from the L1. Crucially, however, if learners access the L1 syntax, the interpretation assigned to questions will be that permitted by the L1 parse.

This leads to clear predictions for the parsing of L2 German wh-questions by L1 English and L1 Afrikaans speakers. Because Afrikaans has the same V2/OV syntactic structure as German, FT predicts that Afrikaans speakers should perform similarly to German native speakers in their interpretation of wh-questions as in (13) and (14), they should provide ambiguous interpretations. An English parse, however, will permit only a subject interpretation of simple tense questions (13) and an object interpretation of compound tense questions (14). Recall that German present tense questions share an identical linear order with English simple present tense *subject* questions while German perfect tense questions are linearly identical to English perfect tense *object* questions. It is thus expected that the tense condition will affect L1 English speakers' interpretation but not the L1 Afrikaans'.

The results of the picture interpretation experiments support the Full Transfer position. The Afrikaans speakers show patterns of interpretation similar to native German speakers (see Grüter & Conradie 2006: 110–111 for more discussion). The more interesting results for the purposes of the experiment presented below come from the L1 English speakers. Responses were coded as either subject only, object only, both (i.e. where a participant checked both possible subject and object answers to ambiguous questions), or neither (i.e. where a participant chose 'don't know'). The English speakers' patterns of interpretation differ significantly compared to the native German speakers. The native speakers recognized the ambiguity in the questions and chose both possible answers at rates of 40.7% in the present tense and 45.3% in the perfect tense (for more discussion see Grüter 2006: 311). The L1 English speakers' did not recognize the ambiguity and never chose both possible answers as a response to a question. More importantly, the tense of the question had a significant effect in the learner group but no effect in the native group. Learners assigned subject interpretations to simple tense questions at a rate of 71.2%, and object interpretations to perfect tense questions at a rate of 97.1%.

Thus, where the predictions of the models of transfer diverge, FT is supported. The comprehension of questions is consistent with learners having transferred the full L1 phrase structure and movement operations in their parsing of L2 input. This is schematized in (15) and (16).

(15) English parse of German simple tense questions:
Was jagt die Katze → $[_{CP}\ WH_{Subj\ C}\ \emptyset\ [_{IP}\ t_{WH\ I}\ \emptyset\ [_{VP}\ t_{WH}\ V\ DP_{Obj}]]]$

(16) English parse of German perfect tense questions:
Was hat die Katze gejagt → $[_{CP}\ WH_{Obj\ C}\ Aux\ [_{IP}\ DP_{Subj\ I}\ t_{AUX}\ [_{VP}\ t_{Subj}\ V\ t_{WH}]]]$

Summarising, at the initial state, these learners seem to show no effect of a general processing limitation. However, the input is apparently filtered through the L1 syntax, thus giving rise to non-target interpretation of L2 clauses. Of course, the studies surveyed did not make use of online processing methodologies, so we cannot say how the time course of sentence processing proceeded. However, evidence from processing in L1 English-L2 German at higher proficiencies also suggests that there is no general impairment in L2 processing.

4. Processing at higher proficiencies in L1 English-L2 German

In a series of studies, Jackson and colleagues have explored the processing of L2 German by L1 English-speaking learners at intermediate at high proficiencies (Jackson 2007; Jackson & Bobb 2009; Jackson & Dussias 2009; Jackson, Dussias & Hristova 2012). Two studies (Jackson 2008, 2010) in particular provide interesting points of comparison with Grüter. These studies also tested the comprehension of simple tense and compound tense wh-questions, but with case-marking information unambiguously marking thematic roles. They used reading time methodologies to test for online processing effects in addition to comprehension.

The clauses tested were temporarily ambiguous simple past tense questions (17)–(18) and perfect tense questions (19)–(20).

(17) Welche   Ingenieurin traf der   Chemiker gestern
     which.NOM/ACC engineer   met the.NOM chemist   yesterday
     Nachmittag im   Café?
     afternoon   on in the café.
     'Which engineer did the chemist meet yesterday afternoon in the café?'

(18) Welche   Ingenieurin traf den   Chemiker gestern
     which.NOM/ACC engineer   met the.ACC chemist   yesterday
     Nachmittag im   Café?
     afternoon   on in the café.
     'Which engineer met the chemist yesterday afternoon in the café?'

(19) Welche   Ingenieurin hat der   Chemiker gestern
     which.NOM/ACC engineer   has the.NOM chemist   yesterday
     Nachmittag getroffen?
     afternoon   met
     'Which engineer did the chemist meet yesterday afternoon?'

(20) Welche   Ingenieurin hat den   Chemiker gestern
     which.NOM/ACC engineer   has the.ACC chemist   yesterday
     Nachmittag getroffen?
     afternoon   met
     'Which engineer met the chemist yesterday afternoon?'

In each case, the initial feminine wh-phrase (*die Ingenieurin*) is not overtly marked for nominative or accusative case. Only the presence of case marking on the second masculine DP (*der/den Chemiker*) disambiguates to either a subject-first or object first order. Studying reading times at the crucial disambiguating DP by L1 English speakers addresses whether learners have integrated case-marking into their German grammar and can use it online to assign thematic roles. Assuming a general subject-first parsing strategy, reading times will be longer where case disambiguates to an object-first clause. Reading times in the different tense conditions show whether learners rely on encountering the lexical verb before assigning thematic roles or whether, like native-speakers, they can assign thematic roles incrementally during processing before encountering the clause-final verb (Jackson 2008: 883–884). The same sorts of questions are explored in Jackson (2010), with the addition of L1 influence as a variable. The same sentences are tested with L1 Dutch learners of German. If there is L1 influence, there would be different processing costs for L1 Dutch versus L1 English speakers according to tense as Dutch word order is identical to German in the clauses tested.

The results overall show a significant effect of the disambiguation to subject-first versus object-first. Subject-first order was easier to process and comprehend across the board in comparison to object-first order (including for native German speakers). In comprehension accuracy, there was an effect of proficiency in the 2008 study, whereby intermediate-level learners were less accurate than advanced learners, but there was no difference between advanced learners and native German speakers. Tense had no effect on comprehension, but there was an interaction of tense and word order for the advanced learners; object-first order caused more comprehension problems in simple past tense compared to the perfect tense.

The reading time results revealed a similar pattern. Overall, object-first questions required longer reading times than subject-first for intermediate, advanced and native speakers. There was an effect of proficiency on reading times at the case-marked DP. Intermediate learners showed no significant slow-down, while advanced and native German speakers patterned together by reading significantly more slowly when case disambiguated to an object-first order. Intermediate learners showed no effects of verb tense. As with comprehension accuracy, there was an interaction between tense and word order for the advanced learners' reading times; object-first order caused significantly longer reading times in the simple tense but not in the perfect tense.

In the 2010 study comparing Dutch and English-speaking learners of German, there were no L1 effects on comprehension accuracy. The reading times replicated the earlier results, with a general preference for subject-first parsing, and thus longer reading times where case disambiguated to object-first order. There were no interactions between tense and word order, tense and L1, or tense by word order by L1. However, at the Adv/PP region following the case-marked DP, there was a significant word order by L1 interaction, and tense by word order by L1 interaction. The English speakers were significantly slower on object-first word order in simple past questions but not in the perfect tense. There was no effect of tense on the L1 Dutch or native German speakers.

Summarising the results, all the learners (intermediate and advanced L1 English, and advanced L1 Dutch) showed a general subject-first preference in parsing, similar to the parsing patterns of native German speakers. At advanced levels at least, learners are able to integrate case-marking online and use it to assign thematic roles. However, there does seem to be an effect of L1, particularly with regard to tense. So while there are general similarities in L2 processing regardless of L1, the "subtle differences that emerged between the two L2 learner groups highlight the difficulty of developing an adequate model to explain L2 processing mechanisms – underscoring that these mechanisms might not be universal, but rather in certain situations, an L2 learner's native language can have an impact on how they process L2 input, even at more advanced levels of proficiency" (Jackson 2010: 224).

Obviously, Jackson's focus was on issues specific to online L2 processing rather than the nature of L1 syntactic transfer and the possible effects of L1 word order in the processing of L2 sentences. However, given the learnability implications of FT and Grüter's initial state findings, one might ask whether the subtle L1 influence detected in the online studies is in fact the result of syntactic transfer. These issues are explored in what follows.

5. Representation, processing and learnability: Predictions for L1 English-L2 German

In light of the results obtained by Grüter & Conradie and Jackson, subtle questions emerge about the relationship between the L1, L2 grammatical knowledge and the parsing of target-language input. It seems that at the initial state, parsing (and thus comprehension) is conditioned by the L1 syntax. At intermediate levels of proficiency, learners already appear to have adopted target parsing preferences during online processing (although they still have problems integrating case-marking). The questions are: what is the nature of the grammar which underlies the parsing? Learners who have a target subject-first parsing strategy need not necessarily have the target German V2/OV grammar. Is there influence of L1 word order? The differences in reading times and comprehension accuracy for different clauses might betray L1 syntactic transfer during parsing (see further below).

Given the initial state results, and learnability considerations in L1 English-L2 German, it would in fact be surprising if there was no effect of L1 syntax beyond the initial state. Consider Grüter's (2006: 87) observation that the initial state "constitutes a crucial factor in determining the course that subsequent L2 development can and must take." The transferred English V3/VO representation will be able to assign formal parses (though possibly with non-target interpretations) to a wide variety of clauses, including declarative SVO, simple and compound tense questions, relative clauses and copular clauses. Under such conditions, where the initial state grammar is relatively successful in parsing a certain range of input structures, a failure-driven approach to L2 grammatical development would predict that L1 transfer will persist into higher levels of proficiency. White (2003: 34), for example, states that "in some cases the L1 grammar may appear to accommodate the L2 input adequately and thus change will not be triggered." A range of findings on L2 German support the notion that target word order is only gradually acquired (see extensive discussion in Meisel 2011: 119ff.). Indeed, Meisel (2011: 132) points out that "[ungrammatical V3 order] represents a particularly persistent pattern in the speech of L2 learners of German." This is supported by research on L1 English-L2 German by Beck (1998), who finds that learners have persistent problems with the V2 pattern. The influence of L1 word order is thus known to persist at higher proficiency levels.

Against this background, it is somewhat surprising that Jackson finds no strong evidence of the influence of L1 word order in parsing. However, as already alluded to, it is possible that the "subtle" L1 effects uncovered in Jackson's experiments *are* in fact a manifestation of L1 syntactic transfer. Recall that the learners with L1 English showed greater processing costs when case disambiguated to an object-first order in simple past tense questions as compared to perfect tense questions. This is compatible with Grüter's findings and the possible continued influence of the L1 during processing. To recap, Grüter showed that English speakers preferentially interpret simple tense German questions as subject questions and compound tense questions as object questions. This provides a possible explanation for Jackson's findings of longer reading times and lower comprehension accuracy in object-first simple tense questions versus object-first compound tense questions. If there is continued influence from L1 English word order, there will be a stronger expectation of subject-first clauses in simple tenses and object-first order in compound tenses. Disambiguation to object-first order would thus violate a stronger expectation in simple tenses, giving rise to the effects Jackson identified; that is, longer reading-times and lower comprehension accruacy. This speculation presupposes that the L1 grammar is available and is activated during processing of L2 input at higher levels of proficiency (as would be assumed by a model such as MOGUL, Sharwood Smith & Truscott 2005; Truscott 2006).

By replicating Grüter's picture interpretation task, and extending it to include relative clauses and case-marking, the study presented below seeks to explore whether L1 English-L2 German learners after the initial state do in fact continue to show evidence of the influence of English word order in their parses of German input. This is tested on the basis of ambiguous questions and relative clauses (21)–(22) and case-marked questions and relative clauses (23)–(24).

(21) Was jagt die Katze?

(22) Das Tier, das die Katze jagt.

(23) Was jagt der/den Hund?

(24) Das Tier, das der/den Hund jagt.

Interpretation of clauses such as (21) and (22) permits predictions with respect to the roles of general parsing strategies versus target or non-target syntactic properties. In the absence of case-marking, any interpretation is of course possible and case will not motivate any reanalysis. We should, therefore, see interpretations licensed purely by the nature of the parse assigned to the input. Because the grammatical properties of English and German license different interpretations, we can use comprehension as a way of judging the nature of the parse assigned to the clauses. The predictions are summarized in Table 1.

It is more difficult to predict the role of case-marking for the pre-intermediate learners who participated in the study. Jackson (2008) finds that her intermediate-level learners do not show reading time effects immediately at disambiguating case-marking. They do, however, exhibit longer reading times at the sentence-final segment on object-first clauses. This may mean that even though they do not *immediately* integrate case-marking into the argument structure of the clause, they do "not completely disregard case-marking information" (Jackson 2008: 899). For pre-intermediate learners, we can thus predict that they will also not immediately integrate case-marking information. In the sort of offline task used for the experiment below, they may, however, be able to use case to arrive at target interpretations, even if they delay assigning interpretation to the end of the clause and cannot yet process case in a target-like way online. If learners can make use of case-marking for interpretation, it is predicted that interpretation of case-marked clauses will be more target-like. If they do not use case-marking, we should see similar effects as outlined in Table 1; if case-marking is not part of the learners' grammars they will have to resort to word order patterns (possibly influenced by L1 patterns) to arrive at interpretations of the clauses.

Table 1. Predictions for comprehension of clauses in L2 German

If general subject-first strategy	→	subject interpretation of all clauses
If target V2 syntax	→	ambiguous interpretation of questions
If target OV syntax	→	ambiguous interpretation of relatives
If non-target V3 syntax	→	subject interpretation of questions
If non-target VO syntax	→	object interpretation of relatives

6. The study

6.1 Participants

15 instructed learners (5 female / 10 male) of L2 German with L1 English were recruited for the study. The learners were in the latter stages of the UK GCSE high-school course in German. This places them at the pre-intermediate or elementary level (A2–B1) on the Common European Framework. This proficiency level was targeted to fill the gap between Grüter's initial state learners and Jackson's intermediate to advanced learners. At this level we should see whether L1 influence persists, which in turn would lend credence to the idea that residual transfer may be identified at even higher proficiency levels.

The learners were remarkably homogenous in terms of their learning profiles. With the exception of one learner who had started learning German at 8 years old, the age of onset was similar for all learners, whose first exposure to German was when it was introduced into the school curriculum (see Table 2). The majority of learners had the same experience with German, which came exclusively from instruction. Only three learners reported that they read or heard German outside of instruction. Input was thus limited mainly to classroom-based instruction, which amounts to approximately 360 contact hours by the end of the course of study.

Table 2. Learners' bio data

Age	Age of onset of acquisition	Length of instruction
16.3 yrs.	11.8 yrs. (range 8–13)	5 yrs. (range 5–8*)

* With the exception of the one learner who started German instruction in primary school, all the learners were in their fifth year of instruction.

Control data for comparison came from 14 native speakers of German tested in Austria (7 female, 7 male; M age = 28.9 years).

6.2 Method and materials

The essential elements of Grüter's picture interpretation task were replicated. Cartoon scenes of animals were projected onto a white screen using MS PowerPoint. Each scene was accompanied by questions / statements which identified (an) animal(s) in the picture. The experiment was preceded by an explanation of the procedure in English and an opportunity to practice. There were a total of 4 different cartoons, each of which was accompanied by 4 sentences. Each scene was preceded by a brief explanation in English, which provided the translation equivalents

Word order and case in the comprehension of L2 German 213

• In the next four scenes, animals are chasing each other. • Ein Tier jagt das nächste Tier. Die Tiere sind: – eine Fliege – a fly – ein Elefant – an elephant – eine Kuh – a cow – ein Fuchs – a fox – eine Maus – a mouse	Das Tier, das der Fuchs jagt. 	Was jagt die Kuh? 

Figure 1. Example of the experimental stimuli

of the names of the animals depicted to ensure that the learners were all familiar with the relevant vocabulary.[1] Presentation of the sentences was timed at 10 second intervals (see Figure 1 for excerpt of the progression of the experiment). The learners' task was simply to record the animals identified by the sentences by circling the appropriate answers in a pre-prepared multiple-choice answer sheet.

The total of 16 test sentences consisted of 2 x ambiguous questions, 2 x case-marked questions, 2 x ambiguous relative clauses, 2 x case-marked relative clauses. The 8 remaining sentences were NVN declaratives which required a true or false response and different wh-question forms. These serve as distracters for the purposes of the results presented here.

As in Grüter's study, responses to ambiguous clauses were coded for type of answer as follows:

i. 'subject' where only the subject interpretation was chosen
ii. 'object' where only the object interpretation was chosen
iii. 'ambiguous' where both possible answers were checked
iv. 'no response' where the 'don't know' option was checked

Given that case-marked clauses are unambiguous, and that the native speakers showed no variation in their responses (see below), the learners' interpretations of case-marked clauses were further coded simply as 'target' or 'non-target'.

---

1. The vocabulary (both the names of animals and the verbs used in the clauses) had also previously been checked with the class teacher to verify whether the learners would be familiar with the lexical items used. In addition, many of the animal names were close cognates in English and German, e.g. camel – Kamel, fox – Fuchs, etc. There should, therefore, have been no major difficulty with the items used.

6.3 Results

Results are presented and discussed separately for ambiguous clauses and unambiguous case-marked clauses.

6.3.1 Interpretation of ambiguous clauses

The results from the native German group's interpretation of ambiguous questions mirrored those obtained by Grüter. They did not consistently detect the ambiguity in the questions and indicated that both subject-first and object-first interpretations were equally possible at a rate of 53.6%. Where they provided just one answer, they preferred an object interpretation (32.1%) over subject (14.3%). This also reflects Grüter's findings and appears to contradict results which suggest that native German speakers have a general subject-first parsing strategy (Bader & Meng 1999; Schlesewsky et al 2000). However, it should be noted that the inanimate wh-word *was* was used in the questions, and so an animacy bias privileges the object interpretation. In any case, the L2 group's pattern of responses was strikingly different to the German natives', as outlined in Figure 2. No learner showed that they had detected the ambiguity in the questions by checking both subject and object interpretations. The L2 group overwhelmingly preferred a subject interpretation of questions (86.6%) versus object (13.4%). Interestingly, this subject-preference is even more marked than for Grüter's initial state learners (71.2%).

The frequencies of the different response types to ambiguous questions were tested in a one-way MANOVA. Using Pillai's trace, this revealed a significant effect of L1, $V = 0.71$, $F(2, 26) = 31.4$, $p < .01$. Univariate ANOVAs for each answer type showed significant L1 effects only on the frequency of subject answers, $F(1, 27) = 15.2$, $p < .01$, and ambiguous answers, $F(1, 27) = 8.3$, $p < .01$. Overall,

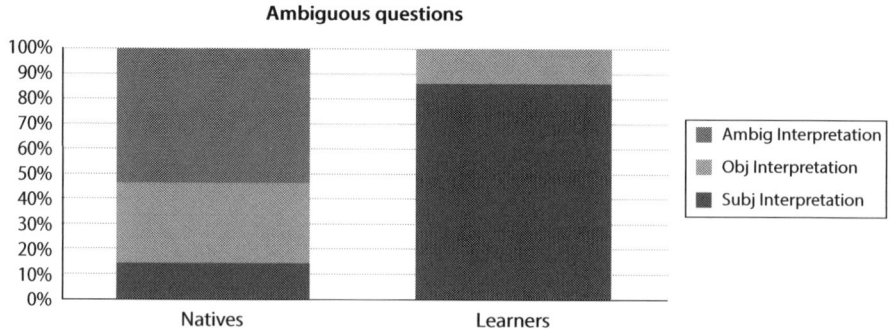

Figure 2. Interpretation of ambiguous questions by native German speakers and learners

the learners are significantly more likely to provide a subject interpretation of ambiguous questions, and less likely to provide an ambiguous interpretation than are native German speakers. Indeed, the learners apparently do not recognize the ambiguity in these questions at all. This is consistent with the learners having been influenced by the L1 syntax, which licenses only a subject interpretation.

Of course, the group results might mask individual preferences which show that some learners are more likely to entertain both possible interpretations. This could be revealed where a learner provides a subject response to one ambiguous question and an object response to another. Only two of the 15 learners provided such a pattern of responses. One learner provided only object responses. The remaining 12 had determinate subject interpretations.

The results for ambiguous relative clauses show a similar trend of apparent L1 influence. Again, the native German group provides ambiguous interpretations to over half the relative clauses (57.2%). Where they provide only one interpretation, subject is strongly preferred over object (35.7 vs. 7.1%). This lends support to previous studies of a subject-first preference in embedded clauses (see work cited above). Again, the learners are strikingly different, as outlined in Figure 3. As is the case in ambiguous questions, no learner provided both possible subject and object interpretations of an individual relative clause. They clearly prefer an object interpretation (82.1%).

The frequencies of the different response types were also tested in a MANOVA. Using Pillai's trace, this again revealed a significant L1 effect, $V = 0.79$, $F(2, 26) = 49, p < .01$. Follow-up univariate ANOVAs showed significant L1 effects only on the frequency of object responses, $F(1, 27) = 16.8, p < .01$, and ambiguous responses, $F(1, 27) = 8.3, p < .01$.

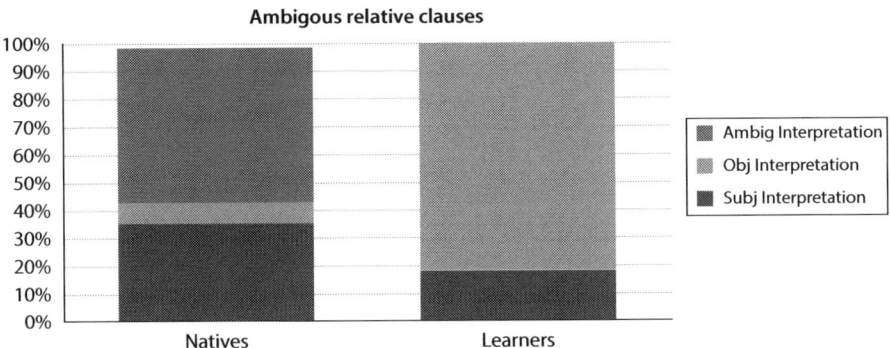

Figure 3. Interpretation of ambiguous relative clauses by native German speakers and learners

The overwhelming preference for object interpretation, in line with what the L1 word order allows, speaks in favour of continued L1 influence. This is particularly striking given findings that object-extracted relative clauses have higher processing costs than subject-extractions (Gibson 1998). If the learners had a general subject-first parsing strategy, one might predict that this strategy, in combination with the relatively more complex computation needed for the object interpretation, would conspire to render the subject interpretation more likely. As this is not the case, it seems that learners continue to rely on L1 word order to arrive at thematic interpretations of L2 clauses.

The pattern of individuals' responses to relative clauses shows more variability than was the case with questions. Five of the fifteen learners assigned an object interpretation to one of the ambiguous relatives in the experiment and a subject interpretation to the other. The other ten learners had consistent object-only interpretations of relatives. This may perhaps reveal that setting the headedness property proceeds more quickly than setting the V2 parameter.

Overall, the results from interpretation of ambiguous clauses indicate continued influence of the L1. Learners provide patterns of interpretation which are significantly different to native speaker preferences. Their different parsing preferences for questions compared to relative clauses appear to be suggestive of having filtered the input through the L1 syntax. They thus provide the interpretations permitted by the equivalent L1 word orders, i.e. WH_{SUBJ}-V-DP_{OBJ} in questions, and $RelPro_{OBJ}$-DP_{SUBJ}-V in relatives.

6.3.2   Interpretation of case-marked clauses

The performance of the L1 German group on case-marked structures shows that they used case appropriately to interpret the argument structure of clauses. They perform entirely consistently and at ceiling, always assigning the interpretation mandated by the case-marking. This might be somewhat surprising given results of online studies which show less than consistent patterns (e.g. Jackson finds less than 100% comprehension accuracy where case disambiguates to the dispreferred object-first order). However, recall that the task parameters were the same for the learners and the native speakers (i.e. each clause was presented for 10 seconds). This apparently allows enough time for native speakers to read (and reread) sentences and arrive at the interpretation required by the case-marking, even if they might have experienced initial online processing difficulties in those cases where case-marking disambiguated to OS order.

For the learners, the role of case is markedly different. Their comprehension of unambiguous case-marked clauses suggests that learners do not use case-marking effectively as a cue for sentence interpretation. Rather, they continue to provide interpretations which are in line with those licensed by the equivalent English

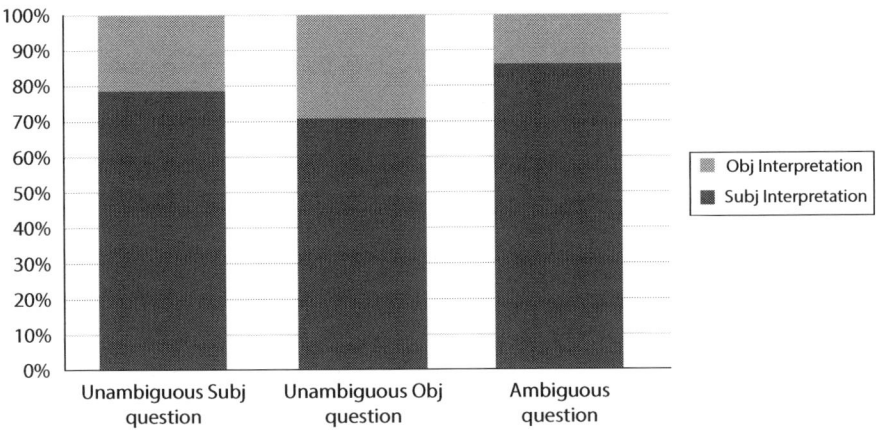

Figure 4. L2 group's interpretation of different question types

word order. Figure 4 summarises the learners' results for all types of question. This shows a similar preference for subject readings of questions across the board, including for unambiguous subject questions (78.6%) and unambiguous object questions (71.4%). Interestingly, the frequency of object readings increased where case-marking unambiguously required an object interpretation. However, paired samples t-tests on the frequency of subject responses revealed no significant effect on interpretation of subject questions ($M = 0.77$, $SE = 0.12$) vs. object questions ($M = 0.69$, $SE = 0.13$), $t(12) = 0.65$, $p > .05$. As a group, then, the learners continue to rely on the L1 word order patterns to parse questions and they ignore case-marking. However, two learners did show target patterns of responses by providing only subject interpretations of subject questions and object interpretations of object questions. It thus seems that individual learners at pre-intermediate proficiency are beginning to be able to use case-marking for interpretation.

The by now familiar pattern also emerges for case-marked relative clauses. The learners persist in providing object interpretations regardless of case-marking information (see Figure 5). Yet again, the rate of object interpretation decreases where it is disallowed by the case-marking. However, paired samples t-tests once again revealed no *significant* effect of case on the rate of object interpretations of object relatives ($M = 0.87$, $SE = 0.09$) vs. subject relatives ($M = 0.8$, $SE = 0.11$), $t(14) = -0.56$, $p > .05$. Two learners provide consistent target-like patterns of response by always assigning object interpretation to object relatives and subject interpretation to subject relatives. These are, however, *not* the same learners who performed in a target-like way on case-marked questions. The status of case-marking and the ability to use it for interpretation thus seems to be unstable in individual learners' grammars.

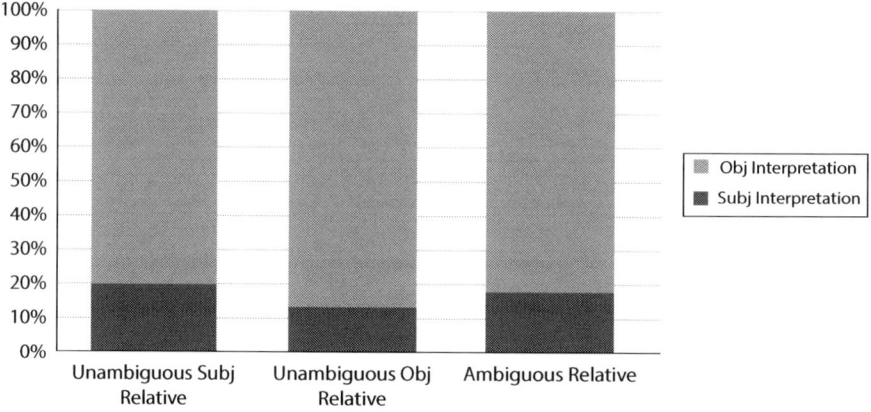

Figure 5. L2 group's interpretation of different relative clause types

7. Discussion and conclusions

A replication of the methodology used by Grüter (2006) and Grüter & Conradie (2006) has found continued strong L1 influence after the initial state. L1 English-speaking learners of L2 German comprehend questions and relative clauses in line with the interpretations licensed by the English syntax. The learners' patterns of comprehension show that they do not use the target syntactic properties of German to parse input, and, in addition, that they do not use German case-marking as a cue to sentence interpretation.

7.1 Transfer, processing and learnability

These findings are compatible with different models of L1 transfer proposed for grammatical representation and for L2 input processing. The important point is that there appears to be some form of L1 English influence in these learners' comprehension of L2 German clauses. Regardless of the ultimate characterization of the nature of this transfer, such L1 effects will complicate L2 development and give rise to learnability issues in L1 English-L2 German.

On the issue of grammatical representation, the Full Transfer / Full Parse model can accommodate these results rather straightforwardly. As already outlined, the L1 initial state in combination with the nature of parses assigned to the input will determine the further development of the grammatical representation. Assuming the L1 grammar transfers in its entirety at the initial state, the task of developing away from the L1 towards a target V2/OV representation will pose significant learnability problems, especially in the case of L1 English-L2 German learners in instructional settings. As has already been noted, the L1 English grammar can formally accommodate a range of German surface clause structures. Failure-driven development of the grammatical representation is thus not assured. Indeed, this issue is even more acute in the high-school instructional setting. The range of structures used in pedagogical materials and discussed explicitly in grammar instruction is necessarily restricted for didactic reasons. For example, accusative case-marking is usually exemplified on the basis of SVO declaratives as in (25), where the case-marked DP remains in a canonical post-verbal position. If learners are accessing the L1 grammar to parse such input, they could assign a syntactic parse and get the correct interpretation here (even without being able to integrate case-marking; indeed, interpretation of (25c) relies on a canonical SVO order as the neuter DP *das Meeschweinchen* has no overt accusative case).

(25) a. Die   Prinzessin küsst den   Frosch.
        the.NOM princess   kisses the.ACC frog
     b. Mein   Vater   bäckt einen   Kuchen.
        my.NOM father   bakes a.ACC   cake
     c. Ich habe ein   Meerschweinchen.[2]
        I   have   a.(ACC) guinea pig

Because these sorts of structures are perfectly compatible with an English syntactic parse, which will also assign a target interpretation, parsing such structures with a non-target V3/VO grammar will not motivate failure-driven development of the syntactic representation. This reflects Sprouse's (2011: 98) reasoning when he states that "[i]t is logically possible that, owing to the initial state, the Interlanguage grammar licenses certain target-deviant linguistic objects from which there is no available input to trigger retreat." Obviously, his thinking applies to the possible end-state of L2 development, but at the proficiency level of the learners tested, it seems likely that there has certainly *not yet* been relevant input to trigger retreat from the L1 grammar.

On the processing side, research in the Competition Model has shown that learners will tend to use cues for interpretation in the L2 which are reliable in their L1 (see Morrett & MacWhinney 2013 for recent discussion). For example, in the case of English, word order reliably marks thematic interpretation, with the first

---

2. These are taken from a BBC GCSE revision site (http://www.bbc.co.uk/schools/gcsebitesize/german), but are typical of the sort of structures which occur in the textbooks to teach grammar at the proficiency level tested. The website is presumably more accessible to readers who would like to explore the sort of input available in instruction than are the textbooks used in the course. The books used in instruction were from the *Na Klar!* Series (Nelson Thornes).

noun in a declarative clause serving as the agent/subject of the clause. Because German permits much freer word order, case is a more reliable cue for interpretation than linear order. Research in the Competition Model paradigm has shown that English learners of German rely on word order for interpretation of German clauses. They tend to assign the agent theta role to the first noun encountered in a clause and do not attend to morphological marking which would contradict a subject-first interpretation (Kilborn 1989; Kempe & MacWhinney 1998).

Kilborn (1989) also finds that in N-N-V sequences, native speakers of English tend to interpret the second noun, i.e. that immediately preceding the thematic verb, as the subject. Such sequences reflect the word order in German relative clauses. And the results of the picture interpretation task reported above show that learners prefer to interpret these sequences as OSV. It is, therefore, possible that the learners are transferring word order cues for interpretation from English to German in their processing of these sequences, rather than the abstract syntactic representation. In any case, the results reported here at least complement Competition Model findings in that the learners do not attend to case as a cue for interpretation and continue to rely on L1 word order preferences.

The results obtained from the picture interpretation task cannot clearly discriminate between Full Transfer and the Competition Model. However, I would argue that it is not possible to discriminate strongly between such models at all. It would be preferable to agree with VanPatten (2010:6), who assumes that the ingredients of SLA are input, processors and UG, but that the presence of all these elements does not guarantee successful acquisition; he points out that "evidence is converging on the role of the L1 in complicating SLA, in both processing and in how UG works."

In sum, L1 transfer, the nature of the input in instructed L1 English-L2 German, and the inability to use case-marking effectively all conspire to make it difficult for L1 English speakers to acquire the grammatical properties of German and assign target interpretations to German questions and relative clauses. They continue to be influenced by L1 English in their parsing of L2 German. It remains for future work to address more specifically whether this L1 influence is in the form of transfer of the syntactic representation or transfer of word order cues.

7.2 Methodological considerations

To conclude, some methodological concerns should be addressed. Firstly, as highlighted by an anonymous reviewer, the participants only answered two experimental items per condition. This might result in reduced statistical power to detect response patterns among the participants and thus the ability to reliably detect non-target performance. This concern could be addressed in an expanded version of the study. However, given that the results replicate Grüter's findings and are relatively clear-cut with little individual variation, they are at least indicative of an effect of L1 English in leading to non-target performance in L2 German.

Secondly, much of the previous discussion has attempted to integrate findings from low-proficiency learners in an offline task (the present study and Grüter) with findings obtained from higher-proficiency learners in an online task (Jackson). In a certain sense, this runs the risk of attempting to compare apples and pears. Obviously, there are likely to be task effects specific to the choice of methodology. For example, even though the picture interpretation task was timed, it included no online measure, so it cannot say anything about the time-course of processing. While the comprehension results seem to show the continuing influence of the L1 for parsing, it is of course entirely possible that the target L2 structures were activated, or target L2 cues were attended to during processing of the sentences but were abandoned, or not accessed for interpretation at some point after reading the whole sentence.

However, in order to get a full picture of L2 development in both grammatical knowledge and processing, it is necessary to try to integrate results obtained from a range of different methodologies into an overarching account which explains how development proceeds. L2 grammatical development and processing are logically bound together (as VanPatten 2010 observed). The acquisition of grammatical properties depends on being able to process and assign parses to input which might conflict with the current state of grammatical knowledge, thus forcing changes in the grammatical representation in cases where the input cannot be parsed. On the other hand, how learners attempt to process input will depend on their grammatical representation for the L2, and thus the sort of syntactic parse they attempt to build for input clauses.

One important way to start to address these interrelated issues would be to heed Mackey's (2013) call for greater use of replication in SLA research. By replicating Grüter's original study, continued transfer beyond the initial state has been identified. Further replication of the same methodology at even higher proficiencies would help to clarify the picture. For example, faced with globally ambiguous German clauses, what interpretation would highly proficient learners prefer? Perhaps in such cases without case cues, advanced learners might prefer interpretations more in line with an L1 parse? Such work would contribute to a more fine-grained picture of if and when transfer persists in parsing at higher proficiency. Similarly, by replicating Jackson's online experiments with lower proficiency learners, we might see different patterns emerge. It is possible that there are online effects of case which do not show up in offline comprehension results. For example, using eye-tracking, Jackson & Dussias (2012) find an effect of case in intermediate L1 English-L2 German while reading sentences. Learners who show no reading time effects do then seem to show effects of having processing cased in some way, even if they do not use it effectively in comprehension.

7.3 Conclusions

To conclude, while several questions with respect to methodology and interpretation remain open, the study presented in this paper contributes further to an already rich picture of development in L1 English-L2 German from initial state (Grüter 2006) to intermediate and advanced (Jackson 2008) to near-native proficiency (Hopp 2006). It would seem that the results from the present study contribute further support to VanPatten's (2010: 6) observation that the L1 is the major complicating factor in L2 processing and grammatical development. Further replications and refinements of the methodologies used in the range of L1 English-L2 German studies would help to address issues of L1 transfer and general processing strategies in more detail. This would go some way to clarifying our understanding of the parallel development of L2 grammar and processing, and would help to answer VanPatten & Jegerski's (2010: 10) call for the debates surrounding L1 influence in L2 processing to progress by moving away from an L1/no L1 dichotomy to ask about "L1 influence under what conditions and for processing of what types of linguistic features?"

References

Agbayani, B. 2000. "Wh-subjects in English and the vacuous movement hypothesis." *Linguistic Inquiry* 31 (4): 703–173. DOI: 10.1162/002438900554523

Bader, M. and Meng, M. 1999. "Subject-object ambiguities in German embedded clauses: An across-the-board comparison." *Journal of Psycholinguistic Research* 28 (2): 121–143. DOI: 10.1023/A:1023206208142

Beck, M.-L. 1998. "L2 acquisition and obligatory head movement: English-speaking learners of German and the local impairment hypothesis." *Studies in Second Language Acquisition* 20: 311–348. DOI: 10.1017/S0272263198003027

Clahsen, H. and Felser, C. 2006. "Grammatical processing in language learners." *Applied Psycholinguistics* 27: 3–42. DOI: 10.1017/S0142716406060024

Dekydtspotter, L., Schwartz, B.D. and Sprouse, R.A. 2006. "The comparative fallacy in L2 processing research." In *Proceedings of the 8th Generative Approaches to Second Language Acquisition Conference (GASLA 8)*, M. O'Brien, C. Shea and John Archibald (eds), 33–40. Sommerville, MA.: Cascadilla Proceedings Project.

Gibson, E. 1998. "Linguistic complexity: Locality of syntactic dependencies." *Cognition* 68: 1–76. DOI: 10.1016/S0010-0277(98)00034-1

Grüter, T. 2006. "Another take on the L2 initial state: Evidence from comprehension in L2 German." *Language Acquisition* 13 (4): 287–317. DOI: 10.1207/s15327817la1304_2

Grüter, T. and Conradie, S. 2006. "Investigating the L2 initial state. Additional evidence from the production and comprehension of Afrikaans-speaking learners of German." In *Inquiries in Linguistic Development: In Honor of Lydia White*, R. Slabakova, S.A. Montrul and P. Prévost (eds), 89–114. Amsterdam: John Benjamins.

Hopp, H. 2006. "Syntactic features and reanalysis in near-native processing." *Second Language Research* 22 (3): 369–397. DOI: 10.1191/0267658306sr272oa

Jackson, C.N. 2007. "The use and non-use of semantic information, word order, and case markings during comprehension by L2 learners of German." *Modern Language Journal* 91 (3): 418–432. DOI: 10.1111/j.1540-4781.2007.00588.x

Jackson, C.N. 2008. "Proficiency level and the interaction of lexical and morphosyntactic information during L2 sentence processing." *Language Learning* 58 (4): 875–909. DOI: 10.1111/j.1467-9922.2008.00481.x

Jackson, C.N. 2010. "The processing of subject-object ambiguities by English and Dutch L2 learners of German." In *Research in Second Language Processing and Parsing*, B. VanPatten and J. Jegerski (eds), 207–230. Amsterdam: John Benjamins. DOI: 10.1075/lald.53.09jac

Jackson, C.N. and Bobb, S. 2009. "The processing and comprehension of wh-questions among second language speakers of German." *Applied Psycholinguistics* 30: 603–636. DOI: 10.1017/S014271640999004X

Jackson, C.N. and Dussias, P. 2009. "Cross-linguistic differences and their impact on L2 sentence processing." *Bilingualism: Language and Cognition* 12 (1): 36–82. DOI: 10.1017/S1366728908003908

Jackson, C.N., Dussias, P. and Hristova, A. 2012. "Using eye-tracking to study the on-line processing of case-marking information among intermediate L2 learners of German." *International Review of Applied Linguistics in Language Teaching (IRAL)* 50: 101–133.

Kempe, V. and MacWhinney, B. 1998. "The acquisition of case marking by adult learners of Russian and German." *Studies in Second Language Acquisition* 20: 543–587. DOI: 10.1017/S0272263198004045

Kilborn, K. 1989. "Sentence processing in a second language: The timing of transfer." *Language and Speech* 32 (1): 1–23.

Mackey, A. 2013. "Methodology in SLA research: Past, present and future." Plenary Lecture at the *Annual Meeting of the European Second Language Association*, Amsterdam, Netherlands, 28–31 August 2013.

Meisel, J. 2011. *First and Second Language Acquisition: Parallels and Differences*. Cambridge: Cambridge University Press. DOI: 10.1017/CBO9780511862694

Morrett, L.M. and MacWhinney, B. 2013. "Syntactic transfer in English-speaking Spanish learners." *Bilingualism: Language and Cognition* 16 (1): 132–151. DOI: 10.1017/S1366728912000107

Pesetsky, D. and Torrego, E. 2001. "T-to-C Movement: Causes and consequences." In *Ken Hale: A Life on Language*, M. Kenstowicz (ed.), 355–426. Cambridge, MA: MIT Press.

Schlesewsky, M., Fanselow, G., Kliegl, R. and Krems, J. 2000. "Preferences for grammatical functions in the processing of locally ambiguous wh-question in German." In *German Sentence Processing*, B. Hemforth and L. Konieczny (eds), 65–94. Dordrecht: Kluwer. DOI: 10.1007/978-94-015-9618-3_3

Schwartz, B.D. and Sprouse, R.A. 1994. "Word order and nominative case in nonnative language acquisition: A longitudinal study of L1 Turkish-L2 German Interlanguage." In *Language Acquisition Studies in Generative Grammar*, T. Hoekstra and B. Schwartz (eds), 317–368. Amsterdam: John Benjamins. DOI: 10.1075/lald.8.14sch

Schwartz, B.D. and Sprouse, R.A. 1996. "L2 cognitive states and the full transfer/full access model." *Second Language Research* 12 (1): 40–72. DOI: 10.1177/026765839601200103

Sharwood Smith, M. and Truscott, J. 2005. "Stages or continua in second language acquisition: A mogul solution." *Applied Linguistics* 22 (2): 219–240. DOI: 10.1093/applin/amh049

Sprouse, R.A. 2011. "The interface hypothesis and full transfer/full access/full parse. A brief comparison." *Linguistic Approaches to Bilingualism* 1 (1): 97–100. DOI: 10.1075/lab.1.1.16spr

Truscott, J. 2006. "Optionality in second language acquisition: A generative, processing-oriented account." *International Review of Applied Linguistics in Language Teaching (IRAL)* 44: 311–330.

Vainnika, A. and Young-Scholten, M. 1996a. "Gradual development of L2 phrase structure." *Second Language Research* 12: 7–39. DOI: 10.1177/026765839601200102

Vainnika, A. and Young-Scholten, M. 1996b. "The early stages in adult L2 syntax: Additional evidence from Romance speakers. *Second Language Research* 12:140–176. DOI: 10.1177/026765839601200202

VanPatten, B. 2010. "The Two Faces of SLA: Mental Representation and Skill." *International Journal of English Studies* 19 (1): 1–18.

VanPatten, B. and Jegerski, J. 2010. "Second language processing and parsing: The issues." In *Research in Second Language Processing and Parsing*, B. VanPatten and J. Jegerski (eds), 3–26. Amsterdam: John Benjamins. DOI: 10.1075/lald.53.01van

White, L. 2003. *Second Language Acquisition and Universal Grammar*. Cambridge: Cambridge University Press. DOI: 10.1017/CBO9780511815065

When Germans begin to learn Swedish
Which is the transfer source for function words, content words and syntax?*

Christina Lindqvist and Ylva Falk
Uppsala University / Stockholm University

This paper explores the role of the L1 and the L2 in L3 oral production, both as regards lexicon and syntax. Previous research has shown that both L1 and L2 are used in L3 oral production, and different explanatory factors have been put forward, e.g. (psycho)typology and L2 status. However, these factors do not explain why function words tend to come from L2 while content words seem to be transferred from both L1 and L2 to a larger extent. In order to explain transfer patterns in L3, we use the declarative/procedural model (Paradis 2009), and hypothesize that syntactic transfer will come from L2; transfer of function words from L2; and transfer of content words from both L1 and L2. We analyze lexical and syntactic transfer in eleven native German speakers' retellings of an episode from a mute video film. The results largely seem to support Paradis' model.

Introduction

The aim of this paper is to explore the role of the mother tongue, L1, and the previously learned foreign languages, L2(s), in third language (L3) oral production. The role of the L1 and the L2(s), or background languages, will be analyzed both at the lexical and syntactic levels. We use the term L3 as it has been defined by Hammarberg (2001): it is the language that the learner is currently learning, after the L1 and at least one L2 (see also next section). We investigate native speakers of German who are in the process of learning Swedish in Germany. The data consists of oral production elicited by means of a retelling task. Previous research on the role of the background languages in L3 learning has shown different results

---

* The study was conducted within the projects *The role of the background languages in third language acquisition. Vocabulary and syntax* and *Lexical and syntactic transfer in third language learning*. Both projects are financed by the Swedish Research Council.

regarding transfer source. There is evidence for both L1 and L2 transfer. Two factors have often been discussed in order to explain the dominance of either L1 or L2: (psycho)typology and L2 status (cf. Bardel & Falk 2007; Sánchez 2011a; Singleton & Ó Laoire 2006a, 2006b). In the present study, we will adopt a neurolinguistic framework (Paradis 2009) with a view to explaining transfer patterns in third language learning.

Theoretical background

In the literature on third language learning, the L3 notion is sometimes used with different denotations. In this study we will make use of an operational definition of L3, namely that of Hammarberg:

> In order to obtain a basis for discussing the situation of the polyglot, we will here use the term L3 for the language that is currently being acquired, and L2 for any other language that the person has acquired after L1. It should be noted that L3 in this technical sense is not necessarily equal to language number three in order of acquisition.
> (Hammarberg 2001:22)

In our case, the participants all have German as their L1, and have then learned English as L2. Some of them have also learned an additional L2, before starting to learn Swedish L3, the language they are currently learning (see also the section Participants).

In research on L3 learning various factors have been suggested to have an impact on the source for transfer (i.e., transfer from L1 or L2). The two most debated factors are (psycho)typology and L2 status (cf. Sánchez 2011a). The term psychotypology (coined by Kellerman 1983) refers to the learner's own perception of language proximity, which enables transfer to come from either the L1 or the L2, depending on whether the learner perceives the languages as close or not. The notion itself is often used as an umbrella term which covers typology, cross-linguistic similarity, language relatedness and psychotypology. Studies have shown that language relatedness is of importance, i.e. that a related language more easily transfers into the target language (e.g. transfer between Romance languages in De Angelis 2005a; or transfer between Germanic languages in Ringbom 1987). Other studies have shown that cross-linguistic similarity can lead to transfer between languages that are not very closely related, but more related as compared to a third involved language (e.g. influence from Spanish rather than from Basque into English; Spanish and English being Indo-European languages; Cenoz 2001). Evidence for the psychotypology factor can be found in Rothman (2011), for instance, who showed that if a learner perceives a background language to be "closer" to the target language, this is the language that will take on the role of transfer source. The studies by for instance Singleton and Ó Laoire (2006a, b) and Lindqvist and Bardel (2013) also acknowledge the importance of the psychotypology factor.

Turning to the L2 status factor, it has its origin in the pioneering study by Williams and Hammarberg (1998), who discovered a general tendency to activate an L2 in the production of an L3.[1] This has later been manifested in various studies (cf. Bardel & Falk 2007; Bohnacker 2006; De Angelis 2007; Falk & Bardel 2011; Klein Gunnewiek 2000; Leung 2005; Sánchez 2011b) in which it is shown that transfer mainly comes from the L2 even in cases where transfer from L1 would have yielded a target-like construction. This suggests that the L2 status factor alone, in some cases, can explain transfer behavior in L3 learning, especially at the level of syntax. However, there are also L3 studies on lexical transfer in which transfer from both L1 and L2 is found (cf. De Angelis 2005a; Lindqvist 2009; Lindqvist & Falk 2013; Williams & Hammarberg 1998), indicating that the L2 status factor alone cannot predict which background language that will be transferred in all cases.

In order to explore the reason for the existence and impact of the L2 status factor, attention has been paid to the many features that L2 and L3 learning have in common (cf. Falk & Bardel 2010, 2011). While an L1, in the normal case, is acquired implicitly, a later formally learned L2 is normally learned explicitly (which also applies to the learning of an L3). This fundamental difference entails features that an L2 and a later learned L3 have in common, in terms of age of onset, outcome, learning situation, and degree of metalinguistic awareness in the process of language learning, for example.[2] These differences between L1 on the one hand and L2/L3 on the other hand might account for the L2 status factor's significance in L3 learning.

By adopting the neurolinguistic approach from Paradis (2004, 2009), Bardel and Falk (2012) aimed at further exploring what is behind the L2 status factor. According to the declarative/procedural model, as proposed by Paradis (2004, 2009), there is a fundamental difference between procedural and declarative memory in relation to implicit linguistic competence (ILC) and explicit metalinguistic knowledge (MLK). Paradis suggests that ILC and MLK are neurolinguistically distinct (and might be dissociated by pathology) and that they have different memory sources. ILC is sustained by procedural memory and MLK is sustained

---

1. The same phenomenon had already been pointed out by Meisel (1983) as a *foreign language effect* and as a *Fremdspracheneffekt* by Ecke and Hall (2000).

2. Cf. Hufeisen (1998: 171–172) who pointed at various factors that are involved in L1/L2/L3 learning, respectively.

Table 1. Memory sources for the different linguistic competences in L1/L2/L3, according to Paradis (e.g., 2009)

	L1	L2	L3
Procedural memory sustains	Phonology, Morphology, Syntax, The Lexicon	–	–
Declarative memory sustains	Vocabulary	Phonology, Morphology, Syntax, The Lexicon, Vocabulary	Phonology, Morphology, Syntax, The Lexicon, Vocabulary

by declarative memory. These memories are responsible for verbal communication. In the L1 procedural memory sustains phonology, morphology, syntax and the lexicon and declarative memory sustains vocabulary. In L2/L3 the pattern is different in that every linguistic level of the language is sustained by declarative memory (as visualized in Table 1).

According to Paradis' perspective, as the table shows, in L1 procedural memory sustains linguistic structure while declarative memory sustains vocabulary (word as form-meaning pairs). In L2, grammatical aspects ("to the extent that teaching of L2 is formal", Paradis 2009:x) are based on explicit MLK, and thus sustained by declarative memory, which also takes care of vocabulary in both L1 and L2/L3. As for the learning of foreign languages, Paradis assumes that:

> Within the framework of the implicit/explicit perspective (...) all late-learned languages (L2, L3, Ln) are sustained to a large extent by declarative memory. As such, they are more likely to manifest dynamic interference from one another than from the native language(s). (Paradis 2008:344)

In line with the framework of Paradis, Bardel and Falk (2012) suggested that these neurolinguistic differences regarding our capacity of verbal communication can explain the strong impact of the L2 status factor in L3 learning of syntax and the variation of transfer source (L1 or L2) as for vocabulary in L3 learning.

Paradis makes yet another distinction of high importance in the present context, namely that between content words and function words. In the L1, function words are processed by syntax, since they are acquired implicitly. In L2/L3, on the other hand, function words are learned explicitly, as they tend to be treated as open-class words. Hence, in L2/L3, function words are sustained by procedural memory. By and large, the declarative/procedural model makes powerful predictions as for transfer source in L3 learning.

Hypotheses

The hypotheses are based on the declarative/procedural distinction. We hypothesize that

1. With respect to syntax, transfer will come from the L2(s).
2. With respect to lexicon:
    a. For function words, transfer will come from the L2(s).
    b. For content words, transfer can come from either L1 or L2(s).

Participants

The participants in the study are eleven German students learning Swedish as an L3 at a technical university in Germany. The data for the present study was gathered towards the end of the first semester of studies. The participants had then studied Swedish for three months and had had about 50 hours of instruction. Table 2 provides information about the participants' age, sex and background languages. As emerges from the table, all the participants had German as L1 and English as their L2. Some participants had knowledge of additional L2s: French (eight participants), Greek (one), Latin (two) and Turkish (one). The proficiency level in the L2s was tested by means of a written standardized test developed at the Swedish Open University (Folkuniversitetet). The tests measure proficiency levels in accordance with the CEFR scale A1–C2 (cf. Council of Europe 2001), and are available in several languages. However, proficiency levels in Greek, Latin

Table 2. Participants

Participant	Age	Sex	L1	L2a	L2b	L2c
P01	21	Male	German	English B1	French B1	Greek
P02	23	Male	German	English B1	–	–
P03	22	Male	German	English*	French*	–
P04	21	Male	German	English B2	French A1	–
P05	21	Female	German	English B2	French A1	Turkish
P06	25	Male	German	English B1	French A1	–
P07	23	Male	German	English B2	–	–
P08	22	Male	German	English B2	Latin	–
P09	22	Female	German	English C1	French B1	Latin
P10	21	Male	German	English B2	French A1	–
P11	21	Female	German	English*	French*	–

* Participants P03 and P11 did not complete the proficiency tests.

and Turkish could not be tested. The age of the participants ranges from 21 to 25; the mean age is 22.

Task

The task was an oral retelling of a short video film (an episode from the clay animated cartoon Shaun the sheep). The participants were recorded in pairs, with a Swedish native speaker also present, and retold the film to each other. The procedure was as follows. After a few minutes' introductory conversation in Swedish, the native speaker of Swedish introduced the task, also in Swedish. The film was shown on a laptop. One of the participants was invited to look at the film and to retell what was happening to the other participant, who would not see the screen. After a few minutes, the native speaker would interrupt and let participant two take over. In this way, each participant would retell about four or five sequences of the film. The participants were told that they could themselves push the pause button at any time. The recording lasted for about 30 minutes in total. The reason for recording the participants in pairs was that they would feel more at ease when having another non-native speaker present. The Swedish native speaker tried not to interfere, but let the two participants solve the task together. However, the native speaker did provide help when needed. This procedure worked out satisfactorily. The fact that all participants did not retell exactly the same portions was not a problem, because we were not interested in comparing the way the participants expressed specific sequences in the film. Also, the task was quite demanding, and it would have been difficult for the participants to retell the whole film by themselves.

Categorization

We identified instances of lexical and syntactic transfer from the L1 German and the L2s English and French.[3] Lexical transfer was identified as formally deviant lexical items, as for example code-switches, i.e. instances of words from the L1 or the L2 that had not been adapted to the L3 (example (1)), and word construction attempts, i.e. words from the L1 or L2 that had been adapted phonologically or morphologically to the L3 (example (2)).

---

3. No transfer from the other L2s was identified.

(1) P11   Hunden **mange** (French)
          Dog-the eats
          'The dog is eating.'
          Target structure: Hunden äter.

(2) P06   Människor **denkar** Shaun är en man or en bonde
          People   think   Shaun is a man   or a farmer
          'People think that Shaun is a human being or a farmer'
          Target structure: Folk tror att Shaun är en människa eller en bonde.

In example (2) the German word *denkt* has been adapted into Swedish by adding the Swedish present tense suffix *-ar*.

Instances of lexical transfer were then further divided into the sub-categories L1 content word, L1 function word, L2 English content word, L2 English function word, L2 French content word and L2 French function word. Paradis' (2009: 18) distinction between function words and content words was followed. Paradis defines open-class words (i.e. content words or lexical words) as "nouns, verbs, adjectives and most adverbs", as opposed to closed-class words (i.e. function words or grammatical words), which are "articles, prepositions, conjunctions". In the present study, phrasal verbs are treated as a special case. There are several instances in the data where the verb and its particle have been separated in a non-targetlike manner by the learner, and, in addition, two different languages have been used, as in the following example:

(3) P04   Hunden **kör**   med bil **weg** (German)
          Dog-the drives with car away
          'The dog drives away with the car'
          Target structure: Hunden kör iväg med bilen.

The German particle *weg* ('away') is here combined with the Swedish verb *kör* ('drives'). In both languages, the notion of 'drive away' is expressed by phrasal verbs: *han kör iväg* in Swedish and *er fährt weg* in German. The methodological problem is that the verb and the particle have been separated, which in this case is compulsory in both German and Swedish (even though the word order differs). As the verb in the infinitive is *wegfahren*, i.e. a content word, it would make no sense to classify this verb into one content word and one function word, only because it is used in the present tense and therefore separated. Thus, all instances of this kind were excluded from the analysis.[4] We also excluded cases where it was impossible to establish source language (mainly the use of *bringar* and *in*. The

---

4. However, this example also shows syntactic transfer. We will discuss this phenomenon below.

former is based on either English *bring* or German *bringen*. The correct Swedish word with the meaning of 'bring' is *hämta*. The latter is a code-switch from either English or German).⁵

Another methodological remark concerns instances of code-switches like *immer noch*, which contains two words that generate one meaning. These cases are interpreted as one semantic unit with the meaning 'still', and are thus counted as one instance.

The second main category of transfer was syntactic transfer. Two sub-categories of negative syntactic transfer were identified in the participants' productions: verb placement in the main clause, i.e. the non-application of the verb-second rule (example (4)), and use of the progressive form (example (5)).

(4) P07 Sen   hunden ligger   på pool
         Then dog-the lies   on pool
         'Then the dog is lying by the pool'
         Target structure: Sen ligger hunden vid poolen.

The word order expressed in example (4) corresponds to both English and French word order.

(5) P10 Hunden   **är** relaxen   på pool
         Dog-the is   relax   on pool
         'The dog is relaxing by the pool'
         Target structure: Hunden vilar vid poolen.

In this case transfer has to come from L2 English, as the progressive form does not exist in any of the other background languages.

Few other types of negative transfer were found, probably due to the relatively low level of proficiency of the learners, and to the type of task. For example, it would have been interesting to look at the use of the negation, but the task does not really allow for using negations, because the participants tend to tell what the protagonists do, not what they do not do. Another interesting phenomenon is the placement of the adjective. However, there are practically no adjectives in the data. Adjective placement in connection with transfer in L3 oral production is investigated in previous work (e.g. Falk et al. 2014).

---

5. An anonymous reviewer pointed out that it would have been interesting to include ambiguous cases since they might represent joint influence from more than one language. As for content words, including a mixed category would not have changed the results, as the model predicts that transfer can come from both L1 and L2. As for function words, only one word, *in*, is transferred.

Results

In this section, we will present the results regarding lexical and syntactic transfer. The two categories of lexical transfer will be presented separately, starting with transfer of content words.

Lexical transfer

Table 3 shows the distribution of content words into the categories L1 German, L2 English and L2 French at an individual level.

As Table 3 shows, transfer of content words comes from both the L1 (67% of the occurrences) and the L2s (33%). The following example illustrates this, where both an L1 word and an L2 word are used in the same utterance.

(6) P09   Han köper en stol och en teve och en **Kühlschrank refrigerator**.
'he buys a chair and a TV and a refrigerator refrigerator'
Target word: *kylskåp*.

Table 4 shows the distribution of function words into the categories L1 German, L2 English and L2 French at an individual level.

Table 4 shows that function words are in 85% of the cases transferred from the L2s, and in 15% of the cases from L1. It is interesting to note that function words

Table 3. Transfer of content words

Participant	L1 German	L2 English	L2 French
P01	4	9	0
P02	16	8	n.a.*
P03	8	2	0
P04	10	1	0
P05	14	3	0
P06	11	1	0
P07	17	8	n.a.
P08	12	5	n.a.
P09	3	7	0
P10	18	9	3
P11	9	2	3
Total	122 (67%)	55 (30%)	6 (3%)
Total	122 (67%)	61 (33%)	

* n.a. indicates that the participant did not have any knowledge of French and that transfer cannot come from this language.

Table 4. Transfer of function words

Participant	L1 German	L2 English	L2 French
P01	0	14	4
P02	2	6	n.a.*
P03	1	2	0
P04	4	3	5
P05	1	0	16
P06	2	3	1
P07	1	11	n.a.
P08	2	4	n.a.
P09	2	1	4
P10	0	0	5
P11	0	1	1
Total	15 (15%)	45 (46%)	37 (38%)
Total	15 (15%)	82 (85%)	

* n.a. indicates that the participant did not have any knowledge of French and that transfer cannot come from this language.

are transferred from both English (46%) and French (38%) L2. The following example shows an utterance where several French function words are inserted.

(7) P05 Bonden har en **autre** affär **et** och oh Gott, **non**, nej, hon har **autre** saker.
Farmer-the has another shop and and oh God, no, no, she has other things
'The farmer has another shop and, and oh God, no, no she has other things'
Target structure: Bonden har en annan affär och och åh Gud, nej, nej, hon har andra saker.

Syntactic transfer

In this section, we will give an account of the results concerning syntactic transfer in the data. All instances of the non-application of the verb-second rule and the use of the progressive form are shown in Table 5. The L1 German column refers to instances of the kind that were shown above, i.e. non-targetlike placement of the verb particle, cf. example (3).

As emerges from Table 5, it is quite obvious that syntactic transfer tends to come from the L2s (96% of the occurrences). It was decided to merge the L2 categories, as the research question only asks whether transfer comes from the L1 or the L2s. Still, the results from each language are shown, as some of the participants do not have French as L2.

Table 5. Syntactic transfer

Participant	L1 German	L2 English	L2 French	L2 English/French
P01	0	1	0	24
P02	0	0	n.a.*	n.a.
P03	0	0	0	4
P04	1	0	0	0
P05	0	1	0	0
P06	0	0	0	3
P07	0	4	n.a.	n.a.
P08	1	2	n.a.	n.a.
P09	0	0	0	1
P10	0	3	0	0
P11	0	0	0	0
Total	2	11	0	32
Total	2 (4%)		43 (96%)	

* n.a. indicates that the participant did not have any knowledge of French and that transfer cannot come from this language.

Discussion and conclusion

In the present study, we investigated the use of the L1 and the L2 in L3 oral production. The hypotheses (here repeated) were, in line with the L2 status factor (Bardel & Falk 2012) explained by the declarative/procedural model (Paradis 2004, 2009) that, with respect to

> Syntax: transfer would come from the L2(s),
> Lexicon: content words would be transferred from either the L1 or the L2(s), function words would be transferred from the L2(s).

These hypotheses are based on the two different memory systems that sustain various components of language depending on whether the language is an L1 or an L2/L3. As for the L1, the procedural memory sustains phonology, morphology, syntax and the lexicon and the declarative memory sustains vocabulary. This is not the case for later (formally learned) languages (L2/L3), for which declarative memory sustains everything and no parts of the language rely on implicit competence.[6]

---

6. Paradis reckons that there are L2 users who reach a near-native level. In these cases there is a possibility that the "L2 grammar in its entirety will be internalized and hence subserved by procedural memory" (2009: 15–16) and the L2 syntax will, in a similar manner to the L1 syntax,

In the present study we found, as hypothesized, transfer of syntax to come from the L2 in 96% of the cases. This negative transfer was manifested as violations of the verb second rule (which applies to both L1 German and L3 Swedish) and transfer of the progressive form from L2 English. Both these syntactic constructions can be traced to L2 English and the former one also to L2 French, of which some of the participants have knowledge. Unexpectedly, there were two instances (4%) of negative transfer that only can stem from the L1, namely when the verb particle was placed in a sentence-final position (a structure that must come from L2 German), however the role of the L1 in syntactic transfer is certainly of minor importance.

Turning to lexical transfer of content words we find that both the L1 and the L2s are used. This is exactly what we expected, since content words are sustained by declarative memory in all languages, no words are supposed to be implicitly learned or acquired (according to Paradis 2009: 114, there is no "optimal period" for learning words, as is the case for the other aspects of language acquisition). All in all, transfer stems to a larger extent from the participants' L1 German (67%), while one third stems from their L2s English and French. French lexical transfer of content words is rare, but two participants make use of their L2 French in this category (cf. Table 3 and example (1) above). As for function words, the declarative/procedural model assumes them to be treated as syntax in the L1 (i.e., sustained by procedural memory) but as open-class words in the L2/L3 and hence sustained by declarative memory. This would for us mean that the transfer source for function words would be L2. In 85% of the cases this is what happens. The transferred function words are almost equally taken from L2 English (46%) and L2 French (38%). Here we also find a few instances of L1 transfer, which was not hypothesized to happen.

All in all, our results corroborate our hypotheses. Our findings are also in line with previous L3 research on transfer. In many studies the L2 status factor has been shown to have a strong impact on syntactic transfer (cf. Bardel & Falk 2007; De Angelis 2005a; Falk & Bardel 2011; Klein Gunnewiek 2000; Leung 2005; Sánchez 2011b). In Bohnacker's (2006) study, which involved the same language combination but in a mirror-manner (L1 Swedish, L2 English, L3 German), the results showed that the learners were not able to apply the verb second rule (which is present in both the L1 and L3) due to transfer from L2 English, which was also the case in the present study. Earlier L3 studies on lexical transfer have shown what could be interpreted as contradictory results since there are studies that found L1 transfer, studies that found L2 transfer, and studies that found

---

rely on implicit linguistic competence. However, this is according to Paradis very rare and only possible through frequent use of the learned grammatical rules.

both (e.g. De Angelis 2005a; Lindqvist 2009; Lindqvist & Falk 2013; Williams & Hammarberg 1998). As discussed above, this is not contradictory, but rather straightforward, when applying the declarative/procedural model. As far as content words are concerned, these are sustained by the declarative memory in all languages (L1, L2 and L3) and therefore interact in a similar way. However, L1 function words are not part of the declarative knowledge, since they are treated as part of syntax, which is not the case with L2/L3 function words. There are a few studies that have acknowledged the different transfer patterns for content words and function words (Bardel & Falk 2012; De Angelis 2005b; Falk submitted). The present study also shows this tendency for function words to be transferred from an L2 rather from an L1 in L3 learning.

Turning back to the suggested role of (psycho)typology (cf. De Angelis 2005a; Ringbom 1987; Cenoz 2001) we do not exclude the possibility of this factor bearing an impact on the transfer source in L3 learning. The declarative/procedural model maintains that content words in all languages that an individual knows are stored in the same memory component. This means that there are no predictions as to which of the languages that will be transferred. However, we do find it plausible that (psycho)typology does have an effect when it comes to the transfer source of the content words. In this study a total of 122 content words were transferred, 67% of these came from L1 German, 55% from L2 English and only 3% from L2 French. The fact that the number of L2 French content words is low might be explained with typology (in both a relatedness and similarity manner, cf. theoretical background), since all other languages are Germanic.

To conclude, this study has shown that the declarative/procedural model can explain transfer patterns in L3 learning and that there may also be interplay with other factors, especially the L2 status factor, and the psychotypology factor to some extent. One of the shortcomings is that there were relatively few participants in the study, and also relatively few instances of transfer, especially as far as syntax is concerned. Future research will have to replicate the results on a larger material and on different language combinations.

References

Bardel, C. and Falk, Y. 2007. "The role of the second language in third language acquisition: the case of Germanic syntax." *Second Language Research* 23 (4): 459–484.
DOI: 10.1177/0267658307080557

Bardel, C. and Falk, Y. 2012. "What's behind the L2 status factor? A neurolinguistic framework for L3 research." In *Third Language Acquisition in Adulthood*, J. Cabrelli Amaro, S. Flynn and J. Rothman (eds), 61–78. Amsterdam: John Benjamins. DOI: 10.1075/sibil.46.06bar

Bohnacker, U. 2006. "When Swedes begin to learn German: From V2 to V2." *Second Language Research* 22 (4): 443–486. DOI: 10.1191/0267658306sr275oa

Cenoz, J. 2001. "The effect of linguistic distance, L2 status and age on cross-linguistic influence in third language acquisition." In *Cross-linguistic Influence in Third Language Acquisition: Psycholinguistic Perspectives*, J. Cenoz, B. Hufeisen and U. Jessner (eds), 8–20. Clevedon: Multilingual Matters.

Council of Europe. 2001. *The Common European Framework of Reference for Languages: Learning, Teaching, Assessment*. New York: Cambridge University Press.

De Angelis, G. 2005a. "Multilingualism and non-native transfer: An identificational problem." *International Journal of Multilingualism* 2 (1): 1–25. DOI: 10.1080/17501220508668374

De Angelis, G. 2005b. "Interlanguage transfer of function words." *Language Learning* 55 (3): 379–414. DOI: 10.1111/j.0023-8333.2005.00310.x

De Angelis, G. 2007. *Third or Additional Language Acquisition*. Clevedon: Multilingual Matters.

Ecke, P. and Hall, C.J. 2000. "Lexikalischer Fehler in Deutsch als Drittsprache: Translexikalischer Einfluss auf 3 Ebenen der mentalen Repräsentation." *Deutsch als Fremdsprache* 1: 31–37.

Falk, Y. Submitted. "Lexical transfer in L3 learning: A cross-sectional study on Swedish."

Falk, Y. and Bardel, C. 2010. "The study of the role of the background languages in third language acquisition. The state of the art". *International Review of Applied Linguistics in Language Teaching* 48 (2/3): 185–220. DOI: 10.1515/iral.2010.009

Falk, Y. and Bardel, C. 2011. "Object pronouns in German L3 syntax: Evidence for the L2 status factor." *Second Language Research* 27 (1): 59–82. DOI: 10.1177/0267658310386647

Falk, Y., Lindqvist, C. and Bardel, C. 2014. "The role of L1 explicit metalinguistic knowledge in L3 oral production at the initial state." *Bilingualism: Language and Cognition*, 1–9. DOI: 10.1017/S1366728913000552

Hammarberg, B. 2001. "Roles of L1 and L2 in L3 production." In *Cross-linguistic Influence in Third Language Acquisition: Psycholinguistic Perspectives*, J. Cenoz, B. Hufeisen and U. Jessner (eds), 21–41. Clevedon: Multilingual Matters.

Hufeisen, B. 1998. "L3 – Stand der Forschung – Was bleibt zu tun?" In *Tertiärsprachen. Theorien, Modelle, Methoden*, B. Hufeisen, B. Lindemann (eds), 169–184. Stauffenburg: Stauffenburg Verlag.

Kellerman, E. 1983. "Now you see it, now you don't." In *Language Transfer in Language Learning*, S. Gass and L. Selinker (eds), 112–134. Rowley, M.A.: Newbury House.

Klein Gunnewiek, L. 2000. *Sequenzen und Konsequenzen. Zur Entwicklung niederländischer Lerner im DeutschenalsFremdsprache*. [Sequences and consequences. About the development in German as a foreign language in Dutch native speakers.] Amsterdam: Rodopi.

Leung, Y.-k. I. 2005. "L2 vs. L3 initial state: A comparative study of the acquisition of French DPs by Vietnamese monolinguals and Cantonese–English bilinguals." *Bilingualism: Language and Cognition* 8 (1): 39–61.

Lindqvist, C. 2009. "The Use of the L1 and the L2 in French L3: Examining Cross-linguistic Lexemes in Multilingual Learners' Oral Production." *International Journal of Multilingualism* 6 (3): 281–297. DOI: 10.1080/14790710902812022

Lindqvist, C. and Bardel, C. 2013. "Exploring the impact of the proficiency and typology factors: two cases of multilingual learners' L3 learning." In *Essential Topics in Applied Linguistics and Multilingualism. Studies in Honor of David Singleton*, M. Pawlak and L. Aronin (eds), 253–266. Switzerland: Springer International Publishing.

Lindqvist, C. and Falk, Y. 2013. "Engelskans roll vid inlärning av svenska som tredjespråk." [The role of English when learning Swedish as a third language]. Paper presented at *Nordand 11*, Stockholm, Sweden, June 2013.

Meisel, J. 1983. "Transfer as a second language strategy." *Language and Communication* 3: 11–46. DOI: 10.1016/0271-5309(83)90018-6

Paradis, M. 2004. *A Neurolinguistic Theory of Bilingualism*. Amsterdam: John Benjamins. DOI: 10.1075/sibil.18

Paradis, M. 2008. "Language communication and disorders in multilinguals." In *Handbook of Neuroscience of Language*, B. Stemmer and H.A. Whitaker (eds), 341–349. Amsterdam: Elsevier. DOI: 10.1016/B978-008045352-1.00033-1

Paradis, M. 2009. *Declarative and Procedural Determinants of Second Languages*. Amsterdam: John Benjamins. DOI: 10.1075/sibil.40

Ringbom, H. 1987. *The Role of the First Language in Foreign Language Learning*. Clevedon: Multilingual Matters.

Rothman, J. 2011. "L3 syntactic transfer selectivity and typological determinacy: The typological primacy model." *Second Language Research* 27 (1): 107–127. DOI: 10.1177/0267658310386439

Sánchez, L. 2011a. "'Luisa and Perdito's dog will the breakfast eat': Interlanguage transfer and the role of the second language factor." In *New Trends in Crosslinguistic Influence and Multilingualism Research*, G. De Angelis and J.-M. Dewaele (eds), 86–104. Clevedon: Multilingual Matters.

Sánchez, L. 2011b. *Crosslinguistic Influence in Third Language Acquisition: English after German in Spanish/Catalan learners in an Instructed Setting*. Ph.Diss. University of Barcelona.

Singleton, D. and Ó Laoire, M. 2006a. "Psychotypologie et facteur L2 dans l'influence translexicale. Une analyse de l'influence de l'anglais et de l'irlandais sur le français L3 de l'apprenant". *AILE* 24: 101–117.

Singleton, D. and Ó Laoire, M. 2006b. "Psychotypology and the 'L2 factor' in cross-lexical interaction: An analysis of English and Irish influence in learner French". In *Språk, Lärande och Utbildning i sikte*, M. Bendtsen, M. Björklund, C. Fant and L. Forsman (eds), 191–205. Vasa: Faculty of Education, Åbo Akademi.

Williams, S. and Hammarberg, B. 1998. "Language switches in L3 production: Implications for a polyglot speaking model." *Applied Linguistics* 19 (3): 295–333. DOI: 10.1093/applin/19.3.295

Cross-linguistic influence and formulaic language
Recurrent word sequences in French learner writing

Magali Paquot
Université catholique de Louvain

This chapter reports on a follow-up study to Paquot (2013) which replicates its methodology to investigate transfer effects on French EFL learners' use of recurrent word sequences. The study focuses on a large dataset of two- to four-word lexical bundles overrepresented in the French component of the *International Corpus of Learner English* (ICLE) as compared to nine other ICLE learner sub-corpora. Results are in line with a usage-based view of language that recognizes the active role that the first language (L1) may play in the acquisition of a foreign language. In accordance with Paquot's (2013) findings, the different manifestations of L1 influence displayed in the learners' idiosyncratic use of lexical bundles are traced back to various properties of French words and word combinations, among which their discourse function and frequency of use seem to play a crucial role.

1. Introduction

Lexical bundles are "recurrent expressions, regardless of their idiomaticity, and regardless of their structural status" (Biber et al. 1999: 990). These repeated sequences of words may be grammatically complete (*by contrast, on the other hand*) or incomplete (*the nature of the, is based on the*). They may be composed of clause segments (e.g. *I don't know what*) or be parts of phrases (e.g. *the use of*). They are "conventionalized building blocks that are used as convenient routines in language production" (Altenberg 1998: 122) and typically function as referential markers (e.g. *the end of the*), text organizers (e.g. *on the basis of, for example*) or stance markers (e.g. *it is possible to*) in written text (Biber et al. 2003). Corpus-query tools often provide an option that retrieves repeated sequences of words of a given length (e.g. two-word sequences, three-word sequences) fully automatically. This method has been used extensively to investigate formulaic language in learner writing and compare the number of lexical bundles, their structural characteristics and discourse functions in learner and native corpora (cf. Paquot & Granger 2012).

Some of the studies have attributed to the learners' mother tongue specific patterns of use of lexical bundles in learner writing. Allen (2011: 111), for example, partly ascribes Japanese learners' repeated use of *it can be said that* to the first language (L1), as its translational equivalent is frequent in Japanese academic writing. However, until very recently, no study had targeted transfer effects on EFL learners' production of recurrent word sequences as their primary object of investigation. In recent research, I have therefore sought to fill in this existing research gap by conducting a comprehensive transfer study of lexical bundles from 2 to 5 words in French EFL learner writing. Preliminary results are reported in Paquot (2013) where I investigated transfer effects on French EFL learners' use of 3-word recurrent sequences that include a lexical verb and reported that the different manifestations of L1 influence displayed in the learners' idiosyncratic use of lexical bundles could be traced back to various properties of French words and word combinations, including their collocational use, function, and frequency of use.

The main objective of the present work is to replicate the method adopted in Paquot (2013) on a much larger dataset of lexical bundles and investigate whether the types of transfer effects identified in French learners' use of three-word lexical bundles with a lexical verb are also traceable in other forms of recurrent word sequences. The study therefore focuses on two- to four-word lexical bundles irrespective of their constituent forms and addresses the same research questions as Paquot (2013):

– RQ1: How much of French learners' <u>idiosyncratic</u> use of lexical bundles can be attributed to L1 influence?
– RQ2: What types of transfer effect (e.g. lexical and semantic transfer, syntactic transfer) are at play?

According to the results reported in Paquot (2013), it is expected that transfer effects will be particularly noticeable in the overrepresentation of lexical bundles whose L1 equivalent forms fulfil specific discourse functions or are particularly frequent, and are consequently deeply entrenched in French speakers' mental lexicon.

To answer the research questions, the study is grounded in Jarvis's (2000) unified framework for the study of L1 influence (Section 2). The learner and native corpus data used are described in Section 3. Section 4 summarises the different steps involved in the methodology. Section 5 reports the results of the analysis of transfer effects on French EFL learners' use of lexical bundles and Section 6 provides answers to the research questions in the light of the preceding sections. Section 7 offers concluding remarks.

2. Jarvis's (2000) unified framework for the study of cross-linguistic influence

Transfer studies have too often fallen into the trap of making a case for L1 influence on the sole argument that the structure exists in the L1, thus relying exclusively on "'shot-in-the-dark' post hoc interpretive guesses which pass for explanations" (Lightbown 1984: 245). To remedy this situation, Jarvis (2000) puts forward a unified framework for the study of L1 influence which is premised on the following operationalizable definition of the construct of 'transfer':

> L1 influence refers to any instance of learner data where a statistically significant correlation (or probability-based relation) is shown to exist between some feature of learners' IL performance and their L1 background. (Jarvis 2000: 252)

This definition of L1 influence translates into a list of at least three potential sources of evidence that transfer studies should consider altogether when presenting a case for or against L1 influence:

i. **Effect 1: Intra-L1-group homogeneity in learners' IL performance** is found when learners who speak the same first language behave as a group with respect to a specific second language (L2) feature. To illustrate this first L1 effect, Jarvis uses Selinker's (1992) finding according to which Hebrew-speaking learners of English as a group tend to produce sentences in which adverbs are placed before the object (e.g. *I like very much movies*).

ii. **Effect 2: Inter-L1-group heterogeneity in learners' IL performance** is found when "comparable learners of a common L2 who speak different L1s diverge in their IL performance" (Jarvis 2000: 254). To illustrate, Jarvis (2000) refers to a number of studies reported by Ringbom (1987) that have shown that Finnish-speaking learners are more likely than their Swedish-speaking counterparts to omit English articles and prepositions. Jarvis (2000) argues that "this type of evidence strengthens the argument for L1 influence because it essentially rules out developmental and universal factors as the cause of the observed IL behaviour. In other words, it shows that the IL behaviour in question (omission of function words) is not something that every learner does (to the same degree or in the same way) regardless of L1 background" (Jarvis 2000: 254–255).

iii. **Effect 3: Intra-L1-group congruity between learners' L1 and IL performance** is found where "learners' use of some L2 feature can be shown to parallel their use of a corresponding L1 feature" (Jarvis 2000: 255). This is the type of evidence that Selinker (1992) produced when showing that Hebrew-speaking learners' positioning of English adverbs parallels their use of adverbs in the L1. The added value of this third effect is that it also has explanatory power by showing what in the first language motivates the IL behaviour.

In a follow-up article, Jarvis (2010) acknowledges the existence of a fourth type of evidence that was not accounted for in his original framework, viz. 'intralingual contrasts', which he defines as "differences in learners' performance on features of the target language that vary with respect to how they correspond to features of the source language" (Jarvis 2010: 175). To illustrate, the author briefly describes Finnish learners' use of the English prepositions *near* (whose translation equivalent in Finnish is the preposition *lähellä*), *under* (whose translation equivalent in Finnish is the postposition *alla*), and *in* (whose translation equivalent in Finnish is the locative suffix *-ssa/-ssä*) and reports that the number, types and persistence of the errors that the Finnish learners produce correspond with how the English prepositions translate into different Finnish structures. As will become clear in Section 4, the focus on overused lexical bundles in French learner writing does not make it possible to investigate this fourth type of evidence.

3. Data

The learner corpus data used for the present study come from the first version of the *International Corpus of Learner English* (ICLE) (Granger et al. 2002). ICLE texts share a number of learner and task variables, which were used as corpus-design criteria. All the learners are young adults who study English as a Foreign Language (EFL) at university and their proficiency ranges from higher intermediate to advanced (Granger et al. 2009: 12). Learner productions are typically argumentative essays of 500 to 1,000 words in length and they cover a wide range of topics (e.g. the death penalty, euthanasia). Learner texts also differ in task conditions.

The focus of this study is on French learner writing but other ICLE sub-corpora were used as comparable corpora to test for inter-L1-group heterogeneity in learners' interlanguage performance (cf. Section 2). Table 1 provides a breakdown of the ten ICLE sub-corpora used. Learner essays in each sub-corpus were carefully selected in an attempt to control for a number of task variables which may affect learner productions (cf. Kroll 1990; Ädel 2008): all the texts are untimed argumentative essays, potentially written with the help of reference tools. Although

Table 1. Breakdown of ICLE essays

	No. of essays	No. of words	Average no. of words per essay
Corpus under analysis			
French (ICLE-FR)	228	136,343	598
Comparable corpora			
Czech (ICLE-CZ)	147	130,768	890
Dutch (ICLE-DU)	196	162,243	828
Finnish (ICLE-FI)	167	125,292	750
German (ICLE-GE)	179	109,556	612
Italian (ICLE-IT)	79	47,739	604
Polish (ICLE-PO)	221	140,521	636
Russian (ICLE-RU)	194	165,937	855
Spanish (ICLE-SP)	149	99,119	665
Swedish (ICLE-SW)	81	48,060	593
Total	1,641	1,165,524	697

essays written without the help of reference tools would arguably be more representative of what advanced EFL learners can produce, untimed essays with reference tools are used here as they represent the majority of learner texts in ICLE.

4. Methodology

The methodology used is based on Paquot (2013) and involves several steps which are specified here. Section 4.1 covers the extraction of lexical bundles from ICLE texts. Section 4.2 introduces the procedures and statistical test used to operationalize Jarvis's (2000) unified framework on learner corpus data. Section 4.3 describes the method used to rule out topic influence and explains the rationale behind this extra step.

4.1 Extraction of lexical bundles

The focus of the study is on potential transfer effects on French EFL learners' use of recurrent word sequences. Lexical bundles of 2 to 4 words were first extracted from the ICLE French sub-corpus with the help of the computer software WordSmith Tools 5 (Scott 2008). A minimum frequency threshold of 5 occurrences was adopted. A Perl program was then used to retrieve relative frequencies per 100 words for each of the selected bundles in the 1,641 learner texts that make up the ten learner corpora. Computing relative frequencies per 100 words in each learner text is crucial to make comparisons between learner texts of different size possible (cf. Table 1 for an average number of words per learner sub-corpus).

4.2 Jarvis's (2000) unified framework and learner corpus data

Intra-L1-group homogeneity is most evident when directly compared with inter-L1-group heterogeneity (Jarvis 2000), and I therefore made use of comparison of means tests to assess these two effects. Unlike in Paquot (2013), however, I used pairwise Wilcoxon rank sum tests to compare French learners' use of recurrent word sequences with that of the nine other learner populations ($p < 0.05$ after correction for multiple testing). In this study, lexical bundles which displayed significant differences in use between the French learner group and at least 5 of the other learner populations as revealed by the Wilcoxon tests were considered to show intra-L1-group homogeneity and inter-L1-group heterogeneity. All statistical tests were performed with R (R Core Team 2012).

While the first two effects readily lend themselves to automatic and quantitative evaluation, intra-L1-group congruity between French learners' L1 and IL performance does not. Assessing this third effect required a more qualitative approach. First, the use of each lexical bundle was carefully analysed in ICLE-FR. The next steps consisted in identifying the French potential "equivalent" of each lexical bundle in context, describing its use in French L1 and comparing learners' L1 and IL patterns of use. For these purposes, I also consulted a 126 million word French web corpus available in the Sketch Engine (Kilgarriff & Kosem 2012).

4.3 Recurrent word sequences and topic variability

Previous research has identified topic influence as an important explanatory factor for the presence or absence of specific lexical bundles in various text types and genres (e.g. Cortes 2004). The unbalanced distribution of prompts across the various ICLE sub-corpora must consequently be addressed adequately in this study. The ICLE French sub-corpus, for example, is characterised by a strong bias towards just one topic ("Europe 92: loss of sovereignty or birth of a nation?"). This topic was selected by c. 40% of all the French learners, and more than 70% of all the texts about Europe 92 in ICLE are to be found in the French component only. To identify potential cases of topic influence, I used the ICLE built-in corpus query tool (Granger et al. 2009) to analyse the distribution by essay prompt of all the bundles that display intra-L1-group homogeneity and inter-L1-group heterogeneity (Effects 1 and 2). If the distribution of a lexical bundle concentrated on French learners' essays on the creation and future of Europe, topic was considered a more likely explanation than L1 influence and Effect 3 (intra-L1-group congruity) was not tested.[1]

5. Results

This section presents the results obtained from the transfer study. The extraction procedure outlined in Section 4.1 generated 3,855 2-word sequences, 1,492 3-word sequences and 350 4-word sequences from the French learner sub-corpus, which were submitted to further analysis.

5.1 Testing effects 1 and 2

An R script was written to assess Effects 1 and 2 for all recurrent word sequences in ICLE-FR. Pairwise Wilcoxon rank sum tests identified 154 2-word sequences, 59 3-word sequences and 15 4-word sequences that present significant differences in use between the French learners and at least five of the other nine learner populations ($p < 0.05$ after correction for multiple testing). Table 2 provides a categorization of the 228 statistically significant recurrent word sequences according to their most frequent function in context (Biber et al. 2003) and shows that the large majority of the overused[2] recurrent word sequences in ICLE-FR are referential expressions.

Table 2. Categorization of statistically significant recurrent word sequences per function

	2-word sequences	3-word sequences	4-word sequences
Referential expressions	138 [89.6%]	51 [86.44%]	13 [86.7%]
Discourse organizers	15 [9.7%]	6 [10.17%]	1 [6.66%]
Stance markers	1 [0.65%]	2 [3.39%]	1 [6.66%]
Total	154 [100%]	59 [100%]	15 [100%]

---

1. The fact that topic is considered a more likely explanation does not rule out L1 influence per se and the opposition between topic-induced and L1-induced lexical bundles made in this study is thus largely methodological.

2. The term 'overuse' is descriptive and refers to the fact that a lexical bundle is found significantly more in the French learner corpus than in the other ICLE sub-corpora.

5.2 The influence of topic

An analysis of the frequency of the 228 recurrent word sequences in the 1,641 learner texts and their distribution by essay prompt reveals that a large majority of them only appear in ICLE-FR essays that discuss the creation and future of Europe (Table 3). Examples of topic-induced recurrent word sequences include *all this, an economic, big nation, different countries, European citizen, European market, great nation, national identity, of a, own identity, the creation, to build, twelve countries, unification of, will also, a new nation, all the countries,* and *political union, countries will be, from an economic, it will be, its own culture, of a nation, point of view, the creation of, the European community, a loss of identity, birth of a nation, the free movement of,* and *United States of Europe*. As already discussed in Paquot (2013), the influence of topic is not only visible in the selection of content words but also in tense preferences. As illustrated in Examples (1) and (2), quite a few overused bundles include the modal verb *will* and are used to discuss Europe's future possibilities and obligations.

(1) Thanks to this new nation **it will be** possible to be at the same level as that of other giants, as the United States or USSR. (ICLE-FR)

(2) Each nation **will have to** forget its own interests and share its wealth with the other countries of the Community. (ICLE-FR)

Table 3 further shows that all the lexical bundles that were classified as 'topic-induced' are referential expressions. By contrast, topic bias does not explain why French EFL learners overuse specific recurrent word sequences that function as discourse organizers or stance markers as these sequences appear in essays covering a wide range of prompts. It could have been expected that a prompt such as "In his novel 'Animal Farm', George Orwell wrote 'All men are equal but some are more equal than others'. How true is this today?" trigger more instances of stance markers such as *it is true, it is untrue,* etc. than other prompts which ask for opinions or comments. Table 4 provides a complete list of the lexical bundles for which topic influence was ruled out and which were therefore submitted to the third test (i.e. intra-L1-group congruity).

Table 3. Topic-induced recurrent word sequences

	2-word sequences	3-word sequences	4-word sequences
Referential expressions	133/138 [96.4%]	49/51 [96%]	12/13 [92.3%]
Discourse organizers	0/15	0/6	0/1
Stance markers	0/1	0/2	0/1
Total	133/154 [86.4%]	49/59 [83%]	12/15 [80%]

Table 4. Non topic-induced recurrent word sequences

Size	Number	Recurrent word sequences
2-word sequences	21	<u>Referential expressions</u>: all this, confronted with, considered as, point of, such a <u>Discourse organizers</u>: are concerned, as far, even if, far as, forget that, in order, in other, is concerned, is thus, let us, order to, other words, speak of, the contrary, we may <u>Stance marker</u>: from being
3-word sequences	10	<u>Referential expressions</u>: considered as a, of the time <u>Discourse organizers</u>: as a conclusion, as far as, far as the, in order to, not forget that, on the contrary <u>Stance markers</u>: according to me, far from being
4-word sequences	3	<u>Referential expression</u>: most of the time <u>Discourse organizer</u>: as far as the <u>Stance marker</u>: is far from being

5.3 Testing effect 3

Testing Effect 3 amounts to checking whether the overused lexical bundles in ICLE-FR have translational equivalent word sequences in French that may induce such overuse. Before doing so, however, a quick scan of concordance lines for the 34 remaining lexical bundles (Table 4) showed that some regrouping of overlapping word sequences was possible, sometimes making up longer and more syntactically complete bundles such as *as far as * is/are concerned* and *most of the time,* or pinpointing shorter but more salient word combinations such as *considered as*. Other word sequences proved to be systematically used in larger structures (e.g. *point of* is always followed by *view*, making up the compound *point of view*). Intra-L1-group congruity between learners' L1 and IL performance was consequently evaluated for nineteen lexical bundles (see Table 5).

The identification of more complete word sequences also made the next task of identifying translational equivalent forms in French easier. For this particular task, I did not rely exclusively on congruency but adopted a form-function mapping approach to translational equivalence instead. So, while En. *in order to* does not have a congruent form in French, it has clear translational equivalent forms, the most frequent ones being Fr. *pour* and *afin de*. Lack of formal equivalence is certainly not a sufficient criterion to prevent cross-linguistic influence and transfer studies also need to account for possible semantic interlingual identifications despite formal dissimilarities (cf. Jarvis & Odlin 2000). I also made sure I selected the most frequent equivalent form(s) in context. To illustrate, the sequence *all*

Table 5. Lexical bundles and their most frequent equivalent forms in French

English lexical bundles	Most frequent corresponding bundles in French
according to me	selon moi
all this	tout ceci, (tout cela)
as a conclusion	en conclusion
as far as * is/are concerned	en ce qui concerne …
confronted with	confronté/es à, (confronté/es avec)
considered as	considéré/es comme
even if	même si
in order to	pour, afin de
in other words	autrement dit, en d'autres termes
is thus	est donc
is far from being	est loin d'être
let us	*1st person plural of the imperative*
let us not forget that	n'oublions pas
most of the time	le plus souvent, la plupart du temps
on the contrary	au contraire
point of view	point de vue
speak of	PARLER de
such a	un/e tel/le
we may	on peut

this is over-represented in ICLE-FR when *this* is used as a pronoun (not as a determiner). The sequence is also very often used in subject position (Example (3)).

(3) **All this** goes to show that somehow wealth corrupts. (ICLE-FR)

The second column of Table 5 provides the most frequent corresponding bundles as identified in the French web corpus for each of the nineteen longer, syntactically complete or more salient lexical bundles. Small capitals are used to represent lemmas rather than word forms.

As will be further demonstrated in Section 6, intra-L1-group congruity between learners' L1 and IL performance is found for all the lexical bundles except two, i.e. *as a conclusion* and *in other words*. Cross-linguistic influence is arguably not the most prominent factor to account for French EFL learners' overuse of *as a conclusion*.[3] Its functional equivalent form in French is *en conclusion*, which

---

3. The word-by-word translation of En. 'as a conclusion', i.e. *comme une conclusion*, only occurs 4 times in the 126 million word corpus and is never used to introduce a conclusion. The sequence *comme conclusion* is slightly more frequent (0.1 occurrence per million words) but is rarely used as a sentence-initial adverbial, which is how French EFL learners use *as a conclusion*. Instead, *comme conclusion* is mainly used to introduce a prepositional phrase (e.g. *comme*

translates neatly as *in conclusion*. French learners' use of *as a conclusion* is most probably better explained as a teaching-induced phenomenon: a number of (on-line and in print) teaching materials targeting French learners list *as a conclusion* as a perfectly correct connector (Paquot 2010:160). Similarly, I was not able to draw a clear parallel between French learners' use of *in other words* and their use of a corresponding L1 feature.[4]

6. Discussion

This section addresses the research questions guiding the study by discussing the more quantitative results provided in Section 5 and specifying how French learners' use of the English lexical bundles can be shown to parallel their use of corresponding lexical bundles in French. A close look at the lexical bundles listed in Table 5 helps identify four major types of transfer effect found in French EFL learners' use of recurrent word sequences, thus already addressing RQ2: (1) transfer of semantic properties, (2) transfer of collocational and colligational preferences, (3) transfer of functions and discourse conventions and (4) transfer of L1 frequency. In what follows, I describe the different types of transfer effect and comment on the extent of the correspondence between each overused lexical bundle and its French counterpart.

6.1 Transfer of semantic properties

Connectors are particularly prone to semantic misuse in learner writing (Paquot 2010:168–172). Several explanations have been provided to account for this phenomenon, most importantly perhaps the fact that connectors are often presented in long lists of undifferentiated and supposedly equivalent items, classified in broad functional categories (Crewe 1990; Milton 1999; Lake 2004). However, cross-linguistic influence also reinforces the conceptual problems often induced by misguided teaching practices. As already argued by Granger and Tyson (1996), French learners' repeated and erroneous use of *on the contrary* instead of *on the*

---

conclusion de cet article 'as a conclusion to this article') and in the larger phraseological pattern TIRER *comme conclusion* (En. 'draw a conclusion').

4. My contention is that French learners' overuse of *in other words* may also be attributed to L1 influence because French makes frequent use of reformulation and apposition markers (see Section 6.3 for comments on explicitness in French) but this would need to be supported by a careful quantitative corpus-based analysis of reformulation markers across languages.

other hand is at least also partly due to an over-extension of the semantic properties of the French *au contraire*, which can be used to express both a concessive and an antithetic link. Similarly, the fact that *même si* can be used to introduce a condition or a concession in French largely contributes to French learners' erroneous use of *even if* instead of *even though* (Gilquin 2008: 19–20) as illustrated in Example (4).

(4) Since in our Western societies, almost everybody is aware of the growing environmental problems – ***even if** almost nothing has been actually done –, we should now turn to the underprivileged parts of the world. (ICLE-FR)

6.2 Transfer of collocational preferences

Collocational preferences in the first language may prompt learners to use lexical bundles that display untypical phraseology in English (Nesselhauf 2005; Laufer & Waldman 2011; Paquot & Granger 2012). The idiosyncratic expression *according to me* is repeatedly used in ICLE-FR (Example (5)) but does not appear in other ICLE sub-corpora except for ICLE-DU and ICLE-SW, where it is however extremely rare. The English preposition *according to* and the French preposition *selon* both mean 'as shown by something or stated by someone'. However, they differ in use: *according to* is usually not followed by the personal pronoun *me* while *selon moi* is frequently used in French to express personal opinion (Paquot 2010: 185–186).

(5) ***According to me**, the prison system is not outdated: it has never been a solution per se. (ICLE-FR)

Cross-linguistic influence is also detectable in French learners' preference for the colligational pattern 'considered as + adjective/noun phrase' over the more frequent 'considered + adjective/noun phrase'. As shown in Examples (6) and (7), French EFL learners' preference for the construction 'CONSIDER + *as*' mirrors the use of French *considérer*, which is typically followed by the preposition *comme* when introducing adjective or noun phrases (Paquot 2013: 402).

(6) Besides childhood is often **considered as** the happiest period in one's life. (ICLE-FR)

(7) L'économie ivoirienne était considérée comme l'une des plus dynamiques d'Afrique subsaharienne, au point d'être qualifiée de « miracle ivoirien ». ("The Ivory Coast economy was considered as one of the most dynamic …")

6.3 Transfer of functions and discourse conventions

As hypothesized, some of the lexical bundles used idiosyncratically in French EFL learner writing have equivalent forms that fulfil specific discourse functions in French. First, the overrepresentation of the lexical bundles *let us* and *let us not forget that* in ICLE-FR results from the fact that French EFL learners transfer their knowledge of French writing conventions and make use of English imperative forms in French-like phraseological patterns and to serve the organizational and interactional functions typical of French imperative verbs (Paquot 2008; Paquot 2010: 188–192).

(8) **Let us not forget that** the new organization of the states will not be accomplished overnight. (ICLE-FR)

(9) **N'oublions pas que** Stendhal est né à Grenoble en 1783. (French web corpus) ("Let us not forget that Stendhal was born in Grenoble in 1783.")

French EFL learners also often use the English verb *speak* with the first person plural pronoun *we* and a modal verb in textual sentence stems, i.e. "routinized fragments of sentences which serve specific textual or organizational functions" (Granger & Paquot 2008: 23), as illustrated in Examples (10) and (11). This probably stems from the fact that in French the verb *parler* ("*speak*") is also often used with the first person plural pronoun *nous* or the indefinite pronoun *on*[5] in introductory phrases to fulfil functions such as introducing a new idea or voicing one's opinion (Examples (12) and (13)) (Paquot 2013: 405).

(10) **We may** here **speak of** a social phenomenon of collective brainwashing ... (ICLE-FR)

(11) **We cannot speak of** a loss of national identity because ... (ICLE-FR)

(12) **Nous pouvons parler** ici d'une action sans intention. (French web corpus) ("We can here speak of an action without intention.")

(13) **On peut parler de** dissociation entre la tête et le corps. (French web corpus) ("We can speak of dissociation between mind and body.")

---

5. The French indefinite pronoun *on* is much more frequent and stylistically very different from the English *one*: it can refer to one or more people, be substituted for all personal pronouns and "has an unclear enunciative status (i.e. relation to speaker or locator and receiver)" (Fløttum et al. 2006: 113). See Tutin (2010) and Fløttum and Thue Vold (2010) for a discussion of the use of the indefinite pronoun *on* and the first plural pronoun subject *nous* in French academic writing.

French EFL learners' overuse of the lexical bundle *we may* is the result of a highly complex interplay of factors including incomplete mastery of the English modal system and features of novice writing (Hyland & Milton 1997; Thewissen 2013). These factors however are also reinforced by interlingual factors and transfer of writing conventions from the L1 (Neff et al. 2003; Neff et al. 2004). Examples (14) to (18) show that French learners' use of the bundle *we may* in sequences such as *we may ask ourselves*, *we may wonder* and *we may hope* to organize discourse and express attitudes parallels the use of corresponding word sequences in French.

(14) However, **we may ask ourselves whether** in our modern world, there is still a place for dreaming and imagination. (ICLE-FR)

(15) **We may wonder** if equality really exists. (ICLE-FR)

(16) Moreover, **we may hope that** if Europe is stronger, all the countries which make it up will also be stronger … (ICLE-FR)

(17) **On peut espérer que** l'avenir permettra de faire toute la lumière sur ce dernier point. (French web corpus)
("We may hope that the future will shed light on this last point.")

(18) **On peut se demander** pourquoi des actions apparemment neutres sont militarisées, comme la mission spatiale … (French web corpus)
("We may wonder why apparently neutral actions are militarized, such as the spatial mission …")

The overrepresentation of *in order to* in French learner writing when compared to other learner populations is arguably brought about by systemic differences between French and English. As put by Hervey and Higgins (2002: 120), "it is more common in French than in English for texts to be **explicitly** structured with connectors (…) that signpost the logical relationships between sentences" (emphasis mine) and a variety of connectors may be used to express purposes in French, e.g. *pour, afin de, de façon à,* and *en vue de*. It may be hypothesized that the English function word *to*, i.e. the most frequent but also the least marked way of expressing purpose, is not explicit enough in the eyes of French speakers who almost systematically resort to *in order to* as a default option to express purpose (Examples (19) and (20)).

(19) In 30 months, I leave the university **in order to** begin a new life. (ICLE-FR)

(20) After having examined some of the measures taken **in order to** protect the environment, it is obvious that … (ICLE-FR)

This phenomenon is certainly compounded by a teaching-induced factor: '*in order to* + infinitive' is often taught as the first (if not the only) means to express purpose. However, transfer of training alone cannot serve to explain why French EFL learners differ from other learner populations in their use of *in order to*.

6.4 Transfer of L1 frequency

Next to congruency and function, the frequency of lexical bundles in the first language seems to play a significant role as well (cf. Selinker 1983; Gass 1983): the more frequent a discourse- or stance-oriented lexical bundle is in French, the more likely French learners are to use its congruent form in English. Thus, the lexical bundle *point of view* has a very frequent congruent form in French, i.e. *point de vue* (77.3 pmw) which is used in similar phraseological patterns (e.g. *de ce point de vue* 'from this point of view', *du point de vue de* 'from the point of view of'). Similarly, the sequence *such a* corresponds to Fr. *un/e tel/le* (127 pmw): both lexical items are used to add emphasis. In Paquot (2013), I suggested that a useful way of verifying transfer of L1 frequency is to check whether the lexical bundles used by the French learners have equivalent structures in another language represented in the ICLE corpus and if so, why these are not transferred into English by the other learner population. Spanish is arguably a good candidate for this purpose: French and Spanish are both Romance languages, and there are often congruent sequences in Spanish for the French word combinations that were pinpointed in this study as responsible for transfer effects. I therefore made use of the c. 117 million word Spanish web corpus available in the Sketch Engine to check the frequencies of Spanish equivalent word combinations.

Frequency comparisons of translational equivalent word combinations in French and Spanish strengthen the case for transfer of L1 frequency. Table 6 shows that there are Spanish congruent forms for English lexical bundles such as *according to me, as far as * is concerned, considered as, is thus, is far from being* and *on the contrary* but they are much less frequent than the French counterparts. As a result, Spanish learners are less tempted to translate these infrequent Spanish word combinations. Thus, word combinations such as *es/está pues* and *está lejos de ser/estar* are rare in the Spanish web-derived corpus and no instances of *is thus* or *is far from being* are found in the Spanish learner corpus.

Transfer effects also interact with input (cf. Larsen-Freeman 1976). French EFL learners differ from the other learner populations represented in ICLE by their repeated use of the lexical bundle *confronted with*. The explanation here is not to be found in the frequency of the French word-by-word translation: *confronté/es avec* is relatively rare (0.3 pmw). Rather, the overrepresentation stems from the fact that, unlike in Spanish for example, the congruent past participle form is frequent in French (*confronté/es*, 27.7 pmw) but most French EFL learners

Table 6. Lexical bundles in French and Spanish

	French	Freq. pmw	Spanish	Freq. pmw
according to me	selon moi	5.5	según yó	0
as far as * is concerned	en ce qui concerne	19.1	en lo que concierne a	2.3
considered as	considéré/es comme	46	considerado/as como	5
is thus	est donc	90.1	es/está pues	2.1
is far from being	est loin d'être	5.7	está lejos de ser/estar	0.5
most of the time	la plupart du temps	10.5	la mayor parte/mayoría del tiempo	2.1
on the contrary	au contraire	80.8	al contrario	16.2

seem to know that *confronted* should be followed by the preposition *with*. This explanation is reinforced by the fact that ICLE-FR is the only corpus in which there are two instances of *confronted to*, which corresponds to the more frequent colligation *confronté/es à* (11.1 pmw). Similarly, frequency effects in the first language and in the foreign language interact in a number of ways. Thus, while both the sequences *tout ceci* ('all this') and *tout cela* ('all that') are used in subject position in French, *tout cela* is three times as frequent as *tout ceci* in sentence-initial position (15.7 vs. 4.1 pmw) and used in patterns such as *tout cela constitue* ('all that constitutes'), *tout cela montre* ('all that shows'), *tout cela relève* ('all that relates to'), *tout cela depend* ('all that depends on'), *tout cela signifie* ('all that means'), *tout cela suppose* ('all that supposes'), and *tout cela veut dire* ('all that means'). French learners, however, use *all this* more frequently than *all that* in subject position in English. The L1 frequency effect is here arguably compounded by the fact that in English the reverse situation is found with *all that* very rarely used in subject position and *all this* often used in textual sentence stems such as *all this seems / comes / sounds / means / suggests / implies*.

Except for *as a conclusion* and *in other words* which were discussed in Section 5, all the English lexical bundles listed in Table 5 have been explained in terms of transfer of semantic properties (*on the contrary, even if*), transfer of collocational preferences (*according to me, considered as*), transfer of functions and discourse conventions (*in order to, let us, let us not forget that, speak of, we may*) or transfer of L1 frequency (*point of view, such a, as far as * is/are concerned, is thus, is far from being, most of the time, confronted with, all this*). Different transfer effects have also been found to work in tandem (e.g. the overuse of *considered as* is explainable by both L1 frequency and collocational preferences).

The seventeen L1-induced 'regrouped' lexical bundles represent as much as 12.3% of the 2-word sequences, 15.3% of the 3-word sequences and 20% of the 4-word sequences that set the French learners apart from at least 5 other learner populations (cf. Table 7). Thus, to answer RQ1, L1-related effects contribute

Table 7. Cross-linguistic influence on French EFL learners' use of lexical bundles

	2-word sequences	3-word sequences	4-word sequences
Referential expressions	5/138 [3.6%]	2/51 [3.9%]	1/13 [7.7%]
Discourse organizers	13/15 [86.7%]	5/6 [83.3%]	1/1 [100%]
Stance markers	1/1 [100%]	2/2 [100%]	1/1 [100%]
Total	19/154 [12.3%]	9/59 [15.3%]	3/15 [20%]

significantly to French learners' use of lexical bundles in L2 together with other factors such as transfer of training and level of proficiency: between c. 12% and 20% of French learners' overuse of lexical bundles can be attributed to L1 influence and the extent of L1 influence grows with the size of the lexical bundles. Global figures for the whole set of overused lexical bundles however hide significant differences between the three functional categories: the overuse of most referential expressions cannot be ascribed primarily to L1 transfer effects and was explained by topic instead while almost all the discourse organizers and stance markers that are overrepresented in ICLE-FR are L1-induced.

Results also show that formal similarity between L1 and L2 word combinations does not necessarily make a word combination in the first language a strong candidate for transfer into the foreign language. Many learner (corpus-based) studies, however, have fallen into the trap of claiming L1 influence on the basis that the structure exists in the first language without further investigation of L1 empirical data. In line with Paquot's (2013) results, findings suggest that two L1 factors may play a prominent role in the transferability of lexical bundles: the function and frequency of the lexical bundle in the first language. These two factors are little documented and well worth exploring in more detail.

Conclusion

This study replicated the methodology developed in Paquot (2013) except for the statistics used and the types of lexical bundles analyzed. In Paquot (2013), I made use of ANOVAs and Dunnett's tests despite the fact that the data was not normally distributed on the basis that "the assumptions normally cited as being required of parametric tests are overly restrictive in practice" (Howell 1997: 646). In this study, I opted for non-parametric tests to escape from this unresolved debate. Pairwise Wilcoxon tests however selected a lower percentage of significant lexical bundles and most of the word sequences analyzed in Paquot (2013) were not identified although the same dataset was used. Examples include *be tempted to*, *deeply rooted in*, *is to know whether*, *role to play* and *to go further*, all of which proved to be L1-induced. This supports the common view that parametric tests are more powerful and suggests that these tests may be valuable tools for exploratory purposes "even when the distribution assumptions are violated to a moderate degree" (Howell 1997:646).

The first study was limited to an analysis of 3-word bundles with lexical verbs and revealed that the first language did not seem to generate obvious errors in the writing of intermediate to advanced French EFL learners. The present study is much wider in scope, i.e. it focuses on lexical bundles of various sizes made up of different constituent forms, and shows that transfer effects may trigger errors, most notably in the form of semantic misuse of connectors (e.g. *on the contrary, even if*).[6]

More importantly, results point to the same types of L1 influence as described in Paquot (2013). The transfer effects on lexical bundles lie at the interface between 'lexical transfer' and 'discursive transfer' to use Jarvis and Pavlenko's (2008) typology. I have identified transfer effects on collocational and colligational preferences and the semantic properties of lexical bundles, L1 influence on L2 rhetorical writing conventions and transfer from the L1 discourse system. Transfer effects are most visible in the learners' selection of unmarked word combinations whose translational equivalents are deeply entrenched in French speakers' mental lexicon because these L1 sequences are particularly frequent or directly anchored to important communicative or metatextual functions (i.e. stance markers and discourse organizers). Interestingly, in a recent study of discourse markers in translated English, Granger (2013) reported that English texts produced by French translators are also characterised by an overrepresentation of the lexical bundles *on the contrary, as far as, in order to, in other words* and *let us not forget*.

L1 frequency also proved to contribute to transferability in a significant way: frequent lexical bundles in the first language are more easily transferred and this is most apparent when different L1 backgrounds are compared with the help of learner corpora such as the *International Corpus of Learner English*. Frequency effects are central in current second language research and theory but they have often been restricted to effects of input or L1 frequency (e.g. Ellis 2002; Ellis & Ferreira-Junior 2009). Results provide empirical evidence to support the claim that L1 frequency deserves a more prominent position in usage-based approaches to second language acquisition (Paquot 2013b).

---

6. With its focus on repeated and fixed word sequences, the lexical bundle approach does not readily provide access to collocational errors, which are not necessarily frequent and may involve sequences of words that are not adjacent. A large proportion of collocational errors, however, are often L1-induced in EFL learner writing (cf. Nesselhauf 2005; Laufer & Waldman 2011).

More generally, the studies reported on here and in Paquot (2013) have also brought to light the considerable potential of a corpus-driven approach to track L1 influence on learner language. Transfer studies have often focused on "bits and pieces of learners' language chosen for analysis because they caught the researcher's eye, seemed to exhibit some systematicity, confirmed some intuition one had about SLA, or had been found interesting in L1 acquisition" (Lightbown 1984:245). The lexical bundle approach is arguably already validated by the fact that it identifies successfully word sequences such as *on the contrary* and *even if* that have already been analyzed as L1-induced in previous studies on French learners' use of connectors (e.g. Granger & Tyson 1996; Gilquin 2008). However, it is much more powerful and represents "corpus linguistic methodology at its most heuristic, i.e. as a raw discovery procedure" (De Cock 2004:227). Coupled with Jarvis's (2000) framework and appropriate statistical tests, it proved most useful to extract fully automatically a number of word combinations that deserved further analysis and consequently identify transfer effects that until now have been little documented in the SLA literature. Lexical transfer has too often been narrowed down to transfer of form/meaning mappings and the third aspect of word knowledge, i.e. use, has rarely been investigated in all its complexity. Further research is clearly needed.

References

Ädel, A. 2008. "Involvement features in writing: Do time and interaction trump register awareness." In *Linking up Contrastive and Learner Corpus Research*, B.M. Diez-Bedmar, G. Gilquin and S. Papp (eds), 35–53. Amsterdam/New York: Rodopi.

Allen, D. 2011. "Lexical bundles in learner writing: An analysis of formulaic language in the ALESS learner corpus." *Komaba Journal of English Education* 1: 105–127.

Altenberg, B. 1998. "On the phraseology of spoken English: The evidence of recurrent word-combinations." In *Phraseology: Theory, Analysis, and Applications*, A.P. Cowie (ed.), 101–122. Oxford: Oxford University Press.

Biber, D., Conrad, S. and Cortes, V. 2003. "Lexical bundles in speech and writing: An initial taxonomy." In *Corpus Linguistics by the Lune: A Festschrift for Geoffrey Leech*, A. Wilson, P. Rayson and T. McEnery (eds), 71–92. Frankfurt: Peter Lang.

Biber, D., Johansson, S., Leech, G., Conrad, S. and Finegan, E. 1999. *Longman Grammar of Spoken and Written English*. Harlow: Longman.

Cortes, V. 2004. "Lexical bundles in published and student disciplinary writing: Examples from history and biology." *English for Specific Purposes* 23 (4): 397–423.
DOI: 10.1016/j.esp.2003.12.001

Crewe, W. 1990. "The illogic of logical connectors." *ELT Journal* 44 (4): 316–325.
DOI: 10.1093/elt/44.4.316

De Cock, S. 2004. "Preferred sequences of words in NS and NNS speech." *Belgian Journal of English Language and Literatures* [New Series] 2: 225–246.

Ellis, N. C. 2002. "Frequency effects in language acquisition: A review with implications for theories of implicit and explicit language acquisition." *Studies in Second Language Acquisition* 24: 143–188.

Ellis, N.C. and Ferreira-Junior, F. 2009. "Construction learning as a function of frequency, frequency distribution, and function." *Modern Language Journal* 93: 370–385. DOI: 10.1111/j.1540-4781.2009.00896.x

Fløttum, K., Dahl, T. and Kinn, T. 2006. *Academic Voices – Across Languages and Disciplines*. Amsterdam: John Benjamins. DOI: 10.1075/pbns.148

Fløttum, K. and Thue Vold, E. 2010. "L'éthos auto-attribué d'auteurs-doctorants dans le discourse scientifique". *Lidil, Revue de Linguistique et de Didactique des Langues* 41: 41–58. Available at: http://lidil.revues.org/index3006.html (accessed January 2014).

Gass, S. 1983. "Language transfer and universal grammatical relations." In *Language Transfer in Language Learning*, S. Gass and L. Selinker (eds), 69–82. Rowley, MA: Newbury House.

Gilquin, G. 2008. "Combining contrastive and interlanguage analysis to apprehend transfer: Detection, explanation, evaluation." In *Linking up Contrastive and Learner Corpus Research*, G. Gilquin, S. Papp and M.-B. Díez-Bedmar (eds), 3–35. Amsterdam, New York: Rodopi.

Granger, S. 2013. "Tracking the third code: A crosslinguistic corpus-driven approach to discourse markers." Plenary talk given at the *ICLC7 – UCCTS3 Conference*, Ghent University, Belgium, 11–13 July 2013.

Granger, S., Dagneaux, E. and Meunier, F. 2002. *The International Corpus of Learner English. Handbook and CD-ROM*. Louvain-la-Neuve: Presses Universitaires de Louvain.

Granger, S., Dagneaux, E., Meunier, F. and Paquot, M. 2009. *The International Corpus of Learner English. Handbook and CD-ROM* (Version 2). Louvain-la-Neuve: Presses Universitaires de Louvain.

Granger, S. and Paquot, M. 2008. "Disentangling the phraseological web." In *Phraseology: An Interdisciplinary Perspective*, S. Granger and F. Meunier (eds), 27–49. Amsterdam: John Benjamins.

Granger, S. and Tyson, S. 1996. "Connector usage in the English essay writing of native and non-native EFL speakers of English." *World Englishes* 15: 19–29. DOI: 10.1111/j.1467-971X.1996.tb00089.x

Hervey, S. and Higgins, I. 2002. *Thinking French Translation. A Course in Translation Method: French to English*. London: Routledge.

Howell, D. 1997. *Statistical Methods for Psychology*. Belmont: Wadsworth.

Hyland, K. and Milton, J. 1997. "Qualifications and certainty in L1 and L2 students' writing." *Journal of Second Language Writing* 6 (2): 183–205. DOI: 10.1016/S1060-3743(97)90033-3

Jarvis, S. 2000. "Methodological rigor in the study of transfer: Identifying L1 influence in the interlanguage lexicon." *Language Learning* 50 (2): 245–309. DOI: 10.1111/0023-8333.00118

Jarvis, S. 2010. "Comparison-based and detection-based approaches to transfer research". In *EUROSLA Yearbook 10*, L. Roberts, M. Howard, M. Ó Laoire and D. Singleton (eds),169–192. Amsterdam: John Benjamins. DOI: 10.1075/eurosla.10.10jar

Jarvis, S. and Odlin, T. 2000. "Morphological type, spatial reference, and language transfer." *Studies in Second Language Acquisition* 22: 535–556. DOI: 10.1017/S0272263100004034

Jarvis, S. and Pavlenko, A. 2008. *Crosslinguistic Influence in Language and Cognition*. New York and London: Routledge

Kilgarriff, A. and Kosem, I. 2012. "Corpus tools for lexicographers." In *Electronic Lexicography*, S. Granger and M. Paquot (eds), 31–56. Oxford: Oxford University Press.

DOI: 10.1093/acprof:oso/9780199654864.003.0003

Kroll, B. 1990. "What does time buy? ESL student performance on home vs. class compositions." In *Second Language Writing*, B. Kroll (ed.), 140–154. Cambridge: Cambridge University Press. DOI: 10.1017/CBO9781139524551.014

Lake J. 2004. "Using 'on the contrary': The conceptual problems for EAP students." *ELT Journal* 58 (2): 137–144. DOI: 10.1093/elt/58.2.137

Larsen-Freeman, D. 1976. "An explanation for the morpheme acquisition order of second language learners." *Language Learning* 26 (1): 125–134.
DOI: 10.1111/j.1467-1770.1976.tb00264.x

Laufer, B. and Waldman, T. 2011. "Verb-noun collocations in second language writing: A corpus analysis of learners' English." *Language Learning* 61 (2): 647–672.
DOI: 10.1111/j.1467-9922.2010.00621.x

Lightbown, P.M. 1984. "The relationship between theory and method in second-language-acquisition research." In *Interlanguage*, A. Davies, C. Criper and A. Howatt (eds), 241–252. Edinburgh: Edinburgh University Press.

Milton J. 1999. "Lexical thickets and electronic gateways: Making text accessible by novice writers." In *Writing: Texts, Processes and Practices*, C.N. Candlin and K. Hyland (eds), 221–243. London and New York: Longman.

Neff, J., Ballesteros, F., Dafouz, E., Martínez, F. and Rica, J. P. 2004. "The expression of writer stance in native and non-native argumentative texts." In *English Modality in Perspective*, R. Facchinetti and F. Palmer (eds), 141–161. Frankfurt am Main: Peter Lang.

Neff, J., Dafouz, E., Herrera, H., Martínez, F., Rica, J.P., Diez, M., Prieto, R. and Sancho, C. 2003. "Contrasting learner corpora: The use of modal and reporting verbs in the expression of writer stance." In *Extending the Scope of Corpus-Based Research. New Applications*, New Challenges, S. Granger and S. Petch-Tyson (eds), 211–230. Amsterdam/New York: Rodopi.

Nesselhauf, N. 2005. *Collocations in a learner corpus*. Amsterdam: Benjamins.
DOI: 10.1075/scl.14

Paquot, M. 2008. "Exemplification in learner writing: A cross-linguistic perspective." In *Phraseology in Foreign Language Learning and Teaching*, F. Meunier and S. Granger (eds), 101–119. Amsterdam: John Benjamins.

Paquot, M. 2010. *Academic Vocabulary in Learner Writing: From Extraction to Analysis*. London/New York: Continuum.

Paquot, M. 2013. "Lexical bundles and L1 transfer effects." *International Journal of Corpus Linguistics* 18 (3): 391–417. DOI: 10.1075/ijcl.18.3.06paq

Paquot, M. 2013b. "L1 frequency effects in input-poor environment: A corpus-based study of word combinations in learner writing." Paper presented at the *32nd Annual Second Language Research Forum*, Brigham Young University, Utah, USA, 31 October – 2 November 2013.

Paquot, M. and Granger, S. 2012. "Formulaic Language in Learner Corpora." *Annual Review of Applied Linguistics* 32: 130–149. DOI: 10.1017/S0267190512000098

R Core Team. 2012. online. *R: A Language and Environment for Statistical Computing*. Available at: http://www.R-project.org (accessed January 2014).

Ringbom, H. 1987. *The Role of the First Language in Foreign Language Learning*. Clevedon/Philadelphia: Multilingual Matters.

Scott, M. 2008. *WordSmith Tools version 5*. Liverpool: Lexical Analysis Software.

Selinker, L. 1983. "Language transfer." In *Language Transfer in Language Learning*, S. Gass and L. Selinker (eds), 98–111. Rowley, MA: Newbury House.

Selinker L. 1992. *Rediscovering Interlanguage*. London/New York: Longman.
Thewissen, J. 2013. "Capturing L2 accuracy developmental patterns: Insights from an error-tagged EFL learner corpus." *Modern Language Journal* 97 (Suppl. 1): 77–101. DOI: 10.1111/j.1540-4781.2012.01422.x
Tutin, A. 2010. "Dans cet article, nous souhaitons montrer que… Lexique verbal et positionnement de l'auteur dans les articles en sciences humaines. Enonciation et rhétorique dans l'écrit scientifique". *Lidil, Revue de Linguistique et de didactique des langues* 41: 15–40. Available at: http://lidil.revues.org/index3040.html (accessed January 2014).